Witchcraft in Early Modern Poland, 1500–1800

Witchcraft in Early Modern Poland, 1500–1800

Wanda Wyporska

© Wanda Wyporska 2013

All rights reserved. No reproduction, copy or transmission of this publication may be made without written permission.

No portion of this publication may be reproduced, copied or transmitted save with written permission or in accordance with the provisions of the Copyright, Designs and Patents Act 1988, or under the terms of any licence permitting limited copying issued by the Copyright Licensing Agency, Saffron House, 6–10 Kirby Street, London EC1N 8TS.

Any person who does any unauthorized act in relation to this publication may be liable to criminal prosecution and civil claims for damages.

The author has asserted her right to be identified as the author of this work in accordance with the Copyright, Designs and Patents Act 1988.

First published 2013 by
PALGRAVE MACMILLAN

Palgrave Macmillan in the UK is an imprint of Macmillan Publishers Limited, registered in England, company number 785998, of Houndmills, Basingstoke, Hampshire RG21 6XS.

Palgrave Macmillan in the US is a division of St Martin's Press LLC, 175 Fifth Avenue, New York, NY 10010.

Palgrave Macmillan is the global academic imprint of the above companies and has companies and representatives throughout the world.

Palgrave® and Macmillan® are registered trademarks in the United States, the United Kingdom, Europe and other countries.

ISBN: 978–0–230–00521–1

This book is printed on paper suitable for recycling and made from fully managed and sustained forest sources. Logging, pulping and manufacturing processes are expected to conform to the environmental regulations of the country of origin.

A catalogue record for this book is available from the British Library.

A catalog record for this book is available from the Library of Congress.

To Pamela, Valerie, John and Krysia, who nurtured me.
To Daniel and Arkady, who are my world.

Contents

List of Figures and Tables	viii
Acknowledgements	ix
Maps	xi
Figures 1 and 2	xiv

	Prologue	1
1	Witchcraft in Context: Histories and Historiographies	6
2	The World of the Witches: Confessions and Conflicts	29
3	Witchcraft and Gender: Intimate Servants and Excluded Masculinities	53
4	Framing the Witch: Legal Theories and Realities	70
5	*Nullus Deus, Sine Diabolo*: The Ecclesiastical Witch	95
6	Beyond Demonology: Blame the Witches	127
7	Sceptical Voices: Ending the Era	151
8	Epilogue: Comparisons and Conclusions	176

Notes	191
Bibliography	220
Index	241

List of Figures and Tables

Figures

1 Jan Ziarnko's illustration for Pierre de Lancre's *Tableau de l'inconstance des mauvais anges et demons* ... (Paris, 1613)   xiv
2 The anonymous work, *Czarownica Powołana* (Poznań, 1639)   xv
3 Occupation of individuals tried for witchcraft in the Wielkopolska sample (where known)   54

Tables

1 Witchcraft trials in the Wielkopolska sample   31
2 Number of individuals tried for witchcraft in the Wielkopolska sample   31

Acknowledgements

This book began life as a doctoral thesis at Oxford University and I am grateful to Robin Briggs, Professor Robert Frost and Professor Lyndal Roper for guidance and suggestions. The research would have been impossible without generous awards from the Arts and Humanities Research Board, the British Association of Slavonic and East European Studies and the Polish government. I would also like to thank the trustees of the Mary Starun Fund at Hertford College, Oxford for electing me to the Starun Senior Scholarship, Oxford University for a Scatcherd Scholarship and the Institute of Historical Research for electing me to a Scouloudi Fellowship.

Working in archives and libraries in both Poland and the UK accrues many debts and I would like to thank the staff of the British Library (in particular the redoubtable Jeremy), the Taylor Institute and the Bodleian Library. In Poland I am particularly indebted to the staff of the Poznańskie Towarzystwo Przyjaciół Nauk, Kórnik Library, Gniezno Archdiocesan Library, Lublin and Cracow archives and the Czartoryski Library, Cracow. Special thanks are due to the unfailingly kind staff at the Archiwum Państwowe w Poznaniu (especially Małgorzata Kaczmarek), the Biblioteka Narodowa at the Pałac Krasińskich and the Archiwum Głowne Akt Dawnych, whose expertise and kindness kept me going. I would also like to thank Mary Spence for maps and Palgrave editorial staff, Holly Tyler, Jen McCall, Clare Mence, Eric Christianson and Ruth Ireland, as well as the anonymous readers.

Thanks are also due to Sophie Ratcliffe Schuman, Katherine Lunn-Rockliffe, Nicola Thomas, Lina Christopoulou, Robert Pyrah, Sarah Hearn, Magdalena, Wojciech and Tymon Wirscy, Olena Krajewska, Bogdan and Jadwiga Lewandowscy, Anna Jagiełło, Anna Ascough, Gloria Freitas Kearns, Debika Pramanik and Charles Abboud. The late Professor Stanisław Eile, Bolesław Mazur and Professor Norman Davies encouraged me and instilled in me a deep love of Polish history, literature and language. My family, Valerie, Krysia and John McNamara have unfailingly supported me and lived with witches for decades. Finally, I owe an indescribable debt to my peerless example as a fellow writer, Dr Daniel Woodley, for his love, support, patience, fabulous dinners and intellectual rigour and also to Arkady

Wyporski-Woodley for giving me a practical understanding of motherhood and the love that it brings.

All translations are my own and for all errors, of course, I take sole responsibility.

Wanda Wyporska
London, May 2013

Maps

Map 1 Contemporary Poland.

Map 2 Wielkopolska showing the towns that heard witchcraft trials.

Maps xiii

Map 3 Apex and decline of Poland in the sixteenth to seventeenth centuries.
Source: Dennis Hupchick and Harold E. Cox, *The Palgrave Concise Historical Atlas of Eastern Europe* (Basingstoke, 2001), p. 26. By kind permission of Palgrave Macmillan.

Figures 1 and 2

Figure 1 Jan Ziarnko's illustration for Pierre de Lancre's *Tableau de l'inconstance des mauvais anges et demons*…(Paris, 1613). © The British Library Board.

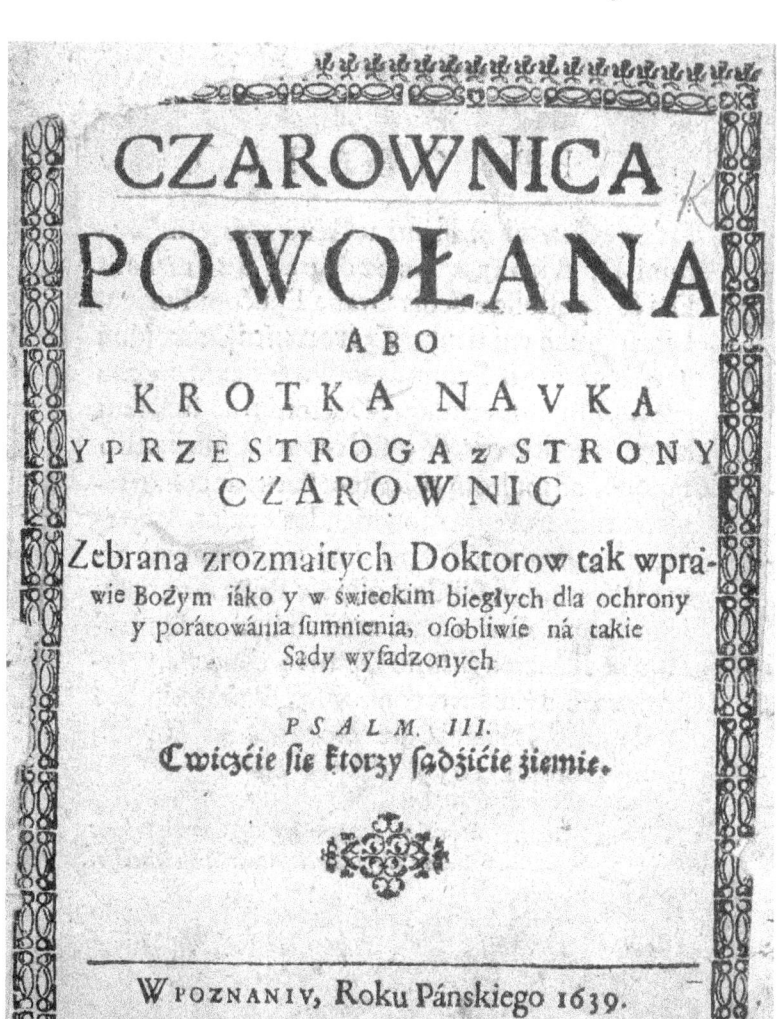

Figure 2 The anonymous work, *Czarownica Powołana* (Poznań, 1639). © The British Library Board.

Prologue

In 1613 the good gentlemen of Kalisz's municipal court arrived in the village of Kucharki to try Dorota of Siedlików and Gierusza Klimerzyna. Listening to a wide range of testimonies, they heard tell of sex with the Devil, ruined beer, stolen milk, a visit to the sabbat and the involvement of both priests and the local nobility. What they heard was typical of some of the many accusations and confessions recorded in witchcraft trials throughout the area of Wielkopolska (Great Poland) in western Poland and would have been familiar to those trying cases as late as the middle of the eighteenth century. When Dorota, the miller's daughter, was arrested at the Kucharki tavern, she claimed that her mother (some five years dead) had taught her to sprinkle cattle with holy water and that she had given people concoctions to improve marital harmony. She sprinkled holy water, invoked the power of the Virgin Mary, and genuflected as part of a ritual to ensure that a man sold all his bread at market. She also admitted that on the advice of Little Casper, her black and hairy devil, she had located stolen objects. These actions had variously been regarded as beneficial rather than malevolent at other times and in other places, but together with confessions to practices more overtly regarded as witchcraft, they sealed Dorota's fate.

For this unfortunate woman had committed the cardinal error of harming the local lord's property and at the heart of her trial was not only her confession that she had buried spells to harm Lord Szkulski's cattle, but also the male witnesses who testified that Dorota had threatened Maciej Gorczyca that he would 'come to ruin' when he accused her of stealing flour. Up until she was subjected to torture, her account contained little that was implausible to modern mentalities, but under torture she began to recite a more elaborate tale. A few Thursdays previously, in despair, she had uttered the words, 'Oh dear God, maybe I will give myself to the Devil like the others so that I can have a good life.' That very night, the Devil, whom she recognized by his cold hand, visited her, but she resisted him by making the sign of the cross. Later, when Dorota was stretched in the torture chamber, she added that she had slept with the Devil – seduced by the promise of butter, money, a black cow, and an escape from poverty. Her devil had also bruised and beaten her, which she complained about to two priests in Kościelna Wieś. Dorota was not the only one to enjoy the attentions of her own personal devil; she claimed the female miller also had sex with a devil called Little Martin.

The trial records testimony that Dorota wreaked revenge on a number of people who had slighted her. Peldowa had refused her bread and called her a hag, so when she subsequently fell ill after taking a powder made from herbs, earth from a grave and human bones, Dorota's name was mentioned. Dorota 'freely' admitted that she had bewitched Kosmalina's cattle because she had not paid her for a distaff and denounced Old Klimerzyna for stealing milk from the seigneur. Klimerzyna confronted her face-to-face, saying,

> My dear Lord, have mercy on me. I will, by God, say what I know dear Lord Szkulski, for a long time you have wanted my health ... By God she is lying about me. Dear Lord, forgive me in my innocence. Because she denounced me, I am denouncing the miller's wife because she harmed people with that Dorota.

Dorota thus corroborated the seigneur's ill will towards Klimerzyna, whose daughter he had harmed, leading Klimerzyna to threaten him with lean times. The women confessed to burying a pot containing various ingredients under the threshold of his cattle byre and were subsequently found guilty and sentenced to the stake.[1]

This trial illustrates many overarching historiographical themes and presents a case for viewing Polish witchcraft cases as similar to those found elsewhere in early modern Europe. Fears centred around the domestic sphere, the role of charity-refused, revenge on a seigneur and the importance of the gender, behaviour, status, age and motives of all those caught up in the witchcraft persecution, are all familiar to witchcraft historians around the globe. However, it is essential to set the stage by identifying common elements of trials heard before the municipal courts in Wielkopolska during the early modern period. On average between one and two women were tried in each case, torture was used to extract confessions, witnesses were called, and it was often the local seigneur who made the accusations and/or claimed to have suffered loss. Accounts of the sabbat, a relationship with a personal devil, quarrels and rivalries, use of ambiguous practices to harm and/or heal and motives for malefice, all reveal the complexities of witchcraft accusations and the community relationships upon which sometimes one's very survival depended. Dorota's testimony illustrates a world of tension, together with many of her own stated motives for causing harm: she gave herself to the Devil to escape poverty, but harmed the seigneur out of anger.

This trial indicates the dangerous ground trodden by those who purported to help people with concerns about illness, marital harmony or improving their lot in some way, as people were quick to turn on practitioners if something went awry. It also confirms the existence of the magical world which people had to negotiate – cunning folk and witches were at work everywhere, employing magical practices and rituals in everyday life. However, the trial highlights the ambiguity with which some practices such as invoking the Virgin, Jesus and the Trinity were regarded and the important role played by those who claimed the authority to interpret them as beneficial or malevolent. Thus the three key themes of this study are: first, to identify who was defining the paradigms of the witch; second, can we establish a composite, recognized body of attributes commonly ascribed to a 'witch'; and finally, did the trials correlate with intellectual discussions of witchcraft?

This study defines witchcraft as a set of beliefs or practices regarded as using supernatural power to harm or heal. The epistemological truth of witchcraft is not important. As Briggs points out, 'witchcraft is itself a reification, an imposed category whose boundaries are anything but clear'.[2] We must also honour the combinations of rich beliefs in varying forms of the supernatural, in God, in the Devil or devils and a host of other entities, in the context of divergent doctrinal demands. This work only begins to hint at just how individuals negotiated varying and fluid formal and informal belief systems. Another of the key aims of this study is to provide an overview of witchcraft trials heard before the municipal courts in Wielkopolska, in tandem with a wide variety of contemporary literature in which witchcraft was discussed. This purview includes so-called 'élite' printed discourse as well as forms of Polish literature produced by and for the 'middling' class. This will enable comparisons between various representations of witchcraft, trials, the witch, the devil and the sabbat, and by using as broad a range of materials as possible, I hope to refute some of the many erroneous conclusions reached about the witchcraft persecution in Poland.

Wielkopolska is the focus of this work and although there are many articles on individual Polish trials, to date there have been only a few regional studies, mainly focusing on Lublin, the Świętokrzyż area and Ducal Prussia.[3] Wielkopolska was a region with its own historical, geographical, religious and political specifics, outlined in Chapter 1, where I shall also provide a brief overview of the history of Poland during the period. Of necessity this will focus in particular on socio-economic and population changes; devastation caused by wars, climate conditions, epidemics and disease; the Counter-Reformation; and the role of the *szlachta*, or nobility, reflecting some of the main historiographical themes. The methodology employed can be succinctly expressed in the title of Briggs's article, '*Many Reasons Why*', and to that end the materials will be analysed in order to see which, if any, of the range of existing causal theories may be relevant to the Wielkopolska sample. I shall also explore the legal frameworks essential for a cogent understanding of representations of the witch.

Representations of the witch in drama, poetry, agricultural manuals and other literary genres have yielded significantly varying conceptualizations of the witch and the Devil, often challenging the dominant negative ecclesiastical stereotypes. Poland, as elsewhere, was also home to sceptics, whose arguments (with the exception of limited debate on demonic agency) were based not on theology, but on heavy criticism of the judicial system, led and sustained by the Polish Roman Catholic clergy. The publication in 1614 of a Polish translation of parts of the *Malleus Maleficarum*, the swift translation and publication of Spee's *Cautio Criminalis* in Poznań in 1647, and the publication of a similar Polish anonymous work, *Czarownica Powołana* in 1639, confirm that Poland was au fait with European intellectual currents of the time. This is also supported by Polish authors' familiarity with contemporary debate, both pro- and anti-witchcraft.[4]

Inevitably this study includes a statistical analysis of the sample of Wielkopolska trials, which should not be extrapolated to represent Poland, but merely provides a preliminary indication of statistics on trial frequency and chronology, the gender of those tried, and the geography of the trials. As Bogucka and Pilaszek, I have eschewed an overall set of statistics for reasons I shall elaborate on later.[5]

Much of the scholarship available in English on the Polish witchcraft persecution is erroneous or has repeated the anachronistic findings in the French summary of Bogdan Baranowski's 1952 overview of the subject.[6] In recent years, however, a new generation of Polish historians has revived the area of witchcraft studies with a host of articles and books on individual cases and several regions. Pilaszek's recent work has provided a comprehensive overview and will be widely read for its English summary. My own study surveys a broad range of factors that played a part in the persecution to present a clear analysis of the witchcraft persecution in Wielkopolska in the early modern period, and in the intellectual context of Polish demonology in its most comprehensive sense. By following the approaches of scholars such as Briggs, Rowlands and Clark, I shall explore the interstices between demonological works and trials. By focusing on Wielkopolska, with its proximity to German lands and its distinct regional identity, I hope to add an important regional study to the tapestry of works available on Polish witchcraft. I hope that this will also serve as a general introduction for the English-speaking reader to demonology in Poland and witchcraft in Wielkopolska.[7]

1
Witchcraft in Context: Histories and Historiographies

A Brief Introduction to Early Modern Poland

As I have espoused a multi-causal explanation of the witchcraft trials, following Briggs and his focus on 'the lives and beliefs of the ordinary people, who were at once the victims and the instigators of most prosecutions',[1] it is essential to provide something in the way of historical context. Although not the place to expound on three centuries of the Commonwealth of Poland-Lithuania's history, a brief overview of early modern Poland and Wielkopolska will set the trials and literature within their social, cultural, economic, political, religious and climatic contexts – all of which may have contributed to the everyday situations leading to accusations of witchcraft.

Poland has long suffered from a reputation for a rather protean geopolitics ranging from a partner in the extensive Poland-Lithuania Commonwealth to its dismemberment and disappearance from Europe's map in 1795. Historians tempted to focus on a retrospective teleology of this period, seek portents of Poland's partitions and demise in every event. Undoubtedly warfare, economic decline, an increase in intolerance, political unrest and climatic problems from the middle of the seventeenth century onwards, contributed to a breakdown in the fabric of Polish society and the conditions under which the population functioned.[2] That this disastrous period coincided with an apparent increase in witchcraft trials deserves closer examination.

The dominant feature of early modern Poland is the all-pervasive power of the *szlachta* translated widely as 'nobility', and since they played a key role as judges, accusers, victims and witnesses in the trials, I shall briefly explain the complexities of this estate. *Szlachta* is a broader term than its nearest English equivalent 'nobility' suggests, ranging from landless nobles and those who had even voluntarily entered into serfdom, to part-owners of a village and great magnate families owning vast swathes of land throughout the Commonwealth. However, all were theoretically equal as *szlachta*, each had a vote in the election of the monarch and their status was fiercely guarded and legally defended.[3] Estimates place their numbers at between six and ten per cent of the population, which remained constant until the end of the eighteenth century.[4] In 1569, it is estimated that this estate owned approximately 60 per cent of land in the Commonwealth, the Church 25 per cent, and the Crown the remaining 15 per cent, but by 1670, 57 per cent of the *szlachta* were landless, possibly contributing to social conflict.[5]

The importance of the *szlachta* was underlined by the division of political power between the king, the *Senat* (Senate or Upper House), and the *Sejm* (Lower House). Nonetheless, the noble estate influenced all aspects of life, with control over the peasantry, the judicial system, trade, the development of cities, clerical appointments as well as foreign policy. From the mid-fifteenth century the monarch required *szlachta* consent to introduce legislation, establish taxes, or call a *levée en masse*. A century later in 1569 *szlachta* domination was almost complete: they had won reductions in land tax, an undertaking that no new taxes were to be passed without noble consent, a noble monopoly on land-owning, and the right to buy municipal houses without taxation. Their political leverage was assured by securing the primacy of the *Sejm* over the *Senat*, restricting senior clerical appointments to the nobility and the right to a sentence passed by a court of peers before land or titles could be confiscated. Importantly, in regard to the jurisdiction of witchcraft trials, peasants were deprived of the right to leave the village without the landowner's permission and of the right to appeal to the Royal Courts in a case against their seigneur. Meanwhile, the Seigneur gained the right to demand work on his land from his peasants. The regulation of weights, measures and prices was also under noble control. Poland was largely run by the *szlachta* for the *szlachta*: and its virtually complete control over the legal system and peasantry is a crucial factor for this study.

Yet the *szlachta* itself was a disparate estate made up of many complex layers. The rapid growth in magnate power in the mid-sixteenth century provoked strong attacks from the middling and Calvinist nobility in respect of the distribution of royal land and this so-called Executionist movement reached a crescendo during the 1560s.[6] Such a concentration of titles and positions among so few was the source of much wrath, and as Frost writes, the 'percentage of starosties in the hands of senators and central dignitaries between 1697 and 1763 varied from one palatinate to another, but nowhere was it lower than 56 per cent (Sieradz) and the highest figure was in Rawa, where it reached 99 per cent.[7] Poland was governed implicitly by a magnate oligarchy and although different families enjoyed prominence for certain periods, such power was a constant factor in checking the throne.[8]

Tensions both within the noble estate and between the nobility and peasantry had many roots. The growth in the magnates' fortunes inflamed conflict among the lesser nobility, at whose expense the former's power had often been augmented. It was exacerbated by the crisis caused by the export of gold and silver and the import of luxury goods. These factors led to even greater consolidation of land by magnates, who increased the volume of exports to combat decreasing purchasing power, thus increasing peasant labour duties.[9] In the *upadek* 'collapse' of the mid-seventeenth century, predictably the middling and lower *szlachta* suffered most and this was heightened by the loss of labour through wars and disease that often forced the sale of lands and possessions.[10] It was well-nigh impossible for Poland to be a strong state economically, but *szlachta* opposition also blighted political and social development.[11] In addition, Poland was a state with very little centralization of power, where the nobility and church owned or leased the majority of the land and acted as they saw fit therein, which significantly weakened the judicial system and resulted in localized variations.

External threats from Muscovy, Sweden, the Turkish state and Saxony further fuelled the tense internal politics of the noble estate. The negotiations necessary between the monarch and the *szlachta* prior to military action increased factionalism. During royal elections these factions (with or without heavy bribes) backed either the *Piast* or 'native' candidate or foreigners.[12] The relatively peaceful economic stability in the last quarter of the sixteenth century gave way to the tumult of the following century, which witnessed the Zebrzydowski *rokosz* or 'rebellion' (1606–08), the First Swedish War (1617–29) and the First Turkish War (1620–21). The currency became ever more depleted and inflation increased. A brief peace with both Muscovy and Sweden was the calm before the proverbial storm as Poland experienced the devastation renowned as *Potop* or 'the Deluge'. The country was beset on all sides, by Chmielnicki's rebellion in Ukraine (1648–57), the First Northern War (1654–60), the Muscovite War (1655–67) and Lubomirski's rebellion (1665–67). Warsaw was occupied, Cracow besieged and the cult of the Virgin Mary gained national importance after the miracle at the monastery of Jasna Góra in 1656, as the Poles defeated Sweden. The Second

Turkish War (1672) preceded the reign of King Jan Sobieski (1674-96), which was marked by his unpopularity among the *szlachta*. Political woes were reflected in the paralysis of the *Sejm* by the repeated use of the infamous *liberum veto* (the veto of legislation by one expression of dissent).

'The sixty-six years which separate the reign of John Sobieski from that of Stanisław August Poniatowski are often regarded as the most wretched and the most humiliating in the whole of Polish history', as Davies remarks.[13] During this time the Saxon Wettin kings August II (1697-1704 and 1709-33) and August III (1733-64) held the thrones of Saxony and Poland simultaneously. August II fought the Great Northern War (1700-21) and by its end, according to Frost, the Commonwealth was in an anarchic stalemate, its international position in ruins, its political system paralysed, and the economy wrecked.[14] It is during the last quarter of the seventeenth century and the first quarter of the eighteenth that the sample shows a peak in the witchcraft persecution – when Poland was sliding towards decline.

Amid this panoply of crises, the dethronement of August II in 1704 and the War of the Polish Succession (1733-38) were particularly important factors in the history of Wielkopolska, bringing the election of local magnate Stanisław Leszczyński to the throne. However, his five-year tenure ended with Saxon and Russian troops marching in to secure the succession of August's son, elected August III. In 1764, Catherine the Great's one-time lover, Stanisław Poniatowski, was elected king of Poland only to preside over the dismemberment and eventual destruction of the Commonwealth in 1795, despite introducing a greater degree of centralization and attempting reform. Ironically Poniatowski set in motion much debate about political reform and the sociopolitical grounds on which the *szlachta* functioned. Indeed, it was during his reign that the *Sejm* passed the statute ending witchcraft trials in 1776.

It was not only the Polish noble estate that differed from its European counterparts. For example, Polish towns played a very limited if any formal political role and only Cracow had the right to be represented in parliament. Towns were either owned by the king (royal towns), by the clergy or privately owned by *szlachta*, which had clear implications for legal jurisdiction. Ownership fluctuated throughout the period and towns developed well up until the first half of the seventeenth century.[15] Even by the end of the sixteenth century, of 900 chartered towns in the crown, only eight exceeded 10,000 inhabitants and the majority of towns consisted of small predominantly rural populations numbering between 500 and 2000. Thus, the majority of the Commonwealth's population was rural and in addition, wars and epidemics of the seventeenth century may have reduced this urban population by as much as 60 to 80 per cent, with the exception of Royal Prussia and Gdańsk. The population was frequently supplemented by influxes of immigrants (for example, from Brandenburg and Silesia during the Thirty Years War) and many nobles, especially in Wielkopolska, welcomed migrants, often settling them with land and preferable conditions.[16] A rich tapestry of communities and beliefs coexisted in the Commonwealth, also home to Jews, Armenians, Tartars, Ruthenians, Germans, Scots, Roma and Lithuanians among others.

Another indirect impact on the persecution was the rise and fall of Poland's role as a leading grain exporter. The intensification of the trade exacerbated the miseries of much of the peasantry, as the majority of estates were run with extremely cheap or free labour and, of course, the *szlachta* had full control over production processes. At the turn of the sixteenth century 'restrictions on the peasantry began to take on a real force as an agrarian boom, brought about a shift from cash rentals to peasant labour services', which helped to increase production, but also resulted in free peasants often being enserfed.[17] Many estate owners increased the days of service required from their peasants to work on the demesne farm, at first to increase profit levels and later to maintain them as prices fell. The decline of Poland's share of the grain trade affected both *szlachta* and peasants, compounding suffering caused by 'the Deluge'. It is estimated that between 1648 and 1660, over a quarter of the Republic's population was lost, heavily impacting on trade patterns and hastening the declining economic role of towns. Hand-in-hand with this went the impoverishment of the peasants, culminating in what Davies notes as 'an irreversible process of economic regression' in the mid-seventeenth century.[18] Others point to the underdeveloped bureaucracy and weak fiscal position that had arisen partially from such a weak monarchy.[19] At the same time, the debasement of the coinage created a further fiscal crisis from 1650, exacerbated by an influx of foreign currency. The collapse of the economy was echoed by the lack of effective centralized political power.[20] Between 1669 and 1762, only 20 of the 53 *sejmy* enacted legislation. Real power lay with the confederacies and the local dietines – in the hands of the *szlachta*.[21] Thus Poland's decline spelt economic misery for the peasantry and degradation in living standards for the lower levels of the nobility, sowing the seeds for increased societal conflict.

Although many historians see the demise of Poland as a consequence of the iron grip of the *szlachta*, the estate can take some credit for the proud tradition of religious toleration of the sixteenth and first half of the seventeenth centuries. This, exemplified by the 1573 Edict of Toleration, earned Poland the sobriquet of a 'state without stakes' and was only possible because of the fierce independence of the *szlachta*.[22] However, by 1660 less than half of the population was Roman Catholic and the Commonwealth was home to: Uniates, Orthodox, Lutherans, Calvinists, Arians, Mennonites, Schwenkfeldians, Anabaptists, Czech Brethren, Karaites, Muslims, Armenians and Jews. By the mid-sixteenth century the Protestant Reformation had been relatively successful, in particular among the *szlachta*, perhaps attracted by the thought of avoiding tithes and other taxes payable to the Roman Catholic Church. Many also found Calvinism appealing, with its notions of the elect, especially those of a Sarmatian leaning.[23] Protestant influence was visible in intellectual debate and Polish students attended the Lutheran University of Koenigsberg and other European Protestant universities. But, however great the gains Protestantism made in Poland, especially among prominent Lithuanian magnates such as the Radziwiłł and Sapieha, ultimately the Counter-Reformation triumphed. The Reformation failed largely due to a widespread lack of support from the peasants, the independence of the *szlachta* and the lack of unity among the Protestant communities – visible in the Sandomierz Agreement of 1570.[24] The identification of certain German communities with Protestantism created a basis for prejudice, exacerbated by Swedish and Saxon looting and violence which saw the Protestant faith often identified in the Polish Roman Catholic psyche with the enemy, in a crude dichotomy of Pole-Roman Catholic and foreigner-Protestant.

Pilaszek suggests that the Counter-Reformation impacted on the witchcraft persecution in a more direct way. She believes that the charge of heresy (within which witchcraft fell) was regarded by the nobility as a weapon wielded by the Roman Catholic Church against non-Roman Catholic nobles, fuelling their fight for jurisdiction over the crime as a measure of self-preservation.[25] Undoubtedly, Poland was one of the great successes of the Counter-Reformation and the Roman Catholic Church gained many converts over several generations. Cardinal Hosius, whose *Confessio fidei Catholicae Christianae* of 1553 ran to 30 editions in European languages during his lifetime (1504–79), was a leading light at the Council of Trent and also introduced the Jesuit order to Poland in 1565. The Order's humanist educational programme was key to Counter-Reformation success, as the high reputation of its schools attracted even Protestant *szlachta*, facilitating great waves of conversions. In 1600 there were 25 large Jesuit schools and colleges in Poland-Lithuania; by

1772 they numbered 115. Educational levels also rose among the clergy during the sixteenth century, resulting in more incumbents remaining in their parishes than in Western Europe, which also probably played an important part in a lack of enthusiasm for the Reformation among the peasantry, yeomanry and burghers. The *szlachta* generation of the 1570s and 1580s returned *en masse* to Roman Catholicism, following the trends for humanistic learning. Poland continued to be largely tolerant until 1658 when the expulsion of the Arians indicated a grave turning point and a wave of radical Marianism swept the land. In 1668 apostasy from Roman Catholicism was forbidden under penalty of exile and by the latter half of the seventeenth century it was rare for non-Roman Catholics to hold positions of power. This coincides with the second wave of Tridentine reform at the turn of the eighteenth century, which Pilaszek contends reached out to the peasantry and finally catechized greater numbers.[26] By 1772, out of a population of twelve million, non-Roman Catholics numbered no more than one and a half million.

It is worth remembering that Polish religiosity of the seventeenth and eighteenth centuries has been described as *ludowa* 'folk' and *swoista* 'of itself', strongly linked to fundamental beliefs, values and customs and with mainly rural characteristics. The increasing pauperization of the countryside may have driven more people to turn to popular piety and seek supernatural explanations for misfortune. Perhaps proof of this can be seen in the Jesuits' many attempts at eradicating popular belief and their increased missionary work.[27] A new ambiguity between the divine and the diabolic and the use of herbs and the sacramental arose, in response to redefining of the orthodox. In a time of increased misfortune, witchcraft provided a ready explanation.[28] The peak of the Polish witchcraft persecution coincided with one of the most destructive periods in Polish history, when power was decentralized and there was a weak centre, when there were political and economic disasters, throughout periods of warfare and destruction, and when a mission to catechize was aggressively winning the day. All these factors contributed to the conditions under which people sought answers to their daily misfortunes within the complex world of witchcraft.

Early Modern Wielkopolska

In the seventeenth century, the estimated population of Wielkopolska was 800,000, of whom 240,000 lived in cities and small towns – a relatively high rate of urbanization. These figures fluctuated when towns thrived or declined, during epidemics, and when rural areas suffered destruction.[29] By the second half of the eighteenth century, of Wielkopolska's towns, 90 belonged to the *szlachta*, 26 to the crown, and 16 to the clergy, although as in the rest of the Commonwealth there was the usual oligarchy of titleholders.[30] The region's separate economic structure and close links to Pomerania, Silesia and its German neighbours gave it a distinctive identity, whilst its political identity was defined by its narrow, educated élite of magnates who were often challenged by a broader layer of educated and politically active middling *szlachta*, especially during times of conflict.[31] The rest of the noble estate consisted of smallholders or even landless *szlachta*, but it was the middling landowners who made up over 90 per cent of Poznań's and 50 per cent of Kalisz's *szlachta* and filled the *Sejm* and *Sejmiki* 'regional dietines'.[32] The political and economic fortunes of Wielkopolska's magnate class depended upon the monarch, the fluctuating fate of crown lands and offices as well as dynastic issues. For example, the Górka and Opaliński families held the majority of crown land in the second half of the sixteenth century, but by the eighteenth century, their fortunes had declined. In contrast, in the Poznań palatinate, 47.5 per cent of noble possessions were held by the so-called fragment-owning *szlachta* and 32 per cent by *szlachta* owning one village. Many even owned a part share, for example the village of Chwałkowo Kościelne had five owners.[33] Wielkopolska was relatively stable in the first half of the period and the religious toleration guaranteed by the Confederation of Warsaw allowed its large dissenting population to live in peace. Wilson argues that this religious plurality lasted until at least 1648 and sees the mid-seventeenth century as the crucial point at which religious toleration broke down and Roman Catholicism became the dominant religion.[34] The dimly viewed capitulation of the magnate Krzysztof Opaliński to the Swedes in July 1655 increased tensions among the *szlachta* (especially against the magnates), xenophobia and intolerance. The destruction wreaked by Swedish soldiers quartered in the area was followed by similar actions by the Brandenburgers. In 1664 the king garrisoned soldiers in Poznań and Kalisz – merely a prelude to the first half of the eighteenth century, when soldiers quartered in the region looted and destroyed its towns as Wielkopolska suffered for its support of Leszczyński. Unsurprisingly, this period was also marked by a slowdown if not a halt in the establishment of new towns in Wielkopolska, which lasted into the eighteenth century, as 60 per cent of existing towns had to be rebuilt and repopulated, with predictable economic consequences.[35]

The towns of Grodzisk, Kalisz and Poznań benefited from their position on the Silesian – Wielkopolska grain trade route and saw many merchants, travellers and itinerants pass through. Wielkopolska was one of the most confessionally mixed areas in the Commonwealth with Germans, Silesians, Czechs, Brandenburgers, Pomeranians, Dutch and Scots, who were predominantly, but not all, Protestants (including Calvinists, Lutherans, Czech Brethren and other denominations) and who were found among all levels of society, along with Jews and Roman Catholics. The rural majority remained Roman Catholic, despite pockets of Protestant strongholds, whereas German communities were mainly resident within towns,[36] including Kościan, Gostyń, Grodzisk, Krzywiń and Poniec, all of which experienced trials for witchcraft. The Thirty Years War (1618–48) and its aftermath saw influxes of migrants to the area, but Protestants were also well represented among the magnate class (predominantly Lutheran rather than Calvinist as in the rest of the Commonwealth), and at this time, their faith was no barrier to their election to the *Sejm* or *Senat*.[37] By 1600 there were 142 Lutheran communities and the Lutheran Church maintained a solid position throughout the seventeenth century, to a greater extent than other Protestant denominations.[38] It was officially accepted in six of the royal Wielkopolska towns – Wschowa, Brojce, Międzyrzecz, Skierzyna, Czaplinek and Walcz – while the number of Roman Catholic churches in Poznań halved.[39] However, later confessional polarization was exacerbated by the Counter-Reformation and a perception that Protestants had welcomed the Swede Charles Gustav during Opaliński's surrender.[40]

The disasters Wielkopolska experienced from the middle of the seventeenth century, coupled with the general collapse of the Commonwealth, all contributed to the environment in which the witchcraft persecution took place. The broader themes of confessionalization, war, epidemics, climate, economic decline and political uncertainty provided a framework for individuals' experiences of destruction, pauperization and religious uncertainty, which may have convinced many that the Devil truly was at work. Belief in witchcraft and the Devil may also have been fuelled by Poznań's position as a crossroads and market town, through which many travellers passed, exchanging tales of witchcraft and gossip. Interestingly, Pilaszek discerns a link between towns that conducted trade beyond their own borders and higher rates of witchcraft trials.[41] One might also speculate that magnates from eastern Poland, who had built up estates in Wielkopolska during the 'Deluge', brought with them witchcraft beliefs from the East, apparently an area rife with witchcraft according to several demonologists.[42] The presence of foreigners, superstitious soldiers and their camp followers might also have contributed to a varied repository of beliefs. We can also only speculate about the

German Roman Catholics who settled in villages belonging to Poznań between 1719 and 1749 from Bamberg, infamous for its large-scale witch-hunts a century earlier.[43] However, these are merely speculations as to what may have fed into witchcraft beliefs.

Historiographies of Witchcraft

Since classical times different notions about witches,[44] or those believed to be able to make use of supernatural power for either good or evil, have existed in various societies. The persecution and execution of witches in Europe, which began in the fifteenth century, increased rapidly in the sixteenth century throughout much of western and northern Europe, reaching a peak, according to most historians, between the 1580s and the 1630s. There is a rich range of studies on the causes of witchcraft, individual trials and an increasing number of regional studies. However, a great deal of attention has been paid to attempts at quantifying the persecution, resulting in estimates of the number of European deaths ranging from nine million women alone[45] to a more realistic figure of forty thousand men and women.[46] Attempts to provide mono-causal reasons for the witchcraft persecution have invariably failed when applied to a broader spectrum, but have produced a rich historiography.[47]

However, Briggs's article *'Many Reasons Why'* encapsulates both in its title and content, the historiographical route that I have followed. I wanted to step back and allow the material to speak for itself rather than impose a framework upon the diverse materials. Witchcraft studies boast a plethora of varied and interesting historiographies and I shall mention but a few strands of interest. For example, some feminist theorists read the predominance of women tried in most areas as a persecution of women, whether as healers, harridans, midwives, mothers, old women, widows or because of poverty, fertility or lack thereof and domestic issues.[48] While some historians see poverty and/or lack of status as conducive to being regarded as a witch,[49] others sense social tension in which women, who were single, independent or just regarded as 'other' were accused of witchcraft.[50] Some historians have concentrated on the role of the élites and linked the persecution to the centralization of the state and state-building processes[51] or to their repression and control of the lower orders.[52] Others have suggested that the causes be found in quotidian socio-economic interactions embodied by the functionalist charity-refused paradigm,[53] or taken psychoanalytic and other interpretations based around birth, fertility and motherhood.[54] While theories focusing on the élites as a driving force have predominantly relied upon readings of demonology, close readings of trial records have revealed that accusations were most often part of a social phenomenon played out within a community, dependent upon individual quarrels and disputes. What most historians can agree upon is that many of those who accused others were convinced that harm had been done to them, their possessions or their community, and many turned to the courts only as a last resort when they had been unable to gain redress from the suspected witch. There are clearly dangers in applying a monolithic causal explanation to a rich and complex phenomenon with local, regional and national similarities and differences.

Historiographies of Polish Witchcraft

I have divided Polish historiography into four periods, with the first contemporary to the persecution and the second period beginning with the end of the persecution and ending in 1952, when Bogdan (Bohdan) Baranowski's (1915–93) overview of witchcraft appeared. Accounts of the Polish persecution have until recently been dominated by his work, which marked an important turning point in the historiography of Polish witchcraft.[55] Many of the authors writing in this period were local historians, ethnographers and legal historians, who based articles on a single court book or trial, but unfortunately, due to extensive damage in the Second World War, some of the pre-war accounts cannot be verified against original trial records and must be viewed with caution.[56] The third period, post-Baranowski, was distinguished by a dependency on his work by the majority of writers, and the fourth is characterized by a new generation, which has challenged his work.[57]

The academic treatment of witchcraft trials in Poland, prior to Baranowski, has been described as dominated by ethnographers with no interest in, or knowledge of, history and historians with no equivalent knowledge of ethnography.[58] Polish historians rarely discussed the witchcraft persecution, eager perhaps to preserve Poland's reputation as a *państwo bez stosów*, 'state without stakes'.[59] Legal historians dominated the field and their articles varied greatly in quality. The synthetic style popular in the nineteenth century produced detailed descriptions of folk customs, law and some trials, so consequently, in the first few decades of the following century, authors privileged accounts of the witches' purported practices within the context of contemporary folk beliefs. Krzyżanowski, in 1844, was one of the first to write about witchcraft trials in the context of their constitutional background, concluding with the controversial Doruchów case of 1775, wrongly believed to be the last legal trial for witchcraft in

Poland.⁶⁰ One of the most frequently cited nineteenth-century works was Łukaszewicz's monograph on Krotoszyń, where he writes,

> In the records of our town in the 15th and 16th centuries, we rarely come across witches, but in the 17th century, thanks to ignorance, incubated in Jesuit schools, there is barely a single page in the alderman's records, without a single accusation of witchcraft...⁶¹

He also suggested that 'witches were not an inherently Polish product... but were brought from Germany by means of the barbaric Magdeburg Law', pre-dating the erroneous modern suggestion that Poland be regarded as an extension of the German persecution.⁶² Łukaszewicz claimed that witches were mainly either poor or argumentative women, so the concepts of the witch as female, poor and a German import were already established.⁶³

One of the studies most useful for locating trials, if not for its theories on Polish witchcraft, was Olszewski's essay from 1879, in which he cited over twenty cases, most of which have been verified. His explanation for the predominance of women accused was based on a linguistic theory about the anthropomorphization of various negative concepts (such as war and death) as feminine. He was somewhat closer to the truth when he touched upon the idea that loose morals were a reason for women being accused of witchcraft, supporting later feminist behavioural explanations.⁶⁴ Despite discussions of demonology, partial reproductions of trials and listings of trials, the nineteenth-century contribution can be characterized by helpful references to primary sources, but little methodological progress.⁶⁵

A new impetus came with the publication of *Wisła* 'Vistula' and *Lud* 'Folk', two journals focusing primarily on folk beliefs and customs, which stimulated a multi-disciplinary approach to witchcraft studies prior to the Second World War. This elicited many different approaches, from literary-psychological explanations under the influence of the 'Young Poland' cultural movement, to a renewed emphasis on the legal context of the witchcraft persecution.⁶⁶ Further transcripts of witchcraft trials were published and articles on Polish demonology began to appear, so that by the time Baranowski published his work in 1952 a consensus on the characteristics of the witchcraft persecutions had emerged. In advance of the functionalist trend evident in the 1960s, Polish writers had already identified social tensions as causes of the Polish persecution.⁶⁷ It is possible that Baranowski drew upon the suggestion that tension between the peasants and their seigneurs fuelled unrest to the extent that the peasantry used witchcraft as a tool of social and personal empowerment or revenge.[68] As we shall see, landowners did accuse peasants and servants of using witchcraft to harm them and their households. While witches were regarded predominantly as women, foreigners such as Finns or Tartars were also suspect, alongside those with 'extraordinary' knowledge such as the cunning folk, shepherds, millers and the Roma. Those perceived as 'other' were more literally demonized in the portrayal of Jews and Germans as devils.[69] In contrast to the consensus that the majority of the accused were women, opinions were divided as to whether noble women were ever accused.[70]

Perhaps the most important debate centred on the extent of the witchcraft persecution. There was a consensus that Poland saw few if any trials during the sixteenth century, but then experienced an extreme increase in the seventeenth and eighteenth centuries,[71] attributed by some to the publication of the Polish translation of part two of *Malleus Maleficarum*, entitled *Młot na czarownice*, in 1614. Some claimed it was used as material for homilies, study and even as an executioner's handbook, but no evidence has been found to support these claims.[72] Many historians were convinced of the large scale of the Polish persecution, claiming variously that every court had passed at least one sentence for witchcraft, that trials were virtually an everyday occurrence and that there was barely a page in a court record book without a trial.[73] The consensus on the extent of the persecution contrasted sharply with dissent as to whether the trial procedures, torture and details were German 'imports', suggested not only on the grounds of geographical proximity but also because of the introduction of German laws, the presence of German communities in Poland and the inevitable cultural flow.[74] However, many Polish ethnographers and anthropologists concluded that witchcraft beliefs originated from ancient Slavonic practices, demonized by Christianity.[75] Prior to Baranowski's work, several German historians had also written on the subject or reproduced trials from Poznań, Braniewo and Gdańsk.[76]

The various examinations of the judicial procedures evoked discussion around the reported practice of shaving the accused, the widespread lack of a legal defence and whether judges were uneducated, illiterate and superstitious.[77] For example, the severity of the torture inflicted suggested that judges were forced to pass death sentences to prevent survivors bearing witness.[78] Other historians claimed that the Roman Catholic Church played an important role in the persecutions,[79] but Gloger's challenge to this view is supported by literary sources and several trial records.⁸⁰ Thus, an effective paradigm of the witchcraft persecution had already been established by the time Baranowski's work appeared in 1952.

The Influence of Bogdan Baranowski

Baranowski was the key name in Polish witchcraft studies after 1949 and some of his archival research in this field is very valuable. He dated the first death sentence for witchcraft in Poland passed in a secular court to 1511 at Waliszew, near Poznań, although he claimed there was evidence that the death sentence had been passed in Bishops' Courts prior to this. He dated the peak of the persecution between 1675 and 1725, gave credence to the much-discredited account of the last death sentence for witchcraft in Doruchów in 1775,⁸¹ and claimed that suspected witches had been beaten and murdered after the repeal of the witchcraft acts. His seminal work *Procesy czarownic w Polsce w XVII i XVIII wieku, The Trials of Witches in the 17th and 18th Centuries,* heralded two decades of writing on the subject. We must bear in mind that it was written before the Stalinist Thaw of 1953, which we may read as a Marxist influence on his conclusions that the witchcraft persecution was adopted from the West, fanned by the Roman Catholic Church and used by the nobility to oppress the peasantry. However, this also reflects a continuum with the opinions expressed by his predecessors. Baranowski was also a proponent of the functionalist view, believing that peasants fought both feudalism and their masters with witchcraft and acknowledging that the trials arose as a result of neighbourly tensions and quarrels. His work is an essential point of reference, as a source quoted by the overwhelming majority of authors (both Polish and non-Polish, who read his summary in French) after 1952, but many of his conclusions are now routinely challenged.⁸²

In *Procesy czarownic* Baranowski focused on the causes of the persecution, statistics and extracts from trials and demonology.⁸³ His statistics became a misleading canon for most post-war authors, especially those who read only his French summary, and although he offered a disclaimer, they were subsequently quoted as definitive figures for Poland. These statistics were based on Baranowski's incorrect and anachronistic calculation of 1250 towns in the part of the Polish Republic of the seventeenth and eighteenth centuries that fell within the 1952 Polish boundaries. Estimating that each town court tried an average of four cases for witchcraft during the period and sentenced two people to death from each trial, he then added to this figure of 10,000 death sentences, 5000–10,000 deaths reflecting illegal murders of witchcraft suspects, resulting in a total of 15,000–20,000 deaths over the three centuries.[84] If this figure were correct, the total number of deaths in Poland would account for 37.5 per cent of the European total, given the recently revised figure of 40,000 executions.[85] This is highly unlikely, however, and it must be ruled out on the grounds of faulty methodology rather than lack of veracity, since the high rate of record loss means that a definitive figure for executions can never be reached. Baranowski's figures also appear exaggerated in the light of recent trends towards progressively downgrading claims of mass trials with large numbers of victims. Clearly the difference in territory between the *Koronna*, 'crown territories' in the seventeenth century, and the Poland of 1952 is evident, not to mention the territorial fluctuations of Poland between 1500 and 1800. However, the author revised his own statistics down to a few thousand in an epilogue to the Polish translation of Baschwitz's work in 1971. Unfortunately many scholars have ignored this, preferring the myth of 15,000 Polish witches.[86]

Beyond Baranowski

One of Baranowski's key claims was that Poland's witchcraft persecution peaked later than in most of Europe, correlating with the Hungarian pattern. Klaniczay attributed the latter to a natural time lag for cultural transmission from the West and later socio-economic developments.[87] Levack suggested Poland be regarded 'as an extension of the German phenomenon' and that the persecution increased with the transfer of jurisdiction from the ecclesiastical to the municipal courts. He attributed the comparative lateness to the sudden outbreak of wars in the seventeenth century, citing Baranowski's figures, albeit with a caveat that he regarded them as too high. Levack also supported the idea that the witches' sabbats and pacts with the Devil were German imports and viewed the translation of *Malleus Maleficarum* as an impetus for further dissemination of belief in the Devil. In his updated work from 2006, he continues to include the discredited trial from Doruchów in 1775 and the 1793 reported execution of two women in the Poznań area, routinely discredited by Polish authors.[88] An examination of the work of the few non-Polish authors who have discussed Polish witch-hunts reveals that they nearly all rely directly or indirectly on Baranowski's publications.[89] Writing in the otherwise excellent *The Athlone History of Witchcraft and Magic in Europe: The Period of the Witch Trials*, Monter also repeats the 'cultural lag' theory. He is of the opinion that since Poland's chronology was similar to Hungary's, but with a population (excluding

Jews and Orthodox populations) twice as large, then we should expect 1000 executions in Poland, that is, twice those in Hungary.[90]

Many of the Polish authors writing in the thirty years following the publication of *Procesy* agreed with Baranowski's conclusions[91] and some, including the respected historian Tazbir, agreed that trials were the result of a class war between the peasants and their seigneurs, writing at a time when a Marxist view of history was de rigueur in Poland.[92] Polish historians have suggested that German Law, the translation of the *Malleus* and the Counter-Reformation all helped to intensify the persecution and have examined similarities between accusations levelled at witches and Jews, without ruling out pagan influences.[93] Other writers reproduced trial extracts, but few offered a coherent explanation for the phenomenon as a whole.[94]

In recent years many more full trial transcriptions and regional studies have been published, as a new generation of scholars has challenged Baranowski. Including the trials published by the pre-war generation, there is now a wide range of transcripts and discussions of trials in Polish, which mainly focus on one trial or town,[95] including one full trial published in English, with more to come.[96] The corpus of Polish witchcraft trials numbers over one hundred trials or fragments, supplemented by more in-depth analysis, such as Wijaczka's work on Royal Prussia and the Kielce area, Szkurłatowski's work on Gdańsk, and a collection of village trials and the analysis and reproduction of some of the numerous Kleczew trials by Wiślicz. A recent survey by Pilaszek in Polish with an English summary has greatly added to our understanding of the subject and Ostling's publication has also provided interesting insights.[97]

Among the first to challenge Baranowski's statistics was Karpiński, who in his work on Poznań, Lublin, Cracow and Lwów between *c.* 1550 and *c.* 1700, found only 78 records of witchcraft trials involving women in the four towns. Pilaszek, in a critical examination of Baranowski's methodology, even doubted the veracity of some of his references to trials, whilst Salmonowicz pointed out Baranowski's work reflected the ideological constraints of its time. Bogucka criticizes Baranowski's works and concludes rather incautiously that Poland lacked an intense persecution because nobles could not afford to lose labour, the Polish devil was a figure of mockery, there was a paucity of demonology and no capitalist transformation took place.[98]

Returning to Ostling, there are many interesting insights to be gained from his examination of the witchcraft trials in relation to magical practices, peasant religiosity and Host-stealing in particular. Ostling sees not only a Marian influence, but also regards Polish Christianity as christocentric, with its roadside passions of the Christ, and Poland's view of itself as the 'Christ of Nations'. His work confirms the importance of the Host as a motif and the vital belief in transubstantiation, which allow us a better insight into the trial confessions. The in-depth discussion of 'prayers' or what might be termed 'spells' or 'incantations' is also interesting and emphasizes their analogous nature, their popularity and their ambiguity, which is also supported by my research. There is no doubting the centrality of the roles of the nobility, of torture or of a mentality that feared the zero-sum nature of resources, on which our accounts both agree. However, as Stuart Clark points out,

> All the more disappointing, therefore, is the book's major ontological confusion about the reality of witchcraft. Witches are throughout described as 'imagined' because witchcraft did not really exist, whereas the book's very subject is the beliefs and actions of those historical agents who for 250 years believed largely that it did, and its declared aim is to allow these beliefs and actions to speak for themselves. We do not have to accept Clifford Geertz's famous suggestions that the real may be as imagined as the imaginary to see that the historian has no business adjudicating the ontological preferences of the past.[99]

However, as interesting as some of Clark's suggestions are, I think it's rather dangerous to regard the confessions as 'explorations of Christian piety', when surely anyone accused of witchcraft would try and deploy all the religious knowledge at their command to prove their piety. That's not to deny the possibility of discovering that piety within confessions, but to read such protestations with a little more distance. The strong links to milk theft and theories of moisture and dryness also make an interesting supposition, but are not suitably convincing to this author. It is his decision to virtually eschew the archives (with the exception of Lublin) that is more troubling, as this can only make sweeping conclusions look rather doubtful, as Pilaszek and I contend.[100] His work was based on a database of 254 trials, which territorially he claims to be based on the crown territories. With the exception of some of the Lublin trials, his database comprises secondary sources and some of Wiślicz's transcriptions of a number of Kleczew trials.[101] It is puzzling, to say the least, that he has used several of the Kleczew trials, but ignored others from the same criminal record book which contains over fifty trials.[102] He includes only two trials from Turek, from a court record book containing the trials of 39 women, none from Gniezno and eight out of at least 15 cases from Warta, where again there is a criminal record book replete with trials, which can easily be found in the archives.[103] The overriding concern must be that the claims made for witchcraft in Poland, as a whole, should be modified to reflect the selective nature of the database. For example, the statement, 'I find Kiszka's brief statement to be among the most interesting texts from the entire corpus of Polish witch-trial testimony', rings somewhat hollow, when we know that trials have knowingly been excluded from the database.[104] To put this into perspective, compared to Ostling's 254 selected cases, Pilaszek has found 867 lay cases and this study, limited merely to Wielkopolska, is based on 225 cases (my own preliminary research yielded mentions of over 800 trials). Lack of contact with the archives also means that out-of-date references are reproduced from secondary sources.[105]

As a result, some of his extrapolations require disclaimers. For example, the claim that 'nearly all the accusations against men are exceptional in some way' is based on four trials against five men.[106] Pilaszek's research found 142 men accused in the crown territories, and although her research includes slander cases, which his does not, this indicates a huge discrepancy. As Pilaszek points out, Ostling claims that in only two trials known to him was a sentence based on written law, whereas Berlich, Carpzov and Binsfeld were mentioned in many more trials.[107]

Pilaszek's magisterial work provides a full geographical survey ranging from Wielkopolska to Podolia and Red Ruthenia. As Bogucka and myself, she rightfully eschews any definitive statistical extrapolation for her research on the basis of the state of the archives and extreme record loss. Her database of 867 lay cases included 721 heard before municipal courts, cases heard before village and military courts, as well as slander cases. She suggests that during the reign of Sigismund III Vasa (1587–1632) there was a twofold increase to almost 10 per cent of trials heard and that this shows a decrease from 25 per cent to 19 per cent in trials from a peak between 1676–1700, compared to 1701–25, in comparison with Baranowski's increase from 23 per cent in the former to 32 per cent in the latter. Thus she regards 1680–1700 as the period when the trials started in earnest, with the Great Northern War (1700–21) acting somewhat as a brake on the persecution. The end, she says, came with the end of the nobility's belief in witchcraft, and she dates the last execution to 1774 in Bełżyce, Małopolska, where a man was hanged for witchcraft.[108]

Her research reveals an execution rate of 42 per cent, comparable to the rest of Europe, and found that 80 per cent of the trials heard before the municipal courts were from villages. Her statistics show that 142 men were accused, or 10.6 per cent, and her findings that cases brought against men were not so different to those involving women support most of my evidence. She suggests several reasons why Poland escaped a major persecution, the first of which depended upon the weakness of the Reformation, an absence of any strong heretical movements and the linking of witchcraft to heresy. Second, the state authorities were not interested in hunting witches and so there was little effective development or organization of the legal system, which was highly localized and limited the number of trials with its accusatorial system. She also ascribes the paucity of trials in the sixteenth century to gaps in both legal provision and in the nobility's understanding of the theory of witchcraft.[109] Despite the high proportion of women tried, Pilaszek claims (after Bogucka) that women enjoyed a somewhat higher position in Poland, especially as wives and mothers, and that capitalism didn't degrade their position, thus leading to fewer trials.[110]

Although Pilaszek accepts that the Roman Catholic Church acted as a brake on individual trials, she sees the second wave of Tridentine reforms and the 'mission' undertaken at the turn of the eighteenth century as key to increasing the number of trials. Despite reforms being implemented in provincial parishes and the rebuilding of seminaries, few candidates for the priesthood spent the requisite two years in training. Pilaszek draws attention to the greater role of wandering preachers, as well as the Jesuit and Piarist missionaries. Since the 'mission' of that period placed great emphasis on the fear of Hell and the Devil, the clergy played an important role in building an atmosphere of danger from evil forces, at a time when people felt less secure and possibly turned to ostentatious Baroque liturgy as a comfort. She also mentions the booming trade in sacramentals and the village clergy who may have come to view para-liturgical practices as acceptable. She also links the increase in the intensity of the persecution in the 1680s and 1690s to an increase in sermonizing by religious orders.[111]

Pilaszek sees a range of other influences, such as the *Potop*, the rise of capitalism, the higher age of women at the time of marrying (rendering them more prone to accusations of infanticide and the use of contraception), women's lack of recourse to the law or use of violence and the publication of legal works by Groicki, Damhouder and Carpzov.[112] Importantly, she dismisses the Constitution of 1543 as the turning point in increasing the number of trials on the basis that it was merely a temporary constitution superseded by those of 1562 and 1565.[113] In fact she makes an original case for Hussitism, which appeared in the fifteenth century, as the real watershed, suggesting that only then did trials increase as the growing network of parishes and the battle for orthodoxy revealed doctrinal errors among ordinary people. Witchcraft was regarded as a heresy denoted as *lèse majesté* and was therefore a public crime. She perceptively suggests that because accusations of heresy had been used instrumentally against members of the nobility, they were determined to control jurisdiction over heresy and therefore witchcraft, which played itself out in a battle with the church over jurisdiction.[114]

She ascribes the higher numbers of trials for Wielkopolska and Royal Prussia to better record-retention and concludes that areas which engaged in trade beyond their local spheres had higher rates of trials, as well as those where there was a higher reception rate for German legal works.[115] She supports these views with an analysis showing that between 1676 and 1725, 60 per cent of the trials heard took place in Wielkopolska and Royal Prussia. Pilaszek's work complements this study, supporting many of the tropes and statistics evident in Wielkopolska.

Reading the Archives

The common practice of destroying the *księgi czarne*, 'Black Books' (books of felonies), or *Libri maleficorum* may have been one reason for the scarcity of interest in Polish witchcraft. My survey of Poland's main archives soon disproved that assumption, revealing that witchcraft trials were to be found in a variety legal record books, including: the Municipal Aldermen's Court Books, the Council Court Books, mixed court books, Village Court Books, or exceptionally in a book established specifically for the purpose, such as that for Kleczew which contains the trials of over 100 people.[116] This poses myriad problems for the researcher, but means that potentially there could be thousands more undiscovered cases. While it is possible to gain a rough idea of the frequency with which witchcraft trials appeared in court record books from the Wielkopolska sample, this is unusual because it represents one of the most complete sets of municipal records. From over 200 municipal court record books examined, only five books contained between 10 and 20 trials, many contained one or two cases per book, whilst the overwhelming majority revealed no cases. The sample used in this study is based on four main types of sources. First, references to trials in secondary literature were checked and the book in which they were found was checked for further trials. Second, the criminal record books for Wielkopolska in both AGAD (Central Archive of Old Polish Records) and Poznań's state archive were examined. The Poznań criminal records 'fair copies' ran between 1502–1600 and 1616–29 and the deposition books covered most of the period between 1652–1775.[117] The *bruliony* 'rough copies' covered roughly 50 years between 1553 and 1723 and the *zeznania* 'testimony' books focused on the middle of the eighteenth century.[118] Appropriately, the last record in the Poznań series of criminal records is a contract between the *Wójt*, 'alderman', of the city of Poznań and the executioner, concluded on 2 January 1763. Third, court books described in the archival catalogues as containing witchcraft trials were thoroughly examined and finally, the Wielkopolska municipal court record books for the period were sampled at a rate of every fourth book.

The aim was to collect the largest number of trials from the sources most likely to contain them, thereby providing a viable sample. The municipal court records were an obvious source as the place where witchcraft trials were officially recorded. This is supported by the sample, which indicates that out of 205 cases for which information is available, in 114 (55.6 per cent) of these the municipal court was deputed to try a case in a village. In addition, a study of village witchcraft trials concluded that although some cases were heard before the village courts, the majority were most likely to be heard by municipal courts because they were better organized, usually retained an executioner and had greater financial resources. As the courts of higher instance, the municipal courts could dismiss village courts' sentences and most importantly they could pass the death sentence.[119] There are many other places where trials may have been recorded, such as the Roman Catholic visitation records, other municipal records, military records and village records, which have not formed part of the sample, but which would benefit from further research.

Wielkopolska was chosen as the best set of records from which to take a sample for several reasons. Despite extensive losses in the Second World War, the Poznań archives were relatively well preserved, regarded by the Germans as part of the Wartegau. This extensive set of records covered a large geographical area that also complemented the contemporary demonological literature originating from Poznań. However, the *Himmlerkartoteka*, held in Poznań and compiled on the orders of Heinrich Himmler during the Second World War, which also has references to many trials in the area, has been omitted from this study because of its poor quality and inaccuracy.[120] The problem of record loss and damage is particularly acute in Poland, since after the Second World War only 800 of approximately 5000 municipal court books from

AGAD survived and only 20 per cent of the 1.6 million documents dating from between the sixteenth and nineteenth centuries.[121] In Poznań, the Poznańskie Towarzystwo Przyjaciół Nauk (PTPN) archive lost 488 of its 788 municipal court records from the fifteenth century and the Biblioteka Raczyńskich also suffered heavy losses.[122] Many Polish archival materials were taken to the then Soviet Union, destroyed, burnt or taken to Germany, and although some records were returned after the war, much was lost or is still missing. The relatively random nature of the surviving records has a distorting effect and precludes any wider geographical or statistical conclusions. Therefore, I must reiterate that the sample can only provide indications of possible patterns within Wielkopolska, but my initial research, which located mentions of around 800 trials (excluding Silesia and Pomerania), allows a conservative estimate of a very minimal figure to be made for a broader geographical area.[123] Given an average of between 1.5 and 2 executions per trial (an average taken from the statistics of the detailed sample from Wielkopolska) this figure would result in a total of between 1200 and 1600 executions, placing the persecution numerically at least on a par with Scotland. However, the population of the Polish regions of Mazowsze, Wielkopolska and Małopolska alone was thought to have wavered between 3.1 million and 3.25 million between 1580 and 1700, against one million for Scotland.[124] Pilaszek's statistics of 867 cases with 1316 accused and 558 executed are regarded by Ostling as being at the low end, although his statistics reveal an average of 1.1 executions per trial.[125]

There are other reasons why statistics cannot confidently be presented. First, while there are undoubtedly felony books containing nothing but witchcraft trials, there are equally hundreds if not thousands of books containing none. For example, the municipal court record books for Rzeszów (not in Wielkopolska) show barely a couple of mentions of witchcraft,[126] whereas the Kleczew book[127] contains only witchcraft trials. The dilemma lies in the so-called dark figure of trials, which cannot be discerned, so it is impossible to estimate the number of court record books lost, destroyed or retained in private collections. Of these, one cannot know how many were free from or full of trials, so even the most chronologically complete sets of criminal records (such as Poznań) may still not reveal the true number of witchcraft trials.

The quality of the extant trial material is varied and consists of partial or full written records of the judicial procedures, denunciation, torture, confessions and sentences of the accused witches. The records are a mixture of first drafts or *bruliony* and 'clean' copies. Some are extremely difficult to read, others are examples of careful and considered calligraphy. The information contained in the records varies from a few sentences of the judicial decree to an annotated account with extensive witness statements, references to other trials, appeals and other accounts of interaction between the judiciary, the accused and the accusers.

Literary Sources

The decision to examine the broadest possible range of printed sources has yielded varied representations of the witch, challenging many stereotypes.[128] Witches and devils were used as devices in a variety of literary genres, including medical and agricultural works (pseudo-scientific reference works), encyclopaedias, chronicles and treatises. Clark's suggestion that for people of the early modern period the discussion of witchcraft was in fact a forum for enquiring into religion, science and politics has encouraged many to re-examine a range of materials and witchcraft tracts in the light of their relevance to broader contemporary debates. Through focusing on understanding the mentalities and motives of both the accused and their accusers, Clark's work proves the vital importance of examining representations of the Devil, the witch and witchcraft in varying forms of texts, such as drama, calendars and poetry.[129] Following his lead, this work examines a wide range of Polish literary forms with the aim of identifying and exploring motives and motifs common to the witchcraft trials.[130]

2
The World of the Witches: Confessions and Conflicts

The previous chapter set the historical and historiographical contexts for introducing the trial records and testing them against selected theories. In this chapter, I shall introduce statistics drawn from the Wielkopolska sample (with the clear proviso that they ought not to be extrapolated to represent any geographical notion of Poland). I will also sketch the chronology and geography that emerge, the evolution of the definition of the crime of witchcraft and identify the demographics of the accused. This will enable us to examine how the paradigms of the witch were defined, whether there was a composite, recognized body of attributes, ascribed to the 'witch', to see how people negotiated belief systems and also to lay the basis for investigating any correlation between narratives and details found in the trials and in the printed sources examined in later chapters. The trial narratives reveal features common to the majority of European witchcraft trials, which emerged through accepted vocabulary, narratives and sequences of events, of which the judiciary and the accused often seemed to have been aware and co-authored. However, secondary narratives also emerged, revealing histories of abuse, misfortune, quarrels within the community or families and details of other crimes, which provide a prism through which to view early modern life. The widespread application of torture predisposed most of the accused to confess and in many cases there are subtle and more obvious differences among confessions prior to and after torture. However, great care must be taken in reading the trial records as texts largely controlled and shaped by the judiciary, for as we shall see, a confession, as often intended in the Roman Catholic Church, was an instrument to encourage people to reckon with their own perceived failings and thus was a catalyst, for releasing private matters into the public domain. We do great injustice to those accused

30 *Witchcraft in Early Modern Poland, 1500–1800*

if we fail to acknowledge their agency in shaping the narratives and in trying to produce answers they thought might either be acceptable or might put an end to their suffering.[1] Through reading the trials, we can add flesh to the statistical bones of the sample and explore not only the most obvious pattern of the gendering of witchcraft, but also determine whether there are indeed links between the trials and selected factors such as climate, epidemics, confessionalization and German influence – all of which have been suggested as possible influences on the persecution.

The Chronology of the Persecution in the Wielkopolska Sample

The sample consisted of 225 cases involving over 460 individuals accused before secular courts between 1500 and 1800. Two controversial and unverified trials reported in Poznań (1793) and Doruchów (1775) have been omitted, as well as several cases heard in Gostyń described by Przybyszewski.[2] However, the reference in an Ostrzeszów case from 1783 to the seigneur of Doruchów interrogating and ordering six women to be burnt at the stake has been included.

The sample indicates an average of less than one trial per year and that two people were tried per trial, confirming Baranowski's estimate. The graph in Table 1 shows increases in the 1580s and the first two decades of the seventeenth century, reaching a peak between 1660 and 1740, with a dip between 1700 and 1710 – a period Frost identified as unstable. Bogucka suggests that 'on the whole, the penalties became more cruel and savage on [sic] the middle of the 17th century, the first few decades of the 18th century in particular were marked by the growth of sadism in the administration of justice'.[3] She also claims that more savage punishments were meted out to curb the increasing crime rate or from indifference to suffering resulting from exposure to wartime cruelty.

In terms of the numbers of individuals tried, the peaks were slightly different (see Table 2), with a third of the trials occurring between 1670 and 1700 and just over 20 per cent between 1710 and 1730. The decline was relatively swift and following the peak in the 1740s, the number of trials was less than half that in the previous decade, between 1750 and 1790 there were fewer than a dozen trials and by 1750 trials were more or less an anomaly. The Wielkopolska sample is especially striking because it has one of the highest proportions of females accused – 96 per cent, compared with 95 per cent in the Bishopric of Basel (1571–1670), 93 per cent in Essex (1560–1675), 92 per cent in the County of Namur

Table 1 Witchcraft trials in the Wielkopolska sample

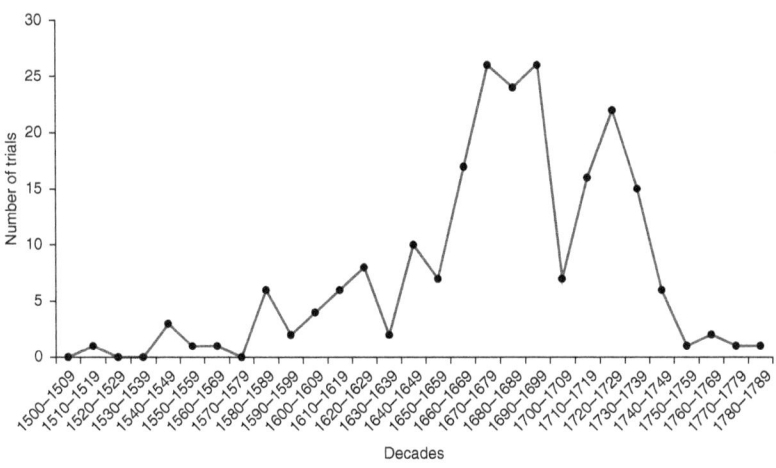

Table 2 Number of individuals tried for witchcraft in the Wielkopolska sample

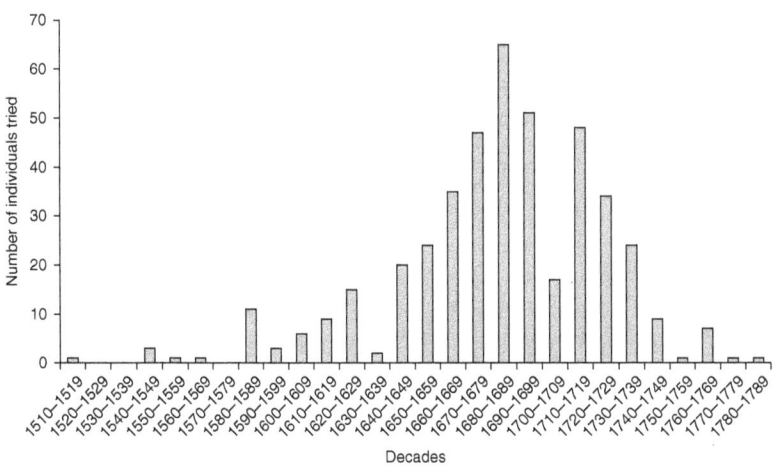

(1509–1646) and 90 per cent in Hungary (1520–1777).[4] We must also bear in mind that Pilaszek's broader research has returned a figure of nearer 90 per cent, but Wiślicz's study of Kleczew accords with my figures, with a total of 95 per cent women.[5] The sample consists of trials heard before the judiciary of Wielkopolska's municipal courts, but 56 per cent of those trials for which a location can be identified were held in villages.⁶ According to Behringer's classification, there were neither 'major persecutions' (100–249 executions) nor 'large-scale witch-hunts' (20–99 executions), and although there were several 'panic trials' (4–19 victims) the majority were what he terms 'witch trials' (up to three executions).⁷ The sample shows that only the municipal courts of Poznań and Kalisz heard cases in the sixteenth century but later there were several relatively intense outbreaks: in Kalisz, 1650–80; Gniezno, 1670–90; and Grodzisk, 1710–20. Courts in Kleczew, Poznań and Wągrowiec heard more than 20 cases; Gniezno, Kalisz, Warta, Pyzdry, Turek and Wronki heard 10 to 20; and the rest heard five or fewer cases. However, according to the sample, only Kleczew, Wągrowiec and Turek tried over 30 individuals. Bogucka is correct in her assessment that a careful estimate is required when bandying about statistics.⁸ My sample confirms that the persecution occurred between the same dates as many other countries in Europe, but that the peak was substantially later. Interestingly, Wiślicz analysed the months in which trials took place and discovered a preponderance in May and June, followed by December, which he suggests indicates pre-harvest tensions. His evidence shows accusations made at these times were predominantly about spoiling crops and depriving cows of milk.⁹

Harming, Healing and Harmony: From Wise Woman to Witch

Definitions of witchcraft evolved throughout the period. The accusations made mainly against healers and cunning women in the sixteenth century targeted a broader range of suspects over the following centuries. According to trial records, witchcraft charges changed from accusations of healing and using ambiguous rituals to accusations of cavorting with the Devil and attending diabolic feasts, requiring only a confession as proof. In Kalisz in 1580¹⁰ itinerant thieves Zofia of Lękno and Barbara of Radom were accused of witchcraft, tortured and subjected to swimming. Zofia drowned, thus proving her innocence, as it was generally believed that pure water rejected sinners. Barbara floated and confessed,

> I was a servant in households in Gdańsk and on St Thomas' Day...I killed a black hen and with a rope I stole milk...I took a spoonful of all the dishes prepared for Christmas Eve, mixed them up and gave them to the cattle...to keep witches away and so that they would keep away from me all year.¹¹ This my mother taught me...'Witches and little witches, don't take my threefold profit, because you will

smell and be as ugly as the white mustard mixed with other things.' Orszula in Szewicze, a royal city, asked me to give her something to abort her pregnancy. I gave her nothing to harm her pregnancy and instead, I gave her herbs and then she had two children, twins.

Furthermore she had confessed to a priest, who refused to absolve her and ordered her to do penance (there is no archival indication that it was he who had reported her). She had sprinkled cows on a Thursday with washing-up water in order to divert their milk to her and when asked what witchcraft she had used to escape the water, replied that she had appealed to the Devil, and said she had yet more war to wage in the world and that the Devil had promised that she would not drown. Barbara was sentenced to death at the stake.

In 1584, Elżbieta of Tyniec, a married female servant, appeared before the Kalisz court charged as an *incantatrix* and,

> Freely said: This year, one day three weeks ago, when her cow gave little milk... wanting to help the milk to come and remembering what she had been taught from good people, with whom she had served, she went to the river, took filled a jug with water and [said,] 'Lord God, by your sweet power and with the help of the Virgin Mary, and all the saints, I don't want a miracle in and of itself, but that all my profit be as it was and return to my cow.' Going home, she washed the cow from horns to tail, she added a handful of earth... [and] washed the cow.

After further interrogation, however, she admitted that she had learnt the ritual from Helszka who poured wax, therefore her previous attempt to ascribe the ritual to 'good people' failed. She survived torture and her death sentence was commuted to exile, in the hope that she would lead a better life.[12] At first glance one may think that this was a simple difference between 'black' and 'white' magic, because Elżbieta's ritual was religious in its nature, but the trials show widespread use of similar incantations.[13] In Kalisz cases heard in 1593, 1613 and 1616, variations of the incantation, '*Bozą Mocą, Panny Marii mocą i wszystkich swiętych pomocą*', 'By the power of God, the Virgin Mary and all the Saints', were mentioned by those accused and later in this chapter we will see how they were used further afield.[14]

The trials also reveal rivalries between competing cunning folk, although few as dangerous as Apolonia Porwitowa's feud with the executioner's wife, Katowa, which came to light before the Kalisz court in 1593. Apolonia had a reputation for keeping a disorderly house, witchcraft and counter-magic, having ruined Sobka's beer and rid Pan Bieniasz's, Pan Labenczel's and Pani Pawłowska' s houses of lice (she was paid variously a bowl of flour and a grosz); the last of whom's husband had brought a case against Małgorzata of Chmielnik in 1587. The invocations she used were part of the standard 'grammar' of spells, appealing to the power of God, the Virgin Mary and all the saints – 'I call upon God's power, Our Lady Mary's power and the power of all the saints... I add these herbs and cast out these insects from this cellar, this beer, and these utensils'. This invocation was followed by three genuflections. After torture she called the judiciary to her cell because she wanted to denounce Katowa, but understandably, not in front of her husband, the executioner. As a footnote to this feud, witness testimony indicated that Apolonia had ruined Bieniaszka's beer and Katowa had restored it. Katowa denied everything, saying, 'I am innocent and not afraid of torture. If I had been able to feel it, I would have been able to agree with you ages ago.'[15] Apolonia also admitted that a woman had asked her for a poison to give to her husband, but she had deceived her by giving her something harmless to administer. Subsequently, as Apolonia told the tale, the wife was pleased because the relationship had improved, however, it might equally have been the case that had the woman poisoned her husband and regretted it, that she might have projected this guilt onto the cunning woman. Inhabiting the powerful nexus of fulfilling desires was a dangerous pastime.

As well as religious invocations, we can see that the spells made use of sympathetic practices and analogy. In a Kalisz trial from 1616, Marusza and Regina confessed that they used ants in rituals to bind and cause harmony alongside their invocations, to bring luck to Kawczik when brewing beer or distilling alcohol. Łukaszowa was given an anthill to put in the cellar and the analogous invocation 'as ants all come together so may the household' was uttered. They also sold herbs to ensure good beer sales at market. In contrast, they gathered earth from Stawiszyń cemetery and threw it onto Ciemny's hay to ruin the beer, saying, 'let his beer repulse people, as the dead do the living'. Discord was also sown by taking such earth and scattering it around the house saying, 'by the power of God, the Virgin Mary and all the saints, let people be disgusted by the house as the dead disgust the living'.[16] Ostling devotes an interesting chapter to analysis of spells and analogous practices.[17]

In the middle of the sixteenth century, Dorota Gnieczkowa's repertoire included: pouring wax to locate a thief, protecting a household from harm, causing hail, putting out fire, finding buried money, carrying out love magic and sowing discord. One client paid Jedynaczka seven groschen to procure rat poison so that she could poison her husband. The client even planned to put holes in a tablecloth to make it look as if a rat had gnawed it. However, a troubled Jedynaczka duly returned the money on the advice of her neighbours.[18]

The methods used by those we term cunning women were many and varied and the trials reveal great ambiguity as to the practices condoned or condemned by the churches, perhaps as the result of an increasing heterodoxy and the ignorance of local priests. They also give an insight into complex relationships between the cunning folk and the gentry; the latter frequently used the services of the former, before subsequently bringing them to trial. At the level accusation, there is no doubt that most of the actions mentioned in the trials probably did take place. The majority of the motives discernible from the trials reveal the desire to harm others or their possessions, to increase profit or to ensure the success of more complex production procedures.

The Devil's Doxy: How the Devil Took Centre Stage

In contrast to the definitions of behaviour that attracted accusations of witchcraft in the sixteenth and early seventeenth centuries, the Grodzisk trials (1702–56) present an entirely different picture, constructing a more diabolic understanding of the witch and diabolizing her previously more neutral attributes.[19] Whereas previously, charges were predominantly brought on the basis of a perception that harm had been done and that the culprit had used a set of practices invoking supernatural powers to achieve this harm, as time went on, more diabolical notes crept into the confessions and the questions posed by the judges.

The 14 cases involve 25 accused, of whom three were male and two were under 16. On average each case involved one or two people, but from 1707, there was an outbreak of denunciations that fuelled the cases heard over the following five years. The cases were conducted, or at least recorded, in a uniform way. A typical trial in this collection began with the much-rehearsed format, beginning with the date, a list of the officiating judge, recorder and other officials present, and then the charge and the names of those bringing the charge (if any). There followed the confession of the accused, torture, further confession and then the interrogation questions. When the accused confessed, she was asked if she denounced certain named individuals. She admitted that she denounced them and in a few cases she renounced the original denunciation.[20] When this happened, the accused often claimed that the person denounced had always been good to them. These cases contain denunciations of over 100 people. However, the trials of only 19 appear in this collection and several were already deceased.[21] The court also recorded witness statements and the questions put to them, but in some of these cases they either do not survive or were not recorded.[22]

The accused was then required to state that she forgave the court for sentencing her. In many cases, this was exacted from the accused not once but three times, perhaps to formally dissolve the court and individuals from any personal guilt. The sentence and the crime were then recorded and in the majority of these cases, submission to the devil was noted at the head of the sins, followed by blasphemy and then the particular legal apparatus invoked. The final part of the sentence was often similar to this, from the trial of Anna Jasińska:

...*iako prawo jest opisane ogniem ztegoz świata na Instantią Instygatora Woyciecha Wołocha y zony jego bydź przez Mistrza Jana z Grodzyska zniesiona, ktorę sąd ninieyszy jemu executią oddaie zleca.*

...as it is written in the law, at the instance of Woyciech Wołoch and his wife, you are to be banished from this world by means of fire at the hands of Master Jan of Grodzisk, to which execution this court hands over and commissions you.[23]

The Devil: Ludic or Loathsome?

One of the most interesting features of Polish witchcraft confessions is the variety in descriptions of the devils.[24] Many women confessed to a specifically named devil, to whom they had given themselves and they also mentioned devils belonging to others. Some devils are described as German (Estonian witches also mentioned German devils), French or Polish and their method of dress varied. The most frequent name for the devil in the Grodzisk trials was Jasiek/Jan (six mentions), followed by Kuba (three mentions) and Woyciech (mentioned twice). The 19 names given include Jarek, Maciek, Stach, Rokitka, Andrzej, Marcin and Malachoski. Wiślicz identified 48 devils in the Kleczew trials, two she-devils, 31 named Jan, Janek or Jaś, then Woyciech, Jakub and Piotr and three Rokitas. He suggests Jan may have been a euphemism for the Devil, although Jan and its diminutives Janek and Jaś are common names given in Poland, corresponding to the English John and Jack.[25] Kazimierz Gracz confessed to having a devil named Rokitka, a diminutive of Rokita, one of the traditional Polish folk names for the Devil.[26] The common Polish terms for the Devil, *czart*, *diabeł* and *szatan* appear in the trials as well as the diminutives *czartuś*, and *diabełek*, 'a little devil', almost forms of endearment and perhaps analogous with a familiar, since rarely was there any reference to familiar-like creatures. However, it also reflects the Slavonic mythological tradition of the *domovoi*, 'house spirits', who were mischievous rather than harmful spirits who looked after the home and had to be placated with offerings of food. Indeed, we have already seen an example of this in Barbara of Radom's confession above. In contrast, the popular and localized names for Polish devils, *Rokita* and *Boruta*, recognized to this day, were absent from treatises.[27] However, colloquial forms of functional descriptive names also appeared in trials, such as *przeklętnik*, 'the cursed one', *pokuśnik*, 'the tempter', or *obłudnik*, 'the cheat' and the terms *oblubieniec* and *polubieniec*, 'bridegroom', referring to initiation through diabolic copulation or marriage.[28]

When it came to appearance, the devil had all the best clothes as well as tunes. Hanykowa's Kuba was dressed fashionably in the German style whilst Oderyna's Kuba dressed in the French style.[29] The German devils were also often described as 'fashionable' and we can speculate that perhaps this reflected the wealthier situation of Wielkopolska's German population. The devils of Debska and Kanczyna dressed in black, whilst the devil Jarek wore green hose, a red hat and black boots.[30] Stach, a devil in the Polish style, dressed in green and was neither old nor young and Barbara Konieczna's devil dressed as a Polish peasant.[31] Małgorzata Kupidarzyna's Jasiek was *młody w sukni zielonej i żółtych botach, czapka barankowa*, 'young, in green dress and yellow boots, [with] a lamb fleece hat', but Teresa Chałupniczka's Jasiek wore red.[32] In some cases there is confusion as to whether the Devil is referred to as wearing black or being a black man. This was a concept more often found in printed sources, where for example, he was portrayed as a black man who breathed fire from his mouth and nostrils, or a small child with a black face.[33]

In the majority of cases the devils were said to have blasphemed against God and Our Lady, calling the latter *stara baba*, 'old hag' or, with a pejorative meaning, Jewess.[34] As if it weren't enough for those accused of witchcraft to be associating with devils who freely blasphemed, they were also accused of having sex with the devil. Anna Chałupniczka confessed that they had sex in her own bed, whilst her husband was there, but Regina Całuyka's devil urged her to leave her husband and beat her during the trial to prevent her from talking.[35] Despite the focus on diabolic detail, there were no mentions of a search for the so-called Devil's mark in this sample and only in cases involving

38 *Witchcraft in Early Modern Poland, 1500–1800*

men is there mention of a pact. However, in this collection of cases there are two accounts of the devil biting the accused in the ring finger, which is the nearest equivalent we can find.³⁶ The following extract from a trial heard before the court of Dolsk in 1710 displays features both typical and atypical of Polish cases. The written pacts concluded by men contrasted with the physical manifestation of a pact associated with the illiterate female:

> Regina... is taken freely for inquisition without any torture, she admitted that she had been to *Łysa Góra*, Jozefka... told me just you do as I do and you will have good, at which she acquiesced and gave me to a devil, to whom I registered in blood from my ring finger unto death, and that devil's name was Jan in red and yellow boots. I have already known him for 15 years...³⁷

Another aspect peculiar to Poland is the accusation of inflicting the *kołtun*, 'matted hair', which appears in the trial of Anna Ladzina. The *kołtun* was known medically as *Plica Polonica* and garnered a great deal of interest from foreigners visiting Poland.³⁸ The condition was blamed on witchcraft and popular belief maintained that if the hair were cut off, then the sufferer would go blind.

The Sabbat

The background for much of the witches' perceived actions was often the nocturnal gathering at *Łysa Góra*, 'Bald Mountain', which became a key part of confessions from the mid-seventeenth century onwards. It was not to be found at one specifically named location, but was often identified as a hill beyond the local village or town. In Polish a range of terms designated this event but none of the printed sources mentioned a *sabat*, 'witches' sabbat' nor the term *szabas*, 'the Jewish or Christian day of worship'. In the Polish translation of the *Malleus Maleficarum* the term sabbat (although rarely used) is rendered as *biesada*, 'feast',³⁹ whereas Chmielowski used the words *sejm*, 'parliament or diet',⁴⁰ *schadzka*, 'meeting' (this also has a sexual connotation), and *bankiet*, 'banquet'. Occasionally the word *sabbat* appeared in the trials but in most accounts the term *Łysa Góra*, 'Bald Mountain', was used generically to indicate the sabbat.⁴¹ *Łysa Góra* is still celebrated in popular belief as the meeting place of witches and a famous hill bearing this name in the Świętokrzyż 'Holy Cross' mountains was reputedly the site of pagan worship, although, or because of this, a monastery was founded there as early as the twelfth century. In one instance *Łysa Góra* was described as the place where *Niemcy chowają*, 'Germans gather (or hide)',[42] and elsewhere Anna confessed that, *ta Łysa Góra się bydz iako dwór albo pałac*, 'this Bald Mountain is like a manor or a palace'.[43]

In this range of cases, as with others in the sample, there was a certain order ascribed to the sabbat proceedings. According to the denunciations, men were usually musicians playing the bagpipes or pipe.[44] There was often a queen of the gathering (which was not called a *sabat* 'sabbat' but a *bankiet* 'banquet'), such as Oderyna in 1707, who wore a gold crown and was surrounded by the children.[45] By 1737 Oderyna had perished at the stake, to be replaced by Niewitecka.[46] Others also had specific duties, such as Mularzewna, a serving girl, the widow Kasperczanka, who milked the cows and Gneska, who poured the beer.[47] The sabbat was an occasion for a variety of activities, ranging from having sex with the devil, to feasting and dancing and *tancowały każda z swoim*, 'each woman danced with her own'.[48] We could also speculate that the low regard with which dancing was held compounded the stigma attached to the accused.

However, opinion as to the contents of the feast varied. Anna Jasińska claimed they ate horse droppings and horse's urine,[49] whilst others confessed they cooked and ate a stolen horse, stolen cows or meat.[50] Occasionally the accused claimed that these animals were specifically killed for the feasts.[51] Jasińska also said that the sabbat took place on Thursdays, a popular association, as we shall see.[52] There were also many ways to travel to the sabbat: a certain Anna went through the chimney at midnight, Jadwiga of Porażyn travelled by normal carriage, while Anna Jasińska went on horseback.[53] Małgorzata Kupidarzyna confessed, *jeździłam na parobku Marcinie*, 'I travelled on Marcin, the labourer', whilst Anna Chałupniczka maintained that *maścią mnie posmarowawszy ześmy leciały*, 'I was smeared with ointment so we could fly'.[54]

Materials of *Maleficia*: The Bleeding Host and Powerful Powders

The Grodzisk trials also provide an idea of how the perceived practices of those accused of witchcraft had changed from the sixteenth century. The details in the trials accorded more with the fantastic printed accounts and the basic attributes of the witch were evolving, with increased ambivalence as to the true nature of hitherto acceptable practices. Attempts to heal or increase profit through using invocations were largely replaced by accounts of despoliation of the sacred Host – an assault on the very body and blood of Christ himself. A scenario recounted many times in these trials is the theft of the Host from churches. According to some accounts, the Christ Child appeared on the Host and even spoke and cried. The Host was then beaten every hour and the blood that flowed from this was collected from the floor and used in the witches' spells.[55] Although at first glance these accounts seem rather fantastic, if we consider the Roman Catholic dogma of transubstantiation (in which the Host becomes the actual rather than the symbolic body and blood of Christ) and the post-Tridentine emphasis on the Eucharist, then these stories illustrate a valid understanding of the magical power enshrined therein. If the Eucharist transformed into the body and blood of Christ during the Mass, then there was no reason why the Christ Child could not appear from it. Its use in witchcraft practices merely drew upon the same magical transformative power. The abuse of the Christ Child entwined the notions of the witches' sacrilege and their infanticidal tendencies, exacerbating society's deepest fears about heretics and mothers. Ostling devotes two chapters to a discussion of Host-theft and desecration. Perceptively he points out that whilst we can learn nothing about Judaism from similar charges laid against Jews, we can learn something about Christianity from the charges laid against witches. He examines the use of the Host in folk magic, the place of the Host in the Counter-Reformation and draws differing conclusions from what he terms 'primary' and 'secondary' Host-theft cases. My research supports his opinion of Host despoliation as an extremely important element of the witchcraft confessions in terms of Counter-Reformation emphasis on the Host and transubstantiation. However, although an interesting approach, I do not agree with his reading of the witchcraft trials as expressions of piety, as I would suggest that anyone accused of witchcraft might seek to appear pious in their own defence.[56]

The relevance of the Bleeding Host and sacramental power lay in people's belief that the power was located within the items themselves, rather than in the consecration of the items. This is why such importance was attached to preventing religious items such as the aspergillum and even rust from the church roof from falling into the hands of witches. Ecclesiastical objects were not to be used by those outside the Church and the ambiguous nature of sacral power was illustrated by earlier cases in Kalisz and Poznań, in which appeals to divine power to heal and protect were interpreted as witchcraft. Simply put, once again, it was the provenance of the power that was important – the power was neutral, to be appropriated either by the good (authorized male priests) or the bad (female witches).

Returning to Grodzisk, the young Anna's trial is an excellent example of Host-theft.

In Poznań, Barbara took my hand and introduced me to a devil named Jasko and I went with him to Łysa Góra in Poznan... where the Germans gather... we smeared ourselves under our arms and went to Łysa Góra and I ate and drank and served the Gentlemen.... There was a queen and others sat around her and I flew to the banquet then with this devil home and he lay down with me and had sex with me on Thursdays only, although he visited me on Tuesdays, he didn't have sex with me, only on Thursdays. When I took communion and after confession, I stole the wafer and took it to Poznań... but the witches beat the wafer, not in Grodzisk, but at Łysa Góra, past Bendykowo, and placed it on a board and the baby Jesus appeared... then they beat him.[57]

Despoliation of the Host was also a charge laid against Jews from the thirteenth century onwards and is part of the tradition of 'miraculous hosts', which deserves a deeper examination than its treatment here. As in France, Germany, Italy and elsewhere, Poland also boasted its own accounts of miraculous hosts, the most famous of which was linked to Poznań – the 1399 miracle of the three Hosts. Although there are no contemporary sources to support the story, historian Jan Długosz gave an account in 1491, followed by others.[58] By the time of the witchcraft trials, the legend was firmly established, embellished from Długosz's mention of a stolen Host sold to Jews and subsequently found in a meadow, to a much-elaborated upon narrative. According to the legend, a Christian servant girl, working for a Jewish family, procured three Hosts for them, and they subsequently set upon the wafers with knives. Unable to get rid of the Hosts down a well or by other means, they threw them into a field. When the Host was raised up in churches the following Sunday, the three Hosts rose up in the air and the cows in the field knelt as if in worship. On that site, the Church of Corpus Christi was founded and many miracles were subsequently attributed to this phenomenon. As Węgrzynek points out, Poznań was the centre of the Reformation in Wielkopolska and although no more than 15% of the population had converted, the Roman Catholic Church had been significantly affected. The Jesuits encouraged the cult of the Host in the second half of the sixteenth century, as they fought against Jews and Protestants and staged theatrical Corpus Christi processions.[59]

According to the Grodzisk confessions, as well as the Host, powder was also used to cast spells predominantly against people and cattle, but also in one confession to cause crop failure. In another case, the Host was thrown into a well to poison the water, the only such mention in the whole sample.[60] Powder, on the other hand, came in various colours and was given by the devils. A certain Anna was given a green powder that caused damage to the legs, she scattered another powder under the bed of Dawidowa to cause illness, put a red powder into hot beer to keep away her fiancé's attentions until after the wedding and also used yellow and black powders. Other ingredients buried in strategic places included bone (particularly horse bone), horse manure, a chicken and herbs.[61] Elsewhere in Wielkopolska, Małgorzata Krystkowa confessed to using black powder to kill cattle on Thursdays but was also given white powder by her devil Jasiek, whereas Teresa Nowaczka of Porażyn only harmed her own pig with the black powder given to her by her devil, as she claimed that she couldn't give it to anyone else. A certain Małgorzata confessed that a gypsy gave her grass with which she bewitched horses, and so the accounts show no uniformity as to the powers of the differently coloured powders.[62]

Many Reasons Why?

Scholars of witchcraft have often been tempted to ascribe the persecution to one cause or factor, seduced into thinking that they have found the Holy Grail – the overarching reason for the persecution which will fit all local, national and confessional variations. However, the consensus now among leading witchcraft historians is that the persecution cannot be regarded as a monocausal phenomenon, which is the approach followed in this study. It is clear though that the twin planks of a legal procedure for prosecuting witchcraft and belief in the devil and supernatural practices had to be in place to provide a framework within which witchcraft accusations could be made. This, I believe is the only common factor, as regional studies are revealing ever different patterns of prosecutions. This framework was contingent on many possible variables or catalysts and it is this contingency which I believe is at the heart of explaining the sporadic nature of the persecution. In addition to the difficulties and implications of taking someone to court and the probability at every step of a trial being dropped rather than going ahead, this may explain why there were so few, rather than so many trials, as Briggs and others have pointed out.[63] This approach could also explain why some of those denounced were accused and why others were not, since the most important catalysts were individuals, their histories and personalities – exacerbated by power and conflict. As Moszyński perceptively noted, *czarownica, to charakter*, 'a witch, it's in one's character', and as Bever noted in his study of Württemberg, 80 per cent of his sample had a bad reputation.[64] There is no shortage of conflict in testimonies and indeed witchcraft trials provide a fascinating window onto everyday tensions within early modern communities. This contingency factors in the powerful seigneur, the peasant with a grudge, the old woman who cursed and threatened others, death and disease, crop failure, cattle illness and many other possible elements dependent on individuals' human nature – ultimately the persecution could depend on the range of insecurities, envy and sadistic tendencies that any individual might display. The key element in the witchcraft persecution was how individuals coped or failed to cope with misfortune and what strategies and power they could deploy – how they negotiated life and belief systems that governed society. These power games are most visible in the seigniorial pattern, but can also be seen not just within the Wielkopolska cases, but also in many European and North American trials, because accusations were often made within the framework of a superior accusing an inferior, according to either reputation or social position. Despite a firm belief in the contingent nature of the trials, it is worth briefly examining several of the most important broader hypotheses historians have suggested, to ascertain whether we can identify a link between the effects of German influence, weather, subsistence crises, war, plague and Tridentine Catholicism on Wielkopolska and its witchcraft persecution.[65]

German Influence

The question of German influence is of particular significance to Wielkopolska, because of its geography, multi-ethnic population and mixed-confessional nature. The desire of some historians to anomalously treat Poland's persecution as part of Germany's, together with some Polish historians' tendencies to ascribe the persecution to 'the old enemy', has prevented many from seeing beyond this rather parochial view. There are clearly many similarities between the German and Wielkopolska persecutions, both on micro and macro levels, for example, much of the Polish legal system derived from the *Speculo Saxonum*, the *Carolina* and Magdeburg Law and the majority of towns in Wielkopolska were founded on the Magdeburg Law. The codices most commonly relied upon by Polish municipal courts were Groicki's collections based on German law, whose publication coincided with the start of the persecution in the sample, so a key plank of the persecution derived from Germany. In addition, to some extent, the territorial make-up of Poland resembled the German lands, because it was divided into areas, villages or towns controlled, ruled or run by a seigneur (or more than one), and although admittedly this was generally on a much smaller scale than in Germany, the pattern in Poland could reap the same bloody harvest, with so much power in the hands of one individual. Just as Johann Georg II Fuchs played a central role in the Bamberg persecution, so also could a Polish seigneur hold sway over life and death in his village. Decentralization of power, numerous property-owning *szlachta* and the lack of reference to superior courts meant that seigniorial will was generally done in Wielkopolska (although this was not the case throughout Poland). This absolutism was compounded by the removal of ecclesiastical jurisdiction over crimes against morality, which was handed, as most power, to the nobles.

The Wielkopolska sample indicates that while there were no waves of trials during the 1590s, the broad period of the persecution was similar to that of Germany. Trials took place from the middle of the sixteenth century and continued throughout Germany's peak (1580–1630), gathering momentum during Germany's second wave in the 1660s and peaking between 1660 and 1740 with a radical dip between 1700 and 1710. Cultural transmission between Wielkopolska and German-speaking lands had resulted in the *Eulenspiegel* tradition swiftly finding its Polish imitators (see Chapter 5), and the concept of devils mirroring sins and German anti- and pro-witchcraft treatises had clearly influenced Polish authors. Similarities in trial confessions have also emerged, most strikingly in the form of invocations based on Roman Catholic rituals found in trials in Poznań and Kalisz as well as in Germany.[66] Both Polish and German women described devils with feathers in their caps, as participants at the sabbat wearing masks and the Devil's member as cold. In Augsburg for example, as in Poznań and Kalisz, prior to 1600, crystal ball gazers, healers, sorcerers and treasure seekers generally fell under suspicion.[67] Wielkopolska trials and German trials also share common descriptions of the Bleeding Host and the Devil's sexual preference for trading in older women for younger counterparts.[68] The revulsion reserved for mothers who had seduced their children into witchcraft was as evident in the case of Margeretha Hörber in Rothenburg in 1627 as it was in Dorota's trial in Gniezno in 1689. At the heart of both cases were the children's claims that their mothers had failed to teach them to pray.[69] Common anxieties around brewing processes are also evident in the frequent accusations of bewitching beer and accusations against innkeepers, in both areas, concurring with Behringer's suggestion that 'landladies were often suspected of witchcraft'.[70] Undoubtedly in parts of both regions disregard for judicial processes accompanied extreme abuse of torture.[71]

However, there remain many significant differences, not least glaringly when it comes to the numbers of victims of the persecution and the mass scale of some German trials. The largest number of individuals in one trial in the Wielkopolska sample was 11, which hardly compares to the hundreds in Trier or Bamburg. Neither were the Polish translation of Spee's work and a similar Polish work credited with having an impact on the use of torture, as in Germany, because the Polish persecution reached its peak after their publication. However, it is clear from the 1689–90 Gniezno trial (examined in the following chapter) that consideration of the *Cautio Criminalis* and *Czarownica powołana* hastened its end. The recommendations of the *Carolina* on seeking university opinions were roundly ignored in Poland, according to my sample, as was the restriction of the death penalty to cases of maleficent witchcraft – again, the extraordinary 1689–90 Gniezno case is the exception, where the court sent a deputation to the Archbishop of Gniezno for an opinion. The lack of an appeal system in Wielkopolska and the loss of the peasants' right to appeal to the Royal Court contrasted unfavourably with the right to appeal to Imperial Courts of the Holy Roman Empire, of which people were both aware and availed themselves. Rowlands's contrast between the 'bark' of demonological rhetoric and the 'bite' of jurisprudential advice, which in most areas restricted the German judiciary from being overenthusiastic in their prosecutions, found little if any reflection in Wielkopolska. The region's trials also differ in the lack of the Devil's mark, witch-finders and *hexenkommissar*, and despite Poland's dependency on the grain trade, Wielkopolska trials rarely mention weather magic. However, there is no doubt that while there were many differences, German influence was crucial in two of the driving forces of the persecution – law and literature.[72]

Natural and Economic Disasters

As outlined in Chapter 1, the period of the persecution was a time of multiple crises, but the real relevance of the disasters that swept Wielkopolska lies in their possible impact on the lives of individuals, which may have rendered them more vulnerable to accusations of witchcraft. From the mid-sixteenth century the Commonwealth was beset by serious and frequent poor harvests and epidemics exacerbated by the European inflation crisis as the silver content of the grosz decreased by two-thirds between 1578 and 1650.[73] Such disastrous conditions provoked an attendant increase in illness and vulnerability and, viewed by many as punishment from God, may have acted as catalysts for persecution – we know that droughts in particular were a notorious excuse for trying women by swimming.

Historians of witchcraft have also speculated on the impact of the Little Ice Age with its attendant crop failure and price increases. Behringer connects the Little Ice Age to the earlier European-wide peak and persecution, but in fact there is a closer correlation with the later events in the Wielkopolska sample. Correlations can be shown between the dates of cold spikes and trials: 1641–43 (one trial), 1666–69 (six trials), 1675 (two trials), 1683–84 (one trial), 1698–99 (three trials). The coldest cycle, between 1680 and 1730, coincided with the peak in the Wielkopolska sample.[74] In 1708, noted as a dry year with a severe winter, there were two trials, while the prolonged heat wave between 1717 and 1719 was accompanied by drought (noted in Polish records), so it may be no coincidence that six trials were heard in Wągrowiec, one in Pyzdry and one in Grodzisk in 1719.[75] We could also speculate, for example, that the serious heat wave of 1616, when wet summers had been the norm between 1600 and 1630, was connected to four trials heard in three locations that year.[76] When hail, severe winds and a plague of locusts were visited upon Gniezno in 1680, at least five and possibly ten women were tried. However, we would need to ask why the trials weren't more widespread during these particular phenomena as the evidence is scant.

Plague epidemics were also common in the wake of marching armies and the malnourished were more likely to succumb to illness, so the cumulative effects of war, bad harvest and epidemics could decimate populations.[77] There is a slight correlation between epidemics and trials: 1588–89, 1599, 1600 (two trials), 1601–05 (two trials), 1623–25 (five trials), 1628–31 (one trial), 1652–62 (14 trials), 1677–80 (five trials each in Kleczew and Warta and four in Wronki) and 1705–12 (eight trials).[78] In 1708 around half of Grodzisk's population were wiped out by plague and when 15 witches were tried two years later, unsurprisingly there was mention of a plague key.[79] The precarious position in which the weather crises, wartime looting and loss of labour through epidemics (including tuberculosis, dysentery, smallpox and typhus) left peasants and the poorer *szlachta* was exacerbated through crop failure and cattle loss. Obviously, evidence is not available for every instance of famine and hunger but again, there is a slight correlation between some of the most severe experiences and trials in the sample: 1598–1602 (two trials), 1620–21 (one trial), 1625 (two trials), 1628–30 (one trial), 1695–97 (six trials).[80] Wielkopolska's huge population losses predictably affected the economic situation and caused mass flight from cities, but it may also have increased fears and superstitious beliefs. In 1585 plague killed two-thirds of Poznań's population and forty years later 6000 of its citizens died of famine and plague.[81] Pyzdry was almost wiped out by plague in 1707; Gostyń's population fell from 1000 to 330 between 1708 and 1712; the number of households in Wągrowiec shrunk from 400 in 1655 to 103 in 1703; and Kalisz's population of 2500 in 1673 had barely reached 700 by 1714.[82] Estimates maintain that the population of Wielkopolska fell by 15 to 20 per cent as a result of the Northern War and plague, especially in the areas around Poznań, Kalisz and Wschowa, and just as the area was recovering, Poznań was hit by heavy flooding in 1736.[83] This is supported by Gieysztorowa's figures for taxed households in the crown, which show that Wielkopolska counted 141,055 households in 1629, which had almost halved to 74,405 by 1661, with pre-Deluge levels only returning in 1776, when figures reached 150,600.[84]

In addition, the quartering of troops and general hardship caused by war, both psychologically and physically, brought fear and hunger to Wielkopolska during the Northern War of 1700–21 and the War of the Polish Succession of 1733–35.[85] Although war in itself did not cause witchcraft trials (in fact it tended to dampen the persecution), the epidemics, poverty, vagrancy and famine in its aftermath could provoke angry repercussions. For example, Hagen claims that during times of war villagers often stopped paying taxes and abandoned their manorial service, which may have provoked repercussions when manorial authority was restored.[86] Interestingly, Rowlands points out that the wartime destruction of parishes meant that those who grew up during times of war were often lacking in religious knowledge and therefore more prone to superstition, and, we might suppose, more inclined towards the comfort of ritual.[87]

The Little Ice Age, together with a disastrous seventeenth century in Poland, brought increasing penury for the peasantry, as the *szlachta* demanded a higher yield from their lands, depending almost exclusively on forcing an increase in the number of days the serfs had to provide their labour to them on the demesne farm. Cattle and crops were the lifeline of the subsistence economy eked out by the peasants and, given the dominance of the grain trade, one might expect more frequent accounts of weather magic. The trial of Grzegorz of Polacewo, who confessed to having stolen the Eucharist for a second time and burying it in order to ruin the wheat crops, is highly unusual in the sample.[88] Weather magic was more commonly found in printed sources, for example one account claimed that if a witch wanted to cause rainfall, she would take sand in her hands and turn her back to the rising sun, exchanging the sand for flint to cause hail.[89] However, weather magic could mask a more sinister motive, namely the collective desire of witches to cause harm to the whole village. Cattle illnesses were frequently the source of witchcraft accusations, along with milk theft. A witch could cause milk from someone else's cow to appear in a receptacle hung on her wall. They could cause the death of pigs and horses, beat, poison or strangle cattle, and pollute or infect the water where cattle drank as well as poisoning fish by throwing diabolic powder into the sea.[90] However, it is the protection or destruction of cows that appears most commonly in Polish trial records from this sample, which is also the focus of the earliest trials from Kalisz in the late sixteenth century. One of the most common practices was to wash the cows with herbs accompanied by an invocation to God and the Virgin Mary, reminiscent of blessings certainly carried out by European parish priests to this day in rural areas. However, in 1544, in a trial heard by the Poznań court, Agnieszka of Żabikowo used the following incantation when cattle dislocated their limbs:

> When Sweet Lord Jesus travelled on earth on his holy donkey with Saint Peter, Saint Paul, the donkey stuck out its foot. – Saint Peter cure – Sweet Lord, I do not know how. Saint Peter, Saint Paul, I will teach you: Let him descend to every christened one and cattle, vein to vein, blood to blood, marrow to marrow, flesh to flesh, by God's power, O the power of sweet Mary, and the help of all the saints.[91]

Interestingly, similar invocations were found in Poznań as well as in a trial from Rothenburg.[92] In 1580, before a Kalisz court, a certain Barbara admitted that she had bewitched a household to divert its milk to her, by placing the cattle under 'diabolic power'. She also claimed that she had carried herbs about her person when they had swum her, which had saved her. In a Kalisz trial (1584) milk was restored by washing a cow with river water and sand and motherwort, millet and fennel were said to improve milk yields. This is also an area that Ostling explores at length. His doctorate included an in-depth examination of the herbs used by witches and, as noted previously, he has written broadly about the construction of spells in witchcraft confessions.[93]

The Counter-Reformation

Another key factor connected by at least one historian to the Polish witchcraft persecution was the strength of the Counter-Reformation,[94] which, through a programme of post-Tridentine re-Catholicization in the first half of the seventeenth century, gained momentum as a considerable number of the Polish-Lithuanian *szlachta* abandoned Protestantism. The middle of the seventeenth century coincides not only with an increased number of witchcraft trials in the sample but also with the introduction of anti-Protestant legislation, including the banishment of Antitrinitarians in 1658 and the prohibition of conversion from Roman Catholicism on the grounds of apostasy in 1668 (any activities by Protestant vicars outside their churches were regarded as an inducement to apostasy). The construction of Protestant churches was prohibited and those built after 1632 were destroyed under legislation from 1717. Just one year later the Calvinist Andrzej Piotrowski, the last dissenting deputy of the *Sejm*, was expelled and intolerance and even violence against dissenters gained ground, evident in the 1724 Tumult of Thorn (Toruń).[95]

The reformations emphasized more heterodox approaches, evident in attempts to eradicate practices condemned by the various churches. This coincided with fewer references in witchcraft trials to the use of holy invocations in the middle of the seventeenth century and a heightened emphasis on Roman Catholic sacramentals and the Host. As Wiślicz points out, 'the post-Tridentine Church was saturated with an idea of supervising the orthodoxy of the cult and of purifying it of any questionable elements'.[96] The removal of a whole layer of protective and popular religion from Protestants led Bogucka to conclude that 'the Reformation intensified reflection on gender relations' and to regard the Protestant downgrading of the role of Mary and the saints as an indication that Eve's sin was still incumbent. Mary had redeemed Eve, but Bogucka suggests that Protestants feared strong women in contrast to the traditional Roman Catholic veneration of St Anne and a host of iconic female saints.[97] Crucially, against the backdrop of such ideological stances, the reforming movements' new conceptualizations of womanhood coincided with a stricter enforcement of social control over morals. The Counter-Reformation brought with it an increased emphasis on Marian devotion, very much encouraged in the Commonwealth and evident, for example, in the establishment of a Rosary fraternity and the Order of Marian Fathers founded by peasant priest Stanisław Papczyński (1631–1701). Kłoczowski suggests that the centrality of the cult of Christ and His Mother was 'informed by old agrarian and family traditions' and that a rich array of Polish sources portrayed Christianity's significance 'at a human and family level'.[98] Exploring the psychological merger of the Holy Trinity with the Holy Family, he suggests a direct link between the opinion of women in society and the veneration of the cult of the Virgin Mary, according with some feminist readings of witchcraft.

In the new post-Tridentine spirit, there was an attempt to establish a seminary in every diocese and religious houses experienced an increase in recruitment. The church now required regular attendance at Mass, home visits by priests, certificates of Easter confession and the registration of births, marriages and deaths, which were often enforced by the manor. By the eighteenth century, a cult of the Sacred Heart had been established and the pope created a special holy day devoted to veneration of the Eucharist for Poland.

However, the iconic role of the Virgin Mary may have strengthened revulsion at her opposite, the witch, and in particular the witch who delivered her own children or others to the Devil. Behringer links Mary with fertility and inversely with 'the female personification of infertility, the witch', noting the 'coincidence of the first witch-burnings in the Bishopric of Augsburg and the Duchy of Bavaria with the founding of the princely Marian Congregation' and the symbolism of the devotional blood pacts with the Virgin Mary of Altötting, signed by Maximillian of Bavaria and Ferdinand Maria.[99] The religious frame of reference underpins the trials, visible in the swearing of an oath on a crucifix and the reference to Exodus and sins against the Roman Catholic faith often found in sentencing. The confessions reveal invocations to God, Mary and the saints, profanation of the Host, the use of a monstrance for restoring milk, washing in Holy Water to enable flight, and feast days, such as Ascension Day, were regarded as significant times when the identity of a witch could be revealed.[100] Contrary to modern popular belief, the Roman Catholic Church was rarely formally involved in the trials – at most local priests made interventions to save the accused. On a wider scale, undoubtedly the religious waves that swept Poland and the catechizing mission re-energized Counter-Reformation Catholicism, encouraging a greater emphasis on orthodox practices and possibly contributing to changes in gendered expectations.

It is clear that Wielkopolska's persecution occurred within a structural and temporal framework common to the rest of Europe, but with a later peak, similar to Hungary. Over time the definitions and perceptions of what constituted witchcraft became increasingly diabolized, as different paradigms were developed on the basis of the term 'witch'.

The general understanding of the term was fluid, with a large degree of ambivalence as to what constituted witchcraft. Some of the macro-level elements that historians claim affected the persecution in Europe may also have played a role in Wielkopolska and epidemics, climatic changes, wartime destruction and the declining economy reinforced the general decay of the Commonwealth, contributing to a mass consciousness that had perhaps developed a greater level of religiosity in the face of such adversity. However structural and environmental elements required the agency of a catalyst (an event or individual) to set a witchcraft trial in motion. While the environmental factors explain why a witchcraft trial might occur in a certain year or period, they do not explain why trials did not occur everywhere that shared the same experience. These factors need to be taken into account together with the notion of individual agency to explain the persecutions, which were often linked to a particular individual or set of individuals. For example, in Germany, the Esslingen persecution ceased with the death of Judge Daniel Hauff in 1665. Many elements both in demonology and in the legal sphere owe much to their German counterparts and it is significant that in a mixed area such as Wielkopolska, the sample revealed only one Protestant involved in a witchcraft trial and he instigated the trial against his own wife.

The sketches of a variety of different trials in this chapter have shown that people availed themselves of witchcraft practitioners' skills from a general desire to improve their domestic or economic situation, whether to gain the affection of a husband or to improve their bread. Motives for employing witchcraft against others ranged from anger at and revenge upon those who had mistreated them, to revenge for a specific deed, such as the refusal to give them bread, whereas motives behind the seigniorial accusations appeared to be fear of economic ruin and harm to their household, which found a convenient expression in a desire to rid the community of witches.

The chronology of the sample is similar to that elsewhere in that it started in the sixteenth century and increased as the century progressed. If the sample accurately indicates the peak of the persecution as between 1660 and 1740, the impetus to persecute those believed to be witches increased at a time when the Commonwealth was undergoing a plethora of crises on both internal and external fronts. Thus it might be supposed that witchcraft was but a symptom of the greater disease destroying the Commonwealth. The era was full of fear evoked by a variety of factors: extreme weather, crop failure, wartime destruction, illness and plague, and spiritual uncertainty. Ideologically, there was also a growing mismatch in belief systems, which saw Enlightenment empiricism gradually replace superstition, but at a varying pace among different levels of society in different regions. Those in rural areas were among the last to cast off superstition and ritual and the sample indicates that the persecution had more or less ended by 1750, after which verifiable trials are rare and sporadic.[101] But it was not until the 1740s that an early or primitive capitalist economy was introduced, bringing with it greater urbanization and industrialization. The population began to increase, as did agricultural production and the balance of export over import;[102] and simultaneously the number of trials for witchcraft decreased significantly. We see over this period a real development in the connection between the witch and the devil and a clear diabolization of practices and attributes associated with the figure of the witch.

3
Witchcraft and Gender: Intimate Servants and Excluded Masculinities

The most striking aspect of this study is perhaps the high number of women accused, but also denounced and involved as witnesses. In terms of demographics, 23 per cent of those for whom occupations can be discerned in this sample were servants (see Fig. 3), often employed by their accusers. When added to the 19 per cent who were serfs, this provides even stronger evidence that witches were frequently servants, supported by research indicating that 33 per cent of female criminals accused were servants.[1] Briggs's paradigm of witches as neighbours can be extended to encompass witches as servants, emphasizing the close relationship between the suspected witch and her accuser as a pre-eminent dynamic.

Detail is often scant about the accused's age, but the sample shows that at least a quarter were widows or married (a fifth were definitely married) and in the few cases where children were involved, they were all the children of the accused. Some women, like men, were accused of witchcraft as a secondary accusation, with the primary charge usually theft, procurement or prostitution. Anna Chociszewska (a noblewoman and somewhat of a rarity among those accused) was tried in Poznań for procuring, theft and witchcraft in 1582[2] and in Kalisz Małgorzata of Chmielnik was accused in 1587[3] by her seigneur of stealing his ducks and geese and harming his wife's health as a preamble to witchcraft charges. The occupations of those accused or denounced also included millers, shepherdesses and shepherds and innkeepers and malters (see Fig. 3), who all appeared as prime suspects in printed sources, as we shall see in a later chapter. The wives of craftsmen also came before the courts; the wives of the saddler, the baker and the tanner all appeared

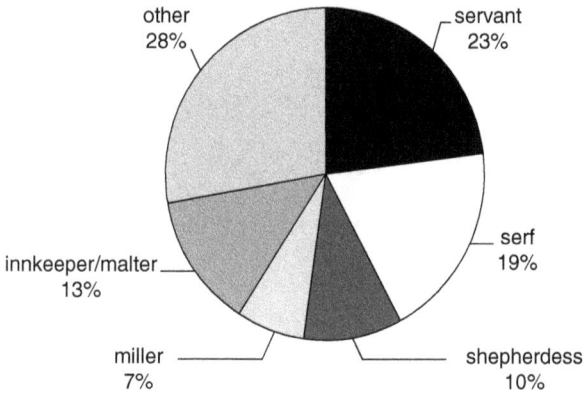

Figure 3 Occupation of individuals tried for witchcraft in the Wielkopolska sample (where known).

before the Gniezno court in 1677; and in at least one instance the wife of a court bench member was tried.[4]

The Gendering of the Witch

Women in the Wider Context: The Position of Women in Poland

As in most early modern spheres, the fate of Polish women depended largely upon their social or financial position and it is no coincidence that noblewomen were rarely accused of witchcraft. However, perceptions of Polish women were varied and contradictory.[5] On the one hand quiet, virtuous and pious women were admired, but on the other, popular belief had it that even the Devil feared them, and although Polish society was undoubtedly patriarchal, strong women were both adored and feared. Some authors were virulently misogynistic, criticizing women for their love of fashionable attire, hairstyles and extravagance, which correlated with the temptations offered by Polish literary devils, as we shall see in the next section. The *szlachta* might have resented high-born women who were more likely to assert themselves, royal consorts who interfered in politics and reform and wives who were socially superior to them or older, but in contrast, some noblewomen ran estates and even the sample reveals one trial instigated by a noblewoman. It's useful to bear in mind Bogucka's perceptive observation on the role of the seigneur and his wife:

> The noble woman also played an important role in contacts between the gentry's manor house and the peasant; she was the person to

whom they came for help and advice, she looked after them when they were ill, she taught them and settled small disputes, she was frequently an intermediary between the serfs and their lord.[6]

However, we know that gifts and favours or dependency were the currency of conflict and the sample shows several cases in which noblewomen sought remedies from cunning folk, whom they subsequently accused of witchcraft.

For many urban and rural women, the household functioned both as a matrimonial and commercial unit in which women's roles often complemented those of their menfolk. It was common for women to preside over brewing beer, housework, milk, making butter, tending the garden, gathering herbs and wild fruits, tending cattle and poultry, spinning linen and wool, weaving cloth and attending the weekly market to sell produce. Thus, most of the basic household economy depended on women, rendering them potentially responsible for failure in the vital task of providing for the family. Selling produce was also a fertile area for tensions and disputes.[7] However, some peasant women worked alongside men in the fields during days of obligation to the manor and others were seasonal paid workers.[8] Karpiński's research on Poznań reveals some extremely independent women who made up two-thirds of tradespeople between 1685 and 1694 and leased town stalls. They predominated among those from craft families, who ran their own workshop, rented property, and dealt in credit. Widows made up almost 20 per cent of the latter and almost 13 per cent of beer brewers, both activities rife with potential for conflict, as the trials illustrate.[9] Although witchcraft trials have often been blamed on a surplus of women, Bogucka believes that in Poland, as a result of wars and destruction, there were actually more men in towns, including migrants, clergy, merchants and vagrants, but concludes that the urban middle class and poor women could act more independently, which may also have contributed to opportunities for conflict. Many women worked as servants and frequently changed employers, thereby making themselves vulnerable and subject to the whims of their employers.

Women's legal rights varied within Poland, for example those under Chełmno law were subject to full community of possessions, whereas the Magdeburg Law protected a woman's rights to her dowry as well as everything which came to her husband's home with her, forbidding the husband from seizing the dowry or using it to discharge his debts. Even so, neither of these laws extended full civic rights to women, so if a woman wished to initiate a legal case, the charge had to be brought by her husband acting in her name. Before the courts, women's fates depended on how the law was practised and on individual judges, as well as their own social standing, previous history, reputation and marital status.

In Poznań at the end of the sixteenth and beginning of the seventeenth century, 90 per cent of family units were traditional two-generational households and the average marriage lasted between 10 and 15 years, with a relatively high rate of remarriage. Thirty per cent of marriages lasted only five years and the 1590 tax record shows that widows with children made up just under 17 per cent of taxpayers. This may well mask a higher figure, as many widows with children may have been under the threshold. Interestingly, 70 per cent of families had children and stepfamilies were relatively common, which may account for many of the trial narratives featuring spousal and child abuse. The household also extended to the manservant and maidservant who lived in the house and were fed and paid once a year. However, their situation declined in line with social conditions and they were often the first to be dismissed when times were harsh.[10] Thus, in the many precarious situations in which women had to earn their living, there were plenty of opportunities for conflict to arise and power to be misused. This was classic territory for negotiation and for those with power to redefine what constituted witchcraft and the witch, in their own interests.

Witchcraft and the Domestic Sphere

> The key to understanding the witch trials lies in their gender-specificity. The details of the cases refer directly to traditionally defined feminine space – the home, the kitchen, the sickroom, the nursery; to culturally defined female tasks or occupations and their direct opposites – feeding (poisoning), child-rearing (infanticide), healing (harming), birth (death).[11]

A focus on the domestic sphere is inevitable because most accusations of *maleficia* concerned health, fertility or productivity – areas generally deemed a woman's responsibility.[12] One of the most striking points in Polish trials is the strong link between fears within the domestic sphere to accusations based predominantly on a diabolic form of poisoning in beer or food, referred to as 'giving the Devil'. Naturally this evokes Jackson's and Willis's paradigms of the witch as a woman who harmed rather than nurtured, an inversion transforming her into one who 'pollutes', which is also a term used in Wielkopolska trials.[13]

Part of the tendency towards equating bad women with witches emerged from women's experiences in the domestic sphere, so crucial to everyday subsistence. As Rublack writes, 'the early modern household was at once a political, productive and familial entity and the space in which people spent much of their time'. She, as others, sees a complementarity in the negotiation of gender between husband and wife within the household as a political unit, where women were considered the binary opposite to men, as well as the implications of sexual tensions and gossip for men's control of women within society.[14] In Zofia's trial in Kalisz (1580) the court noted that she had lived in Poznań for ten years brewing beer, but had a reputation for disorderly living. After the death of her husband and two children, she travelled around markets earning a living through theft and prostitution. Apolonia Porwitowa was noted as keeping a disorderly house and Regina Dereciowa was judged guilty by association for living with Marusza, who had already been executed as a witch, as well as losing four of her five children.[15] In many of these narratives men were absent and, just like single mothers today, women without men were demonized.

The exemplar for both Roman Catholics and Protestants was the Holy Household, additionally furnishing Roman Catholics with the paragon of the Virgin Mary, while the new Protestant template of womanhood pitted the approved, married woman, running a successful household, providing a religious education for her children and containing sex within marriage – against the single, childless, sexually indiscreet woman, often subject to another woman within the household. According to Luther, when a woman turned to the Devil or witchcraft, she was not only showing insubordination to God, but also to her husband, revealing the rebellious character of a bad wife.[16] Women on both sides of the Reformation found themselves measured against often impossible criteria and, not surprisingly, frequently found wanting. The theme of the bad woman or the woman lacking in virtue runs throughout Polish printed sources as well as in trial records. We can identify tropes such as: the mother who rid herself of a child either before or after birth; the procuress; the mother who failed to instruct her children in religion (imperilling their souls); and the notorious wicked stepmother. These characterizations also link to the notion of witchcraft as a hereditary trait, as we saw in the trial of those related to witches, such as Agnieszka of Mnichowo, the daughter of a witch and Marianna, the niece and daughter of executed witches.[17]

Fears around Fertility

Roper's fascinating study of witchcraft trials in Augsburg drew out the complex tensions around motherhood and fertility. Her exploration of women's fears and fantasies around childbirth showed that they often translated into accusations against lying-in maids or midwives when disaster struck. Roper embraced a multi-causal explanation, but suggested that fears of an attack on fertility were prime concerns projected through contemporary art, literature and social conflict onto predominantly old women, thus broadening the genre of materials consulted. As she wrote, 'at the heart of the story, I believe, must lie the emotional dynamic of envy, dependence and terror', reflecting the fraught battle for survival in which fertility played such a vital role.[18]

This theme is also resonant in the trials, although expected references to abortifacients and love magic were relatively rare and few narratives directly involve midwives, but there are clear accusations of causing miscarriages. The confessions of those who had internalized their guilt as bad mothers for killing an infant or miscarrying also bear out Jackson's conclusions and some striking insights emerge from trials held in Turek in the middle of the seventeenth century. When some women subjected to swimming subsequently floated, they were asked why the water (a pure element which cast out sin) had rejected them.[19] A spirited defence was initially put up in the first case in 1648, involving seven women, when they complained that they had been thrown into the water in different ways, some on their sides and others by the leg. However, the experience prompted Zofia Kaliscina to admit that God was punishing her because she had buried a child, which she had failed to confess to the priest. Dorota Gabryska was convinced she had floated because she ate bread on Friday but also retorted that they had thrown her in sideways. She added that she had previously been swum and had not floated because she had not borne children.[20]

In Korytkowo Zofia Fiertayka floated and then admitted that the water had rejected her because she shed something from her vagina, having suffered from a vaginal discharge for three months, and because she had not confessed bad deeds committed in her youth. In the same case Małgorzata Fretówna confessed that the water had not taken her because she had given birth to a small hand, which she had thrown away without her husband's knowledge and to which she had never confessed. She also said that her mother had beaten her and sometimes injured her with a knife. In 1660 Dorota Budzina was convinced that she had floated because she had borne two children in adultery, whom she had crushed at the breast when young and another two of her children had burnt to death during a fire in the village. However, her testimony that she had escaped twice (once from jail) suggests previous brushes with the law. Agnieszka, a servant, admitted she had given birth to a dead child, whom she had thrown away in the dung.[21] It is not insignificant that many of these women were servants, who may have been subjected to sexual advances from male members of the household or others. All these admissions were expressions of particularly female experiences and guilt that reached to the very core of what it meant to be a woman and a mother.

Bad Mothers and Cruel Husbands

Marriage was yet another key aspect of the domestic sphere and details in the trials correlate with Rowlands's account of German women who spoke of their relationship with the Devil as a bad marriage, telling of a cruel and bad husband who beat and deceived them. The internalization of feelings of inadequacy or sin were visible narratives where women spoke of the Devil rejecting or beating them because they were old or were not virgins. These accounts support Rowlands's observation that part of the women's dynamic with the interrogators may have been based on their experiences as beaten women telling their spouse or master what he wanted to hear.

The submissive role is also visible in the trope of the older teacher, usually female and sometimes a procuress, frequently named during a trial. The vast majority of accused women revealed the names of their supposed teachers, often naming their mothers, but many of them were already deceased or had been denounced. Unsurprisingly, there were strong elements of submission evident in women's confessions, which were not simply explained by torture, and which may have been connected to low self-esteem or the traditional role of many women within a patriarchal society.[22]

Male Judges, Female Victims?

The work of historians such as Sharpe, Holmes and Monter remind us that the gendering of the persecution was by no means a clear cut case of female victims and male perpetrators. They have also examined the various roles women played in the persecution; as the possessed, as reporters of physical searches on witches' bodies, as witnesses and crucially as denouncers. Undoubtedly, women could both mobilize men and be mobilized by them, since in a patriarchal society women were often concerned about gaining men's approval. As Briggs writes,

> Early modern Europe was a society in which women got a raw deal in many respects, but this did not often take the form of direct persecution; rather it operated through indirect pressure that frequently led to women accusing one another.

He also points out that 'women typically responded with threats and curses, which then became part of the evidence for their malevolence' and argues that gender was only one of the many causes of the persecution.[23] Other explanations for the preponderance of female victims include male fear of female insubordination, women turning to witchcraft to compensate for their physical weakness and their submission to the dominant intellectual binary polarity of the period, which by default cast bad women as the natural opposite of good men.[24] However, even with such a high rate of female accused as the Wielkopolska sample shows, I would still agree with Larner's often-cited view that the witchcraft persecution was 'not sex-specific but...sex-related'. She claimed that accusations were aimed at witches rather than women and that social position rather than gender played a larger role; women were rendered more exposed to the investigation of secret crimes against the family encouraged by confessionalization. She argued that this enabled the 'hunting of women who do not fulfil the male view of how women ought to conduct themselves', which Rowlands elaborated on, convinced that 'From the context of beliefs about witchcraft which were potentially gender-neutral, then, emerged accusations of witchcraft which were gender-biased although by no means gender-specific.' Rowlands also suggests that the greater preponderance of women was a result of communities believing women were more likely to practise *maleficia* and due to the gendered division of household labour, nurturing and dairy tasks.[25]

Some of the main gendered theories of witchcraft can be supported by at least one trial if not more from the Wielkopolska sample. For example, most accusations centred on the failure of domestic duties regarded as a woman's responsibility and many women internalized their apparent domestic and maternal failures, judging themselves harshly. Women were identified as the main protagonists and most of the *maleficia* was regarded as inverse nurturing. However, although it is difficult to directly assess the impact of new religious ideals on the narratives, Protestant ideologies cannot be dismissed out of hand in a confessionally mixed area like Wielkopolska (although one suspects not by many peasants in everyday contexts).[26] The notion that those accused of witchcraft were 'old, unmarried, widowed, or poor' is more difficult to assess, because most of the cases furnish little detail at this level. This also prevents any real assessment of the suggestion that accusations were in part projections of fertility concerns on those who were past child-bearing age. Fertility was certainly an important aspect of the trials, but was expressed directly most often in the loss of cattle, health and milk, as opposed to weather magic and love magic, which were rarely mentioned. Midwives were also rarely accused, but we can speculate that the narratives describing miscarriage and sexual experience illustrate fears around sexual continence and incontinence, fertility, abuse, shame and guilt.

Male Witches

Although the sample has shown a very small proportion of men accused of witchcraft, nonetheless it is worth briefly examining the contexts in which they appeared before the courts, because they embody a significant shift in the recognizable idea of the witch and display different attributes. The trials of male witches partially conform to Rowlands's five main categories derived from her Rothenburg research: self-confessed boy witches, cunning men carrying out both beneficent and maleficent practices, alleged sabbat attendees, secondary witches (those related to women accused of witchcraft) and those carrying out maleficent witchcraft but with no previous reputation.[27] I have found no examples of the first two categories in the Wielkopolska sample, but the types of witchcraft cases in which men were involved reflect a pattern similar to those for women, with a few prominent male-specific exceptions.

Men at the Sabbat

The involvement of men as protagonists in witchcraft trials begins with those named as attending the sabbat, usually denounced in a long line of others, such as Dorota Rudniki's husband, named and tried at Kalisz in 1600. His wife had sent him to collect birch from the gallows, for which he was convicted of witchcraft alongside her and banished.[28] A pipe player at the sabbat, Wawrzyniec Dziad of Jarocin was tried with five women and subsequently confessed to renouncing God, the Most Holy Virgin Mary and all the saints as well as killing cattle. More unusually he confessed to having escaped from the barrel in which he had been held by the authorities and the Pyzdry court sentenced him to the stake in 1719. In a trial from Grodzisk, Grzegorz of Połacewo played the dulcimer at the sabbat, renounced God and the Virgin Mary and gave himself to a devil called Kuba, although there is no mention of diabolic sex or a pact. Grzegorz was accused of stealing the Eucharist, not once but twice. The first he gave to another witch, the second he buried to harm the wheat crop, and he was also accused of spoiling a neighbour's milk. These examples reveal that men were often, but not always, denounced when details of the sabbat emerged.[29]

The case of a certain Jan, heard before the Wągrowiec court in 1727, is an excellent example of the same attributes of, and charges filed against, both men and women. Over 30 cases for witchcraft were heard before this court between 1689 and 1736, involving over 60 people. In the year of his trial, the court heard three cases involving at least six women and over the previous decade over 25 people had been brought to trial on charges of witchcraft.[30] Jan was from an outlying village, whose owner was a kinsman of Colonel Ludomir Dorposki. Dorposki accused Jan of harming his cattle and claimed that he was a *prawdziwy czarownik*, 'a real male witch' (a rare mention of the masculine form of *czarownica*, 'female witch'), and played an instrument at Łysa Góra. After torture he confessed that he was a witch and had been taught by Katarzyna, a woman from the next village – she had already been burnt as a witch. He denounced nine people and confessed that whilst others had travelled to Łysa Góra on horses and dogs or in a carriage, he had travelled on a pig. He also revealed that Stachowa had a key with which she could summon rain.[31] He admitted to all the charges brought against him, adding that he had also put insects into wheat, scattered powders and seen the Devil appear to him disguised as a wolf. He was sentenced to death. In another case from Wągrowiec in 1738, although little remains of the record, we discover that the accused, a certain Grzegorz, was 'tied up as a duck and swum on the lake'. When brought for questioning, he confessed that he had renounced God and worshipped three devils. He was freed when the village swore a collective oath on his behalf.[32]

Sons and Lovers

In 1721, the Wągrowiec court tried Michał Switaj together with his wife Hedwiga (Jadwiga) for harming their seigneur's cattle, horses and wheat. Michał was tortured first and claimed that Francek (it was unusual for a male teacher to be mentioned) had taught him witchcraft and how to take the harvest from the fields using sympathetic magic. Michał claimed that he just wanted to be lucky in life and also confessed that he had taken the harvest for his children. He had met the Devil in a wood near the meadows, who had instructed him which people, cattle and cows to harm. He claimed to have signed a blood pact on paper with the Devil, which was in his trunk along with his receipts and army documents. The rest of the confession was fairly standard – his devil was even called Jasiek. He smeared himself with ointment and flew to the sabbat on Thursday, where he ate horse manure and drank urine and played the double bass. More damningly, he confessed that his wife had also been there, and had cooked and then danced with her devil Kuba. He had known for some time that she was a witch, because of her nocturnal absences,[33] and these suspicions had been confirmed at *Łysa Góra*. He denied that he had killed the horses, claiming he had merely taken them because there had been nowhere for them to pasture. He denounced his wife to her face, as she continued to steadfastly deny the accusations, and she confessed only after a second round of torture. According to the sentence, Michał was found guilty of harming 30 heads of cattle and they were both sentenced to death.[34]

In an echo of hereditary cases involving females, sons were also accused with their mothers. Szymon Ladzina (described only as young) came before the Grodzisk court in 1737 after his tortured mother Anna denounced him for attending the sabbat:

1. Do you Szymon admit that you stole many communion wafers at the behest of your mother? I do.
2. Do you admit that you gave them to your mother and Niewitecka? I do.
3. Do you admit that you were at *Łysa Góra* with your mother and Niewitecka? I do.

Niewitecka had already been executed as a witch by then and Szymon subsequently retracted a number of denunciations – we can see the names crossed out in the records – but he was still sentenced to death, and beheaded as an act of clemency before his body was burnt.[35] His confession reveals none of the wild accounts that often appeared in children's confessions such as that of the teenage Anna, tried in Grodzisk in 1707, discussed in the previous chapter.

A Man of Substance

Although the cases above have demonstrated a commonality in the paradigm of witchcraft applied to both men and women, the next cases demonstrate clear differences, and in some cases, such as the following, it may have been down to class and influence. In 1728 Jan Głodek was denounced by a woman accused of witchcraft before the court of Wągrowiec. He travelled to Gniezno for documents and approached two local men of substance, one of whom had offered him a letter of support. It seems strange that he was not imprisoned, but allowed to petition for help and subsequently enlist the aid of his friend Josef. Głodek had also been to Klecko to a priest who advised him to go to the Clerical Chancellery at Gniezno. When the court re-adjourned with the seniors of the village at the orders of the Palatine of Kalisz, Głodek was accused of being a witch and a musician at *Łysa Góra*. He had been denounced by Mikołayka and Robarska and was sentenced to banishment from the village and the surrounding ten miles on threat of a return to court if he caused anyone harm. He forfeited all his goods, his estate was apportioned, court costs were paid and debts were recorded on the register. Pan Zaleski earned 30 *grzywien* for his pains, plus 20 for appearing at the trial of Josef, who had been found guilty of trying to pressure one of the witches into renouncing her denunciation of Głodek. According to the guard, Josef had taken beer to the witch and asked her whether she had denounced Głodek. She had, but subsequently withdrew the denunciation. This trial is a rare example of outside help being sought, or at least recorded, and we are even told that one witness, Simon Kapica, claimed he was offered money to withdraw his testimony.[36]

Male Witches as the 'Other'

The cases described so far have more or less conformed to the stereotypical patters of witchcraft trials, with some exceptional features, such as men as musicians at the sabbat, no sexual experiences with their devils and sometimes having enjoyed more lenient sentences. Thus, men were usually involved in cases of witchcraft, either on the basis of an accusation against them as the result of denunciation or occasionally in defence of their wives. However, the following cases rely on definitions of the accused as 'other'; on grounds of religion and sexual practices.

The 1620 trial of Salamon Juddus, before the Kalisz court, reflects the projection of the Devil onto a Jew. Helżbieta Bienkowa and Katarzyna Jagiełczyna from the village of Sobotka had been accused of witchcraft, of stealing the Eucharist, and selling it to Salamon. This fascinating case casts the Jew as the Devil, as it is he who supposedly encourages the women to sin, which, we can speculate, may account for why the Devil is rarely mentioned. Bienkowa claimed she had been selling eggs when Salamon asked her to steal a Eucharist before Easter – she haggled over the price, which exacerbated her crime in the eyes of the court. Ironically the women claimed that they bought a Mass out of the payment and Bienkowa also claimed the priest had encouraged her to denounce Salamon.

When next interrogated, the women admitted they had both encountered the Devil and been to Łysa Góra, but they were not asked to denounce anyone. Katarzyna denied receiving any money, perhaps attempting to distance herself from the whole episode. After they had both been tortured, it emerged that a certain Marcin had encouraged them to revoke their testimony against Salamon; the women were caught between the priest, Marcin and the court. When they were asked if anyone from the Kalisz municipal court or the clergy or the local noble had asked them to denounce Salamon, Bienkowa claimed that Brodatski had promised her a dress.[37] She repeated her claim that the priest had told her to accuse the Jew and added that Salamon had sold meat on a fast day, when he claimed to have been in Poznań on business. Katarzyna was asked again by Marcin and Salamon not to corroborate her friend's denunciation.

Despite being tortured several times, Salamon denied everything and explained that he had travelled around the local towns a lot before Easter and that he was at home on Good Friday, when this was supposed to have happened. As he remarked, Jews knew better than to be seen out on this particular Christian feast. He consistently claimed that he would suffer in the next world if he lied while on trial, although he admitted that he had argued with Bienkowa and taken her to the *Wójt* to settle the matter. He continued to deny the charges, and when he was imprisoned he begged the *Wójt* to release him from jail, as his clothes and purses had been taken and he had been attacked by servants. He called attention to the strictures of his faith that forbade him even to look at the Eucharist, and claimed the charge was ludicrous. The evidence points towards a conspiracy, as further details suggest that Salamon was on familiar terms with some of the *Wójt*'s circle, and there appeared to have been at least two attempts to bribe Bienkowa to name Salamon. The accusation of stealing the Eucharist was sufficient to convict the women, and that of buying the Eucharist was enough to convict Salamon, but why was there a need to introduce witchcraft and the Devil? Unfortunately this remains a mystery, as the ending of the trial does not appear to be in the record book.[38]

We can pose a similar question from the remaining fragment of the next case from the 1730s, in which a man was indicted for sodomy with a cow and a mare, but also eventually claimed he attended *Łysa Góra* and played the fife. He was burnt at the stake with the animals, which was the normal sentence for bestiality.[39] We may surmise that the additional charge of witchcraft reflected an underlying premise that someone who had committed such acts must be in league with the Devil, or perhaps seizing an opportunistic moment to bolster fear of witchcraft within the community.[40]

The Devil's Pact

In contrast to some of the previous trials, those of Andrzej Bocheński (Poznań 1722) and Walenty Musiałowski (Poznań 1746) amply illustrate an exceptional 'male' paradigm of the witch, with different attributes and a more generous reading by the judges, of diabolic complicity. They display a more élite interpretation of the label *czarownik*, 'male witch', and differ significantly from the witchcraft accusations women faced. In both cases the men confessed that they had actively summoned and made a pact with the Devil. Bocheński, originally from Grodzisk, testified,

> My name is Andrzej Bocheński, I attended many schools in Warsaw and Poznań and I graduated in Philosophy here in Poznań. Then I worked as an inspector in many courts and then I spent half a year in the Cistercian monastery suffering from depression. There I wrote a contract with the Devil and I signed it with the blood the surgeon had let, while I was ill. Then Father Bledewski saw the pact and took it and after a suitable penance I had to burn it, but it was only for money.[41]

He was also accused of apostasy, idolatry and blasphemy. He claimed to have written his pact in blood, renounced Christianity and given up his soul. Having lost his parents at an early age, interestingly, he described suffering from melancholy. During a spell of illness he dropped the pact in the monastery. When it was found, he was ordered to leave and to burn the pact, whereupon he admitted he had done it for money and pretended not to remember any further contents. He left the monastery and continued to drift, finding it difficult to settle within a community. As a result of this travelling and perhaps also his education, he may have been regarded with suspicion. He was constantly on the move, either at his own whim or with the help of his family, who were of sufficient merit to secure him positions with the Customs Administrator of Royal Prussia, in Toruń, with a dignitary in Poznań and in the treasury at Malbork. However, he did not remain in one place for more than six months and worked long enough to accumulate some money and then spent it swiftly. In Malbork he contracted 'the French disease' and subsequently took himself off to the vicinity of Lwów, gathered more money and returned to Toruń, staying with relatives for nine months. Finally he entered the service of Pan Załuski in Pyzdry where he served for nine months, but evidently not without trouble, since it was at Załuski's request that he was brought before the Town Hall.

Bocheński complained vociferously about his treatment by Załuski, claiming that he had received little money and inedible food. In fact he was in such dire straits that he wrote another pact, on Corpus Christi, again signed with his blood. This second pact was either, he said, in the Consistory in Poznań or at the Town Hall. After another altercation with Pan Załuski, Bocheński then ran away and a barrel of beer was offered as a bounty. At this point, Załuski ordered his possessions to be gathered up and it was then that they found the pact. Bocheński was clapped in irons and taken to the Town Hall. Rumour abounded about a third pact, which he had left on the table at his brother's house in Toruń, so that they would see his desperation and take pity on him. He hastened to add that that particular pact was signed in ink and not blood. His relatives took the pact to the Jesuits in Toruń, who summoned him, ordered him to go to confession, where he received a penance and burnt the pact. During the last session of the court, it emerged that he had offered his soul to Lucifer (a term rarely used) in exchange for wisdom, knowledge, fortune, luck in marriage and money. He had placed all hope and faith in the Devil, for which he was sentenced to the stake, but his sentence was remitted.[42]

Twenty-four years later, the Poznań court tried Walenty Musiałowski, a herder, who hardly knew his mother, and who was under the impression that he was 20 years old.

> I went to the inn and I drank on the Thursday before St Anne's day, before the harvest, then I was herding the cattle on the fields from the afternoon and then sat down for beer and owed seven zloties and I didn't have it. I started to become desperate and I called upon the cursed Devil with these words, I call upon you cursed Devil, bring me some money and I will sign over my soul to you. Having said that I lay down and I was afraid and jumped up and there I saw the Devil standing over me in the figure of a man dressed in red German/foreign clothes who started to say to me, what is your name, I said Walenty. Then he said to me, listen, you called me, will you sign yourself over to me? I will give you money. I said nothing as I was so scared, then I just said I sign myself over to you.

The young man was gripped by fear and saw the Devil standing over him in red German clothes. The Devil struck his deal, asked him to renounce God, the Virgin Mary and the saints, as well as his patron Saint Valentine, and then scratched him on the right hand on the middle finger and drew blood (a practice admitted by some women in Wielkopolska trials). Then the Devil showed him the money he had requested and he sighed with regret, upon which both the Devil and the money disappeared. Overtaken by remorse, Musiałowski claimed not to have taken any money. Later, he was taken to a priest where he stayed for a week, confessed his sin and lay prostrate as a penitent. Subsequently he signed up with the Brothers of the Rosary and was admitted to communion. According to the account, when he returned home and started work, as a farmhand, he was advised to give himself up to authorities at the Town Hall. His sentence was also commuted.[43]

These accounts are a striking contrast to those of women accused of witchcraft because they feature neither the sabbat, witnesses, denunciations nor *maleficia*. Both these cases feature narratives bordering on accounts of high magic and pacts and they were also dealt with more much more leniently – there is no mention I can find of torture. It seems that both were brought to the Town Hall by specific people and straightforwardly told their stories.

Why So Few Men?

There are several plausible explanations for the relatively low percentage of male witches. First, patriarchal Polish society regarded witches as predominantly women, as evident from demonology.[44] Second, the perception of what witchcraft itself consisted fell mainly within the domestic or female sphere, but as we have seen, accusations of spoiling milk, for example, could be associated with men. The question then remains of why relatively few men were tried on such charges of witchcraft, since the trials above demonstrate that men could be perceived as witches not only in the same circumstances as women (with the exception of charges relating to female fertility) but additionally in connection with sodomy and bestiality and pacts with the Devil that all but approach high magic. Despite this evidence, the predominant stereotype portrayed in Polish printed sources remained that of a female witch, perpetuating the intellectual paradigm, as public executions perpetuated its popular counterpart. The seigniorial pattern discerned in these trials and expounded upon in the following chapter (where frequently charges were brought and/or supported by the local seigneur) also facilitates and may even partially explain the greater number of females accused, since so many of the accusations consisted of giving the Devil in food or beer. Lastly, as we shall see, accounts in printed sources, and the instruction of the well-known legal author Groicki that women be more harshly punished than men, may have heavily influenced the concept that a witch was a woman. The question of male witches is one that clearly requires much more research, as it is interesting to see that many of the trials conformed to the stereotypical 'female' paradigm of the witch, with small exceptions. In the exceptional male cases of Bocheński and Musiałowski, the diabolic attributes of the witch were somehow disregarded and leniency was shown – whether this was because they were men or because the trials were heard towards the end of the persecution, we cannot be sure.

4
Framing the Witch: Legal Theories and Realities

The Legal Definition of a Witch

Since we have already seen that the legal system was rife with abuse, it's useful to compare and contrast two portraits of the legal system – one, the theoretical framework found in various legal codices, the other based on what we can glean from the trials. This is one way of discerning differences and similarities between the printed sources and the trials and will also inform our thinking on how the paradigms of the witch and witchcraft were formed. By examining the trials first, we have a good idea of how the accused and the judges negotiated varied belief systems, a theme developed throughout this work. One would expect the legal system, in addition to papal bulls and church decrees, to provide more standardized definitions of witches and witchcraft, but as the previous chapter illustrated, definitions differed greatly and evolved over time. Literature, treatises and the trial records can be juxtaposed against this legal background to illustrate the failings, successes and influence of legislative power and to identify whether the learned ideas of the judiciary interplay with the beliefs of the peasant and middling classes. The lack of centralized power predictably impacted on the Wielkopolska's various legal systems, which were often ignored in favour of fragmented localized power. Villages and small towns might be under the jurisdiction of the local nobility, clergy or royal statutes and in order to try a peasant who lived in another jurisdiction, permission had to be sought from their seigneur. Trial records demonstrate how influential the power of even minor *szlachta* was, turning private and leased towns and villages into little more than personal fiefdoms.

In theory the legal system should provide a non-biased framework against which to read trial records, but it is clear that the system was very far from objective. On the one hand, judicial personnel were able to impact on the dynamics within trials through the questions they asked and the answers they wrote; but equally the accused could reclaim power by shaping their own narratives and responses, denouncing others, denying charges, requesting to undergo swimming (to prove innocence) or by refusing to speak. In fact the trial itself was a conduit for many linguistic, cultural and belief exchanges between the male and, sometimes, educated judiciary and the frequently female, mostly illiterate women, but as we saw in the previous chapter, we should not fall into the trap of reading trials as simple binaries. Although it is frequently claimed that many judges were illiterate, there is evidence that some were at least aware of a range of legal codices, which were cited in the sentences. The trial of Ploszaika in Poznań in 1629 was presided over by Georgius Janecius, a Doctor of Philosophy and Medicine but such an educated judge is a rare find in the Wielkopolska sample.[1]

By examining the legal system, we can also trace the evolution of legal conceptualizations of witchcraft from the earliest mentions in synodal decrees in the thirteenth century to the trials of the eighteenth century, which fixated upon the relationship between the Devil and the witch. This correlates with the developing diabolism of the trials and shifting ambivalence. In the fifteenth and sixteenth centuries, as we have seen, practices such as sprinkling cattle with holy water, causing impotence and a reputation for witchcraft were considered valid reasons for bringing an accusation of witchcraft before the ecclesiastical courts, and in the absence of any mention of the Devil, the focus appeared to be on *maleficia* rather than diabolism. Other protective measures, for example herbs found about an individual's body to ward off the pain of torture, were also regarded as witchcraft.[2]

In contrast, by the middle of the seventeenth century far more emphasis was placed on accusations of meeting the Devil and attending the sabbat, indicating a shift from the pragmatics of *maleficia* to ideological grounds, from harm as the objective to harm as just one weapon of apostasy. The crime of witchcraft was projected onto the individual in such a way as to transform them into the personification of evil, a threat to the whole community, and indeed, the whole of Christendom, in common with European ideology of the sixteenth and seventeenth centuries. As one sentence declaimed, 'the Law is clear that those who renounce the Lord God and the Most Holy Virgin, and are wedded to their own devil and have sex with him, are to leave this world through fire'.[3]

Witchcraft in Ecclesiastical Legislation

In the Polish territories, the first mention of witchcraft as a crime dates from a statute issued by the Synod of Buda in 1279, which defined witchcraft as summoning the Devil and using religious items. It indicated that such practices were widespread and forbade anyone other than the Bishop to absolve them[4] and instructed parishioners to inform on those they believed to be witches during Church visitations.[5] In 1359 a charter issued by Kazimierz Wielki permitted ecclesiastical courts to pass sentences to be executed by lay courts, expanding the scope of punishment from excommunication and interdict.[6] The earliest extant recorded trials for witchcraft come from the ecclesiastical courts of Poznań, Płock and Gniezno, with the first appearing before the latter's consistory court in 1413, followed by at least a dozen more before 1500. Contrary to popular belief, there was no mention of trial by ordeal for witchcraft and although swimming was practised (even in Poland apparently as late as 1836)[7] it was a practice initially to determine whether a person should be brought to trial as a witch. The Inquisition heard only one case.[8]

In the mid-sixteenth century the ecclesiastical courts' jurisdiction over witchcraft was ratified by the temporary *Sejm Walny* in Cracow of 1543[9] and a year later the Wielkopolska sample shows that the first of a trickle of witchcraft cases came before the secular municipal courts in Poznań and Kalisz. The conflict over jurisdiction between the lay and ecclesiastical courts was discussed well into the eighteenth century. However, in reality Pilaszek maintains that this battle was really an attempt by the *szlachta* to limit ecclesiastical jurisdiction over its own religious affairs and that the temporary statute was revoked by the Piotrków parliament of 1562/3.[10] The formal reversal deprived the ecclesiastical courts of executing sentences other than excommunication and interdict. Karbownik suggests this was the real reason for the change that caused witchcraft cases to be brought before municipal and lay courts in preference to ecclesiastical courts. It was a vital blow to the Roman Catholic Church's power, especially in the wake of the initial success in Poland of the Reformation, which had already rendered its punishments ineffectual for those who had embraced the new faith.

The start of the secular Polish witchcraft persecution in the mid-sixteenth century coincided with the beginning of a series of ecclesiastical regulations and decrees that certainly went unheeded in many areas.[11] In the absence of a cohesive central government, the Roman Catholic Church's synod was one of the only national decision-making bodies. However, in the general decline of the *Deluge*, no provincial synods were held after 1643 and power devolved to the diocesan level, although discussion on reclaiming jurisdiction continued in synodal resolutions and episcopal regulations from 1542–1762. After 1643, most decisions within the church were communicated in episcopal pastoral letters containing regulations often passed in a later synod. In 1682, Bishop Kazimierz Florian Czartoryski issued the Vatican's *Instructio* from 1657 criticizing witchcraft trials in lay courts, which was heavily drawn upon as an exemplar. In these letters, clergy often criticized judicial abuse and torture, denunciations by hostile neighbours and damaging gossip and the refusal of appeals. They also questioned the refusal of a Christian burial to those who had died during torture as well as the continued use of trial by ordeal.[12] As we shall see in Chapter 7, clerical voices were strongly critical of the persecution, directing a great deal of their opprobrium towards secular courts.

In 1739, Bishop Teodor Czartoryski went as far as to deny that a woman's admission to cooperating with the Devil was admissible evidence on the grounds that it could not be proven. He also suggested a bishop's committee where those educated in theology, law and medicine ought to pass verdicts in witchcraft cases either to free the accused or confirm their guilt, before the case was passed on to a lay court. Responsibility would then fall upon the priests and deans to inform the bishop of the need to appoint such a consistory committee and if the lay courts attempted to prevent a committee going about its work, then an interdict or excommunication could be imposed. The clergy also invoked the monarch's aid, by-passing most of the legal system with the result that the *sąd asesorski*, 'Assessorial Court', passed decrees in 1672, 1713 and 1745 forbidding municipal courts from passing sentences before the cases had been heard before the ecclesiastical courts. According to Czechowicz (writing in 1769), the decree of 1745 threatened village court judges with death and municipal court judges with a fine of 1000 Hungarian złoties if they passed the death sentence in witchcraft cases.[13] The last decree coincided with the end of the peak in the Wielkopolska sample, but we can only speculate as to whether the repeated need to pass such legislation indicated a frequency of witchcraft trials.[14]

Secular Legislation on Witchcraft

While the clergy and the nobility argued over the theoretical implications of jurisdiction over witchcraft trials, in reality these debates were important only internally. Justice was a luxury rarely afforded the peasantry.

On privately owned estates, the owner *posiadał pełnie władzy prawodawczej w swoich dobrach* – 'was in complete possession of legal power in his estates' – operating within an alternative and absolutist legal jurisdiction.[15] For the most part, those accused of witchcraft in villages were brought to the nearest town's municipal courts or the judiciary would be deputed to villages to formally sit as a court. Village courts did hear witchcraft trials, but relatively few of the cases survive and the village courts could not pass death sentences.[16] Apart from this private rule of law, there was of course the formal legal system and although, as in many other areas of Europe, there were occasionally statutes or judicial decrees dealing exclusively with the crime of witchcraft, judicial authority was more often to be found in the codices that with time evolved into the law of the land. One of the earliest statutes on witchcraft, issued by Kazimierz Jagiellończyk in the Lithuanian statutes of 1468, stated that if a thief were found to have herbs about him, he was to be tried as a *zeljanin*, 'one who has herbs', translated in Polish sources as *czarownik*, 'male witch'. According to Koranyi, the herbs were most commonly hidden in the hair or armpits,[17] ostensibly the reason for accounts of shaving the accused, to prohibit the Devil from hiding in hair.[18]

By the middle of the sixteenth century a number of codices were in circulation. In 1505/6 Łaski's *Commune incliti Poloniae regni privilegium constitutionem* was published[19] and in 1523 the Parliament of Bydgoszcz published the *Formuła processus*, eventually adopted by the rest of the crown. Jaskier published a collection of law in Latin in 1535, translated into Polish by Szczerbicz in 1581, followed by Sarnicki's *Statuta y metrika przywileiów koronnych*, 'Statutes and Register of the Privileges of the Crown', in 1594, which affirmed the clergy's jurisdiction over *wróżki, czary, czarnoksięstwa*, 'fortune tellers, witchcraft, sorcery'.[20] Military law also provided for the expulsion and handing over of any man to the laws of 'God and the Crown', who was an 'idolator, male witch, fortune teller, cursor'.[21] Jan Cervus Tucholczyk and Jan Cerasinus Kirsteyn compiled legal codices in Latin, but it was Bartłomiej Groicki's Polish-language collections published in 1558 and 1559 that were to prove most popular.

Polish municipal law was based on a variety of sources: natural law, Kazimierz Wielki's statutes (one of the first codifications of Polish law), the *ortyle*, 'sentences' of the *Weichbild*, 'Magdeburg Law' (used as precedents), the *Zwierciadło Saskie*, 'Saxon Law', the *Constitutio Carolina*, Polish law and other regional variations. The majority of Polish towns were founded on the basis of both the Magdeburg Codex and the Saxon Law – together commonly known as the Magdeburg Law[22] – which were introduced mainly into areas with large German populations, particularly in Wielkopolska. In addition, the *Carolina*, issued in 1532 by Emperor Charles V of the Holy Roman Empire, was also partially adopted and more importantly was outlined in Groicki's work *Ten postępek wybrań jest z praw cesarskich, który Karolus V kazał wydać po wszystkich swoich państwiech...*, This is Taken from Imperial Law, Which Charles V Ordered to be Published throughout All His States... (1559).[23] The constitution recognized a number of varying types of law in addition to the three main codices, including customary law, statutes passed by parliament, and so-called eternal and temporary constitutions. From the end of the sixteenth century all statutes passed by parliament were published as a complete body of law known as the King's Constitution, but the monarch could also issue additional edicts (usually for religious or military purposes) or decrees (for matters concerning business or customs). At a local level the *sejmiki*, 'dietines' issued *lauda*, 'local statutes' covering local issues, which did not require the monarch's confirmation.[24]

However, Groicki's works proved the most popular[25] and his compilation of the Carolina was supplemented by *Artykuły prawa maydeburskiego, które zową Speculum Saxonum...*, Articles of the Magdeburg Law That Include Saxon Law... (1558),[26] and *Porządek sądów i spraw miejskich prawa maydeburskiego w Koronie polskiej*, The Order of Courts and Municipal Cases according to the Magdeburg Law in the Polish Crown Lands (1559).[27] Since legal historians generally agree that his work enjoyed the status of an official codex in towns,[28] let us examine it as a theoretical framework for comparison with the realities of the trial procedures, bearing in mind Pilaszek's observation that his versions sometimes mitigated the originals.[29] Groicki clarified that he had not included all the articles, but those usually pertinent to Poland. Interestingly his motivation for writing was a damning indictment of the judiciary and the nobility,

> So that in small towns, where there is a lack of good practitioners [of the law]... that the nobility and officials... would be able to and know how to judge and they are to recognize justice, so that they do not judge at whim but according to written law.[30]

A firm believer in the importance of natural law, at the end of *Porządek sądów*, the author added a list of biblical verses used in legal cases,[31] rendering Exodus 22.18 as *[z]łoczyńcom nie dopuszczaj żyć na świeci*, 'do not permit wrongdoers to live on the earth'. Groicki's works provide an insight into the theory of how a trial should proceed, by defining crimes and appropriate sentences, the criteria required to be a witness, theoretical restrictions upon torture and who was qualified to sit as a judge. Interestingly, in his register to *Porządek*, he writes, 'women, who have committed the crime of witchcraft or poisoning, are to be punished more severely than men, always by fire'.[32] Although there is a consensus that Groicki's work was widely used and we shall return to his work as a benchmark later in this chapter, I have found no citation of it in the Wielkopolska sample with its high number of death sentences.[33]

The Structure of the Polish Courts

In the early modern period Poland's judicial system was extremely varied on a regional, local and village level, as a result of decentralization and the virtual monopoly of noble power.[34] Comparatively Poland's legal system continued to be quite distinct in the greater influence of customary law over established law, whereas in France, for example, Roman law was increasing in significance. However, elements of Roman law had passed into Polish law through the corpus of legal literature. Strikingly, in the seventeenth and eighteenth centuries there was a rise in the *palestra*, or class of professional lawyers and legal representatives, as the middling and lower *szlachta* seized upon this profession as offering a path to increased wealth and social standing as well as opportunities to gain powerful patronage.[35] Ironically in a state with a minimal centralized administrative apparatus, there were numerous court officials, patrons and magnate plenipotentiaries all wielding influence over the legal system at local, regional and national levels. Shortcomings in the statutes were overcome by the use of alternative codices or opinions, which is evident from the Wielkopolska sample, in which the *Carolina*, Mollerius and Damhouder were cited.[36] There is little evidence that the *Malleus* was consulted, but it is known that the Poznań apothecary Jan Frycz, the town's scribe (1585–1607) Krzysztof Zabłocki and Vicar General and Canon Mikołaj Oleski all possessed copies.[37] In addition, town councils issued regulations, precedents were sought and the owners of private towns issued statutes. The Polish legal system was made even more complex by the variety of courts, which included the Parliamentary Court, the Assessorial Court, the Relational Court (held in the monarch's presence which also heard cases concerning the Orthodox churches) and the Chancellor's Court (restricted to the immediate locality of the monarch's residence, the aim of which was to keep the peace at court). Many sectors of society also had their own courts, such as Jews, Armenians, the clergy, the army and the guilds.[38]

The social standing of the accused also determined which courts would hear their trial and predictably the *szlachta* had the right to be tried by peers in the *sądy ziemskie*, 'Land Courts' (requiring the presence of a judge, deputy judge and a scribe), which declined in the seventeenth century and in some areas did not meet for decades. An increase in the jurisdiction of the *sądy grodzkie*, 'Town Courts' (whose judge was appointed by the *starosta*, independently of the dietine), led to a growth in the number of Town Courts' functionaries, as their competence was increased to include both civil and criminal matters. As a consequence, in the sixteenth century the practice of recording actions in the court record books required the *urząd grodzki*, 'City Office', to open daily. The monarch was the supreme judge in matters concerning the *szlachta* and also acted through his court's court, the *sąd nadworny*, until 1578 when the Crown Tribunal was established, with the monarch as its judge. This court sat in Lublin to hear Małopolska's trials and Piotrków to hear those from Wielkopolska. Since these tribunals consisted of members of the *szlachta*, this estate had achieved self-jurisdiction. At the opposite end of the scale, villages had *sądy dominialne*, 'Manorial Courts', and village aldermen's courts led by a manorial official. Other aldermen's courts met under the direction of the village administrator and were supplemented by yet more specialized courts, but it was usual for village courts to use German law, customary law and seigniorial ordinations.[39]

The format and jurisdiction of the municipal courts depended upon whether the town had bought the influential office of the alderman and whether or not the town was privately owned, so, despite German law and municipal privileges, in practice the seigneur could issue legislation or override it in private towns and villages, which takes on great significance in witchcraft trials.[40] In general the *sąd ławy miejskiej (ławniczny)*, 'Aldermen's Court', heard criminal cases and the *sąd rady miejskiej (radziecki)*, 'Town Council Court', usually heard civil cases. There was no prerequisite for the members of the council or the aldermen to be present during a trial and in general a minimum of six constituted a *quorum* in addition to the judge and scribe. The two courts sometimes sat together as the *sąd radziecko-ławnicze* and their own record books were generally retained in the Town Hall.

The Legal System in Wielkopolska

In the 1380s the city of Poznań bought the position of *wójt* to enable the council to take on the role and it duly elected a *wójt* annually to stand at the head of the aldermen. This was not standard practice, for example

Kościan only bought the position in the sixteenth century,⁴¹ while it was not uncommon for the owner of a private town to buy it, or for the *starosta* to hold it in crown towns. It was a limited electoral system and both the town council and the aldermen's court consisted of elected townsmen. However, in the first half of the sixteenth century Poznań introduced a greater degree of democratization in its elections when the *starosta* appointed six councillors and two mayors each year from 24 candidates chosen at a meeting of all the oldest guilds of Poznań. By the end of the seventeenth century, King Jan Sobieski decreed that Poznań must return to a system of a lifelong council of 12, including two mayors appointed by the *starosta*.⁴²

Poznań's council court acted to a large extent as a high court over the jurisdictions under German law and was, in effect, a high court for the 33 Wielkopolska towns that subscribed to the *tortoralia* tax for use of the town's executioner. In this period, the court had a college of aldermen as well as a college of councillors and issued verdicts to other towns in Wielkopolska until 1628. Although the majority of witchcraft cases were heard before the Aldermen's Court (theoretically unless *szlachta* were involved),⁴³ the Council Court was able to hear both civil and criminal cases. The criminal courts sat every six weeks during this period and the administrative courts sat fortnightly, but charges were recorded in the administrative courts, which were open daily from the sixteenth century. The *sąd potrzebny*, 'Court of Necessity', dealt with urgent cases and sat as and when needed, including Sundays and feast days.⁴⁴ Although it was the court's obligation to appoint a legal defence for those accused of witchcraft, this was lacking in most of the trials examined.⁴⁵ Not every urban court felt competent to hear witchcraft cases, so some invited the neighbouring city's court to hear them instead – in 1728 Warta's judiciary was invited to Kozminek to hear several cases.⁴⁶ Theoretically an oral appeal could follow the sentencing, while the court was still in session, but had to be heard before a higher court within six weeks. Appeal courts were held in Piotrków in autumn and winter, where representatives of the *szlachta* were chosen at the dietines as deputies.⁴⁷

The Judiciary

Let us turn now to one of the most important aspects of the legal system – the judicial team – which consisted of at the very least a judge, his deputy and a scribe. We are left in no doubt as to Groicki's concern about the judicial system. He gave judges short shrift, writing, 'judges are to judge in a state of sobriety, and are not to eat or drink whilst the court is in session'.[48] He also described the qualities that judges ought to have: 'fear of God, truth, wisdom, prudence, lack of bias, love towards all equally, knowledge of the law, and power. He is to judge without haste, anger, hatred, love, friendliness, fear, or bribery.'[49] If the judge did not understand all of the evidence or how to conduct the case, he was to record the evidence and send to the nearest town for a competent replacement.[50] Groicki stressed that a judge ought to be competent in the law, to judge accordingly and to pass sentence, not according to his own whim, but according to the evidence presented and the requirements of the law. The position was barred to those who were mad, deaf, blind or dumb, those who were under 21, those who had been excommunicated or banished, and non-Christians and Jews were also prohibited. Needless to say women, the illegitimate and those who had been dishonoured were also barred. Groicki's contemporaries echoed his disparaging and perhaps hyperbolic remarks and often painted judges as licentious, drunken and corrupt.[51]

Pilaszek maintains that although the trials look schematic at first glance, judges 'abandoned the time consuming cause-and-effect interrogation and asked questions which referred only to the most important details of the crime'. She continues, 'by meeting social expectations they gained popularity, eminence and the gratitude of the local inhabitants. They consolidated their position.'[52] In contrast to contemporary criticism of judges, she sees no reason to doubt that the small-town judiciary were conversant with legal literature, suggesting that judges complied with the instructions in Groicki's *Artykuły Prawa Maydeburskiego*. However, she concedes that there is not enough extant material to recreate much of a picture of the judiciary, and that most of the key players in the trials cannot be examined in depth.[53] She and others defend judges, but she admits that the beer consumed during trials could have been up to ten per cent in strength.[54]

One of the many contemporary critical sources,[55] Gdacjusz, the seventeenth-century Protestant preacher, remarked upon the judges' fondness for bribes, which limited their concern to the rich.[56] Serafin Jagodyński, in his collected epigrams (1618) entitled *Grosz*, also developed this theme, as did the influential Krzysztof Opaliński.[57] Baranowski suggested that it was quite common for judges to be drunk and to drink vodka before hearing a case. He claimed that the town councillors and aldermen were usually merchants and craftsmen with very little legal knowledge and that in small towns some were even illiterate, signing documents with a cross.[58] This suggested incompetence of judges was matched by a rise in crime in the seventeenth century, as Bogucka describes:

> The inefficiency of the law courts and the sense of impunity this created may have been the reason why in the 17th century the crime rate, already quite high in the previous century, acquired dimensions which jeopardized the normal functioning of society... The hard times after the Swedish invasion and other wars in the middle of the 17th century and the military operations in the early 18th century, as well as the growing poverty, promoted crime, and so did the anarchisation of relations in the country, the disintegration of the judicial system and the decline in the prestige of authority.[59]

The Theory of Justice

Groicki's works are also useful for reconstructing theoretical trial procedures, a useful contrast to the realities of the trial records. The first step was for the complainant to bring a private accusation or denounce the accused in good faith. They were not supposed to be a known enemy of the accused nor a criminal and were supposed to have witnessed the incident, recalling both the time and the scene of the crime. The accuser must have lived a moral life and not be acting from enmity, jealousy, on the basis of a previous argument nor to make profit, and this was often reflected in the oaths sworn by accusers and witnesses at the start of a trial.[60] In theory, witnesses were also subject to certain criteria. A criminal could give evidence, but had to provide details of the exact time and place of the crime, the instrument used and whether other people were present. According to *Porządek sądów*, a criminal was prohibited from giving evidence as a witness – theoretically this would have prevented the majority of denunciations. Furthermore, women were not allowed to be witnesses because they were inconsistent in their testimony and should only testify in the presence of a chaperone. Witness testimony from those under twenty years or over seventy was also prohibited in serious criminal trials. The evidence we have seen in the previous chapter demonstrates the extent to which these stipulations were ignored.

The nobility, as might be expected, were protected because a servant could not bear witness against their master. Drunks, prostitutes, pagans and non-Christians could not bear witness against Christians, whilst Jews could bear witness only if there were two Christians and another Jew present. If a witness had a bad reputation, was wanted for a crime, was mad, had not attained their majority or had been bribed, then they would not be admitted to court. Hearsay was supposedly insufficient as evidence and a case could not be heard on the basis of a single witness, preferably there were to be two or three witnesses, or seven if possible, and judges were to compare witness testimonies which would all be recorded by the scribe. However, even Groicki pointed out that this custom was not adhered to everywhere. On witchcraft in particular, he wrote in Article 22 of *Articles of the Magdeburg Law*, that anyone who admitted to sorcery or witchcraft should be questioned about their reasons, where the spells were buried (so that a search could be made), what incantations were made and the time and method of the crime. Significantly, the accused was to be asked who had taught them such knowledge, which was an important part of the denunciation process in the sample of trials.[61] Theoretically, many checks and balances were in place, but as we have already seen, when we examine the reality of the trial proceedings, they were of little if any consequence because of the lack of central or otherwise enforcement.

Torture was an essential part of judicial procedure in an inquisitorial system governed by the maxim *confessio est regina probationum*. Since empirical evidence of witchcraft was virtually impossible to obtain, a confession was usually the only admissible proof. Although torture was officially limited to three sessions, evidence from trial records contradicts this. Theoretically, several groups of people were exempt: land-owning nobility, municipal patricians, officials, academic doctors, children, the elderly and pregnant women. According to Article XXVIII of the Magdeburg Law, torture was to be 'mild' and commenced only when some proof of guilt was to be discovered.[62] A denunciation unsupported by any other evidence of guilt was not an acceptable basis for torture and an admission of guilt or testimony given during torture was to be repeated the following day 'freely' as confirmation.[63] Groicki rightly regarded the testimony of the tortured as 'uncertain, incorrect and dangerous'. In theory if there was sufficient evidence and an admission was still not forthcoming after torture, then neither side was judged to have been at fault and the evidence alone could be brought before the judges. Groicki recommended clemency if there was any doubt about the use of torture or the innocence of the accused.[64] Clear guidelines were also laid out as to the types of torture to be applied, and yet again Groicki was critical of judges who decided on methods of torture at whim, stipulating that if the accused died during the ordeal (as we know occurred) the judge should come under suspicion for not adhering to the legal limits and acting mercilessly. The second and third sessions of torture were supposed to become gradually less severe, although trial records suggest otherwise.[65] Finally, the court was to pass sentence only after obtaining a satisfactory confession.

Groicki clearly differentiated heresy from witchcraft, writing, 'He who has broken with the Christian faith is to be burnt. A witch and poisoner is also to meet this death.'[66] The death sentence was common to all the codices in use, except crucially in the *Carolina*, which reserved it only for cases in which witchcraft had caused death.[67] Pregnant women were to be spared the death sentence until after the birth and the mad were also exempt. In theory the condemned had three days to make their confession and recollect their sins after sentencing. They ought not to be drunk when the sentence was carried out.[68] In most cases leave to appeal was to be granted within ten days of the sentence but it could take up to six weeks.

According to Groicki, all had the right to appeal, but paradoxically if the judge believed there was no real reason for an appeal, then he could refuse leave. In felony cases if there was an admission of guilt or what was perceived to be clear evidence of guilt, then leave to appeal was automatically revoked.[69] In reality, the right to appeal was often dependent upon local custom or the will of the seigneur and there are few such examples in the Wielkopolska sample. As Pilaszek points out, the small number of appeals extant is the result of record damage and the judges' reluctance to give access to the higher courts, as they saw themselves as the final instance. She suggests they felt that confession obviated any need for an appeal.[70] In Małopolska it was possible to appeal to the High Court of German Law at Wawel Castle, Cracow, and eventually to the Court of Six Cities, and occasionally the Parliamentary Court overturned sentences imposed by lower courts.[71] Although Groicki's collections are regarded as the predominant source of law, the trials reveal a variety of sources used in sentencing, such as Damhouder's *Praxis rerum criminalium*[72] and Carpzov's *Practicae novae imperialis Saxonicae rerum criminalium* (1635). And in my sample, the Bible, *Speculo Saxonum* and the Magdeburg Law all appear.[73] Legal procedures clearly setting out the duties of judges, witnesses and others involved in the trials were in place, as well as the conditions under which torture could be applied.

The Theoretical Procedure in Municipal Courts

In municipal courts, the writ or summons was initially carried out orally, as opposed to the written document required by the courts hearing the *szlachta*. However, during the seventeenth century there was an increasing demand for a report of the writ's delivery and for the beadle to testify in court that he aimed to record it in the appropriate books. So the writ had to be recorded in the appropriate register as well as in the court session case lists. Municipal law assigned a separate system for criminal cases, dealt with by both the judge and investigating officials. This had to be formally recorded, held in open court, and the accused was to be encouraged to procure their own defence, even if as a last resort it was from the town's administrative office. The first phase of the trial consisted of a general interrogation aimed at establishing the facts and identifying whether a crime had been committed. It was followed by an investigation, often assigned to the *instygator*, 'public prosecutor', with the court having the final say over whether or not the case would be heard. If it was decided that the case would proceed, then the suspect could be held in custody in a suitable place, often the Town Hall. The second phase of the proceedings involved the special interrogation aimed at obtaining a confession.

The accused was given the opportunity to freely admit to the crime and often witnesses were summoned, but if the accused denied the charges, then they were shown the torture room and its instruments. If still reticent, then they were sometimes stripped, tied up and tortured by the executioner. After one session, the victim may have undergone more torture to elicit further details or denunciations. In witchcraft cases in particular, individuals were sometimes tortured beyond the prescribed three times or for longer than the specified 'one good hour'. The confession subsequently had to be freely repeated in front of the judge, who considered the evidence, sentenced the accused and summoned the executioner. Alternatively if the accused had been tortured three times and the evidence was poor, then they were to be released, and this is supported by at least one trial in which the local seigneur ordered an individual to be released. The town employed at least one scribe to record cases, which survive in varying conditions and states of legibility and included rough copies from which clean copies were to be recorded in the appropriate books.[74]

The Reality of Witchcraft Trials

It is worth considering the theoretical legal proceedings and the theoretical legal strictures at such length because in Wielkopolska, and possibly other areas of the Commonwealth, abuse was rife. That's not to say that this was atypical of European courts dealing with witchcraft, but in examples from the Paris Parlement or Rothenburg, to name but a few, the legal system's checks and balances appear to have limited the abuses to a much greater extent. Such flagrant disregard for legal guidelines apparent in the majority of cases mark out Wielkopolska and possibly other areas of Poland. Despite discussion as to whether witchcraft cases should be held before village or municipal courts, illustrated by the statutes discussed previously, the seigneur often played a very influential role in local justice and his or her right to invoke capital punishment was not abolished until 1768.[75]

However, there has been very little research carried out into the crucial process of how the cases reached the courts. Mikołajczyk's account of the case of Gertruda Zagrodzka in Małopolska is one of the few to examine this area and is worth investigating.[76] The process began with registering the complaint, so that charges could be laid and the court could ask for witnesses to be produced at a later date. At this point the person bringing the charge could request the arrest of the accused at once. This is illustrated in a Borek case (1624), when Stefan Lobeski asked 'for her arrest so that she cannot flee, [and the sequestration of] all of her goods from her maternal and paternal side and property and movable goods by this decree'.[77] The accused was then arrested and jailed, summoned to the court where the prosecution put the case, while the court decided whether or not there was a case to answer. Of course rumour would often reach the accused before those tasked with her arrest and unsurprisingly some fled.[78]

In the trial of a certain Agnieszka, heard before the Gniezno court, the charges were read out, she denied them and the defence and the prosecution subsequently put forward their cases so that the court could decide what action to take, while her accuser, Bardanoski, was asked to produce witnesses.[79] Individuals were interrogated by the Aldermen's Court or Town Council Court, which consisted of at the very least a judge, a deputy judge and a scribe, and may have included the full complement of 12 good men. In Grodzisk, for example, the prosecutor passed a list of questions to be asked of the accused to the judicial bench.[80] Often the prosecutor's list of questions to put to witnesses and/or to the accused is all that has survived from a case.[81] In a trial in Poznań in 1681, the following questions were asked:

> Interrogation of Jadwiga by the prosecutor about the crimes of sacrilege and magic
> 1. Why, being able to before Easter communion, did she go to confession only on Easter Sunday and even then she went after Mass had been celebrated in church?

2. Why did she remove the Host from her mouth and put it in her pocket and what did she use it for?
3. Why for a few years did she pray outside the Franciscan church in the evening when it was closed?
...
5. Why did she give the Devil to Anna who works for Pani Toczkowa?
6. Why do respectable people accuse her of being a witch?
7. If ever the possessed chased and beat her and who protected her and what did those evil spirits say to her?[82]

In other cases swimming was used as a preliminary test, which, as elsewhere, entailed tying the suspect's left leg to their right arm and vice versa, and tying a rope around their waist before throwing them into water.

If necessary, a court hearing could take place in a private home with only the *wójt* and two or three assistants, including a scribe.[83] In many cases the Municipal Court was deputed and invited to hear trials in a village or a neighbouring town.[84] For the most part, the accused were generally informed of the charges against them and questioned about them before torture. Even if they made a full confession, the accused might still be tortured to elicit further information and in some trials the initial charge included a request for torture.[85] Torture required a special order to be passed by the court, which often, but not always appears in the court records and was sometimes issued on the basis of one or two witnesses swearing on oath as to the veracity of their charges and their request for torture.[86] Sometimes it was merely noted in the records that the accused had been consigned to the executioner to face torture. Theoretically if an individual withstood three sessions of torture without admitting guilt then they were to be freed. Although even after three rounds of torture, Agnieszka Mierzycka refused to confess, nevertheless she was executed due to pressure from the public.[87]

Whilst witnesses were not always called, there are cases where a significant number appeared, for example eight male witnesses and two female midwives testified before the Kalisz court in Magdalena Klauzyna's trial in 1750.[88] The court could also refuse witnesses, as Marcin Winiarski discovered when he was refused permission to appear at Garbarka's trial before the Gniezno court (1680), possibly because of his involvement in a number of previous witchcraft cases in the city. In another Gniezno case from 1675, Pan Bardanoski laid charges against Agnieszka of harming his household and offered to testify.[89] Interestingly, Bogucka claims that in many towns there were individuals who gathered around courts prepared to act as false witnesses.[90] Despite Groicki's prohibition, hearsay was frequently admitted as circumstantial evidence, which allowed second- or even third-hand accounts to be presented, and witnesses often prefaced evidence by saying 'I heard that...' or 'others say that...'.

Whilst either side had the right to call for an adjournment, the defence more often took advantage of the procedure to gain time to provide more evidence, but occasionally the prosecution was actually ordered to find more evidence. Garbarka's defence gained an adjournment in a case heard by the Gniezno court in Jędrzejewo (1680) while he obtained a letter from a convent testifying to her good character. This successful tactic procured her release, the restitution of her goods and the punishment of her accuser Maciej Baran, who was found guilty of bringing the charge with malice.[91]

The prosecution rarely produced physical evidence in court and only occasionally ointment or powder was exhibited. In Magdalena Klauzyna's trial (Kalisz, 1750) powder was given to a dog, which subsequently died.[92] However, since confession was the 'queen of proof', the emphasis was on alternating question and torture sessions to extract as much information as possible from the accused, as well as securing a consistent story and a confession. In most cases the accused was able to withstand one round of torture, but by the second round the majority in the sample confessed their guilt. Most confessions contained denunciations of sabbat attendees or others who had practised witchcraft, or helped or taught them. The judiciary, anxious perhaps to deflect blame from themselves, insisted on forgiveness from the condemned and many trials record the convicted witch swearing as much as three times that they forgave the judiciary before they were taken to be executed:

> Odpusczacz nam ze dekret wedle spraw twych złych wedle prawa wydamy. Radit Odpuszczam. Pytam cie po drugieraz y trzeci radit odpuszczam.
>
> Do you forgive us for the sentence we pass for these evil things, according to the Law? She said, 'I forgive you.' I ask you for the second and third time. She said, 'I forgive you.'[93]

The sentence was read out to the waiting crowd both to demonstrate the court's authority and to serve as a warning to others. Great emphasis was placed on the apostatic nature of the crime. In cases where women had admitted to diabolic sex, the adulterous nature of this act was underlined, along with their renunciation of the Roman Catholic faith, God, the Virgin Mary and all the saints. Many of the sentences are suffused with Roman Catholic imagery, reinforcing the apostatic nature of the crime. There are several accounts of women who were released, however. Agnieszka of Żabikowo was sentenced to death but subsequently survived, only to be tried in a second trial.[94] The sentence for witchcraft was usually death at the stake, although beheading sometimes preceded this as an act of clemency. Earlier in the period the sentence more commonly took the form of banishment, flogging and even fines. Even on the way to or at the stake, there was still time for the accused to retract a denunciation or to denounce others.[95] Pilaszek mentions a few appeals in Wielkopolska, one of which was heard before the Nobles' Court.[96] She concludes that where cases reached appeal, there was a tendency to relax sentences, but that we cannot ascribe the relative lack of trials to the appeals system.[97]

Alternative Legal Realities: *Ja Pan, Ja Prawo* – The Lord Is the Law

Abuse was not only the domain of the judiciary. Within the Wielkopolska sample I have identified a 'seigniorial pattern', so-called because the majority of the trials were instigated by the seigneur on the grounds that harm had been done to his household, cattle or family. In rural cases the procedure was for him to invite the municipal court to hear a trial, so his involvement was vital and, unsurprisingly, many of these rural cases were based solely on harm to manorial possessions. Pilaszek's research backs this up, as she sees the relationship between the accused witch and the owner of the village or estate as key.[98] Wiślicz also finds that 'among the accusers and witnesses the most numerous group consisted of the gentry, usually owners of the nearby villages, convinced of the evil deeds of their subjects'.[99] His view may be influenced by the appalling actions of Wojciech Brzeza of Wąsosze, who, convinced his son had been killed by witches, embarked on a series of trials that ended with the death of ten women and the banishment of two between 1688 and 1691 in a small settlement recording only eight taxpayers in 1673.[100] He suggests plausibly that 'it was not the Devil who threatened a gentleman, but this gentleman's subjects, who would not shrink even from scheming with the Devil – hence the special emphasis on the estate solidarity of the gentry in the face of witchcraft'.[101] The legal power of the seigneurs reached its apotheosis in the Kleczew trial of 1691, when the Bench, invited by Paweł and Marcin Zbierzchowski, owners of a small village, declined to find the accused guilty and refused to try them. However, they did rule that the court was relieved of any responsibility, but that the brothers could take responsibility for the burning by fire of one of the accused.[102]

The petty noble Jan Łańcuski is an excellent illustration of the strong influence one man could wield. The wave of five trials in the village of Jędrzejewo in 1675, 1677, 1678 and two trials in 1680 (heard by the Gniezno court) was fuelled by the involvement of this litigious individual, also mentioned in the 1689–90 trial. In 1675 he accused Agnieszka Goroska Rusinska of harming him and his wife through putting the Devil in their beer in the form of powder, and threw in an accusation of harming his cattle for good measure. In the same year he brought charges against Regina Pieczarzyna, whom he insisted ought to be swum, but she managed to escape trial until three years later. Meanwhile Goroska's husband brought a complaint to court about the wives of Jan Łańcuski and Bartłomiej Czablikowicz (another official involved in the cases) on the grounds of slander and unsuitable talk of witchcraft connected to his wife. Gogolkowicz, supported by witnesses, also accused Łańcuski's wife of calling his own wife a witch.

Goroska subsequently denounced Pieczarzyna as well as Serdeczna, the wife of a member of the bench, claiming she was one of the elders at the sabbat and had asked her to steal the Host. Predictably this set in motion a chain of trials, involving Łańcuski and a cast of frequent participants. One such litigant was Ostrowski, who accused Goroska of burying a powder under his threshold to kill his geese and cause his wife to miscarry. Three years later, Ostrowski's wife accused Pieczarzyna face-to-face of bewitching her infant to death. Czablikowicz, another familiar figure in these trials and one-time member of the court bench, also testified that when Goroski had gone with him on a trip against his wife's wishes, she had caused his cart to overturn. He insisted that Goroski had also blamed his wife, which seems unlikely given that Goroski not only defended his wife, but also took the risky strategy of bringing a charge against Czablikowicz's and Łańcuski's wives. Marcin Winiarski also appeared as a witness in this trial claiming that the accused had cursed Łańcuski's house. In the confusion of charge and counter-charge, Goroska's defence tried to refer the case to Prince Czartoryski, Archbishop of Gniezno, but the court dismissed him. Finally, Goroska admitted she had been seduced into witchcraft by another woman, smeared herself with ointment to fly through the chimney to *Łysa Góra*, married a devil and renounced God, the Holy Trinity and all the holy angels of God. Contrary to most accounts, her devil had a hot mouth and hands and interestingly the devils addressed one another as *szlachta*. Goroska also admitted stealing the Host, which she gave to Serdeczna, under whose instruction she had been (along with Ofiarzyna) to harm Łańcuski because they were angry with him. We could surmise a conspiracy involving the petty nobles, Łańcuski, Czablikowicz and Ostrowski, in which their wives had become dangerously entangled.

Two years later in 1677, Serdeczna was tried for spoiling Pan Zabłocki's beer with a black powder and for harming Pan Chrystian. In her denunciations, among others, she mentioned the 'late' Goroska and Pieczarzyna. Łańcuski and Winiarski were again witnesses in this case, and testified to Goroska's earlier denunciation of Serdeczna, while Czablikowicz was a member of the court bench. Pieczarzyna, denounced by Goroska, Serdeczna and Dobrogostówna, was finally brought to trial together with Bulewiczówna and Dobrogostówna a year later, accused of harming Pan Piotrowski's beer and Pani Ostrowska's child. The last trial in this chain was not instigated by the *szlachta*, but by Maciej Baran, who accused Małgorzata Garbarka, previously denounced by Dobrogostówna, of harming his wife. Czablikowicz's wife had also complained about her, but other than that the familiar cast was not involved and Winiarski was even rejected as a witness. Consciences may well have been stirred by then, because as we saw above, Garbarka was freed.

In one aspect these cases are typical of a pattern evident in the Wielkopolska sample. Although the *szlachta* was heavily involved, it was most often the petty *szlachta*, who were convinced that harm had been done to them, their families or their cattle. Their zeal in bringing the perpetrators to justice may have indicated a confluence of belief in witchcraft, economic losses, the impact on their family, their changing levels of control over society, guilt and even fear of other individuals. Although some cases relied solely on seigniorial testimony, often other witnesses supported the charges with further accusations, perhaps drawing on an individual's reputation. However, it is clear that noble households were not averse to consulting cunning folk. Apolonia Porwitowa had worked for several noblemen and used blessed herbs for Pawłowski's wife's beer. Regina Dereciowa of Stawiszyń had been paid by Panna Piątkowska to locate someone to find her a husband through love magic and a certain Jadwiga had restored Pan Siekiera's beer in Kalisz. Trials frequently arose when the interactions between the noble households and the cunning women soured. Several other scenarios are also plausible, for example peasants may have spread rumours about damage done to the manor in order to rid themselves of rivals, and certainly rivalries were evident between cunning women, as we saw in Chapter 2. The *szlachta*'s legendary bad treatment of their peasants was noted by contemporaries such as Krzysztof Opaliński and the confessions reveal the peasants' grudges against their masters and mistresses. As Hagen has observed, peasants had both motives for and opportunities to harm the manor, adding to the insecurity of the seigneurial household, which confession narratives support.[103] In Nieszawa in 1716, we gain a wonderful insight, as Sebastian Kusnierczyk named a list of adulterers, gossips, a woman who wanted to poison her husband and details of who was sleeping with whom, saying, 'In this place Nieszawa, there is no-one honest, only whores and witches, apart from Pani Kowalska...Pani Janowa Dziwlewiczowa is a witch and poisoned Marcin, the son of Pan Tomasz Fabiszkowic, in white bread.'[104]

However, not all seigneurs were keen on bringing trials and clearly the majority of them did not. We cannot know how many used their influence to settle disputes before they reached the courts, but some intervened directly in trials. In 1624, Andrzej Borzewski of Borek overturned the court's verdict against Dorota Markowa and her daughter Anna. However, he was in the minority, since charges of harm to the manorial household were brought in at least half of the Wielkopolska sample trials.[105] Undoubtedly seigneurs who felt threatened by witchcraft when they saw their family sicken or their cattle die were also concerned about economic issues, and although attempts to rid the community of a witch were aimed at eliminating evil, curtailing material losses was also vital. The trial records show us that the ideas of zero-sum in relation to resources and magical theft were popular, as people complained about their 'profit' being taken.[106]

While witches were undoubtedly neighbours, many more were servants or serfs and were often accused by their masters. In the *szlachta*-controlled Commonwealth, it should be no surprise that we can detect a 'seigniorial pattern'. The prevalence of this pattern underlines the sporadic nature of trials, which largely depended upon the individual seigneur and the likelihood that he would prosecute, either of his own volition or through persuasion. This seigneurial pattern also highlights the precarious nature of the relationship between the manor and the peasants and provides at least one explanation as to why the majority of the trials heard before municipal courts originated from villages. On the intellectual front, Polish literature had discussed and ridiculed witchcraft even before the persecution began in earnest, which may explain why it was predominantly the largely uneducated petty *szlachta* who, according to the sample, indulged in persecution. As Hagen writes,

> In no central or eastern European land did noble landlordism and village subjection hold more untrammelled sway than in the Polish

Commonwealth, nor in the historical literature is any other system more notorious for its abuses and impoverishing effects upon the common people.[107]

The Decline of the Persecution

As we shall see, the persecution's decline owed much to the refusal of the higher echelons of the nobility and the clergy to continue to believe in witchcraft. However, it seems that the petty nobility took longer to rid itself of such prejudices, which we shall explore by looking at the five trials that took place after the mid-eighteenth century: Kalisz (1750), Kiszkowo (1761), Pyzdry (1761), Kopanica (1775) and Dobra (1781). Magdalena Klauzyna's trial in Kalisz in 1750 contains many elements typical of earlier trials, but is remarkable because she was a 60-year-old midwife (rare within the sample) who had long been regarded with suspicion. Eleven witnesses testified against her, including three other midwives and, as expected, the accusations centred on fertility. She claimed an abortifacient she had provided had actually induced fertility and was in turn accused of inflicting the *kołtun* (matted hair). It emerged that Magdalena had been expelled from Wrocław on suspicion of witchcraft and for having made a wax image of a child, which later died. Significantly when she was asked whether she had harmed women in labour and children, she was accused of threatening Kapitanowa, that she would not give birth to a child without her. Many men testified that children she had helped bring into the world had departed shortly thereafter and Magdalena was burnt at the stake. We could see an attempt to raise levels of evidential proof in this case, because so many witnesses were called and the court tested the powder found on her, on a dog, which subsequently died. Also it is clear that it had taken several deaths to occur for her to be tried – perhaps the catalysts for accusations were much more serious by this time. As Levack writes, 'under certain circumstances the prosecution of witches could continue indefinitely'.[108]

In 1761 the criminal court of Kiszkowo heard a case in the village of Gorzuchowo, owned by three Szeliski brothers, after courts in Gniezno and Pobiedziska had refused, but the Szeliskis, together with the nobleman Jaranowski, were determined to bring the case to court. Educated opinion was clearly against trying witches in Gniezno and Pobiedziska, which had both experienced trials. Ten women were accused of witchcraft, including two pairs of mothers and daughters and old Dorota, the seigneurs' servant. Only the sentence survives, from which we can see accusations redolent of the previous century. Allegedly they had renounced their Roman Catholic faith, engaged in diabolic sex, attended the sabbat, stolen the Eucharist and buried destructive spells. This trial also demonstrates the seigniorial pattern. A village split between three seigneurs suggests multiple conflicts and tensions, exacerbated by noble poverty, and it may have been Jaranowski who wielded influence behind the scenes. However, this case which has a large number of accused for Wielkopolska, combines some classic accusations, such as incantations and theft of the Eucharist, proving that at such a late stage judges were still willing to convict and sentence so many people to death.[109]

In the same year in the village of Obra the Pyzdry court instructed the nobleman Jan Szarzyński's servant Maryanna to be subjected to swimming, for allegedly harming his family, children and possessions. She floated and after torture admitted that she had put powder in Szarzyński's wife's food, but then she had been unable to harm Szarszyński's child, so she took him to the priest. Maryanna claimed her devil was with her in the stocks and during torture had ordered her to say nothing. Quoting the Magdeburg Law and the *Speculo Saxonum* the court duly passed the death sentence. A deputation of priests and a noble immediately went to the Szarzyńskis to request her release, and she was banished from within six miles of the city and fined. This action and its success indicate that there were people who were no longer prepared to send an individual to the stake even though she had admitted to diabolic activities and to using poison. The Szarzyńskis must have recognized that they would not be able to get away with carrying out the sentence, maybe from fear of ridicule, pressure from the Church, or the tide of public opinion against them.[110]

The campaign to end witchcraft trials waged by clerics in the mid-eighteenth century was largely concentrated around pastoral letters and synods thanks also to the efforts of K.F. Czartoryski, S. Załuski and A. Dembowski. The formal process of repealing the witchcraft acts began in 1774, with the Palatine of Gniezno, August Sułkowski's vigorous campaign, culminating in repeal in 1776, when the Castellan of Biecz Wojciech Kłuszewski successfully proposed an end to the hearing of witchcraft cases and the use of torture,[111] celebrated by the striking of a commemorative medal. By this time a definitive intellectual shift away from belief in witchcraft dominated among the élite circles, with the increasing influence of humanism and general distaste for the death sentence, mirrored by the decline in the number of trials recorded in this sample and elsewhere.[112]

Although the decline of the legal witchcraft persecution in Wielkopolska can be dated roughly to the middle of the eighteenth century, it is obvious that most of the towns and villages examined in the sample experienced sporadic outbreaks, sometimes as the result of a denunciation. In reality, the persecution ended in different places at different times. For example, in Gniezno doubt set in when the Metropolitan refused to issue an opinion and when many women had already been sent to the stake. As for illegal punishment and lynchings, it is impossible to speculate on when and where they occurred and therefore when they ended. Although there were trials in other parts of Europe in the eighteenth century and the last executions took place in Scotland in 1722, Germany in 1775 and Switzerland in 1782, the bulk of the persecutions had ceased by the middle of the seventeenth century. Levack ascribes the decline of the persecution to a more secular and rational age and the waning of religious zeal and enthusiasm. However, for the Commonwealth the middle of the seventeenth century had a very different significance and, according to the sample, the Wielkopolska persecution had yet to peak. The improvement in the socio-economic changes that hastened the end of belief in the Devil as purveyor of all misfortune also occurred much later in the Commonwealth.[113]

For the most part, *szlachta*, influenced by Enlightenment thought and possibly peer pressure, stopped believing in witchcraft as the cause of their misfortune and ceased to bring trials. Scepticism and the increasing requirement for more empirical evidence also played their part in the decreasing number of trials. Such a change in judicial habits also impacted on those who persisted in accusing people of witchcraft and their cases were increasingly treated as slander, illustrated by the following 1781 Dobra judgement, which fell in-between slander and witchcraft. A woman accused of inflicting the *kołtun* and taking milk from the plaintiff's cow was admonished and both she and the plaintiff were ordered to desist from such behaviour in future.[114] As the eighteenth century progressed and Enlightenment thought prevailed, witchcraft was ridiculed. Growing scepticism among the upper ranks of the nobility had a notable effect on the judicial system, evidenced by the decline in the number of trials, the reluctance of courts to hear witchcraft cases (as the refusal of the Gniezno and Pobiedziska courts testified) and a preference for trying witchcraft accusations as slander cases. The social dysfunction and chaos caused by trials was also a contributing factor in many towns.

As the Commonwealth stumbled into disaster, the *szlachta* was wracked by broader problems that placed its hitherto petty concerns in a wider context. The mood of Sarmatian absolutism among the petty *szlachta* declined along with their fortunes, as the Commonwealth was beset by war and economic, political and urban decline. At the same time there was a dearth of new literary sources discussing witchcraft. Towards the end of the Commonwealth, the *szlachta*'s control of power was under threat from Poniatowski's reforms, which attempted to create a stronger centralizing movement, and tried to curb the anarchic chaos of the noble estate. Many of the lower tiers of *szlachta* were forced by circumstances to sell their lands to their wealthier peers, who consolidated their estates. Fewer lands in the hands of the petty *szlachta* who were most likely to bring charges meant fewer prosecutions, and so in their fall from grace is the persecution's demise.

5
Nullus Deus, Sine Diabolo: The Ecclesiastical Witch

An Introduction to Demonology

While the legal system adapted to the practicalities of prosecuting witchcraft, intellectual debate was greatly fuelled by the clergy, evident in the enduring portrait of the witch as apostate, blasphemer and handmaiden of the Devil. This image largely emerged in the fifteenth and sixteenth centuries and created a largely stereotypical set of attributes for the witch and ascribed to witchcraft. Descriptions of witchcraft were mainly to be found in demonology, 'that branch of knowledge which treats of demons, or of beliefs about demons',[1] and although a demon in the ancient Greek sense of δαίμων was a spirit rather than a devil, the terms demon and devil became almost coterminous. In this study, I shall interpret demonology in its widest possible sense, including drama, agricultural manuals and other works, so my interpretation is closer to what Stephens terms 'witchcraft theory'.[2] This approach reveals the wide range of sources in which the rhetoric of witchcraft constructed differing paradigms of the witch, which can be compared to the details we have seen in the trials. By analysing a broader range of 'demonography' we can further dispel the notion that Poland's witch-hunt was merely an extension of the German phenomenon. Interestingly, in contrast to Hungary, Poland boasted a relatively rich range of demonography.[3] I have divided the printed sources into three distinct areas; ecclesiastical, secular and anti-witchcraft discourse.

As Stephens pointed out, 'trials and treatises shared themes, they implicate concerns common to both those who prosecuted accused witches and those who wrote treatises...Unless we read treatises as carefully as we read narratives, we can be misled by unexamined assumptions about what motivated concern with witches.' Criticizing the teleological approach to witchcraft texts, he maintained that 'witchcraft theory was far more than a demonology. It was not an anomaly in the history of Western Christianity. It was an expression of Christianity's deepest and truest logic, although in oversimplified form.'[4] Stephens emphasizes the significance of biblical literalism, patristic writings and ecclesiastical opinions, regarded by many early modern intellectuals as worthier than empirical proofs. Compounded by the opinions of learned doctors, they were synthesized and marshalled behind the discourse of witchcraft to construct an influential argument.

Despite sceptical voices, theological arguments were further bolstered by the public confessions of the convicted witches. Since witchcraft provided an explanation for otherwise inexplicable phenomena, beliefs could be manipulated to support different agendas. We can speculate about the effectiveness of the deployment of witchcraft rhetoric during the intense catechizing mission following the Second Tridentine reforms. Although it was rare in my sample, that the church directly instigated charges of witchcraft, as Pilaszek maintains, there can be little doubt that the church played a role in promoting belief in forms of witchcraft. The convergence of a triumvirate of institutional powers consisting of the moral power of the Roman Catholic Church, the social and political power of the *szlachta* and the legal power of the judicial system, was a constellation against which the witchcraft persecution was able to occur. In Wielkopolska, with its multi-confessional population, the very elaborate and visible liturgical practices of the Roman Catholic Church provided fodder for attacks by Polish Protestants, whose discussion of witchcraft differed greatly in many aspects, but was fully abreast of debate in Western Europe. The Roman Catholic Church's influence thundered forth from the pulpit, as preachers distinguished in their own particular way between good and evil, miracles and illusions and diabolic and divine practices.

One of the key aspects of witchcraft belief – the gendering of the witch as female – is interesting to examine in terms of attitudinal changes towards women and their changing social roles. This ideological shift is often overlooked by those reluctant to move beyond a narrow focus on the *Malleus Maleficarum* as sole proof of the church's misogynistic attitudes, although Stephens's examination of textual editing in this work has strongly refuted the exaggerated importance placed on it as a misogynistic diatribe. Stephens suggests that the significance of the witch lay in her experience of the spirit world through sexual intercourse and commerce with the Devil, through which the female witch confirmed the existence of the spirit world: therefore witches had to be women, because they could receive a spirit sexually and could be penetrated, which dismisses sodomy. This interesting interpretation might throw some light on why judges were so keen to question suspects about their sexual activities with the Devil, as the Wielkopolska sample demonstrates.[5] As we have seen, male witches generally confessed to signing a pact with the Devil, in contrast to the sexual pact of their female counterparts and even where they named a personal devil, they mentioned no sexual encounters with them.

In Poland, the sceptics' main critical focus was on the judicial system rather than the ontology of witchcraft. Regardless of genre, as elsewhere in Europe, both Roman Catholic and Protestant sources used inversion as the primary literary device, portraying the antithesis of a godly community, under the control of the Devil, but ultimately answerable to God. As Clark has observed, the contrariety that coloured all aspects of debate was a dominant literary convention, so as a result, the inversion of Christian values, ceremonies and beliefs produced in the minds of the educated an equivalent diabolic reality based on a contrary world order, with St Augustine's *City of God* as a model.[6]

Despite an assumed consensus on the inherently evil characteristics of the Devil and the witch in religious discourse, which created a particular paradigm, their portrayals in Polish drama, poetry, medical and agricultural manuals, and in trial records are extremely varied, which inconsistencies possibly incline towards a ludic Polish or Slavonic phenomenon or to the survival in popular culture of traits associated with pre-Christian gods, goddesses and spirits. A Slavonic or popular devil–witch paradigm, distinguishable from the Christian devil–witch paradigm, can be identified within several Polish early modern works and accords with differences in trial accounts. Pre-Christian diabolic beliefs existed in Poland, of course, and given the prevalence of the ludic devil and spirits, it is useful to draw on their heritage and trace their possible influence on the anthropomorphization of evil, and the nature of beneficent and maleficent Slavonic spirits.

The Influences of Slavonic Paganism

There is evidence to suggest that rituals and beliefs associated with the pre-Christian religious system were still apparent in Poland as late as the sixteenth century[7] and conflicting views among historians and ethnographers as to the nature of Slavonic pagan beliefs provoked great debate.[8] One theory suggests an Ancient Greek-style pantheon of

Slavonic gods and goddesses with responsibilities for individual spheres, while others argue for monotheism. The earliest mentions of Slavonic gods come after Poland's official acceptance of Christianity in 966 but are catalogued by foreign chroniclers writing between the eleventh and thirteenth centuries, such as Saxo Grammatico, Thietmar, Helmhold and Adam of Bremen.[9] The renowned Polish chronicler Jan Długosz, writing in the latter half of the fifteenth century included a pantheon of pagan gods in his *Annales*. This is also disputed on the grounds of evidence of a god named *Czarnobóg*, 'black/dark God', which led some scholars to surmise there must have been a dualist *Bialobóg*, 'White God'.[10] The lack of sources for the period makes a conclusive answer unlikely, but there is consensus as to the strong belief in demons and spirits, who dwelt in rivers, lakes and woods, and those who also lived within the home and were placated with gifts, especially in the eastern regions.[11] A plethora of named spirits, included the *południca*, a female spirit who came to the fields in the afternoon and harmed or killed people; *uboże*, the house spirits that hid behind the oven; and *topielec*, the spirit that encouraged people to drown. We catch glimpses of some of these ancient Slavonic beliefs in trial confessions and *belles-lettres*. If the theory of a monotheistic pre-Christian religion is accepted, then at the risk of courting controversy, I would suggest that the effects of Christianization (officially dated as 966) upon the Polish lands were analogous to those of the Reformation and if the conversion of Poland can be seen as a more gradual reformation, then the tolerance of lingering customs assimilated into a popular form of Christianity is more easily comprehensible. Alternatively, a hostile conversion, with punitive measures against the old customs, might have been more successful in wiping them out. Clearly we can do little more than speculate, but we do know that Poland's Christianization was associated with predominantly German foreign missionaries and appointees, although the country had formally received Christianity from the Czech princess Dubravka (Dąbrówka), whose very name (originating from the word for oak tree) evokes paganism. However, truly accepting Christianity involved a huge change in perception of the human cosmological position,[12] with a significant increase in personal responsibility and duties towards others. No longer could an individual rely on propitiatory offerings to familiar household and local spirits (later replaced by Roman Catholic saints) who would intercede, and so a visible level of protection was formally removed from the general populace. In its place was a new value system imposing constraints on behaviour, as personal responsibility replaced the collective personification of events, rituals and processes.[13] The attendant personification of evil can be compared with the identification with individual devils, more strongly developed in German *Teufelbücher*.[14] The reformations gave birth to an increased awareness of self-culpability, as Urbańczyk maintains, Christianity removed direct access to gods or spirits and restricted access to a hierarchy of priests (initially foreigners). A universal system replaced a localized religious system.[15] The Church became the highest authority – the arbiter of legitimacy, a supranational, supraterritorial authority and the simple rituals and general communal knowledge of pagan worship were replaced by dogma, more strongly emphasized through the Reformation and Protestant emphasis on a hermeneutic reading. This was particularly significant in Wielkopolska, with its relatively large Protestant and German communities and exposure to German and Silesian traders.

Although difficult to prove, Pełka makes the case for assimilation of pagan customs, writing,

> It came to pass in this way that specifically Polish conceptualizations of devils were formed, popular, noble, and town (for example Boruta of Łęczyca or Rokita of Rzeszów, becoming figures of demons of the woods and marshes)...with the vision of the Christian devil.[16]

He saw the witch as analogous, since the practices associated with them were magical but reflected the use of Christian symbols such as holy herbs. The new interpretation of previously acceptable practices as maleficent was inevitably the source of confusion for both the clergy and the lay population, because within pagan systems individuals had generated magical power by collecting certain plants at certain times or performing rituals. Removed from individuals, this power was now theoretically monopolized by the church, which alone retained the power to bless herbs, water and salt. In reality many pagan structural elements remained the same and the most important ceremonies took place at the same points in the year. Słupecki went as far as to suggest that the Slavonic god Weles was a prototype of the Christian Devil and that deities driven out of their strongholds into the groves, waters and mountains were thus demoted to the rank of spirits.[17] The illustrious Polish ethnographer Brückner pointed out that Dziewanna and Marzana, from the Slavonic Olympiad, appeared in *Postępek prawa czartowskiego* (1570) as female devils sent especially to Poland. Marzana was also the name of an effigy of winter taken from villages and drowned at the beginning of spring, symbolizing the end of winter and highly reminiscent of the swimming of the witch.[18]

In contrast to pagan and popular beliefs, the Bible played an essential role in shaping portrayals of the Devil and the witch and as the highest authority for the Christian world, its interpretation, prior to the Reformation, was jealously guarded. It is only towards the end of the Old Testament that our acquaintance with a more unified concept of evil as the adversary of Christ begins. Certain biblical episodes were used in a stock manner by the Roman Catholic Church to illustrate the ease with which diabolic power could be misinterpreted as divine, which also usefully reinforced reliance upon the church for guidance. A narrative constructed from biblical and patristic writings illustrated how the Devil fought with God for the souls of humankind, using witches to recruit others. Such biblical debate was stimulated by translations into the vernacular and the new Protestant emphasis on close reading.[19]

Although the characteristics of a witch were not defined in the Bible, the authority to execute a witch was established by Exodus 22.18 (challenged principally by Johan Weyer, 1563) and in addition varying definitions of the witch were also found in papal bulls.[20] Biblical episodes illustrated how to differentiate between the diabolic and the divine, such as the confrontation between Moses and the Egyptian pharaoh's magicians in Exodus. Although the actions of the magicians and prophets were ostensibly similar, the difference lay in the intention and the origin of the power used. Several examples show Christian saints (for example St Silvester and St Makary) performing magic in order to convert pagans, but individuals were taught that although magic and miracles could take on the same external form, the provenance of the power behind them was the essential determinant of their divinity or evil.

Thus the church had established many fundamental concepts upon which to build a fear of the Devil and throughout the sixteenth, seventeenth and eighteenth centuries, representations of the witch and the Devil evolved within religious and secular writing, both influencing one another to varying degrees. Protestant and Roman Catholic churches alike sought to provide role models for good Christians and as fundamentally patriarchal institutions, also attempted to dictate female mores through providing explicit examples of saintly women as positive role models as well as proscribing certain behaviour and attitudes. It cannot be a coincidence that many of the sins traditionally connected with females were those attributed to the witch.[21]

Although Mieszko's baptism in 966 signified the formal conversion of Poland to Christianity, the worship of pagan Slavonic gods and spirits continued in tandem with Christian worship. Traits of the old spirits lingered, shaping a more ludic devil, elements of which were still to be found in popular belief centuries later. Some traditions of female deities and spirits had been moulded into the fearsome figure of the Slavonic *baba-jaga*, a child-eating female who survives to the present day in fairy tales. In contrast, the Slavonic devil was a harmless fool, who could be outwitted by peasants or women, a parallel creature to God's majestic opposite number, responsible for all the evils of the world. The eradication of pagan beliefs is a subject beyond the scope of this work, but the omnipresence of Slavonic deities in the home, the field, woods and water suggests they were firmly entrenched in everyday belief. Further evidence comes from the varying accounts of pagan revolts in 1022 and 1034–39 and a sermon from the second half of the fifteenth century in which parishioners were admonished for carrying out practices viewed as pagan. Indeed witchcraft was even referred to as 'pagan superstition' in a witchcraft trial in Turek, and as late as 1595, Marcin z Urzędowa commented on the singing, dancing and devil worship that had been occurring around Whitsuntide.[22] The possible early presence of Cyrilomethodian Christians in the south of Poland may also have added to dogmatic confusion. Again, we can only speculate as to the precise nature of pagan interaction with Christian cosmology, but through examining a wide range of sources there is more scope to investigate this theme.[23] However, by the sixteenth century the most pressing problem for the Roman Catholic Church was not the remnants of paganism, but a multitude of Protestant challenges, especially in Wielkopolska, with its Protestant and minority ethnic communities, and where Protestants even formed the majority of worshippers in some areas.

The Protestant Appropriation of Provenance

The multi-confessional nature of Wielkopolska makes it essential to examine Polish Protestant writings on witchcraft as a theme appropriated by both Reformation and Counter-Reformation discourse. Based on principles of exclusion and literal demonization, it could be applied by one group to any other as a useful polemical tool for propaganda. Protestants believed no less in the perils of witchcraft, but their remedies were largely confined to prayer and fasting (as also advocated by Roman Catholics) and introspection of personal piety. The outbreak of the witchcraft persecution (dated by Monter to the 1560s for most of Europe) coincided with a new phase in demonological writing, the implementation of Tridentine reforms, and a fierce battle against heterodoxy and social deviance.[24] Clark sees the impact of this growth in literary activity as 'to encourage the witchcraft persecutions, or at least to justify and explain them'.[25] This is less resonant in Poland, which by then had experienced very few trials. Although the literary and theological debate was chronologically similar to the rest of Europe, it predated the persecution peak, according to the sample and other estimates.[26] While Protestants railed against Roman Catholic corruption of the faith and what they regarded as superstitious practices, Roman Catholics decried Reformers as heretics who had invoked the wrath of God. Writers of all denominations were bedevilled by the same key ideological debates: metamorphosis, demonic agency, abuse of sacramental power, exorcism, abuses of the judicial system and its liberal use of torture, the validity of confessions, biblical interpretation and medical explanations.[27]

Discourse was even more intense in Poland, where some of the more extreme Protestant groups such as Anabaptists and Antitrinitarians had settled, and so religious, if not demonological debate reached more challenging boundaries.[28] While the Roman Catholic Church recommended regular and frequent confession, communion and genuflection as an antidote to temptation by the Devil, typically it was those same protective rituals that Protestant writers across Europe attacked as witchcraft. Scribner, in his excellent examination of Catholic Germany, also pointed out the development of many rituals that mocked the church, which both Protestants and Catholics criticized and were keen to end. The blurring of lines between the use of sacramentals and witchcraft was furthered by the use of blessed water, candles, herbs or flowers to protect against witches, as we have seen. When the priest led a procession to ward off bad weather and allowed people to place items under the altar cloth to infuse them with sacred power at the moment when the Eucharist was raised, then ambiguity around notions of witchcraft, magic and holy rituals abounded. Scribner maintained that many of these customs survived in Protestant areas, particularly in mixed areas, which may also have impacted on Wielkopolska.[29]

Although most of the witchcraft persecution occurred later in Poland, the country's Protestant writers were certainly abreast of demonological trends. Jan Seklucjan and Marcin Krowicki published works in 1545 and 1560 respectively, prior to Johan Weyer's famous work *De Praestigiis Daemonum* (1563), and were followed by those of Marcin Czechowic and Szymon Budny in 1575 and 1576, preceding the key work of Reginald Scot (1584). These Protestant writers employed the vocabulary of witchcraft to decry the Pope as the Antichrist, scorning Roman Catholic rituals as superstitious.[30] Krowicki went as far as to declare such practices as apostatic, claiming that the use of holy water, wax or oil was merely papal devilment and that if ashes had the capacity to cleanse, then they must be a form of witchcraft. He reserved particular scorn for elaborate Easter rituals accusing priests of practising witchcraft stamped with the name of God – and claimed no biblical support for exorcism.[31] Budny typically linked the rise of the Antichrist (the Pope) to a rise in the prominence of Roman Catholic rituals, which in his view were nothing short of pure superstition. His work may have been influenced by the French Calvinist Daneau's *De veneficiis* of 1564, a vociferous attack on papist superstition that proved so popular it was translated into French, German and English.[32]

A Calvinist Catechism

In his *Wykład katechizmu* of 1579, Paweł Gilowski, a leading Polish Calvinist, explained that the Devil had provoked sin, and, as many Protestant writers, referred to the trials of Job, which God had permitted the Devil to inflict. Warned by this example, he urged humankind to guard against bad spirits in the form of devils waiting to tempt them into committing particular sins. There is a visible parallel in his work between those misfortunes ascribed to the devil and those blamed on the witch, for example, debauchery, illness, destroying cattle and crops, controlling weather, theft, murder and plague. Clearly intellectual debate on witchcraft had begun in the sixteenth century, prior to more widespread prosecutions. Gilowski accused those who had recourse to male or female witches (interestingly he uses both terms) of idolatry and linked superstitious belief in local demons written about by St Augustine to popular Slavonic spirits:

> Because earthly demons, spirits of the home, woodland satires, water spirits, highland hags, spirits of the air, a variety of geniuses, maritime Leviathans, are seen...all of whom harm mankind in various ways and at the time when they serve them or have an agreement in whatever way with them, and superstitions, then serve them happily in a carnal way.

Although few works of demonology appear to have survived from the sixteenth century, Gilowski claimed that, although he could write further about what devils do through their magicians, conjurors, divinatrices and witches, 'others have written enough about this, I will leave it'.[33]

The Protestant Pulpit

The next extant work, a collection of Adam Gdacjusz's sermons, did not appear until 1644, over sixty years after Gilowski's work. Perhaps this indicates that it was somewhat of an anomaly, or given Gdacjusz's reputation, that it was a work of self-publicity rather than scholarship. The preacher was a controversial character, closely connected with the Polish Protestant community. His discussion of witchcraft provided an insight into practices regarded as superstitious, as he thundered forth from the pulpit against protective rituals. He described the feeding of a part of every dish from the Christmas Eve meal to cows, in order to protect them from witches,[34] which Barbara of Radom confessed to, claiming that her mother had taught her the practice (Kalisz 1580).[35] Others apparently threw poppy seed into each corner of their house, which was one of a host of beliefs, practices and superstitions connected to virtually every holiday or ritual in the life cycle. Gdacjusz also discussed whether witches could cause bad weather or drought and unusually for Polish accounts, he described the confession of witches from a case in 1553, in which they claimed to have taken and dismembered a child in a ritual aimed at ruining the harvest, but sadly for us provided neither a reference nor a location. Such a colourful description is more likely to have been taken from the *Malleus* or another source, given that narratives featuring the Devil were still a rarity in Polish trials of the sixteenth century. The preacher maintained (in line with the Protestant view) that the women had deluded themselves and that the Devil or *Stary Physik*, 'The Old Physik', knew when the weather would change and therefore deceived witches into believing in their own culpability. Gdacjusz drew on these examples to condemn belief in both witchcraft and superstition, reiterating the fact that ultimately everything that happened to humankind was the will of God.[36] This work is also interesting because it appeared towards the end of the era of religious tolerance in Poland and is one of the few written by a Protestant.

Reformation Challenges

The Reformation's strong challenge to the Roman Catholic Church's monopoly on assigning holy provenance furnished a key point of attack in Protestant discourse, alongside fierce criticism of the panoply of saints and their intercession. The intensely privileged role of the Virgin Mary, together with the routine and popular nature of local piety, village ritual and remnants of pagan practices, provided more grist to the Protestant, and indeed the post-Tridentine, mill. As the Roman Catholic camp primarily associated witchcraft with heresy, Protestants associated witchcraft with ritual, and by utilizing the vocabulary of witchcraft, Protestant writers reassigned the provenance of sacred items, rendering them diabolic. In the confessional war of words, even the ability of the Roman Catholic clergy to bless and protect was regarded as a trick of the Devil, who now resided not in hell but in Rome. The Roman Catholic clergy had become the magicians of the Egyptian pharaoh.

In common with Clark's findings on Protestant authors on witchcraft (which do not include Poles), Polish Protestant demonologists were also predominantly pastors. However, whereas Clark found that Protestant authors devoted a great deal of attention to a providential explanation, which he believes removed the need for complex exegesis and was more readily supportable from biblical sources,[37] this was not a topic developed in the Polish Protestant works examined here. The punitive aspect of witchcraft, emphasized by Protestant authors, was also propagated in some Polish Roman Catholic literature, namely the Łagiewniki and Krynice accounts examined below. Those accounts had the advantage of being subject to neither doctrinal nor dogmatic censorship. Therefore, the finer nuances of theological differences were often lost in the enthusiasm of those eager to write confessional propaganda.

There is little of the apocalyptic Calvinist approach to battling witchcraft evident in the works of Henry Holland (1590), James I and VI (1597), William Perkins (1610) or John Stearne (1648), or any emphasis on the pact with the Devil as the antithesis of Perkins's Puritan Covenant, which came too late for Polish Protestant commentaries on witchcraft (with the exception of Gdacjusz's work) published between 1545 and 1579.[38] Calvinist thought in Poland rarely touched upon witchcraft, perhaps due to the atmosphere of toleration, but more likely because Poland's witchcraft persecution did not really get underway until the middle of the seventeenth century, by which time most of its Protestant communities were greatly reduced through reconversion, migration or expulsion.

The Roman Catholic Paradigm of the Witch

Predictably there were many more pro-witchcraft demonological works written by Polish Roman Catholic clergy, bound by their faith to believe in the true presence of the Devil and demonic agency (although debate on the latter did not form a large part of their discussion). In Europe, following on from the *Malleus* and the works of Molitor, Nider and others, the sixteenth century saw the Reformation breathe new life into demonological debates, as the differing denominations staked out their theological ground. Many Catholic authors refuted Protestant or sceptical works, such as Bodin in his attack on Weyer's work in *De la démonomanie des sorciers* (1580). Bodin's defence of witchcraft relied on the authorities of the past and displayed a staunch belief in the relationship between the Devil and the witch. Among other points, he dismissed Weyer's argument that innocent old women were being burnt as witches when often merely suffering from melancholy, and called for Weyer himself to be prosecuted as a witch. He also used cases he had been involved in as evidence of the truth of his arguments, as did Boguet in his *Discours des sorciers* published a decade later, with new editions following in 1602, 1603 and 1611. Boguet's vision of witchcraft as a dangerous sect threatening civilization was reinforced by prurient descriptions of the Devil's copulation with witches of both genders. This was a tactic deployed by Remy in his *Demonolatry* of 1595, in which he also described cases he had been involved in as proof of belief in the Devil's mark, flight to the sabbat and witches' inability to harm judges. These three important pieces of writing underline a contrast with Polish demonology, as Catholic pro-witchcraft writing was strictly the domain of the clergy. Also lacking, to date, is any evidence of demonological works written by Polish judges, pamphlets mentioning trials or references to identifiable trials, depriving the researcher of important sets of sources.

In Europe, the Jesuits superseded the Dominicans in their propagation of demonology towards the end of the sixteenth century. Most notable of these authors was perhaps Del Rio and his six-volume *Disquisitiones Magicae* (1599–1600), which to some extent replaced the *Malleus* as the authoritative Roman Catholic work, emphasizing the importance of the Devil's pact and the Reformation as the real causes of witchcraft. Another encyclopaedic work was the Ambrosian Guazzo's *Compendium Maleficarum* of 1608 (reprinted in 1626), which weaved together examples from court records with a synthesis of Italian and French writers of the previous century. The *Compendium* is particularly famed for its elaborate woodcut illustrations of diabolic ceremonies, rivalled perhaps only by the Polish artist Jan Ziarnko's illustration in Pierre de Lancre's *Tableau de l'inconstance des mauvais anges et demons* (1612; see Fig. 1). De Lancre was another member of the French judiciary who painted a salacious picture of witchcraft and its dangers, purportedly based on his own experiences. Of course there were many more Roman Catholics writing in support of the persecution, but it is instructive to mention this particular set of works because they appear to have no Polish equivalent. The lack of such apparent reportage on the Polish persecution sets limits on our interpretations.

Although the Reformation placed a premium on theological difference, we must not take a polarized view, forgetting that there was a shared understanding of the basic concepts of sin, despite substantial differences in opinion on provenance and providence.[39] Gilowski's Protestant catechism shared many similarities both with the liturgy of sins ascribed to witches and with Białobrzeski's Roman Catholic catechism of 1567. Many such works indicated a common shift in the emphasis on personal culpability for sin, following newer humanist notions of sin as trespass against others,[40] reflected in the new dominance of the Decalogue over the more internalized seven deadly sins. Ultimately blame for misfortune was directed away from one's own weaknesses towards others, which is extremely relevant in the context of the witchcraft persecution. Bossy's chapter, 'Moral Arithmetic: Seven Sins into Ten Commandments', offers an excellent insight into its effect on witchcraft maintaining that within the framework of the sins, weakness was concentrated on the neighbour, rather than on God, and that holiness was not the business of ordinary people but of 'religious men and women'. The seventeenth-century increase in catechizing actions universalized the Decalogue, which he describes as 'an event in the moral history of Europe...which nevertheless had important consequences in a number of areas'. 'Decalogue ethics' had shifted the focus onto false worship as Christians' worst offence and with that, the Devil underwent an important change. He continues: 'under the old moral regime the Devil has been an anti-type of Christ...Under the new regime he became the anti-type of the Father, the source and object of idolatry and false worship.' According to the seven deadly sins schema, witchcraft had been loosely contained under wrath, but now it was elevated to false worship, evolving from mere *maleficia* and wrath to apostasy and false worship, breaches of the first commandment.[41]

The Jesuit Influence

This shift was illustrated well in one of the most prominent Polish works of the century, *Harfa Duchowna, A Spiritual Harp*, written by the Jesuit and court preacher Marcin Laterna. First published in 1585, with seven reprints during his lifetime, it ran to 25 editions by the end of the eighteenth century.[42] The work condemned witchcraft within Roman Catholic dogma by identifying both witchcraft and superstition within the first commandment, which not only included reading, listening to or keeping forbidden books or knowledge, but also building *zborów kacerskich abo bóżnic pogańskich*, 'heretical Protestant churches or pagan synagogues'. Laterna also mentioned other transgressions traditionally linked to witchcraft, such as its explicit use to harm people and cause matrimonial discord, or its implicit use to damage fertility within marriage, force others into sin and to wish for someone's death in anger. Interestingly, within the sixth commandment of prohibiting adultery, he included dancing and bodily contact – reflecting sabbat practices.[43] The importance of this work lies in whether it was used by the clergy as a confessional aid, and we can deduce its influence from its frequent reprints.

While we can only speculate about Laterna's influence, that of the Jesuit Woyciech Tylkowski can be clearly traced. His *Tribunal Sacrum* (1690) is reflected and cited in many later works, including the first Polish encyclopaedia, *Nowe Ateny, New Athens* (1745–56) and Duńczewski's *Kalendarz, Calendar*, of 1759. *Tribunal* may also have served as a handbook for the clergy, since Tylkowski, like Laterna, discussed sin within the context of the Decalogue and confession. Superstition, incantations and unorthodox ceremonies were included in discussions of the first commandment, together with healing using incantations or words written on papyri and herbs, whereas the use of magical practices to cause death was regarded as a breach of the fifth commandment. Tylkowski advocated the efficacy of communion to repel demons and reinforced belief in demonic agency, claiming that the bewitched were being punished for their impiety.[44]

Although Tylkowski was highly critical of judicial abuses, it was not because he did not believe in witches, as his writing reveals that he regarded those who divined, effected cures through words and other magical arts and procured abortions as witches, concurring with details in sixteenth- and seventeenth-century Wielkopolska trials. He reiterated the common beliefs of the pact with, and submission to, the Devil and renunciation of faith, but also encouraged people to distinguish between witches and simple old women carrying out superstitious practices, echoing sceptical opinion from the previous century. This is a surprising note in what was otherwise a standard Roman Catholic prurient exegesis of witchcraft, because Tylkowski did not engage so much in ideological or theological debate, but focused on detailed descriptions, emphasizing the abhorrent. For instance, he described the witch's chrism as made from water mixed with sulphur, salt and urine, and an unguent made from a corpse, flour, almond oil and human hair. He urged the clergy to ensure women did not remove consecrated items from the church, to prevent them from perverting sacred power for their own profane uses.[45] If this work was a confessional aid for the clergy, he refrained from advising priests on what to do should someone confess to witchcraft (as trials from the sample show they did), but instead detailed the skills that a confessor needed in order to identify a witch. Since this work was published during the peak of the persecution, it is a valuable source of witchcraft beliefs and remedies in circulation in Poland at the end of the seventeenth century, when demonological debate in Western Europe had more or less been successfully challenged by Enlightenment thought. It confirmed many of the common motifs of beliefs about witches, for example that they made a pact with the Devil, abjured their faith, were unable to cry, made malicious confessions, had sex with the Devil and committed sodomy. They flew through the use of an ointment made from the bodies of dead, unbaptized babies, which they had killed and offered their own children to the Devil. Witches harmed fertility, bore the Devil's mark and incited dishonest love among others. Their apostasy was underlined by the reversal of many Christian practices such as singing hymns in the Devil's praise, replacing guardian angels with devils and denying God, Christ, the Virgin Mary, godparents and the saints. Of course the sacraments were also renounced and witches were rebaptized and initiated by the Devil, as they inscribed their names in the book of death and promised to make sacrifices to him. Witches blasphemed, abused sacramentals, committed sexual acts with animals and devils, trampled on the Eucharist and sang obscene hymns.[46] It is important to enumerate this diabolic litany, which illustrates the recurring motifs of successive works and shows synchronicity with other European accounts. These motifs also underline the prurient pictures painted in works aimed at the clergy, based on diabolical reversals of Roman Catholic rituals with more unorthodox sexual practices thrown in.

However, a key plank of Tylkowski's work was his criticism of the Polish judiciary, possibly influenced by the German school of writers such as Laymann, Meyfart and Spee writing earlier in the century. He claimed that judges were ignorant and negligent – judging according to their own interests or personal gain and refusing appeals (confirmed by the Wielkopolska trials and other contemporary sources) and he condemned the excessive pressure placed on the accused to confess. He called for evidence to be substantiated and for the accused to confess with a clear conscience under light rather than serious torture. As a clergyman he was extremely concerned that judges sentenced to death those who were merely in need of a confessor and who confessed as a result from torture, referring to the *Instructio Romana de Iudicijs Sagarum* of 1657, published in 1680.[47] His views were a blend of belief in the prurient, in punishment for those who truly were witches and in compassion for those who were innocent according to his criteria.

The Pastoral Visit

Over half a century later, *Kolęda Duchowna, The Pastoral Visit* by Marcin Nowakowski (1753) was another excellent exploration of the spiritual dimensions of witchcraft in which the author claimed that sin was the result of the Devil's active temptation of humankind, rather than human freewill. Although he believed in salvation through Christ's birth, he also believed in the hereditary nature of witchcraft. His focus was on a punitive God who inflicted retribution for sins through witches and plague (more typical of Lutheran and Calvinist writers). Such sins included using herbs (described as a sign of turning to the Devil and away from God) and indulgence in clothes, music, food or drink. He, like Laterna, agreed with the Puritan idea that dancing was especially evil and a sin thought up by the Devil. However, Nowakowski believed that the individual was not only responsible for their own sin, but also partook in a collective responsibility for sin, suggested in a lively dialogue between a priest and gentleman. When the gentleman expressed scepticism about clerical ability to drive out the Devil, the priest replied that the clergy drove out the Devil in baptism and confession, confirming the efficacy and importance of the sacraments.[48] Nowakowski accused the clergy of sowing profane practices through their own ignorance, but was careful not to accuse them of deliberately seeking to deceive people, viewing the practices largely as superstition, idolatry (for example, turning to the Devil in one's hour of need or addressing the moon as God and dawn as Mary) and *vana observatio* (including eating, wearing or using certain objects in order to invoke or maintain happiness or friendship).

Nowakowski was writing at the end of the era of the persecution and his work provides a snapshot of how witchcraft beliefs had evolved in Poland. He regarded the swimming of witches as manifestly a superstition, long condemned and banned by the Roman Catholic Church. This criticism of the practice supports evidence from the Wielkopolska sample that swimming was still very much in evidence. Nowakowski included descriptions of both formal and informal methods of identifying witches, such as overturning the suspect's broomstick and carrying around cheese made on the Tuesday before Easter and licking it daily until Good Friday.[49] His description of the witch matched the usual Christian paradigm as a figure who abjured God, pledged allegiance to the Devil, made offerings of her children and killed them before their christening. She taught others her arts, seduced them away from confession and tried to persuade them to steal the Eucharist. A deliberate emphasis was placed on the witch's anti-sacramental tendencies and on her propensity to prey upon unbaptized children, reflecting popular and ancient fears of child-stealing women. More importantly, it underlined the importance of baptism as a fundamental Christian ritual and the vulnerable nature of those who had not yet been received into the Christian community. On a pragmatic level, a swift baptism prevented hesitation between denominations.

Much like Skarga[50] a century and a half before, Nowakowski reinforced the importance of the sacraments and used the threat of witchcraft against the impious. As an example, he related the following tale. There once was a baker whose bakery had been bewitched, but when he started to make his confession every month, carried an *Agnus Dei* and had the bakery blessed, all was well. One day he was almost killed by a terrible smell, which disappeared only when he genuflected, and once again, all was fine for a year until he lapsed in his piety and the problems resumed. Predictably once he returned to pious ways, all was resolved. This didactic narrative, resembling a parable, linked lack of piety in the simplest way to witchcraft, identifying it as a punishment from God. This contrasts with the more common paradigm of the innocent victim of witchcraft harmed by the malevolent witch. As expected, the author advocated Roman Catholic rituals as protective measures against witchcraft, instead of focusing on the more fantastic and sensational aspects of witchcraft.[51] Published towards the end of the witchcraft persecution in Poland in 1749, one might speculate that in this work the author was playing on the remaining superstitions of the populace. Whatever his motives, he was writing at a time when sceptical opinion on witchcraft had been firmly established for well over a century and when the rest of Europe, and indeed many in Poland, had privileged empiricism over the supernatural.

A New Athens, an Old Demonology

Around the same time as Nowakowski's work, *Nowe Ateny* (whose full title was *A New Athens, or the Academy Replete with All Science, Divided into Various Titles as to Classes, Erected as a Memorial to the Wise, as a Study to Idiots, as Practice to Politicians, as Entertainment to Melancholics*) by Benedykt Chmielowski appeared in four volumes between 1745 and 1756. By the nineteenth century, some editions omitted the section on witchcraft and the work was heavily criticized by later commentators, but its author, the sometime Jesuit Canon of Kiev, attempted to test his hypotheses, reported his results and often supported his facts with citations from learned doctors.[52] In the context of Western European witchcraft theory of the time, this work would appear completely anomalous, when Enlightenment thought had all but triumphed and trials for witchcraft more or less ended. Indeed, Polish contemporary debate was also predominantly sceptical by this time, although witchcraft legislation was not repealed until 1776.[53] The main significance of this work is its reputation as a handbook for local parish priests, which if true would render the chapter on witchcraft of immense importance in connecting élite and popular belief systems, albeit almost in the wake of the persecution. However, there is a stronger argument for regarding it as part of the wonder-book genre, as a compendium of representations of witchcraft in circulation in Poland. It comes into its own for this study as a useful synthesis against which to compare details recorded in witchcraft trials.

Chmielowski devoted a chapter to fulsome descriptions of witchcraft and counter-magic, which makes an interesting comparison with the trial details. Despite his critical attitude towards women, he placed no emphasis on gendering the witch, for the most part using names, so that this aspect was clear.[54] Chmielowski divided magic into the God-given power to perform natural magic based on the polarities of nature; artificial magic, describing otherwise inexplicable feats such as moving statues and guns that fired by themselves; and finally demonic magic regarded as true magic. In a section entitled 'On Maleficia and/or Witchcraft', Chmielowski described specific acts attributed to witches or demonic agency. These were mainly reproduced from Tylkowski's *Tribunal Sacrum*, which in turn was influenced by the Jesuit Georg Vogler's 45 arts of the witch, with its emphasis on prurient details such as menstrual blood, semen, goat's brain, hyena womb, frog's skin, crocodile and skin from the head of a newly-born foal.[55] These materials contrast with the use of powders, the Eucharist and wax attested to in trial confessions of this period, but Chmielowski, like other Polish writers, disappointingly did not quote identifiable Polish examples despite having lived through the peak of the persecution. However, in contrast with other Polish authors, he told of how familiars (occasionally mentioned in Wielkopolska cases) served witches in their tasks, reported news and lived in the corner of the house or in a ring.[56] They supposedly caused destructive weather magic, infected water sources and caused impotence.[57]

This work once again confirms belief in the diabolic appropriation of power and its corollary, the divine power of the sacramentals, sacraments and rituals. More sensationally, Chmielowski described a range of elaborate parodies of Roman Catholic rituals, for example, the witches stole a mitre for the Devil, who dressed in bishop's robes and celebrated weddings between magicians and witches. Quoting extensively from Tylkowski's works, he recalled parodic confessions, anointments and ceremonies for each day of the week. For example, Thursday was the day of profanation of the Eucharist and sodomy and Saturday was for bestiality and disrespect towards the Virgin Mary.[58] The parody of only four sacraments – of baptism, confirmation, the Eucharist and marriage – may reflect the Protestant reduction of sacraments. On a simpler binary level, psalms were adapted and sung in praise of Lucifer, *Ave Maria* was sung to the mother of the Antichrist and an inverted Trinity consisted of Lucifer, Leviathan and Beelzebub.[59] There was a clear implication that those who did not respect the Virgin Mary and the full range of sacraments and sacramentals formed a non-Roman Catholic collective constituency barely distinguishable from heretics, apostates, Protestants and witches. Chmielowski, as expected, emphasized piety as protection against the Devil, but the most disappointing aspect of the work, given its publication date, was its lack of reference to actual trials.

Instead, the work offers elaborate accounts of the sabbat and the Devil. According to Chmielowski, transvection to the sabbat could occur through the Devil's power, by means of a goat, cane or broomstick or grease extracted from young children strangled before baptism. If the witches wanted to be taken abroad then they slept on their left side and they could also hear what was going on at *seymy*, 'parliaments' (he never used the term 'sabbat'), without seeming to have left the house. He also quoted Remy's opinion that witches travelled to the sabbat on foot, but he described their destination as *Góra Wenera*, 'Venerian Mountain', rather than *Łysa Góra*, 'Bald Mountain' (perhaps a reference to the sexual aspect of the meetings).[60] Despite attending the gatherings, the witches' bodies still appeared to be at home because the Devil could only create the illusion of a body. In contrast to most of the trial accounts, Chmielowski described dishes of tasty stolen food preceded by a benediction addressed to the Devil and followed by an orgy,[61] and the Devil as the President of the Congress sitting in majesty or in the guise of a dog or goat whilst he received the homage of his followers as they variously worshipped him kneeling or with their legs in the air, offered him candles or a baby's navel, kissed him on the backside and celebrated Mass in his honour.[62] Those who did not join in the hideous rituals were beaten accordingly. These accounts also share the hierarchical nature of the gatherings with sabbat descriptions in trial confessions, but markedly in the Wielkopolska trials there were queens of the sabbat. The witch was naturally forbidden to worship God or the Virgin Mary or to venerate saints, their relics or images. She was prohibited from anointing herself with holy water or holy salt, making her confession or genuflecting.[63]

Chmielowski garnered a variety of descriptions of the Devil, including those from Del Rio, Majolus, Trithemius and Metaphrastes. The Devil was described as a spirit of angelic nature with no body but invisible eyes, who took a body from the air, from the thick vapours of the earth or a human or animal body, which then remained cold and moved mechanically as God prohibited the bodies from warming.[64] To saints he appeared in the form of varying animals, as a beautiful woman or even as Christ, which is why Chmielowski disagreed with received opinion that the Devil would not take on the forms of the symbols of Christ, such as a lamb or a dove. Surely if the Devil had appeared as Christ himself, he would not be abashed at taking the form of a dove? This contrasts starkly with descriptions in witchcraft trials in which the Devil almost always appears as a man, although often with one animal feature.[65] Descriptions of the numerous guises of the Devil were underlined to highlight his omnipresence and ability to deceive, emphasizing that the only sure protection against him was consistent piety.

It was essential for the Roman Catholic Church's reputation to be seen to provide remedies for witchcraft, in addition to prayer, piety and regular communion. The author divided such methods (some might call them counter-magic) into those condoned by the church and those not. Chmielowski also recommended the destruction of instruments known to be used by the Devil, such as snake's skin, feathers, animal fur or bones.[66] The Devil was also thought to fear certain predictable items such as salt added to holy water, doves, lamb, fish, bread and the words *per ipsum, cum ipso, in ipso.*[67] He avoided the pious and when he took on the form of a human body, he usually retained one of his characteristics such as fingernails, a tail or a hoof. He was also said to fear the words with which an exorcism ends, *per eum, qui venturus est judicare vivos et mortuos,* 'through him who has come to judge the living and the dead'. Some unofficial remedies included in the section on counter-magic were described as either witchcraft or Jewish practices and emphatically dismissed as having no place in the knowledge of Christians.[68] It is interesting to note the differentiation between ascribed provenances – while Protestants used the vocabulary of witchcraft to denote Roman Catholic practices, Roman Catholics used it to describe 'Jewish' or pagan practices.

A Time to Write?

Białobrzeski's catechism was published in 1567 and Laterna's work in 1585, but because the latter enjoyed 25 editions until the end of the eighteenth century it spanned almost the entire period of the witch-craft persecution in Poland. Tylkowski's work was also highly influential from the time of its publication in 1690 right through to Chmielowski's heavy borrowings from it in the middle of the eighteenth century. By no means was there a constant stream of pro-witchcraft publications. The gap between the first two publications (1567 and 1585) and Tylkowski's work in 1690 suggests that either the subject of witchcraft was not vexing Polish minds during the seventeenth century or that alternatively reprints of works such as that of Tylkowski and Skarga's *Lives of the Saints* were satisfying literary appetites. As with Protestant pro-witchcraft literature, the seventeenth century appears to have seen a dearth of true debate, as both Nowakowski's and Chmielowski's works are better read as wonder books rather than as further contributions to demonological debate. This lack of pro-witchcraft sources during the very period of the persecution is significant and also means that there are no identifiable first-hand accounts of trials or confessions, no pamphlets and few references in secondary literature. Of course, we cannot know the full canon and work only from what is extant or mentioned in other works.

Thus, Polish demonology stands almost hermetically sealed from the persecution itself, due to a lack of self-reference. We could speculate that the dearth of pro-witchcraft works published during the persecution may well be because witchcraft was accepted as a given, but this was not the case in other countries, where the trials themselves formed part of the commentary. Polish pro-witchcraft opinion really experienced its heyday in the sixteenth and the beginning of the seventeenth centuries, following contemporary European trends and predating Poland's own persecution, but by the middle of the seventeenth century, sceptical voices were in the ascendant and, in tandem with intense criticism of the judicial system, formed a dual attack on the persecution.

Witches and Saints, Devils and Miracles

The Lives of Female Saints

One of the most significant works of the era was the *Żywoty Świętych*, *Lives of the Saints*, written by Piotr Skarga (1536–1612), a Jesuit priest and court preacher to King Sigismund III. The hagiography's popularity was attested to not only by its 16 reprints and Skarga's royal patronage, but also by its place in virtually every noble manor and parish.[69] The *Vitae* presents piety not only as the road to salvation but also as protection against witches and is of particular interest for this study from two perspectives. The first is the portrayal of the Devil and his interaction with the saints in parable-like narratives, which provided role models for how good Roman Catholics ought to repulse him. The second important aspect of the *Vitae* (dedicated to Anna of Lipnicka Kormanicka) was Skarga's representation of the highest ideals of women in his descriptions of female saints. Given the prevalence among demonologists of constructing a binary opposite, we would naturally expect to read the saint as the opposite of the witch. However, the criteria used to construct the paradigm of the saint were extremely similar to those of the witch, because both were privy to preternatural power, but it was the provenance of that power which decided not only their status, but often also their fate. Skarga portrays the Devil, together with his retinue, tempting people into adultery or drunkenness. Skarga's discussion of theodicy was confined to the frequently quoted example of Job, illustrating how the Devil was subordinated to God, although the Devil manifested himself in both physical and psychological guises, as a seductive woman, or as an internal voice. As Skarga emphasized the actions of the saints as role models, he admonished his audience for their own religious lapses. He offered them practical protection against the Devil – more frequent communion, prayer and fasting.[70]

Over a third of the saints in this hagiography were female, which provides an excellent opportunity to investigate Skarga's attitudes towards female saints and women in general. These women's actions did not conform to sixteenth- and seventeenth-century ideals of acceptable female roles, so it is interesting to examine how Skarga grappled with conflicting agendas, portraying female saints as exceptions to the social mores of the time, permitted to transgress gendered boundaries of behaviour only for the greater glory of God. Their virtue (established in some lexical definitions as an antonym to witchcraft) was acquired through resistance focusing mainly on the body, mirrored in witchcraft trials. Although some might see in the figure of the female saint a role model for female behaviour, narratives of sainthood tended to fall into two categories – virgin-martyr and sinner-saint, reflecting what Warner has called the 'diptych of Christian patriarchy's idea of woman'. Whilst Mary Magdalene appears to be foremost of the sinner-saints, St Pelagia (Margaret), St Mary of Egypt and others prove that this was a favourite theme serving to emphasize the power of redemption. It is these examples, as Warner notes, which strengthen 'the characteristic Christian correlation between sin, the flesh, and the female', and which reinforce the tradition of Eve, identifying women with sin and concupiscence.[71]

The story of St Pelagia (Margaret) reinforced notions of women as concupiscent, easily won over by the Devil and tempted by material goods, supporting the stereotypes of the corporeal and material weakness of women. Pelagia had been a prostitute and great lover of finery and jewellery, but was converted to Christianity after a successful exorcism by Bishop Nonnus. Although she had renounced the Devil, he woke her on one occasion and promised to give her fine jewels if she would save him from becoming a laughing stock among Christians. She confidently told him that God would fight for her as she overcame temptation. In a similar vein St Agatha was also tempted by fine clothes, jewellery, food, music, dancing, flattery and such amusements as women were perceived to enjoy. The beautiful St Catherine Virgin of Alexandria resisted the sexual advances of Emperor Maxentius, instead converting him to Christianity. She reviled the gods he worshipped as devils for leading him and his people into shameful deeds and sexual debauchery. The emperor was so impressed by her arguments in favour of Christianity that he ranged the cleverest philosophers against her, all of whom she defeated.[72] The broad didactic theme was clear – God's mercy was so great as to redeem even such fallen women and transform them into saints. Witches were only to be redeemed through fire.

In reality, however, such actions were completely unbecoming to most accepted notions of female behaviour in the early modern period. In Skarga's commentary on the life of St Catherine Virgin, he attempted to juxtapose her overtly non-feminine behaviour with the Pauline teaching on the silence of women, by claiming that there were occasions when women should not be silent in their knowledge of Christ's teaching. Despite her gender, St Catherine was inspired by the Holy Spirit to speak out against an impious tyrant, which Skarga justified with the redemption of a large number of souls. However, he admitted that God had bestowed upon the 'white, weak sex wisdom and a courageous heart to carry out His work'.[73] Having established that it was only permissible for women to be so outspoken in extreme cases, Skarga then turned his attention to describing the role of real, rather than saintly women.

Women, he wrote, should pray and work more and had no need of knowledge, with the exception of women in distinguished houses who would otherwise idle their time away. A woman with talent and natural intelligence should be allowed to learn, but expressly for the greater glory of God's work and only under exceptional circumstances. The majority should remain silent, restricting their efforts to worship, work and the home. Skarga's intellectual struggle reflects the huge chasm between the expectations and the reality of the female role, which we may speculate became even more pronounced during the radical Marianism of the Counter-Reformation. The intense devotion paid to the cult of the Virgin Mary in Poland may have directly or indirectly contributed to how women were regarded in society.

'The grammar of the sacred'

The discourse of inversion allows the witch to be viewed as a natural inverse to the ideal of womanhood represented by the Virgin Mary and the female saints, but as Klaniczay and this study have argued, they are linked by a shared and common characteristic – their experience of the supernatural:

> Witchcraft is also related in many ways to the cult of saints. As for the morphological structure describing the operation of (beneficent or maleficent) magical power, the cult of saints (with the belief in miracle working relics) and the popular notions of witchcraft represent two analogous (though opposed) poles of the wider universe of popular religious conceptions about magic.

I would suggest that a natural inverse to Klaniczay's notion of the 'grammar of the sacred'[74] is a 'grammar of the diabolic', and clearly the differentiation between opposing appropriations of power by the witch and the saint relied upon its provenance. In both paradigms, individuals were singled out, may have suffered physically at the hands of men in authority and/or experienced encounters with the Devil. They both claimed supernatural powers and sometimes marriage to Jesus or the Devil. They often displayed bodily abnormalities, such as stigmata or the mark of the Devil, privileging the body as a site of resistance to torture or temptation. Both saints and witches suffered deaths that were often violent and defined by their perceived status and in witchcraft trials we hear of women claiming that they had resisted the Devil, called upon God and the saints for aid and invoked the Virgin Mary.[75] Sallmann writes brilliantly on the allocation of divine or diabolic provenance and the ambiguity of certain practices such as prophecy. He even locates this to local rivalries between Neapolitan Theatines and the Jesuits who apparently battled for 'l'appropriation du monopole de la sainteté prophétique'.[76] The burden of proof of sainthood, as with the witch, lay with the accused and the failed saint was demonized by default. In an investigation of five candidates for sainthood in Naples, in the same period, Sallmann showed that of the five (four of whom were women), four were rejected and subsequently accused of immoral behaviour, or of encounters with the Devil. Indeed one woman was accused of holding orgiastic meetings and having had five abortions – echoing the sabbat and infanticide motifs associated with witches. In Sallmann's words, 'exclusion from sainthood was rapidly transformed into condemnation'. Candidacy as a living saint was a zero-sum gamble; one was either confirmed as a saint or condemned as a witch. Contraventions of desirable female behaviour had to be explained, either by saintly divinity or a witch's diabolism. Nowhere is this interplay better illustrated than in the case of Joan of Arc, as sympathies, countries and confessional factions sought to label her in the light of their own changing propaganda interests. Once condemned as *heretica relapsa, apostata, idolater*, as Warner comments, 'Joan had trespassed gravely. It mattered less what colours one flew than who bestowed these colours. The ritual was legitimised only by the legitimacy of the performer, not by the words themselves.'[77] This underlines the importance of legitimization. Joan's story illustrates one of the most radical transformations, from witch to saint, and the complexities of the political and religious motives behind the decisions.

The issue of gender played a significant part in the judgement of provenance because women were not recognized as repositories of direct power, although there had been a tradition of saintly women in the royal houses of Central Eastern Europe, such as St Jadwiga and the blessed Kinga in Poland.[78] I would suggest that contraventions of desirable female behaviour and the appropriation of power by women had to be explained, either by divinity or diabolism, which was one reason why powerful mistresses, consorts or queen mothers were often rumoured to have been witches.

Local and Popular Piety

Seeing one's neighbour burnt at the stake and hearing from her own lips how she had bewitched people and had sex with the Devil reinforced widespread belief in witchcraft. At ground level, the panoply of saints and local saints to whom Roman Catholics could appeal was extremely popular as protection from misfortune. The Counter-Reformation emphasis on local and national shrines reinvigorated popular religion and the more enterprising sites of worship attracted large crowds by claiming miracles had been wrought through holy images or by engaging the clergy to perform exorcisms.

Wiślicz's account of miraculous sites highlights the ambiguity with which they were regarded by the church. He writes that the

> attitude of the clergy towards them was, at least, unfavourable, and in the 18th century openly hostile. Usually the bishops or archdeacons, after a thorough interview, forbade the faithful to gather at the unofficial miraculous sites under the penalty of excommunication.

The early modern period was the era of growth for the sites, most of which were devoted to the Virgin Mary, and he believes that their ambiguity could be characterized as 'a conflict between a cult of religious character, realised in official sanctuaries, and a folk superstition at spontaneous miraculous sites – i.e. with the superstition to which, somehow a priori, could be ascribed a magic character [sic]'.

The books of miracles contained accounts of healing and good fortune, which were, in essence, magical remedies. Therefore, as Wiślicz continues,

> many of the miraculous occurrences recorded in books of miracles acted as automatic magical remedies – uttering the right formulas and making particular gestures caused immediate, necessary intervention of the sacred... Seeking divine help at miraculous sites by the faithful, especially those from the lower strata, usually resembled magical practice. The Church efforts to pull them away from the witches or unverified forest sanctuaries towards official pilgrimage sites could be regarded as an attempt to substitute traditional magic for Christian magic. It would have to be consistent with the clergy policy towards popular religion. The Church offered the faithful an opportunity to practise magic within the framework of Christian rituals, for example ministering sacramentals, giving the benediction etc. The substitution of Christian magic for traditional magic was perceived by the Church hierarchy as a significant step towards eradication of pagan relics, idolatry and superstitions.

He concludes, 'thus it is rather impossible to determine the exact distinction between religion and magic in [the] case of the miraculous sites of the pre-partitioned Poland. The unconflicting nature of them seems, however, somewhat anachronistic for the early modern period.'[79]

It is no coincidence that the two shrines we are about to examine gained prominence in the mid-seventeenth century, in the wake of the Marian miracle at the Pauline monastery at Jasna Góra in Częstochowa, when the monks and others repelled the Swedish army. This was one of the most significant political and religious moments of the second half of the seventeenth century, in honour of which in 1656 the Virgin Mary was proclaimed Queen of Poland. Inevitably there was a resultant increase in Roman Catholic religiosity and popular local religion, which played an important role in the Counter-Reformation campaign.

In 1723, Marcin Kałowski published *Informacya o początkach y dałszym progressie cudnowego mieysca Łagiewnickiego, Information about the Beginning and Further Progress of the Miraculous Place Łagiewniki*. This work is rich in description of so-called miracles ascribed to St Antony of Padua and exorcisms. It is a useful account because such works provide an alternative opportunity to examine the interface between witchcraft and popular religion, particularly in the ambiguous sphere of saints and miracles. In typical Counter-Reformation style, the work was infused with a strong pro-Marian stance, ending its introduction with an apostrophe to the Virgin Mary. The very sensationalist nature of the work illustrates a shift in witchcraft discourse towards narrative. Dates, names and locations of events were provided, but to date have not been verified. Although this work was written in 1723, Łagiewniki had been a site of pilgrimage since 1676, and Krynice, the subject of the second work, since 1662. The plethora of holy places and images in Poland was noted with Częstochowa singled out as a place of international renown.

Among the countless tales of exorcisms, we find the story of Zeleski, a nobleman, who in 1675 blamed the loss of 500 sheep, cattle and horses on witchcraft and ordered the village women to be swum. He was about to send for the executioner, when his wife took pity on the women and successfully pleaded with him to show mercy. Another story told of how a 16-year-old noblewoman, bewitched by her wet nurse, had been taken to *Łysa Góra*, but fortunately the noblewoman was wearing a scapular that protected her from the Devil. In 1721, a townswoman had apparently been deluded by the Devil in the guise of a handsome foreigner who had lived with her as a husband for four years. Under his influence she neither admitted this nor went to confession and it was not until the poor woman was possessed by a second devil that she finally decided to confess and was freed of them both. The clergy also claimed that people had been freed from shackles, handcuffs and even prison as the result of pilgrimages to the site and supplication to St Antony. The location of lost items was only one of the many ambiguous practices interpreted here as a miracle, but elsewhere, and in the Wielkopolska sample, as witchcraft.[80]

Krynice cudownych łask Maryi z Jurowickich Gór wynikaiące, *Krynice, from the Miraculous Mercy of Mary of the Jurowicki Mountains*, by the Jesuit Franciszek Kolert, was published in 1755. Thanks to a holy image of the Virgin Mary, miracles similar to those described at Łagiewniki were apparently wrought. It was commonly believed that the Devil was unable to act against the Virgin Mary and that devils were driven out at the mere mention of her name. Although, as with the stories from Łagiewniki, the majority of narratives dealt with possession, there was an interesting comparison between possession as a punitive measure and as an affliction of the innocent. Jakub Sąkowski had abandoned God and virtue and was completely debauched. He was subsequently possessed by 40,000 devils, because he had neither heard sermons and nor made his confession. Numerous wolves, wild lions and bears raged within him and he suffered from stomach problems, tears and long fainting spells. If this were not enough, he was also plagued by four regiments of devils and an apocalyptic vision of hell was revealed to him, during which fire was cast into sinners' eyes and the damned were fettered to balls and chains, screaming and yelping like dogs. The earth opened up, the flames of hell burst forth and Sąkowski was about to be thrown out of bed when he heard a voice telling him to supplicate Mary of Jurowice, which he did. The Virgin Mary appeared to him and he subsequently made the pilgrimage of nine miles to Jurowice on his knees. In this story, the vision of hell and of the Virgin Mary redeemed the sinner, but the supernatural experience did not mean that he was regarded as a saint. Thus another construct emerged which permitted people to see visions and hear supernatural voices, but which did not confer upon them the status of either witch or saint. The only narrative involving witchcraft in this work supposedly occurred in 1731, when a woman rumoured to be fluent in the arts of ligature, symbols and other instruments visited nobleman Michał Rutski. Subsequently some of his children died and he suffered problems in one leg, which was cured by a visit to Jurowice.[81]

The *Malleus Maleficarum*

One cannot write about witchcraft without mentioning the *Malleus Maleficarum*. For centuries the huge influence of this work on the witchcraft persecution has been somewhat exaggerated. The publication of the Polish translation of part two of the work, entitled *Młot na czarownice*, *A Hammer of Female Witches*, in 1614 was credited with a wide readership and responsibility for spreading witchcraft beliefs in Poland.[82]

There is little evidence to show that the translation had any significant impact on the persecution. It was quoted neither in trial sentencing nor specifically in subsequent Polish demonology, and the *Malleus* (1486) in its original Latin form was already known to the Polish intellectual élite of the time. Within witchcraft historiography, debate rages on as to the real significance of this work for the European witchcraft persecution, and despite having long been credited to the Dominican inquisitors, Sprenger and Kramer, it is now regarded solely as the work of the latter. Its infamy as the so-called 'handbook' of witch-hunting, however, remains a popular myth and whilst many within Polish circles believe that it was literally used in this way, citing it as an example of vicious misogyny, the influence and role of the *Malleus* is undergoing a revision.[83] There were over thirty reprints between 1486 and 1669.

The importance of the work for this research lies in its citation in Polish literary works and in its significance as the first and only known translation in the early modern period. Translated into Polish by Stanisław Ząmbkowicz, in 1614, it was dedicated to Prince Janusz Ostrogski, Castelan of Cracow, a first-generation Roman Catholic. However, the translation was only of part two, which addressed the methods by which witchcraft was wrought and remedies against it. We may question why, despite being a lawyer, the translator did not translate part three, which described judicial procedures and furnished the belief in the *Malleus* as the judges' handbook. This supports the hypothesis that the work was not in fact used in this way in Poland. Part two could be viewed as a wonder book, of interest for its sensational value and clearly not as a source of legal knowledge. The Polish version also included Nider's *Formicarius* and Molitor's *De Lamiis*, again suggesting that the works were translated with a more general readership in mind.

Although these works had been circulating in Latin in Poland, Ząmbkowicz's introduction provides an opportunity to gain an interesting insight into perceptions of witchcraft in Poland in 1614. He lamented the minimal interest in trying witches because of general scepticism and lack of belief in witchcraft among the general populace and in the courts, supported by the small number of trial records extant from that period. It was the heroic task of the dedicatee, Ostrogski, to prevent the visitation of God's anger upon the populace by persuading people of the omnipresence of witches, so they could be eliminated. Ząmbkowicz described the typical motifs apparent in accusations against witches – confirmation of some of the criteria for witchcraft in Poland at the time of writing.

He described witches (referred to in the feminine) as those who harmed the health of humans or beasts, broke up marriages, sowed hatred, killed children, offered their children to the Devil or caused hail or thunder. They made an explicit pact with the Devil and feasted and copulated with him. He relied upon the authority of the Bible, quoting the stock examples of the Egyptian pharaoh's magicians and Simon Magus, claiming that there had been witches in all times and all places, and in such a potentially crucial work, Exodus 22.18 was translated as 'do not permit male witches to live', cited along with Leviticus 19.31. Ząmbkowicz also quoted Roman legal tables advocating 'cruel torture' for those who harmed harvests or crops by words or verses and Constantine's Constitution advocating the death penalty for witchcraft. Ząmbkowicz agreed with Kramer that women were more likely to be attracted to the Devil's service, because 'women's thoughts gather round dishonesty and evil'.[84]

Like others, Ząmbkowicz defined witchcraft as an even greater crime than *lèse majesté*; rather it was treason against God, a *crimen exceptum*. Witchcraft was a crime without excuse, was indefensible and deserved the death penalty. He recommended that the full weight of the law be applied not only to those who practised witchcraft, but also those who asked witches for advice, and he regarded 'white witchcraft' as equally evil. The translator claimed that many were afraid of the retribution visited upon the Commonwealth for its complacency towards the punishment of witches in his criticism of legal officials. However, he claimed they did not punish those crimes because of their own belief in superstition and because they were too lazy to root out witchcraft. He clearly thinks that either people did not believe in witchcraft or they ignored it and expressed a hope that his translation would open people's eyes to this crime, encourage officials to carry out their duties and encourage people to protect themselves against witchcraft.[85] In reality, the contribution of *Młot na czarownice* to later Polish witchcraft theory or to the trials for witchcraft is rather underwhelming, as it reveals little information that would shed further light on the Polish persecution, which had barely begun by then.

From this chapter it is clear that while Poland could not boast the rich variety of French or German works on witchcraft theory, both Protestant and Roman Catholic authors engaged in contemporary debate, following the broad arguments of their European counterparts. The Polish Roman Catholic Church's theoretical paradigm of the witch shared the same characteristics as those axiomatic to the figure circulating in the rest of Europe, a construct so powerful that it has virtually retained its hold on the definition of the witch many centuries later. This particular paradigm was established on the basis of binary opposition, through a diabolic mirror-image of the divine, which paradoxically proved the efficacy of the sacraments, sacramentals and Roman Catholic rituals through their appropriation by the Devil and witches as a source of power. However, the Roman Catholic voice was not alone in the field of Polish demonology and it is interesting to note the nature of contemporary debate among Polish Protestant writers. If we consider publication histories, then we see, as Clark points out, that discussions of witchcraft were not always connected to an outbreak of trials. He notes that they were also to be found in England and the Dutch Republic on the eve of repeal, and it seems also in Poland.[86] The publication of Polish demonological works ceases, in effect, by the end of the seventeenth century, but in the 30 years prior to repeal, hyperbolic works appear, such as those of Nowakowski and Chmielowski and the two works from Łagiewniki and Krynice. If they were intended by their authors to be didactic works, then they were clearly out of line with contemporary intellectual trends and largely do not correlate in detail with the trials in the sample or the paradigms of the witch defined therein.

Interestingly there was also a hiatus in the publication of sceptical works between 1669 and 1733 and of literary works between 1693 and 1729.[87] We can only speculate that the intensity of the persecution meant that there was some danger in expressing an opinion on the subject, supported by the anonymity of the author of the anti-witchcraft work *Czarownica powołana* and the posthumous publication of Gamalski's *Przestroga pastyrska*, which will be discussed later in this study. It is also striking that none of the Polish works describe identifiable Polish cases, and although the majority of works predate the persecution, even in those published during or after the persecution there is little mention of cases, in contrast to the French authors and judges for example. Whether the publication dates can give some indication of the mood in Poland is debatable, although it is virtually impossible to speculate on the impact of these works and their readership. However, there are similarities between details described in some of these works and those found in confessions to witchcraft in the Wielkopolska sample. The lack of Polish pamphlet materials means that the researcher is missing one of the most important sources revealing interfaces between the trials and printed sources. However, it can be concluded that in the sixteenth century, Polish intellectual trends on demonology were cosmopolitan and au fait with contemporaneous debate.

Another crucial issue illustrated by this chapter is the importance of the legitimization of the sacred and the church's monopoly of this power. This monopoly was essential because access to supernatural power could render one a saint, a witch or a sinner. Since the same construct evoked multiple interpretations, the authority to legitimize or demonize was significant, for individuals as well as communities. This also impacts on our reading of the importance and stability of the composite body of tributes or differing paradigms of the witch and witchcraft, as the same actions could be interpreted in opposite ways. The frameworks within which saints, witches and witchcraft were understood could be turned on their heads.

The discourse of witchcraft was clearly used to encourage piety, as we saw in Nowakowski's parable about the baker, but there is little evidence of the clergy actively encouraging witchcraft trials. Finally, it appears that the intellectual groundwork had certainly been laid by the beginning of the seventeenth century to facilitate the external projection of blame in tandem with a new humanist attitude towards judicial punishment, favouring juries over ordeals. As historians and anthropologists have noted, in appropriating a monopoly of power and regulating the life of the individual by spiritual means, the church also had a responsibility to produce an explanation for the failure of this power. The figure of the witch, as moulded by ecclesiastical literature, was one device that fitted this requirement for an external blame mechanism.[88]

6
Beyond Demonology: Blame the Witches

Although many historians have examined demonology in tandem with trials, most have focussed on ecclesiastical paradigms, at the expense of a broader range of literature.[1] I would argue strongly that as many representations of the witch and the Devil as possible ought to be examined, so as to better comprehend their many guises and to inform our investigations into the attributes of the witch and the creation of varying paradigms. By investigating a broader range of literary genres, the more or less standardized ecclesiastical stereotype of the witch is not only challenged, but stood completely on its head. The Devil and the witch, when inhabiting the liminal space of fiction, were often the subjects of irony and parody, as this chapter will illustrate. In addition, the very nature of the literary genres used could influence the interpretation and representation of motifs within witchcraft discourse. For example, in the Polish literature predating the trials, the figure of the witch was clearly a general literary signifier of old, allowing authors to depict and manipulate the motif freely. I would argue that the presence of the figure of the witch or the Devil in such a variety of spheres confirms the widespread influence of witchcraft belief, supporting Clark's view that demonology was in fact a vital forum for the debate of many issues in the early modern period.[2] From the use of Exodus 22.18, 'Thou shalt not suffer a witch to live', as justification for the execution of witches, to agricultural calendars, drama and poetry, the rhetoric of witchcraft was deployed under many guises. However, it must be noted that on a comparative scale, a minuscule proportion of Polish literature of the period mentioned witchcraft, suggesting that fear of the Devil was not the overriding feature of early modern Polish culture.

Authors regarded as Polish, such as Witelon (c. 1230–c. 1314) and Mikołaj of Jawor (*De Superstitionis*, 1405) explored witchcraft and the role of demons and devils. These authors were followed by early Polish chroniclers such as Jan Długosz, Marcin Bielski and Maciej Stryjkowski, who wrote about various legends and devils, as well as the burning of heretics and Jews. However, their accounts mentioned no identifiable witchcraft cases, which supports evidence that few witchcraft cases were heard in Poland before the sixteenth century. During this time medieval accounts of the Devil as the propagator of sin gave way to a renewed interest by Renaissance European intellectual circles in classical authors. Discussions of Aristotelian and Neoplatonic concepts of magic influenced early modern debate, reviving classical prototypes of female witches. Evocations of Circe, Medea and Dido breathed new life into representations of feminine guile and seduction, which, combined by the late sixteenth century with biblical, patristic, Jewish and pagan Slavonic characterizations of evil, produced a rich and ebullient Polish demonology, evident in trial confessions, treatises and sermons.

My analysis of a broader sample of printed sources is one of the key contributions of this study, which challenges the presumed dominance of the largely ecclesiastical stereotype of the maleficent witch. Although a fundamental set of characteristics ascribed to the witch and the Devil are identifiable, they relate to differing religious, secular and popular ideas of the figures. Some of the previous depictions of the witch in legal and ecclesiastical contexts were constrained by institutional strategy and dogma, in contrast with those investigated in this chapter. The appropriation of witchcraft discourse by a variety of authors from differing social groups reveals some of their motives for writing, as well as suggesting individuals' motives for using witchcraft or for being witches. It also confirms that a variety of layers were added to the composite body of recognizable attributes, to form differing and more pictures of, and complex uses for, the figure of the witch and witchcraft.

A Miscellany – Agriculture, Medicine, Alchemy and Fortune-telling

In light of the trials, it seems germane to begin by examining the works that emphasized the importance of threats to cattle, crops and health to the household, the survival of family units and the well-being of the community. The corollary to this was the importance of healing remedies (never referred to as counter-magic in Polish sources), which is probably why so many agricultural and medical publications contained a range of recommended practices, which share characteristics with accounts in the trials. One of the most famous works, Marcin Siennik's

Lekarstwo doświadczone, Medicine Tried and Tested (1564), devoted a whole chapter to remedies for witchcraft and poison, confirming a link that was not merely semantic, but also a traditional popular belief. Perhaps the prominence given to these remedies suggests that fear of witchcraft was fairly widespread in the middle of the sixteenth century in Poland. Curiously, the list of cures included many for male impotence, often attributed to witchcraft within the intellectual debate, although mentioned rarely in Polish witchcraft trials. We cannot be sure, for example, whether Siennik's condemnation of the popular use of mandrake, long associated with witchcraft and magic, suggested its use in Poland or that he was following European debate.[3] Naturally, he also described the preparation of various ointments, along with their legitimate uses, reflecting their ambiguous nature, but the work's main focus was on protection against unwanted love magic.

This was also the subject of Syreniusz' *Zielnik, Herbalist*, published in 1613. Its author claimed that love magic was used by the mothers and wives of kings of countries with warm climates – perhaps a reference to rumours that King Sigismund August's mother, the Italian Queen Bona Sforza, used the services of witches. Syreniusz claimed these practices derived from pagan knowledge, often acquired from 'disgusting old women, female and male witches, from quacks and swindlers who wander from town to town'. However, he did not dismiss all love magic, just herbal magic, ritual ablutions carried out by old women, the use of written characters and/or actions prescribed by male witches. He did not regard 'customary' love magic as being of 'Satan's matter and his instruments'. Indeed, he advocated herbal protection against witchcraft and harm to brewing and baking processes, at a time when women were accused and sentenced to death for those very same practices.[4]

Perhaps the most celebrated Polish herbalist of his time was Jakub Haur and his works *Skład albo skarbiec, A Store or Treasure* (1689), *Oekonomia ziemiańska, Estate Stewardship* (1675) and the later compilation of both works published as *Wybór oekonomii, A Selection of Husbandry Methods* (1730).[5] Surprisingly, a remedy for the apparently widespread Polish condition of the *kołtun*, 'matted hair', was not to be found under remedies for witchcraft, despite popular belief that it was caused by witchcraft[6] and it symptoms were thought to include blindness, broken bones and disorders of the blood.[7] Haur's discussion of the *Plica* included a recommendation to wash the head in alcohol or beetroot soup. He did refer to witchcraft trials, which is interesting when we consider that he was connected with Cracow from the 1670s onwards, where there is evidence that at least a dozen, if not more, witchcraft cases were heard.

Perhaps from knowledge of these trials, he described a range of motives including anger, jealousy, lust and misery, as well as diabolic copulation.[8] He criticized the many people who did not believe in witchcraft or possession and advised them to go to deepest Ruthenia, where they would certainly encounter witchcraft,[9] and claimed that it was most widespread in Wielkopolska, Silesia, Germany and Hungary, because individuals there were less pious. Ironically, he noted towards the end of the seventeenth century that Poles returning from Spain, France, Italy and other Christian lands observed no witchcraft in those countries.

These comments are all the more significant because Haur was born at the end of the peak in the Western European persecution and lived through a significant period of its peak in Poland. Like most authors, he omitted any definition of witchcraft, perhaps because the herbalist's broader purpose was to provide a list of remedies based mainly on the principle of sympathetic treatment, which the author claimed was scientifically tried and tested. For instance, Haur recommended the protective properties of human excrement and urine, on the basis that the Devil hated and feared them, and his claim that witchcraft materials were often found under a threshold, in cattle stalls, in bedding and in distilleries or breweries was borne out by trial confessions.[10] He also advocated gathering herbs before sunrise, which were to be dried and drunk in a mixture as protection against witchcraft,[11] which paradoxically was precisely the practice that had led more than one woman to the stake over a century previously.[12] Haur warned that 'where there is an inn, there is a Bald Mountain', which teases out an analogy between witchcraft and alcohol, a motif excellently developed in *Wódka z elixierem*, an anonymous work explored later in this chapter.[13]

Just as Haur located the Devil in the vicinity of an inn, *Dunczewski's Calendar* of 1759 countered with *gdzie Pan Bóg kościół buduje, tam diabeł kaplicę stawia*, 'where the Lord God builds a church, there the Devil places a chapel', echoing the belief *nullus deus, sine diabolo*, that there was 'no God without the Devil'. This work coincided with the last quartile of witchcraft trials and provides a synthesis of the beliefs still in circulation towards the end of the period. The text is instructive and uses a different range of vocabulary from that found in more traditional types of witchcraft theory, but the calendar's section on witchcraft and remedies may have reinforced the view that they were an integral part of agricultural knowledge. Yet again, Tylkowski was the main source for this work, so predictably there was an emphasis on some of the prurient details already enumerated here. The section opened with biblical quotations proving the existence of witches, suggesting, perhaps, that by this time one could not assume that belief in witchcraft was widespread. This late work also supports the view that few works published after the middle of the seventeenth century could truly be regarded as demonology, rather than as wonder books. Added to the general hyperbole was the exoticization of witchcraft as used in the east by infidel Tartars, underlining its apostatic nature. Witchcraft provided an explanation for enemy victories, such as the Tartar victory at Lignica (1240), the Turkish victory at Cecora (1620) and Chmielnicki's successes in the lands recovered by Ukraine (1648–57). Duńczewski's calendar described a wide range of witchcraft practices, suggesting either that such practices were still well known in 1759 or that they were included purely for sensationalism. Although the work was published between 1725 and 1775, the section on witchcraft remedies only seems to have appeared in one of the 1759 editions. Content varied between years and editions and there was often more than one edition per year.

The *Calendar* discussed witchcraft on a national scale as well as addressing farmers' concerns about harm to fertility and dairy produce, and conducting weather magic through the use of herbs, images, powders and a variety of other substances, such as human bone, gallows ropes or cat or goat brain, often added to the Eucharist. As usual, witchcraft discourse featured weather magic, although it rarely appeared in Polish witchcraft trials. The *Calendar* also mentioned the swimming of village women after a long drought, supported by evidence from trials, despite the Roman Catholic Church's ban.[14] The work described how witches abjured their faith, submitted to the Devil at orgiastic sabbats with banquets of horse dung and urine and their usual blasphemous abuse of sacramentals. Such a catalogue of evil practices projected intense evil onto an individual, rendering them a threat to the community and deserving of removal.[15]

The author also offered a list of remedies, beginning with those condoned by the Church, again predominantly gleaned from Tylkowski. He began with exorcism, perhaps reflecting a shift from witchcraft experienced as *maleficia* to possession. However, we must remember that there was a much stronger link in Polish popular belief between witchcraft and possession, because many descriptions featured the Devil being 'given' to the victim in food or drink, which caused bewitchment, illness or misfortune. Although the possessed was often held to be the innocent party, as we have seen in the previous chapter, possession could also be interpreted as a punishment. Reading between the lines of Duńczewski's long account of the exorcist's suitability and preparation and insistence upon an impeccable character and piety, we may deduce that this was not always the case. Along with the usual range of protective sacramentals, he also recommended supplication to saints reputed to have repulsed the Devil, such as St Dunstan, St Margaret Virgin Martyr and St Patrick. In contrast to the trials in Wielkopolska, Duńczewski regarded holy incantations as remedies, because the Devil was said to fear them.[16] In fact, this reflects the claims of many of the accused who called upon God, the saints and the Virgin Mary. Despite his great powers and knowledge of nature, the Devil could supposedly be repulsed by particular plants, mainly those with telling colloquial names such as *czarcie łajno*, 'devil's dung', *boże drzewko*, 'God's little tree', and *rączka Pana Jezusa*, 'the little hand of the Lord Jesus'. The author disapproved of the use of counter-magic, but described ways of identifying witches, presumably to punish them rather than to secure a remedy. One suggestion was to obtain the suspect's excrement and put it in the right shoe of the bewitched: when the latter placed their foot in the shoe the witchcraft would be lifted. It was not only the costliness of judicial proceedings which drove people to seek a cure, but also the fear of provoking a chain of denunciations, not to mention sheer desire to be rid of the bewitchment. Many practical manuals contained remedies for witchcraft, which contrasts glaringly with the sample of trial records, where seeking a remedy was rarely mentioned.

The traditional connection between foreigners and witchcraft was further endorsed in *Wróżki, Fortune-tellers*, a treatise on the evils of divination, published in 1589. The author viewed the underworld in an Augustinian manner, privileging binary inversion as a device – men became women, the stupid clever and the rich poor, reminiscent of other familiar inversions, such as the Christian Beatitudes and carnival. His work was chiliastic, judging the ills of the period as God's punishment and viewing eclipses, miracles and other signs as predictions of the end of the world. He regarded this discord as the result of lack of respect for Christian duty, virtue, God and the priest, which all heralded the last days in which people ought to prepare to meet their maker.[17] The recent bad harvests and lean years were attributed to Poland's spiritual crisis, a punishment from God rather than the result of individual acts of witchcraft punishable by the judicial system.[18] This apocalyptic view was one shared by both Roman Catholic and Protestant witchcraft theorists.

Six years later Poklatecki's treatise on alchemy cited Leviticus 19.31, 'regard not them that have familiar spirits, neither seek after wizards, to be defiled by them' (King James Bible), as he insisted that alchemy was a madness sweeping Poland which affected all social estates, to such an extent that it was dangerous even to write about it. Perhaps this explains the lacunae in the publishing histories of various types of demonography? He contributed to confusion over the provenance of magical power by claiming that written characters were mixed with both holy and cursed items to perform witchcraft practices, thus appropriating holy power. He raged on, describing how the Devil was conjured up by the use of candles, crosses, ceremonial ablutions and images touched by a virgin, and how sacrifices were made to the Devil, Christ was abjured and people were led into adultery, witchcraft, theft and other impious acts. Poklatecki refers to both male and female witches having sex with *incubi* and *succubi* and claimed that over five years, 48 women had been sentenced to death for sex with *incubi* but provided neither dates nor locations. Controversially he also claimed that although witchcraft should not be used as a counter-measure against witchcraft, a male witch's advice was extremely helpful. However, confession, prayer, alms and pilgrimage were the preferred methods of counteraction against witchcraft – confirming the Roman Catholic emphasis on the importance of works over grace.[19]

The Witch as a Literary Device

The exploration of fiction provides rich examples of the 'accessorizing' of the basic body of attributes ascribed to the witch. It is in fiction that the *dramatis personae* of the Devil and the witch inhabited their natural theatrical and poetic constructs. Fiction also tended to associate magical motifs with foreigners, reinforcing their identification as 'the other', as we have seen in clerical accounts, but not in trials. Although research has overlooked the witch in Polish literature to date, it is useful to consider a little of what has been said elsewhere on the relationship between demonology and witchcraft persecutions. Willis expressed surprise at early modern English portrayals of the witch 'contaminated by multiple traditions', a consequence she ascribed to the playwright writing for, and originating from, the 'middling sorts'. She argued that the literary witch was a one-dimensional figure, caricaturing evil and sexual appetite in a world subject to inversion. Never a serious figure, she was usually a conceit of irony or parody or associated with feminine seductive powers, unruliness or the disruption of normal gender rules.[20] This is certainly true of some Polish characterizations of the witch predating the trials. However, most of the English works on which Willis based her research were published during the Elizabethan and Jacobean periods. Subsequently their work displayed certain idiosyncrasies in their portrayals of women and witchcraft.[21] Willis also wrote about the participation of aristocratic women in witchcraft evident in Shakespearean literature, a motif missing from Polish literature, but not from Polish history.[22] Although Polish literature obviously appears in a different context to its English counterpart, it is useful to consider Willis's general arguments about the witch as a literary device. Purkiss also saw a clear differentiation, and wrote,

> Plays do not reflect any single discourse of witchcraft, but instead manufacture not one, but many literary witches of their own that have only a tangential relation to the figures in other people's texts, much less the figures on the scaffold at Tyburn.[23]

Her words correspond with the evidence from Polish sources, which points very clearly to multiple paradigms of the witch in various genres of literature and in the trial records.

The first fictional work examined, the anonymous play *Postępek prawa czartowskiego, A Trial of Diabolical Rights* (1570, Brześć Litewski), reflected the European, and particularly German, trend for such works based on trials or parliaments. Its main theme was the fight by Lucifer and his devils to regain their place in heaven, having been supplanted by the human race. It's one of the earliest detailed accounts of demonography and witchcraft. *Postępek* reveals contemporary ideas on the extent of human free will, the survival of practices regarded as superstitious and attitudes towards women and sin. The use of classical and biblical characters such as Circe (cast as the prototype witch who seduced women into witchcraft), the *Parcae* and the witch of Endor established the stereotype of female witches, deployed in preference to alternative male biblical prototypes such as Simon Magus or the pharaoh's magicians.[24]

One of the highlights of this work is the panoply of devils and their role in encouraging particular sins, for example the account of Adam's temptation, which gives way to a discussion of the question of human free will and responsibility.[25] We can read the devils' responsibilities in their telling epithets, for example, *Rozwod* (sic), 'separation', caused marital problems. However, despite such diabolical power, the author maintained that human free will was so strong that it had to be overcome either by cunning persuasion or alcohol, and that drunkenness not only caused men to commit many sins but also to forget them by the following day. This work reinforced many other standard European beliefs, but also replicated details from witchcraft confessions, such as the teaching of witchcraft, Thursday as the favoured day for carrying out witchcraft and the notion that witches also prayed and made offerings to the Devil to cause harm and bad weather, to enable them to fly and to predict the future. Thus by 1570 there was a definite composite body of witchcraft beliefs common to both trials and contemporary demonology. *Postępek*, like most Polish works, revealed scant detail of any Polish specifics, apart from the mention of seven sisters sent to Poland to wreak diabolical havoc, among whom were Jędza, Dziewanna and Marzana. The first name was a generic term for 'hag', and the others referred to Slavonic pagan goddesses, whose significance has already been discussed. The work also reinforced the axiomatic connection between females and witchcraft, playing on traditional criticisms of female weaknesses, illustrated in accounts of the temptations resisted by female saints. It was *Strojnat*'s 'Dandy', the mission of which was to tempt women to take inappropriate pride in their appearance, purportedly causing them to change their clothes ten times a day. He claimed that even in times of plague they were more concerned about impious clothing and luxury, reserving special scorn for noble women.[26] From this drama it is apparent that by 1570, when the persecutions began to peak in Western Europe, a composite idea of fantastic characteristics attributed to the witch similar to that found in Western Europe was circulating in Poland. This picture described the stereotypical maleficent witch, who flew, cast spells and worshipped the Devil, but it did not reference witchcraft trials.

The *Sowiźdrzał* or *Eulenspiegel:* Through the Looking Glass

One of the most fascinating aspects of Polish fiction in this period was the *Sowiźdrzał* or picaresque school of literature, borrowed from the literary tradition of the character of Till Eulenspiegel, who appeared in Germany in the fifteenth century. The 95 tales describe episodes from the life of Till, from his birth to his death, and even include a short tale of how he outwitted the King of Poland's jester. The humour is scatological, with no sense of fate ever catching up with the trickster, whose main targets are the middle and upper classes, especially those who employ the labour of others. Till's adventures highlight the absurdity of life, especially through the key device which sees him treat all speech literally, and it is this inversion through his 'distorted looking glass' which plays into the inversion evident in witchcraft. The character and his adventures were translated into many languages, but the early translation into Polish reinforces Poland's conformity to contemporary European trends.[27]

In his discussion of what he calls *literatura błazeńska*, 'jester's literature', Ziomek contends that the sixteenth century saw traces of such tradition that also included the characters of ancient Ezop, medieval Marchołt and early modern *Sowiźdrzał*. In his etymological discussion of the name *Eulenspiegel*, the 'owl/wise looking glass', he refers to the theory of the owl as the symbol of the wisdom of nature rather than that of culture, which certainly reflects more accurately the essence of *Sowiźdrzał*,[28] a satirical genre highly critical of the middle and upper classes, functioning as a distorting mirror held up to society.[29] While there is dispute about the date of the first copy of a Polish version of *Eulenspiegel*, one edition had been published by 1540 at the latest, and by 1745 there were 12 editions.[30] The most famous works of this genre (it did not just concern the *Eulenspiegel* tales) were published around the beginning of the seventeenth century. Based on antinomies of contemporary social, cultural and literary trends, they were an obvious forum for the figures of the witch and the Devil, the primary protagonists of religious inversion. *Sowiźdrzał* was the literature of carnival and contrariety, of the rogue and the rebel, of those on the margins, and a genre suited to being read aloud at the inn, to raucous laughter. In opposition to literary norms, dedicated to great patrons and featuring the heroic, the idealistic and the noble, *Sowiźdrzał* literature features the anti-hero opposed to the feudal way of life, with little moral conscience. It was, to some extent, the literature of Małopolska, penned by teachers, rectors of parochial schools and wandering students, whose social and academic progress was hampered, possibly by lack of social status. Although teachers by profession, they expressed themselves through literature that was suggestive and full of compensatory humour.[31] They relished mocking social mores, the divisiveness of the social hierarchy and the importance of the preservation of social position, primarily through the liberal use of irony and parody. This produced yet another analogous anti-world, in which criticism was levelled at the very authors of conventional literature – the nobility and the clergy. The genre was in opposition to, and perhaps a reaction against, Polish delusions of noble grandeur in the guise of Sarmatism. In particular, the genre highlighted the absurdity of the world order seen from the perspective of the lower classes, which makes its portrayal of the witch and the Devil particularly appealing. The majority of *Sowiźdrzał* literature examined in this chapter was published between 1605 and 1615 and enjoyed many reprints throughout the seventeenth century. The frequent use of a collective pseudonym (Januarius Sowizrzalius) guaranteed anonymity, allowing the authors to take full advantage of their freedom of speech to paint a portrait of society that mocked the cosy bucolics of contemporary Polish writers.

Drama also featured in the *Sowiźdrzał* repertoire and included *Sejm piekielny, The Parliament of Hell* (1622). The renowned bibliographer Estreicher noted at least ten known editions from 1622, after 1628, around 1650, around 1690, 1730 and 1752. In a fashion similar to their characterization in *Postępek* and many *Teufelbücher* (German devil books), devils 'personified' individual sins. The work juxtaposed the devils' power with their ludic abject fear of women. The devil Smołka was regarded as the most unfortunate, because he lived among women and confessed to being terrified whenever he had to sit next to a *baba*, 'old woman', in case she harmed him. This fear of women is a strong motif in Polish folklore and appears in the Polish tale of Pan Twardowski from where the popular saying comes 'Where the Devil fears to tread, send a woman'. However, despite this fear of women, one hapless devil, Rogalec, was responsible for witches and even travelled by broomstick. He boasted that he had made witches of good women even in the middle of pious Christian cities, reinforcing the fear that devils could tempt everyone, everywhere, in their quest to win souls for Satan. In *Sejm piekielny* those who could heal or carry out divination by using wax, the so-called cunning folk, were demonized for using power originating from the Devil – demonstrating the importance of provenance. The devil Ashmodeus was the patron of love magic, which he claimed was a typical topic of conversation among women. Of course, he encouraged this and advised them on how to bewitch animals by sprinkling water over them, which we can see is an old practice visible in trials.[32]

The common motif of the old crone also appears in *Komedia rybałtowska nowa, A New Minstrel's Comedy* (1615), in which a character named *Baba* or 'Crone', 'Biddy' was immediately recognizable as a witch, not only by her name, but by her actions. She uttered incantations, flew on a stick, used herbs and implicitly had a pact with the Devil. He appeared at her bidding, but their relationship was not harmonious, as he addressed her as *szpętnico, czarownico*, 'ugly one, witch'. In contrast to the learned Latin invocations described by demonologists, in this work the witch's incantations are a mockery of rhyming rubbish, devoid of any sophistication. Unusually, the ability of the witch to summon the Devil implies a less subservient relationship than that usually assumed.[33]

The witch fared better in *Statut Jana Dzwonowskiego, The Statute of Jan Dzwonowski* (1608–25), even emerging as a praiseworthy heroine and a figure to be envied, in a work parodying Groicki's legal codices of the mid-sixteenth century in its structure, which made liberal use of binary inversion. The introductory apostrophe to the reader advised them to act according to the law if they wished to be a real rogue, whereas the witch emerged as an early capitalist heroine, who knew how to turn a profit. The moral was that since virtue clearly did not pay, it was better to cheat, reaffirming the semantic link between lack of virtue and witchcraft. Under conditions where there was a real battle for resources, a housewife who made milk from water and butter from milk derived from a rope (a form of witchcraft) was to be praised and the household where there were always cakes and fat cheeses was to be envied. However, while this was obviously advantageous for the individual, in a society that had a zero-sum view of resources, the advantage of one was clearly to the detriment of the rest, which was viewed as magical theft. Certainly this provoked feelings of inadequacy and envy, which could contribute hugely to tensions within a community. In imitation of Groicki's codices, there were also sentencing guidelines, which subversively decreed that those practising witchcraft should not be punished for making a profit and confirmed that gossip often led to the tribunal – evident from trials.[34]

Peregrynacja dziadowska, *Beggarly Wanderings*, also began with a subversive agenda in the introductory apostrophe to the reader. Conventional medicines such as mercury were decried in favour of alternative methods, such as those used by two male characters named Bałabasz and Marek, who used herbs for beneficial purposes and mostly to aid petty noblewomen in childbirth. They also taught the noblewomen their arts, concurring with accounts in trial records, if we disregard, of course, the fact that these protagonists were male. The two men blessed various household utensils, butter churns, pots, cow byres and pigsties in order to protect them from witchcraft. The 'Old Beggar' encapsulated the ambiguity with which herbal remedies were regarded in claiming that people had great difficulties in discerning harmless practices from witchcraft and that paradoxically they were advised to consult the Devil or a witch. Another character, the 'Old Ringer', practised herbal, love and image magic, could help at births, could bewitch animals and also claimed to be able to cast the evil eye. She boasted of her knowledge, and despite being drunk on a daily basis, divulged none of her secrets. However, she embodies a motif recurrent in both trials and demonology, with her revenge-laden words, 'When someone angers me, it is difficult to protect against [me].' Significantly, these accounts closely resemble the charges made against some of those accused of witchcraft examined later in this study.[35]

The witches in this work were characterized by their epithets. However, instead of young, seductive witches such as Circe or Medea, inversion created lame, ugly and battered old hags. *Chroma Baba*, 'Lame Old Biddy', claimed that there were few who did not know the magical arts, and that they received their schooling from their mothers – affirming the popular notion of hereditary witchcraft. She also boasted that she could open locks by means of herbs and complained at having to stay by the oven (a position usually ascribed to witches' devils or familiars) since she would much rather be out and about gathering knowledge. To relieve her obvious boredom, she occasionally threw old women into the pond. She was accompanied by her bruised and battered colleague *Guza baba*, 'Bruised Old Biddy', who had been rejected for domestic service due to her looks and had turned to the Devil out of discontent. In spite of her close association with the Devil, she was still able to quote holy rites, hymns and sermons by rote. The third witch's name, *Latawica*, often translated as 'incubus', is discussed at length by Ostling, who sees the spirit as signifying unbaptized babies, treasure-hauling demons and an incubus, supporting his arguments with citations both from trial records, and nineteenth-century folklore.[36] In this work, however, *Latawica* was obviously a hybrid of various Slavonic spirits: at night she was the large woman called death,[37] in the afternoon *przypołudnica*, 'afternoon spirit', and in the evening she was *wiedźma*, 'crone' or *latawica*, 'incubus'. Equally at home in the air or in water, she claimed to control the elements and always acted maleficently. Like the 'Old Ringer' above, she threatened revenge, warning, 'Whoever dares to harm me, I will harm him more from anger, than he harms me.'[38] An episode in *Synod klechów Podgorskich, The Synod of the Teachers of Podgórze* (1607, with four editions before 1646), also contained motifs common to witchcraft trials. The eponymous teachers were outraged when women used the Eucharist as food for their cows and for witchcraft. Such an appropriation of sacral power was underlined by the decree not to give witches objects from the church, such as wax, water from the font and even rust from church bells. Holy water, the aspergillum, herbs and motherwort were also not to fall into their hands, and they complained that there was, at that time, more talk of the Devil than of God. Importantly for this study, the work recognized the key role of anger in invoking evil and witchcraft, as the maxim here illustrated, 'become angry, if you wish, you will gain an evil spirit'. As in so many of these works, revenge was a strong and frequently expressed motive. Although this work was ostensibly about the plight of parish teachers and control of schools, witchcraft and the

Devil were occasionally mentioned, reflecting the wide range of genres in which witchcraft rhetoric was found.[39] There was also more than a hint of misogyny and it is clear that women were regarded grudgingly, mentioned in passing as brokers of power, and viewed as a way out of poverty, but also referred to as a 'Devil-wife'.

Wonder books, so popular throughout Europe, were also evident in Poland, and the one Polish work examined here, *News from Joseph Pięknorzycki of Mątwiłaiec's Courier's Bag, Found in Nalewayki*, included an account of a male witch in France who challenged a soldier to a duel.[40] The popular notion that witches were more prevalent in the East was also reinforced by the tale of the witch from Kiev, whose husband never saw her at home after sunset on a Thursday (the traditional day for witchcraft and sabbats according to both literature and trial records).[41] When he questioned this, she turned him into a stork and was also said to have kept a ring made from human nails, which rendered her invisible.[42] In Słonim, a woman was apparently sentenced to drowning for poisoning her husband, but floated back to the shore, which prompted a suggestion of witchcraft and discussion as to whether God or the Devil had saved her. Although she was released, the author remarked that she was likely to indulge in so-called 'unvirtuous' behaviour, a euphemism for witchcraft. An interesting aside in this work reveals the importance of the proverb 'never a lender nor a borrower be' in maintaining a good friendship and avoiding the neighbourly tensions that so often contributed to formal and informal accusations of witchcraft.[43] This was also illustrated by an episode in *Statut Jana Dzwonowskiego*[44] when women cursed each other with the threat of one hundred devils for not being willing to lend items, emphasizing the importance of reciprocity and interdependence as parts of the vital currency of early modern communities.

Poetic Pragmatism: Contemporary Insights into the Persecution

Domestic Demands

The striking feature of the literature discussed in the previous section is the challenge to the assumed negative interpretations of the witch by a more positive and perhaps pragmatic interpretation of witchcraft. Also, while the attributes may be the same, such as producing more milk, the attitudes towards them differ. We have also seen witchcraft described as an instrument used by those whose motives were revenge, envy and ill will. The following two works will provide a remarkable insight into how contemporaries viewed these motives, the individuals who practised witchcraft and some of the real motives behind the trials. Despite the fact that their authors were from the élite sphere, the poems elicit sympathy for the witch and provide a realistic understanding of individuals' motives for turning to witchcraft and for the persecutions.

Szymon Szymonowicz's fifteenth idyll (1614) was simply entitled *Czary, Witchcraft,* and revealed witchcraft as a tool of revenge within a domestic household. The female narrator, although never overtly labelled as a witch, was defined as such by the recognizable actions and motives of a 'witch'. She was angry because her husband had not returned home, evidently not for the first time, and her strong desire for revenge is evident when she says, 'an evil deed deserves evil in return'. The setting of this work within the household is significant, placing witchcraft firmly within the domestic feminine sphere and painting witchcraft as knowledge shared between women. Furthermore, this link is compounded by the woman's introspection as she first judges herself as a good housewife, questioning whether it is she who has caused her husband's absence. Her self-reassurance is based on an enunciation of her domestic skills. She tells herself that she was not to blame, she came from a good home and was a good wife, who managed the household so well that they even had a servant. Satisfied that the fault did not lie with her, but with her husband, she embarked on her revenge, conscious of the implications, saying, 'I know that it is a great sin, I know that all witchcraft is harmful'. And she ordered her servant to help her carry out a veritable catalogue of witchcraft practices aimed at bringing her errant husband home, including sympathetic, image and ligature magic, the last two of which are rarely found in Polish trials.[45]

By locating this example in a domestic scene, rather than portraying the witch at the sabbat or killing babies, Szymonowicz challenged the diabolical interpretation of witchcraft found in clerical works. His witch was not murdering unbaptized babies, but at home lamenting an errant husband. She was operating in an environment where she could neither physically nor verbally revenge herself upon her husband, so she resorted to the secret weapon of females, witchcraft. This parodic idyll, or idyllic parody, polonizes a work by Theocritus and portrays witchcraft as a revenge mechanism, in one of the most common and understandable household situations. The work's popularity was attested to by nine reprints before the end of the eighteenth century, significantly throughout the period of the Polish persecution.

From Satire to Stricture

In 1650, when the peak of the persecution was still raging in Western Europe but Poland was yet to experience the worst, the eminent Wielkopolska intellectual and nobleman Krzysztof Opaliński satirized the witch as an all-purpose scapegoat. His scepticism may have been in part due to the intellectual stimulation of Wojciech Regulus, his one-time teacher.[46] The owner of a printing house in Poznań, Regulus had published several treatises critical of the witchcraft persecution, including a Polish translation of Spee's *Cautio Criminalis* dedicated to Opaliński and his brother Łukasz, published in 1647, and Wisner's anti-witchcraft treatise, again, dedicated to Opaliński.[47] Opaliński's *Satyry*, Satires, heavily criticized the state of Poland and its nobility, painting a society paralysed by evil, deceit and crime, and a lack of centralized power. He warned that the *sroga oppressya*, 'harsh oppression', shouldered by peasants was a key factor in Poland's social chaos. He accused his peers of placing the work of twenty peasants on the shoulders of ten, so that peasants had no time to tend to their own meagre plots of land, thus fuelling unrest. Among the many insights into the plight of the Polish peasantry, he produced a remarkable critique of the mechanism of blame and denunciation inherent in accusations of witchcraft:

> When Spring comes and there is no rain in May,
> Blame the witches. When first one then another ox dies,
> Or a child, blame the witches.
> Then they order an innocent old woman to be taken for torture,
> Until she hands over another fifteen. The executioner racks and burns
> Her until she tells all and denounces the whole village;
> As for the old woman, it is strange that neither a Sir nor a Lady is denounced,
> Who could be rather burnt for innocently
> Ordering their own to be tortured and killed without reason.
> And if there are thirty people in a village,
> and fifteen are burnt! What – for God's sake
> Is the reason? The Lord is ill and unable to manage
> He withers and his children often die at home.
> Just as droughts and natural death
> Were they not sent from God himself!

The *Satires* were published in 1650, 1652 (two editions), 1654, 1691 and 1698 (three editions) spanning the early years of the persecution.

This realistic interpretation is supported by evidence in trial records and it reminds us that there were sceptics among the educated classes who were well aware of exactly what was happening. Opaliński and Szymonowicz question the charges of witchcraft in their contexts, providing us with contemporary micro and macro views. Together with portrayals of the witch in more pragmatic and even admirable terms by the lower educated classes in the *Sowiźdrzał* literature, we see that Polish works challenge the stereotype of the negative representation of the evil and blasphemous witch. Opaliński attached no notions of fear to his description of a witch, indeed precisely the opposite, deconstructing popular diabolic notions to reveal a pitiful old woman as the innocent scapegoat of the superstitious ruling classes, forced to betray her neighbours. His assertion that the local seigneur often instigated trials for witchcraft when his household or family had fallen ill confirms my suggestion of a seigneurial pattern. Moreover, in the very year this work was published, Marusza Staszkowa was tried for witchcraft in Opalenica. After his death in 1656, six more women were tried there and many of the witches tried later by the Grodzisk court came from Opalenica.

While it is possible that Opaliński had heard of Staszkowa's case, we know for certain that he was involved in a case much closer to home, which he discussed with his brother in their correspondence. In a letter written in March 1642 (a decade prior to the publication of *Satyry*) he noted that, 'Mrs Łukomska, *nulla ex causa*, only *ex rancore*, ordered an honest female citizen of Pobiedziska to be tortured, she was supposed to have poisoned her husband, without any proof, *et quod maius*, without our knowledge.' He suggested a letter be sent to Łukomska and later, in May, received news that she had thrown the letter on the floor, refusing to read it. He noted that the executioner was so disgusted by the whole affair that he had refused to execute the accused, even forfeiting the fee. Łukomska then admitted to Opaliński that she had also imprisoned the accused's husband, leaving an infant daughter Teresa without care, who later died.[48] The trial records show that Marianna Rogowczykowa and her husband brought a case against Łukomska and the citizens of Pobiedziska, which reveals her account of the torture to which she was subjected. She was imprisoned for four weeks and deprived of food and sleep. At the time, her 12-week-old daughter was still at the breast and subsequently died as a result of being away from her parents, who had both been imprisoned. Marianna was chained at the neck, the hands and the feet, and at one point salt and water were poured into her mouth. The executioner made clear his disquiet at this particular episode and refused to continue with the torture, even refusing his fee. Łukomska, the scribe and the mayor sent to Poznań for a replacement. Eventually Marianna was released, given medical care and taken away to Sieraków.[49]

The Lesser of Two Evils: Alcohol v. Witchcraft

Another fascinating, but anonymous work, was *Wódka z elixierem*, *Vodka with an Elixir*, published in Poznań in 1729. It was ostensibly an attack on the widespread abuse of alcohol in eighteenth-century Poland and drew a significant analogy between alcohol and witchcraft. Alcohol was consistently shown to be by far the greater evil, because drinking provoked sin, resulted in catastrophe and ultimately led to the loss of one's soul. The discussion of the effect of alcohol on church attendance, taking communion and attending confession suggests that the author was a Catholic clergyman, supported by his claim that witchcraft trials ought to be heard before the ecclesiastical courts.

Since alcoholism was predominantly a male problem, little was said specifically about women, but it was noted that the sight of a drunken woman caused a great deal more shame than her male counterpart. One verse devoted to the shame of women harked back to the golden past when women did not drink, but were paragons of virtue and truly pious until they aped the actions of men. Eve lost paradise through food, and now her daughters were drinking it away. He claimed that many women who purported to be possessed were in fact drunkards, describing their indulgence as the 'spirit of alcohol' that visited a woman at any time of the day. This bears a close resemblance to the Slavonic spirit *prypołudnica*, 'the afternoon spirit', said to cause people working in the fields to sleep in the afternoons. Strikingly, the author portrayed alcohol as a witch, whilst simultaneously criticizing witchcraft trials and the swimming and burning of witches, illustrating the multiple levels of definitions of the label of 'witch' that could be understood by one individual.

Although it was a useful literary device as an analogy, the real so-called witch, the figure of the woman accused of using supernatural power to harm and who would inevitably be condemned to the stake, aroused sympathy and pity in the author. In a verse entitled *Czarownica gorzałka*, 'The Alcohol Witch', a litany of harm reminiscent of that connected with witchcraft was blamed on alcohol: it killed the old, caused marital discord, crippled people, caused hatred and intrigue and made judges pass death sentences on innocent people accused of witchcraft. Previously, we have discussed how blame was shifted from an internalized notion of the self tempted by the Devil to the external mechanism of the witch, and this work reveals a further transfer of blame from the witch to alcohol, from the self to an impersonal third party. Alcohol was blamed for illnesses such as madness, blindness, the *kołtuń* or 'matted hair', and for shortening life expectancy. It also led people to blaspheme, to mock preachers and confessors and to avoid worship or communion. The author even claimed that alcohol was worse than the Devil, because at least the Devil could be repulsed by holy objects, or exorcized (another reason to suspect the author was Roman Catholic). Even the possessed were luckier than those who drank alcohol, since they at least heard Mass, took communion and visited places such as Łagiewniki. This widespread drunkenness was responsible for all social estates' poverty and the reason why innocent women were burnt to death.

The author showed great disdain for superstitious practices, deriding all, from guilds to housewives, who carried out rituals either before they began work or to aid them in their endeavours. Without such practices, butter would not be made, nor cows milked, nor would a tailor pick up his needle. Without such superstitious practices, no food would be prepared, no one would be seated at a wedding, no cabbage would be sown, and likewise, no one would be buried. He claimed that if superstition were instead viewed as witchcraft, then thousands would have been burnt at the stake every day. He fulminated that the real crime was punishing the superstitious rather than alcoholics. Like Opaliński and Szymonowicz, he provided a contemporary explanation of how suspicions of witchcraft arose in Poland. If someone had either good fortune or misfortune, then witchcraft was assumed to be the cause, and his comment 'a neighbour's envy ascribes it to witchcraft' echoes Opaliński's words from over seventy years earlier.[50] The author turned to the motif of Circe, claiming that even such a famed witch only used one form of alcohol to turn Odysseus and his men into swine. How much worse was the situation in Poland, replete with so many varieties? Away from the abstract discussion of witchcraft discourse, a picture of those accused of witchcraft emerged, as well as accusations against the judiciary, who were accused of ignorance of what truly constituted witchcraft, corruption, drunkenness and a lack of legal knowledge – the failings Groicki had lamented in the sixteenth century. The anonymous author of *Wódka* claimed that in the main towns courts were more reluctant to hear witchcraft trials, which they regarded as extremely difficult, and passed them to the clergy first. However, in small towns and the countryside, foolhardy judges took on cases, calmed their nerves with alcohol and were then unable to differentiate between truth and lies. He further accused them of ignorance of the signs of witchcraft and the procedures connected with calling witnesses, which resulted in many innocent people losing their lives. All the witches in this work were female and we can link this to his succinct comment on the importance of reputation: 'Protect yourself from this one: don't chat to this one, / Keep your distance from this one, / Don't spend time at her house: don't drink milk from her.'

As in other works, witches were blamed for a myriad of misfortunes, which in this piece included scorched fields, rainfall, thunder and gales – in contrast to the Wielkopolska sample, where weather magic rarely featured. The author pleaded for people to remember God and his omnipotence, convinced that many of the occurrences blamed on witchcraft could be explained by medical theory. Interestingly, he claimed that Lutherans and Calvinists also suffered misfortunes but did not blame other people for their afflictions, and neither burned nor swam witches. Although this was patently untrue, by the mid-eighteenth century executions for witchcraft in predominantly Protestant countries were extremely rare. The author's words suggest either that witchcraft trials were widespread in Poland (or at least in Poznań at this time) or the use of literary hyperbole. However, the author had lived through one of the most intense periods of the persecution in Poland, but referenced no identifiable trials. He claimed to be of good conscience, did not drink and therefore did not fear witchcraft, writing, 'All alcohol infects, witches barely, there is no worse witchcraft than Ruthenian vines.'[51] The author was unstinting in his criticism of the conduct of witchcraft trials, from the practice of denunciation as a form of accusation to the use of torture, and claimed that documentation was falsified, incomplete evidence was allowed and women were accused of witchcraft when they were really drunkards. He heavily criticized the swimming of witches, outlawed by both secular and ecclesiastical law, which he illustrated with the story of a nobleman. When all the local women and girls of an age to speak were thrown into a pond and subsequently floated, he judged them guilty and rounded them up. A small boy was also thrown in and his father begged the nobleman for mercy, as he watched his son float. The moral of the story was that water, as vodka, deceives, which is an inherent pun in Polish, because *wódka* meant both 'vodka' and 'alcohol' and was derived from *woda*, 'water'.

Perhaps the most instructive narrative was to be found in the story of the priest who had returned to his home village for a visit when he spotted a crowd gathering in a field. They had taken a *baba*, 'crone', to burn for causing her neighbour's orchard to wither. Since she had already admitted to causing harm and failed to sink when subjected to swimming, she was certain to be tried as a witch and was subsequently being held in a barrel. The priest released her from the barrel and barely recognized her face as human, so wracked was she from torture. She admitted that she was a witch but claimed that she had done nothing wrong. She begged to be burnt, saying that she was going to meet her maker and she had admitted to the charges brought against her under torture, but nothing more.[52] This narrative is significant because, whether fact or fiction, the woman finally admitted to the priest that she had used mercury to harm the orchard because she hated her neighbour, but she denied any involvement with the diabolic. The judges were determined to believe that the woman had wielded supernatural power, even in the face of empirical evidence, so even though she had not harmed through witchcraft, her ill will or wish for revenge had to be punished. Unfortunately we have no evidence of any reaction to the more prosaic confession, but this episode confirms what the trial records say, that malice was a strong motive and furthermore was recognized as such by contemporaries.[53] The priest, as occasionally evident in witchcraft trials, stepped in and saved the woman, forcing the judges, whom he derided as 'simpletons, fit to keep neither sheep nor swine', and the accusers to pay the woman twenty Polish zloties. He treated them to an angry speech in which he pointed out that *kołtuń*, 'matted hair', illnesses, death and marital problems could all be caused without the aid of witchcraft. The author concluded that such mistakes were plentiful, as a result of which a large number of alleged witches had already perished at the stake. The final challenge of the work was to decide whether alcohol or witchcraft was the greater evil. Can we see in this a claim that they were equally widespread? He wrote, 'many people drink alcohol for no reason, even more beat the innocent for witchcraft'. However, since most witches were innocent, they would enter heaven and had an opportunity at the stake to repent and carry out a penance, but those who drank did not regret their alcoholism and would lose their souls. In short, alcohol ruined lives, marriages, the economy and health and the author finally concluded that witchcraft was the lesser evil.

Drama as a Coda

In the last work examined in this chapter, witchcraft was again used as a device, but this time to portray ignorance and superstition. *Czary, Witchcraft*, a drama by Father Franciszek Bohomolec, appeared in 1775, just one year before the laws on witchcraft were repealed. The drama was based on the Molièresque conceit of two pairs of lovers for whom marriages to undesirable partners had been arranged, indulging the typical conceit of the couples attempting to rectify the situation. Witchcraft was used here as a device through which to dissuade one of the partners from marrying the intended spouse and it was introduced indirectly – witches were mentioned but never seen and all accounts were mediated through hearsay. This drama derides belief in witchcraft and provides a comical scene in which the sophisticated theatre-going inhabitants of the capital could laugh at the superstitious beliefs of the rural gentry. In case any doubts remained, and a character declaims that it is madness to drown or burn a witch.

One of the characters, the country gentleman named Drągajło (tellingly a name of eastern origin), described a visit to Warsaw where he had seen small devils dancing. His companion promptly expressed shock that the people displaying these devils were not punished, but were actually paid. Drągajło was extremely superstitious and described how on his estate, after a witch had been sentenced and failed to drown, he was so convinced of her guilt that he ordered a stone be attached to her neck. Bohomolec also reflected the functional explanation of witchcraft, describing how the witch's neighbours had brought accusations following a quarrel, whilst we are also told that she had flown to Łysa Góra, 'Bald Mountain', and turned into a horse.[54] We have seen how the witch in drama began as a fantastic figure, making sacrifices to the Devil, flying and acting as the agent of a variety of devils, but by the end of the eighteenth century, belief in such a figure elicited ridicule. If this popular work is indicative of the attitudes of the literate population, then fear of the witch had effectively disappeared within educated circles and Bohomolec's play provided an appropriate coda to the era.

In this chapter, I hope to have demonstrated the value of exploring the broadest possible range of literature, which has illustrated shifts in literary paradigms of the witch that, under a variety of influences, produced differing figures. However, these varying portraits were based on a common framework of attributes, from which elements could be added and towards which attitudes could be either positive or negative. From a brief examination of drama and poetry, certain common attributes of the literary figure of the witch have been established. The witch was almost exclusively female, but rarely connected with seduction, prophecy or love magic, rather with maleficent acts, or even occasionally portrayed as a victim. She used herbs and a variety of rituals, which inhabited an ambivalent area of practices perceived as beneficent and/or maleficent, which concurs with my sample of witchcraft trials. The figure of the witch fulfilled a variety of functions, from pure entertainment, as a stock, almost pantomime character, to the instrument of social satire. Representations of the witch in agricultural and medical works shared more traits with the witch of ecclesiastical writings and of the trials, while the *Sowiźdrzał* witch at times was seen as a positive, even heroic, figure. Meanwhile, Szymonowicz, Opaliński and the anonymous author of *Wódka z elixierem* provided overviews that seem more realistic to us in the twenty-first century, but which also correlate with details in the trial records.

Willis's hypothesis has been partially proved, since the witch was undoubtedly a one-dimensional character within these genres of drama and poetry, but was neither noble nor seductive. This is probably because most of the works in which the witch appears as a character predate the trials and are not, like some English literature, influenced by pamphlet literature. The construct of the witch is clearly contaminated by a variety of traditions and the more ludic *Sowiźdrzał* witch and devil may display characteristics of Slavonic pagan beliefs, since they appeared comfortable within the everyday social and spiritual spaces of folk society, perhaps harking back to a time when supernatural power remained in the hands of the community. The overwhelming impression is of witches, not as the ultimate enemies of humankind, but as those who could effect change for a variety of reasons. The emergence of the domestic as a paradigmatic setting for witchcraft and the importance of female virtue continue to provide an environment within which witchcraft can be contextualized. A significant number of sources support the theory that revenge was a key motive, and crucially, that contemporaries recognized this, and most of the situations in which witches were portrayed in the sources examined in this chapter provided plausible and pragmatic excuses for the use of witchcraft.

Whilst it is clearly impossible in this research to gauge the impact these works had on readers, much can be gleaned from looking at them in terms of publication dates – whether they appeared prior to, during or after the peak of the persecution. Most of the works published before 1650 (Poklatecki, Januszowski and most of the *Sowiźdrzał*) used the witch and the Devil as literary devices and signifiers – trials had occurred by then but the persecution had not yet peaked. The hiatus in publishing works on witchcraft or demonology in other genres examined in this study suggests that between 1650 and 1725 few works were published on the subject. Perhaps tension caused by the persecution at its height engendered fear of writing on the subject, as Poklatecki suggested? Alternatively, with so much happening in Poland's history at the time, the witchcraft persecution may well have garnered little interest. In addition, no pamphlet material emerged, which also points to a lack of enthusiasm to draw upon the trials for literary inspiration, as the majority of Polish authors who wrote on witchcraft made no mention of identifiable Polish trials. So there is an absence of intertextual traces within Polish documentation and no circularity of information between the trials and demonology of any form. It is also possible that since many of the trials involved the local seigneur accusing and trying his servants or others, he may not have wanted such matters widely publicized. Another pertinent factor is that since it was common practice to burn criminal records, it is not entirely surprising that few details of Polish cases emerged, but it is notable that some practices condoned by the authors describe those which had formed the basis of accusations made against female witches in the sixteenth and early seventeenth centuries.

An analysis of the religious texts in the previous chapter reveals a general hiatus in the publication of new works on witchcraft between 1644 and 1745, with the exception of reprints and Tylkowski's work. A similar look at the publication histories of anti-witchcraft works shows that there was a gap between 1647 and 1742, and the only work published within that period was Czartoryski's, based on Vatican recommendations. Four categories can be distinguished among the works examined in this chapter published or reprinted during the peak of the persecution: works published anonymously (*Wódka z elixierem*); works written by the powerful (Opaliński's *Satires*); practical books containing remedies (Haur's works); and reprints of works that first appeared before the peak of the persecution (*Sejm piekielny* and Szymonowicz's *Sielanki*). We can only speculate that this indicates that only those authors who were not in a position to be intimidated or pilloried were free from the danger of publishing works on witchcraft. Finally those works published after the peak (Duńczewski's *Calendar* and Bohomolec's *Czary*) may be regarded as wonder books, intended for entertainment rather than as a didactic source. Bohomolec's play really indicates the final curtain for any credibility in witchcraft beliefs among the educated classes, and as such its discussions of witchcraft reflect the reality of an incident where women were swum, whilst at the same time providing an arena for witchcraft beliefs to be mocked as superstitious nonsense.

7
Sceptical Voices: Ending the Era

So far we have encountered a fluid conceptualization of the witch, in myriad guises, which contrasts sharply with the prevailing ecclesiastical orthodoxy that appropriated the witch as fundamentally evil. This ambiguity lies at the very heart of the doubt and confusion as to the true nature of a witch and of witchcraft and the appropriation of supernatural power, to which the authors examined in this chapter contributed greatly. The publication of anti-witchcraft literature in Poland fell into two main periods. The first, between 1639 and 1647, was dominated by the influential Poznań publishing house of Wojciech Regulus (Krzysztof Opaliński's tutor) which published Spee's *Cautio Criminalis* in Poland in 1647, several years after publishing the anonymous work *Czarownica powołana, A Witch Denounced* (1639), regarded by some as a polonized version of the *Cautio*. Some even claimed that Regulus himself was its author,[1] and in the same year he published Daniel Wisner's *Tractatus brevis de extramagi lamii veneticis*. It took more or less another hundred years for sceptical works to find another voice (at least from the works extant or mentioned). However, in between these periods many synodal decrees and pastoral letters were also published, and two such documents approved by Bishop Kazimierz Florian Czartoryski were distributed posthumously in 1682.

Since the Wielkopolska sample seems to be indicative of the wider phenomenon, then the witchcraft persecution was on the wane by the time the next extant work, *Przestrogi duchowne, Clerical Warnings*, by Serafin Gamalski was published in Poznań posthumously in 1742 (but written prior to 1733). Gamalski's objections were based on personal experience as a confessor to those condemned to the stake, like Spee over a century earlier, and his extraordinary work would certainly merit in-depth study. A few decades later in 1766, Bishop Andrzej Załuski's criticism of the swimming of witches in the work *Objaśnienie...*, *Clarification...*, appeared, followed by a theological polemic within the Polish Roman Catholic Church, initiated by the Jesuit Jan Bohomolec, brother of the author of the comedy *Czary, Witchcraft* (1775).[2] This polemic raged between 1772 and 1777, encompassing the repeal of the witchcraft statutes in 1776.

It is interesting to make a brief comparison between the anonymous work *Czarownica* and Spee's work, since the two entered Polish intellectual consciousness at approximately the same time. The bibliographer Estreicher observed that there was some debate as to whether this was a calque of Spee's work, but although the two pieces have much in common, further analysis shows this not to be the case. *Czarownica* was undoubtedly a pioneering Polish work, which demonstrated Poland's synthesis of European intellectual trends, and deserves analysis since it introduced many of the stock arguments influencing later works.

The Poznań Circle

The Poznań-published literature suggests the existence of a circle of intellectuals seriously engaged in discussion of the witchcraft persecution, who dissented from contemporary orthodox views on its justification. More importantly this group was of sufficient social standing or enjoyed significant enough patronage to be able to freely express and promote these views. Second, it identifies concerns in Poznań about witchcraft, raising the question of whether this was merely hyperbole or whether it corroborated the theory that trials for witchcraft were more numerous in Wielkopolska, as Polish historiography has often claimed. One of the most significant works to emerge from the city was *Czarownica powołana, A Witch Denounced* (1639), and the dedication of the Polish edition to Krzysztof and Łukasz Opaliński leads Estreicher to believe it was published at their behest. He supports his case further with the facts that: Krzysztof wrote the anti-witchcraft satire examined in the previous chapter, Regulus had been their tutor and Wisner's anti-witchcraft treatise (1639) was also dedicated to the brothers. However, Estreicher also makes a case for Andrzej Szołdrski, the Bishop of Poznań, as its author, on the basis that he wrote its *approbatio*. We must consider that whoever the author was, he was clearly influenced by Spee's work, published anonymously in Rinteln in 1631 and followed by a second edition a year later as well as Polish and German translations in 1647. I do not consider that *Czarownica* was merely a calque of the German work, but there are many similarities. Spee's work is much longer, consisting of 52 questions which examine a greater variety of issues and provide much more comprehensive answers. Not only does he criticize judges heavily, as does the Polish author, but he also attacks rulers and those who advise them badly. Spee's work remains one of the most damning attacks on all aspects of the dynamics of the witchcraft persecution. He magnificently employed his experience as confessor to the accused and his formidable command of logic and casuistry to argue effectively on behalf of the innocent against judicial abuses and to highlight the appalling conditions in which prisoners were kept. In contrast, the extensive material on popular witchcraft practices in *Czarownica* is not to be found in Spee.

The formulation of the questions in *Cautio* makes it clear that the author believes in the innocence of the victims in contrast to the more neutral language of *Czarownica*'s author. Both works use the familiar interrogative framework, but the Polish author poses only 13 questions, some of which focus on areas covered by the *Cautio*, such as: what constituted witchcraft; how judges should proceed against the accused without a great deal of evidential proof; on the basis of what signs or indications could a judge proceed to torture; the role of denunciation and whether this refuted the need for evidential proof; and the fate of those who died during torture or in jail. The Polish author also wrote at greater length about superstition, remedies and swimming witches as well as including examples from his own experience and from Wielkopolska, making this one of the most valuable Polish sources, although I have not been able to identify any trials from the sample. He, like other contemporaries, concluded that gossip and revenge were two of the key elements in the witchcraft persecution. He was writing just prior to the peak of the Polish persecution, but at a time when Poznań had experienced at least a dozen trials and Wielkopolska many more. Unlike the *Cautio*, generally credited with removing a significant aspect of the rationale for torture in Germany, *Czarownica* could lay claim to no such influence since its publication coincided with an increase in the number of trials in Wielkopolska, according to the sample. However, both works were referenced in a large trial in Gniezno between 1689 and 1690.[3] It was also highly unlikely that one work would have been able to deploy such influence on the Polish judicial system, not only because of its highly decentralized nature and lack of regulation, but also because the *szlachta* were more or less a law unto themselves. We cannot discount the possibility that *Czarownica* may have persuaded certain individuals of the evils of witchcraft trials, but, as Spee wryly pointed out in his introduction, it was generally a case of preaching to the converted.

Leaving aside the comparison, the first edition of *Czarownica* was dedicated to the respective mayors of Grodzisk and Kościan (both cities whose courts heard witchcraft trials) with an *approbatio* by Bishop Szołdrski of Poznań. A second edition incorporated Bishop K. F. Czartoryski's publication *Instrukcja rzymska* in 1680, which addressed the citizens of Poznań and a third similar edition was published in Gdańsk in 1714, addressed to its citizens. Like most authors of sceptical treatises, the author asserted that the primary focus of the work was not to discuss the ontology of witches, but to ascertain whether judges were abusing their powers in witchcraft trials. From the outset the author based his attack firmly on criticism of the judicial system, lamenting the widespread failure to abide by the correct judicial procedures and contrasting the frequent contravention of legal obligations with the opinions of many doctors who were 'well-versed in law' and Polish legal statutes.

Rarely have commentators delved beyond the frequently cited phrase from *Czarownica*'s opening page, 'our Wielkopolska has extraordinarily increased its number of executions for witchcraft, whether the witches are real or alleged', using it to extrapolate high numbers of deaths in Wielkopolska and Poland. Although the main focus of the work is the examination of judicial procedures, the author paints a sympathetic picture of witches as victims, through personal anecdotes, tales and descriptions of superstitions.[4] His writing suggested he was not persuaded that a conviction was any real indication of the individual's guilt and even the language used suggested a firm distinction between *powołana*, 'denounced' witches as opposed to fewer mentions of *wierutna*, 'real' witches, similarly to the anonymous author of *Wódka z elixierem*.

The author set a precedent for the next 150 years by discussing the 'appropriated jurisdiction' – in other words, the temporary statute passed in 1543. He quoted it at length in both Polish and Latin, suggesting that judges read the constitution. He also implied they had denied its very existence, and engaged in a discussion of the merits and precedence of customary law, constitutions, Magdeburg and Caroline Law and plain reason. Rather predictably he warned that the practical removal of jurisdiction over witchcraft trials from the clerical to the secular courts had led to widespread abuse, which would have been avoided had the clergy retained jurisdiction. We can only speculate as to whether he, as many since, truly believed that the statute was lawful, or whether he simply wanted to bolster his argument.[5]

If the author were a clergyman, as may be supposed, one might expect him to focus on theological rather than legal arguments against witchcraft.

However, just as subsequent critics, his focus is on the judiciary. He accuses judges of causing death, depriving people of their good reputation and destroying the health of the accused; their actions were leading them to eternal damnation. He proposed the mixed forum of both lay and clerics for the judgement of witchcraft trials. Although the author had strong doubts as to the legality of the judges' actions, he was concerned for the well-being of the judges' fate in the hereafter.

Paradoxically, here, as in many other works, it is through suggestions of good practice that we catch a glimpse of the shortcomings of the judicial system. He paints a keen picture of dereliction of judicial duty, where no proofs were established prior to sentencing and Groicki's guidelines were ignored. Most importantly the author refocused attention on the biblical message of mercy and the importance of innocence, citing Matthew 18. Having condemned the personal behaviour of judges as individuals, he moved on to the rife procedural abuses. He evidently sympathized with the accused and recognized that they were at a complete disadvantage in a system which denied them knowledge of the charges against them, access to a defence or even the appointment of an investigator, who was supposed to establish the fundamental details of the crime such as evidence, motives, location, time and method. Not only were the accused often not even conversant with the facts of their case, but denunciations were accepted on the flimsiest of pretences, with scant regard for probity. The author realized that women were often caught in a state of confusion with little time to think and no access to either the money or time to engage a legal defence, which significantly decreased their chances of obtaining justice. He was concerned that women or simple people without any education could generally neither speak for themselves nor act appropriately. Whilst he was convinced that a wise judge would investigate thoroughly and reject doubtful evidence, he also squarely placed the burden of responsibility on the judge, who, after all, had sworn an oath to uphold the law.[6]

Obviation of the law and judicial abuses were often justified by the treatment of witchcraft as a *crimen exceptum*, but the author warned that because the law recommended extreme caution in the inquisition of heretics to prevent loss of innocent life, those judging witches should take even more heed. To them it fell to ensure that the veracity of the accused's account was confirmed beyond all doubt and that the evidence had been freely admitted. He supported his call for diligent interrogation by citing Farinacci's dismissal of confessions obtained as the result of torture and the lack of a legal defence.[7]

One of the key results of circumventing legal stipulations (manifest in the liberal use of torture) was prolific denunciation – potentially a key mechanism for prolonging trials and stimulating further accusations (for example, Anna of Grodzisk denounced over 70 people).[8] The author felt it was open to abuse, with judges frequently suggesting names to the accused during torture, and he regarded denunciation as an inadequate basis for the torture or imprisonment of the denounced. It was to be avoided, he suggested, by restricting judges' interrogations to certain proven matters and accomplices. Although these questions were imperative to the trial, they should not have been used as an opportunity for the judge to suggest names or settle scores, and while most victims of denunciation were blameless, they were subsequently stigmatized by the damage done to their reputation. He did not believe that reported attendance at the sabbat was sufficient proof for being brought to trial – the inconsistency of denunciation and retraction was confirmed by trial records.[9] Although there are instances such as Kleczew and Gniezno 1689–90 to a lesser extent, where denunciation fuelled the dynamics of chain accusations, it is relatively rare that these chains of denunciations reached their exponential potential. Paradoxically, the Magdeburg Law stated that criminals, women and minors could not act as witnesses and testimony was not to be accepted from criminals, alcoholics or those with a bad reputation.[10] The author claimed that even if the denunciation had come from a 'real' witch, it needed evidential support in order for it to be used as the basis for arrest, torture or questioning. This was especially true if the person denounced had previously enjoyed a good reputation. However, the legal system contained an in-built gender bias because it was commonly believed that witches and other women forswore oaths and that a woman's nature was naturally revengeful and secretive. Many contemporaries and most witchcraft historians realized that the accused might have taken the opportunity to denounce personal enemies.[11]

Apart from denunciation, another method of 'identifying' witches, as we have seen, was to swim them. Although the practice had been banned by the church, there are plenty of descriptions of swimming women in trial records and popular belief in its efficacy lasted late into the nineteenth century.[12] The author lambasted those who believed in this practice as uneducated and ignorant of their *paternoster* and Decalogue. The sample trial records reveal that it was frequently local seigneurs who instigated this practice.[13] The author argued that swimming was a form of preliminary torture and reminded his readers of those considered by law to be exempt from torture. Young people and small children could not be tortured but could be shown the torture chamber. Second, old people could only be frightened but not tortured, but there was no clear definition of the terms 'old' or 'frightened'. Third, pregnant women were exempt from torture on the grounds of danger to the foetus, so questioning was to be postponed until after the birth. Finally, the privileged, defined as the nobility, senators, secretaries, princes, royalty or doctors were also exempt.

The author did not condemn the use of torture per se, merely its abuse, and in a view similar to those held elsewhere (in Rothenburg for example), he concluded that there was no justification for torture if the accused had already confessed or there was clear evidence of guilt.[14] Questioning was not to be too severe, the executioner was to apply the rack in such a way that the accused was able to withstand it, and should only apply torture once to establish the evidence and not inflict it again on the pretext of confirming evidence. The only justification for recommencing torture was if the victim subsequently retracted evidence admitted during torture. Tellingly at that point he described a victim who had suffered from depression and subsequently admitted everything in order to escape torture in the hope of a swift death. As we've seen from trials, on occasion the accused died during the trial, which prompted the question of where she should subsequently be buried. It was common practice to presume guilt and therefore deny the victim burial in consecrated ground. The author suggested three acceptable solutions. If the victim had committed suicide then her body ought to be burnt or hung; if she had freely admitted to carrying out witchcraft and then committed suicide, her corpse could be burnt, which merely pre-empted the death sentence; but in the third instance, if nothing had connected the person to the crime and she had died during questioning, then burial in consecrated ground ought to be permitted, in public and with normal church ceremonies.[15]

Although this work is essentially concerned with criticism of the judicial system, inevitably the author had to make clear his position on the existence of witches, and although he distinguished between 'real' and 'denounced' witches, he admitted that there was a fine line between a *zabobonica*, 'superstitious woman', and a witch. He regarded witchcraft as 'an insult to God's majesty and his sacred things and [its use] harms the possessions or health of those close to them'. He correctly observed that even pious women were superstitious, that such practices led people into the hands of the executioner and that those accused were commonly widows or others deemed to hold grudges. Unsurprisingly, contemporary opinion concurs with modern historiographical theories and research which reveal revenge as one of the frequently stated motives for bringing charges of witchcraft or denunciations.[16]

Czarownica's first question focused on definitions of witchcraft, but as we have seen, there was concern about the ambiguous nature of various practices, which prompted the author to speculate that there would not be enough trees from which to make stakes for every superstitious person sentenced. In an effort to differentiate between superstition and witchcraft, he cited a Thomist typology of superstition consisting of: idolatry or blasphemy; divination; and observations, cautions and the teaching of superstition.[17] He defined divination as news of secret things (including tracing stolen goods) and knowledge that could not be acquired naturally[18] and criticized those who claimed to be able to identify witches and the causes of bewitchment. This is particularly interesting because in my sample of trials there is no mention of professional or even informal witch-finders, a figure visible in many parts of Europe. In light of witchcraft accusations in sixteenth- and early seventeenth-century trials, it is instrumental to note that in 1639 this author regarded the pouring of wax or lead accompanied by holy invocations as superstition, rather than witchcraft, emphasizing the ambiguity with which such practices were regarded. However, the author also enumerated a diabolic litany of 'real' witches' acts that they performed for self-satisfaction, because of their controlling nature, or for profit (and this latter phrase is reminiscent of the incantations used in trials). In one example, a man sold his soul to the Devil for a wife but another settled for four red zloties, which was more in keeping with trial confessions, in which the Devil promised a cow or money.[19] The author believed that the Devil enabled witches to control the elements, as well as humans and cattle, and to affect the soul. The Devil controlled witches and their fantasies (perhaps a nod towards the Protestant theory of the delusional power of the Devil), which was why those accused freely admitted to such fantastic events before the courts. However, as in other works such as *Wódka z elixierem*, concurrent discourses separate treatment of 'real' witches from the plight of those wrongly accused of witchcraft. The author reversed the orthodox logic by claiming that it was the denunciation of innocent people and the actions of the judges that were diabolic, rather than the actions of the condemned. He also ascribed hallucinations (including sleepwalking, transvection and lycanthropy) to medical conditions or strange humours in the body and credited witches with healing (rarely mentioned in Polish literature but frequently in trials), claiming that it was one reason for doctors losing both custom and their reputation (another popular historiographical explanation for witchcraft in the twentieth century). He explained that counter-magic or healing was regarded as rebellion against the Devil, who would not allow one witch to throw off the spell of another.[20]

In *Czarownica*, we find an explicit discussion of gender in which the author admitted that the reputation of women had been much maligned in contemporary generalizations. He argued against the Polish proverb, 'there are as many clever wives as there are white crows', mentioning outstanding women in Poland's history such as Dąbrówka (Dubravka, a Czech princess), the wife of Mieszko who brought Christianity to Poland, and Jadwiga, a Polish queen who brought Christianity to Lithuania. He drew his answers from commonly consulted demonological authorities but then cited other less charitable views on women, such as Laymann's opinion that women were easier to deceive than men, unable to control their emotions or desires, credulous about their dreams and bore grudges. He also cited contemporary Galenic theory and the belief that women were thought to cause strange illnesses and harm to others when subject to unusual appetites, often connected with pregnancy, thus revealing some typical issues concerning the female body in the early modern period.

He also finds room to discuss remedies for witchcraft, mainly reproducing those from Leonardus Lessius, but perhaps the most interesting part of this section is the warning against so-called prophets who claimed to be able to identify the possessed and witches, whom the author regarded as magicians and cheats who deserved the gallows. This is a rare mention of witch-hunters in a Polish source, but I have found no evidence in the sample to support their existence. Instead of falling victim to such charlatans, the author stressed how important it was to follow doctors' advice and not to claim witchcraft was the cause of matters as trivial as an injured finger.[21] A substantial number of remedies were attributed to the Roman Catholic Church and its demonifuges (items or practices designed to protect against the Devil), which usually included: the sacraments, exorcisms, holy water, holy relics, incense, herbs, salt, bread, wheat, fervent prayer, alms, fasting and invocations to Jesus, Mary and guardian angels. The author reminded readers to put their trust completely in God, who would not let a hair fall from their head, and concluded by describing the complexity of trying witchcraft cases, due in no small part to the spiritual danger posed to the judge. This anonymous author set the tone for succeeding critical works but, more importantly, he was exceptional in furnishing the reader with anecdotes and examples of Polish witchcraft and superstitions.

Daniel Wisner's *Tractatus brevis de extramagi lamii, veneticis* (1639)

Wisner was another cleric and prominent member of the Poznań circle associated with Krzysztof and Łukasz Opaliński and dedicated the *Tractatus* to Krzysztof, with a long paean to the greatness of the Opaliński clan. Although published in 1639, it was written a year earlier and Wisner made it clear that the tract was intended to be didactic, warning of the disturbing nature of the material and that it was not to be read for amusement or wonder. Perhaps this was a reference to other works that had used the motifs of witchcraft to entertain or as an oblique reference to the Polish translation of the *Malleus Maleficarum*, published in 1614. Wisner's primary aims were to instruct ignorant judges, rescue the innocent and salvage reputations from infamy (echoing *Czarownica powołana*), and he painted a Poland rife with magic, superstition and sacrilege. Setting the tone of the work in the introduction, he described the bad conditions often found in prisons, torture carried out in woods, the abuse of torture and the use of hot irons. His main recommendation was that a mixed forum should hear trials for blasphemy, with ecclesiastical courts wielding superior jurisdiction (as in *Czarownica*). Although he stopped short of calling for a return to ecclesiastical jurisdiction, he viewed the ecclesiastical and secular legal systems as 'twin gladiators' working together to defend Christians. This supports Pilaszek's views on the temporary nature of the 1543 statute.

Wisner's attack on witchcraft trials was also located within criticism of the abuse of judicial procedures rather than in theological debate, and he was in no doubt about the existence of witches, but in common with the author of *Czarownica*, he distinguished between those innocently accused of witchcraft and 'real' witches. He began his deconstruction by criticizing the arrest of suspects (providing one of the few descriptions of Polish conditions) and the squalid conditions of prisons. He wrote that the book is

> to instruct those judges who are without verse, to rescue the innocent in mind and body and those of good name from infamy... People are imprisoned in the most miserable places, their hands and legs are tied with a thick rope and with hot iron *ligatis propinando*. Then they are led to the woods, tortured... and a great number of women suffer from miscarriages.[22]

He described how many honest men and matrons had been violently dragged out of their houses to be detained in extremely bad conditions and pointed out that according to the Second Constitution of Emperor Maximillian I and Charles V from 1548, the accused were entitled to receive advice about questioning and defence representation. He rehearsed the recommendations that all the relevant points in a case be recorded during questioning and recommended that no questioning ought to proceed without having established those vital points, the full circumstances and the names of any accomplices. Furthermore, details about the accused's reputation, their known enemies and the consistency of their confessions were also to be recorded. Wisner, underlining the importance of reputation, in common with the anonymous author of *Czarownica*, bemoaned the loss of a person's good reputation without proof and the scandal that ensued after such an accusation. Therefore, he regarded it as a fundamental point that the judge disregarded any *mala fama*, 'bad reputation' attributed to the accused in the absence of clear proof. Whilst Wisner praised those who judged according to the law, in good conscience, with legitimate documentation and witnesses, he didn't hesitate to accuse the majority of erroneous and arbitrary judgements.[23]

The similarity of Wisner's criticisms to those voiced in *Czarownica* fuelled suggestions that he was its author, although as we have seen, these criticisms were widespread. Wisner decried the use of criminals' confessions, witness testimony as proof, interrogation methods and the absence of any advocate for the defence as well as the obvious hostility between the various parties, denunciation and the use of torture to elicit a confession. He dismissed the hereditary principle invoked to accuse the children of the accused and advocated mercy for the innocent, even at the risk of overlooking the guilty. Wisner repeatedly stressed the importance of proof as 'clear as daylight', without which trials should be declared null and void, and suggested that a denunciation had to concur with at least two other witness accounts in order to be admitted as evidence. Any subsequent confession from the denounced extracted during torture was not to be admitted as a reliable form of evidence. He pointed out that there was often insufficient evidence to warrant torture, viewing multiple sessions of torture as tyrannical and the swimming of witches as 'purgatory by water'. He also dismissed at length the presumption among judges of failure to cry as proof of guilt and questioned the retraction of a denunciation at the stake by dismissing the assumption that those about to meet their maker would always tell the truth.[24]

Roman Instructions and Polish Concerns

Bishop Kazimierz Florian Czartoryski (1620–74) was instrumental in proposing and passing synodal statutes critical of erroneous judicial practices apparent in witchcraft trials. Scion of a family that was to become one of Poland's most prominent, his letter from 1669, known as *Mandatum pastorale ad universum clerum et populum Dioecesis suae de cantelis in processu contra sagas adhibendis die XI Aprilis* or *Universo populo*, was published posthumously in 1682 together with the Vatican's *Instrukcja rzymska o sądach y processach jako maią być formowane ... przeciw czarownicom ...*, *Roman Instructions on How Courts and Trials against Witches Are to be Formed*.

The *Instructions* open with the usual catalogue of criticisms of judicial error, but since it was originally issued from the Vatican, the focus in this first part of the work was on the obviation of the rights of the Holy Office of the Inquisition, which also served to link the crimes of witchcraft and heresy. Rome expressed concern for judges' consciences, but the focal dissatisfaction was with their ineptitude, mistakes, abuse of torture, failure to obtain clear evidence and general incompetence. The instructions offered alternative empirical explanations for judges who tended to see witchcraft in all misfortunes, including credible medical diagnoses for common illnesses often regarded as witchcraft. Witchcraft was not to be dismissed out of hand, but regarded as a last resort, when reputable doctors had exhausted all other possibilities. When illness struck, the doctor was to enquire among members of the household before a diagnosis was offered, and only then if he remained convinced of witchcraft was the judge to proceed.

The *Instructions* recommended taking the accused to prison, questioning them about the circumstances and producing evidence of guilt. The accused's house was to be searched not only for items that could be used as evidence, but also for holy books, holy palms, incense, candles, gold and oil. If the oil contained fat, it was not to be automatically assumed that it was for the purposes of witchcraft, while items (including feathers, a ball of wool and needles) found in a bed were not necessarily signs of witchcraft, but, as the author logically points out, were part of women's domestic accoutrements. It was even suggested that the Devil himself had placed such items there in order to throw suspicion upon a certain individual, since nails and needles were often vomited up by the possessed.

The themes raised in the *Roman Instructions* reflect concerns common to those found in Polish and other European works. The shortcomings of judges and their manifest failure to adhere to legal regulations were contrasted with recommendations for appropriate behaviour. While the probity of evidence admitted by judges was examined here, as elsewhere, particular attention was paid to the acceptance of gossip and ramblings of the possessed as evidence that ought to have been ruled inadmissible, implying that they were not. When inefficient exorcists asked the possessed to identify witches, they gave a voice to the Devil who identified in which food or drink the possession had been transmitted and its donor, leading to false denunciations against many innocent people. The author concludes that judges often conducted cases against the accused on the Devil's evidence and firmly believed that their view of possession was deeply erroneous. The Church's considered view was that the possessed had been afflicted with God's permission, not through witchcraft, and it was clear that some people falsely believed themselves to be possessed and subsequently carried out a variety of deceptions. Gossip, slander and the denunciation of ugly old women were condemned and not to be taken seriously as proof of witchcraft in isolation.[25]

Crucially the work claimed that divination and incantations did not necessarily constitute apostasy, and therefore these practices were not automatically regarded as witchcraft, in contrast to Wielkopolska trials in the sixteenth and seventeenth centuries. Moreover, there was support for not judging women as apostates since it was believed that they naturally had more of a tendency towards superstition, fulfilling the will of others and indulging in machinations dealing with love and hatred. Although the *Instructions* tell us that judges required a true sign of guilt from God, there was no indication of what that might have been. However, this work does provide a rare insight into arrest and prison procedures, with the author recommending that to avoid problems in trials, arrests ought to be made on an individual basis rather than en masse and that prisoners should not be held together in one prison. The prisoners should not be promised forgiveness in return for leniency or clemency, nor be allowed to admit to experiences that they had merely dreamt, whilst questioning should only be carried out during the court session without undue pressure. The accused should be fully conversant with the charges against her and be asked to disclose known enemies and disputes, as well as personal information, such as: her lifestyle, sexual life, frequency of communication and confession, knowledge and use of superstitions, and from where she had acquired this knowledge. The accused ought to have recourse to a legal representative or at least to an official from the Holy Office who could find them a representative, and, crucially, those charged should be given time to recollect and ponder their plight.[26]

Naturally, the use and abuse of torture was as much a concern in the Vatican, if not more so, as it was in Poland, but Rome was able to call upon its institutional power and stipulated that torture was not to be carried out before the Holy Office had been consulted. Questioning was not to be conducted during or before torture and if the accused began to speak, it was crucial to record their words. Although the use of weights attached to the legs was forbidden, the use of the strappado was permitted. Torture was only to be repeated in the most serious cases and only after consultation with the Sacred Congregation or the provincial Holy Office, but was to last no longer than one hour. Failure to cry during torture was not admissible proof of being a witch, and confessions extracted during torture had to be treated with the utmost care, especially if women had admitted to apostasy, turning to the Devil or attendance at the sabbat. The judge was to identify whether there was a case for apostasy on the basis of sabbat details found in confessions. Subsequently, he was to either verify the claims or dismiss them. Discrepancies in the accused's accounts were to be regarded as an indication that they had fabricated the confession out of fear of torture, and in such cases the judge was advised neither to ask questions nor admit evidence based on denunciations or claims of sabbat attendance. In these *Instructions*, it is clear that the sabbat was regarded as a delusion caused by the Devil, which interfered with the conduct of witchcraft trials.[27]

The *Mandatum pastorale* also known as *Universo populo* was Czartoryski's addition to the *Instructions* and he continued to criticize the judiciary, noting the role of revenge as a contributing factor to witchcraft trials. He described how many judges would charge, torture and execute a woman for *maleficia*, which were clearly the result of drunkenness, bad hygiene or bad food. He criticized over-reliance on the possessed for information, swimming women to identify them as witches, lax provision of a defence (permitted to all other criminals) and the frequent suppression of evidence. Czartoryski went as far as to condemn all these travesties as the work of the Devil, claiming that the Father of Lies had encouraged people to harm the innocent and deceived them into believing they had feasted in palaces and attended sabbats. This work provides a lot of information about how witchcraft trials had been conducted in the first half of the seventeenth century and supports much of the evidence discussed throughout this study. According to Czartoryski, appeals to a higher court were not uniformly permitted and new forms of illegal torture were applied to elicit the answers desired (supporting findings from Wielkopolska). He suggested that torture was an excellent opportunity to suggest names to victims at their most vulnerable and described chains of denunciations running into tens of victims that often encompassed whole villages, warning that arrests only came to a halt when the judge himself or his wife was the next to be tortured.[28] He urged judges not to hand people over for torture lightly, not to rely on an individual's reputation or the word of the possessed and not to subject suspects to swimming. Predictably he lamented the loss of clerical jurisdiction over witchcraft, blaming it for loss of lives and likening it to the biblical notion of weeding out the wheat from the chaff.

Despite the severity of his criticisms, Czartoryski was at pains to stress that true witchcraft ought to be punished accordingly, but he was also swift to threaten inept judges with excommunication. He, like others, was concerned that those who died from severe torture in prison were denied burial in consecrated ground and buried under the gallows, even if they had neither admitted their guilt nor been convicted, and pointed out that it also misled the simple folk, who believed that this was justice. Czartoryski wrote this missive to highlight these issues and to inform the masses about witchcraft. It was to be hung up on church doors, read out and impressed onto the minds of the community.[29]

Where God Builds a Church, the Devil Places a Chapel

In 1742 the Bernadine Serafin Gamalski's (c. 1675–1733) work *Clerical Warnings for Judges, Investigators, and Investigators of Witches, Written by Father Serafin Gamalski*, dedicated to Archbishop Szembek, was published in Poznań. It was another work highly critical of the judiciary and another work published posthumously. Gamalski, like the rest of the authors examined previously, denied neither the appropriateness of the stake or the sword as the death sentence for witchcraft, nor the existence of real witches, and wrote, 'let judges and inquisitors learn caution and circumspection in matters pertaining to alleged witchcraft from the example of his Highness [Szembek] so that prisons will not be filled with the innocent and that the guilty will not escape'. Thus Gamalski's arguments did not differ so very greatly from those of his predecessors a century previously, despite the fact he had lived through the peak of the persecution. He revealed a more enlightened, empirical approach, while somehow maintaining a Roman Catholic theological belief in witchcraft.

As a confessor to women who had been accused of witchcraft, Gamalski had a rather more intimate view of witchcraft trials, but supported his criticisms without sentiment. He condemned the torture of witches because it broke secular law, Church law and natural law, urging adherence instead to Matt. 18, but he reversed some of the previous arguments in his devastating critique of lay magistrates. Gamalski invoked the wrath of God, not upon the witches, but on those who persecuted them, claiming that the laments of the tortured could be heard by God and that his anger was aroused at the sight of stakes, quoting accounts of God's wrath in Exod. 3.9, and Pss 40 and 37. However, he contrasts the ignorance and incompetence of secular judges in meting out punishment with that which they would be dealt at the Last Judgement, and so transforms the witch into the righteous victim with a claim on God's mercy. Having set such a scene Gamalski launched his attack on public prosecutors, claiming that unjust courts would be punished. Interestingly, he regarded the incompetent judiciary and torture of witches as elements unique to Poland. Echoing the author of *Czarownica*, he wrote,

> One does not hear of such fulsome excesses and sudden and rather illegitimate executions in other nations and states as only in our unfortunate Poland, where there will soon be insufficient woods and forests for all the stakes, and probably in the towns and small towns and villages, people will more swiftly cease to be moved by such fires.

Gamalski explained that he was not defending real witches, whom he defined as those who had contracted a pact with and sworn to serve the Devil. He discussed the connection between witchcraft and heresy and recommended that Inquisitors of the Holy Office be summoned when a suspected witch had been arrested, in keeping with the *Roman Instructions*. He noted that prior to sentencing, suspects 'had been kept in barrels, logs, stocks, benches, and in lay judges' prisons'. This is one of the most reliable accounts we have, considering his experience as a confessor.[30]

Gamalski was not reticent in suggesting causes of the persecution – revenge, fantasy, melancholy and hypochondria. He questioned the reasons, needs and occasions behind accusations and denunciations, writing, 'works that simple folk understand as miraculous should not always be left in this erroneous belief'. As he pointed out, on the one hand people were fooled by human artifice, which they often mistook for supernatural events, and on the other even judges made similar mistakes, confused as to whether a particular matter was *ex natura rerum* or diabolical. The author prudently recommended erring on the side of caution and did not condemn the use of prayers in conjunction with natural medication, concluding that they often worked, which appears close to condoning practices regarded as witchcraft in the sixteenth and seventeenth centuries by both judges and treatise writers.[31] However, he did emphasize the need to investigate cases thoroughly, suggesting that judges were confused about what constituted natural astrology, superstition, divination, *vanae observationes* and *sortilegia*, although he clearly saw little need to define the terms for the educated audience he was addressing. This confusion, he observed, also extended to ordinary people, because either they did not understand the so-called books of justice, or they were illiterate, which echoed Czartoryski's concerns. He argued against the use of torture where there was strong evidential proof and recommended it be applied only as a last resort, blaming the inefficiency of the Polish legal system. Although the regulation limiting torture to one hour had been confirmed by the Holy Congregation in 1657, in Poland it could be prolonged to two or three hours, or even half a day, and continued into a second or third day. This, he argued, was the real work of the Devil. His critique extended to demolishing many witchcraft beliefs. For example, he did not believe that the Devil helped suspected witches to sustain torture nor that the inability to cry or speak was any indication of guilt. The reason that victims were unable to cry, he wrote, was probably that they had already shed so many tears at their arrest that their humours had been affected. Their silence he attributed to sheer fright and pain.[32]

The Bernadine confessor clearly regarded denunciation as the work of the Devil, whose aim was to send as many innocent people as possible to the stake, while both the executioner and the seigneur profited. He noted, but proffered no real reason for, the gender disparity, quoting the popular Polish proverb, 'where the Devil fears to tread, send a woman'.[33] He also disputed the questioning of women about the sabbat, which he believed should only occur after sentencing, when the convicted witch was preparing for execution, and he cast doubt over retractions and denunciations made at the stake. The author believed in innocent until proven guilty, deeming it essential to establish the truth of evidence presented and to detect any rancour, anger, enmity or jealousy between those involved in the case, or evidence of a deal, bribery or property disputes.[34] He raised concerns similar to Wisner's in regard to witnesses and viewed foreswearing with the same severity as murder. His accounts reveal that the accused were beaten, tortured, tied up in prison and forbidden to have visitors, and they support claims by other authors that the accused were denied a defence lawyer or any legal representation, because judges claimed witchcraft was a *crimen exceptum*. The work ended with a plea to judges to open their eyes to the truth and dismiss false evidence. Despite his severe criticism of judges, Gamalski acknowledged the difficulty of sitting in judgement over witchcraft trials and called for judges to be far more rational, contrasting the situation with that of similar felonies heard before a jury which warranted the right of appeal (supporting the presumption that appeals in witchcraft cases were rare, at least in Wielkopolska). Gamalski concluded by challenging the orthodox logic, claiming that since those accused of witchcraft were tortured, dragged to the gallows and denied legal representation and advice, it was indeed the court which had been possessed by the spirit of 'evil, ignorance and cruelty', and ought to be exorcized.[35] Thus, he claimed, the legal system, the key instrument of God's justice, had been subverted by the Devil – the instrument of the Devil was the judge and the witch was a victim worthy of God's pity.

The Swimming of Witches

Bishop Załuski was a prominent clergyman, already renowned for speaking out against the persecution of practices erroneously mistaken for superstition at synods. His work *Objaśnienie*, published in 1766, was a longer commentary on the condemned practice of swimming witches. As his sceptical predecessors, he argued that courts were lax and levels of evidential probity were low, resulting in the deaths of many innocent people, so his solution was an increase in clerical visitations to root out *gusła* and *zabobony*, 'superstition'. The author condemned both divination and locating lost items but recognized that many people unwittingly practised witchcraft through ignorance, reminding priests that it was their responsibility to report those people and to use the array of methods at their disposal such as sermons, the confessional and the threat of the punishment awaiting transgressors. This work also discusses resolving such issues within the immediate community and the passing down of superstitious practices through families and within communities. Załuski believed that most individuals acted out of ignorance and custom and therefore they needed to be made conscious of their sin. There were also some who did not regard their actions as wrong, because they healed without diabolic intervention. The cleric dismissed this, warning that the Roman Catholic Church meted out great punishment to those who indulged in such practices.

Załuski described swimming (the Lateran Council of 1215 had forbidden exorcism and benediction before swimming, as a mark of the church's disapproval) as tying the witch up and throwing her from a bridge and claimed it was natural for the victim to sink, thus fatally proving her innocence. Although it usually took place in a pond or river, swimming was also practised in a large vat of water, and as we have seen, there are many accounts of it in the Wielkopolska sample. Załuski effectively discredited swimming and noted cases where innocent individuals had floated, claiming that in Poland between ten and twenty women at a time could be sentenced to the stake following this type of test. Disappointingly he provided no details of identifiable cases, although he was writing a decade before the witchcraft acts were repealed and at a time when the persecution had virtually ended. He condemned the execution of so many women, which had fuelled debate among the learned, and mocked Scribonius's theory that since witches were possessed by the Devil, they were lighter than others. Załuski also expressed concern about the shaving of witches prior to trials and the number of deaths occurring in prison as the result of torture (confirming the tendency to subsequently burn the bodies). The bishop ended his work by reiterating the primacy of clerical jurisdiction over witchcraft cases, which would have recommended a penance appropriate to the severity of the crime, such as fasting and prayer.[36] This was a work which had little discernible impact on the persecution, published as it was in 1766 when the persecution was already on the decline, but it provides an interesting commentary on swimming, supporting findings in the sample that it was reasonably widespread.

The Figure of the Devil

The Jesuit Jan Bohomolec was one of the only Polish authors to truly engage with the metaphysical nature of the problem of witchcraft, and one of his works, *The Devil in His Figure from the Occasion of the Question if Vampires Are Revealed to the Eyes: Part One* (1772), synthesized the views of selected philosophers and theologians displaying a large degree of scepticism (similarly to his playwright brother). Although the title indicated that the treatise dealt with the question of vampires, in fact it also provided a basis for the discussion of the nature of spirits, the Devil and his powers. In contrast to the other works examined in this chapter, Bohomolec's argumentation against witchcraft beliefs did not criticize judicial abuses, but instead explored the logic and philosophies of Leibnitz, Wolff, Spinosa and Descartes. In addition, by 1772 trials for witchcraft in Poland had all but come to an end and more sophisticated Enlightenment arguments had emerged, which turned on the interaction of the spiritual and material worlds and the true nature of the functions of the body. Bohomolec's more forensic approach dismissed a variety of beliefs, such as metamorphosis (described as a reflection of people's credulity to which he had never discovered witnesses), the Devil's capacity to form a baby in the womb, a witch's ability to cure and the veracity of the Devil's pact. As a cleric, Bohomolec's dilemma lay in combining scepticism about witchcraft beliefs with the logic of the mechanical nature of the body, whilst maintaining a belief in God's omnipotence and avoiding any denial of the existence of witches. The key to his argument over the interstices between the spiritual and corporeal was the pre-eminence of God and the role of the soul, so he argued that the spirit could neither move nor control material, and like other authors examined in this chapter, used biblical references to differentiate between genuine miracles and works of the Devil.

However, one of the most pressing arguments was the nature of apparently supernatural occurrences, fuelling accusations of and belief in witchcraft. Some maintained that the Devil executed his power over people through external agents such as alcohol, poison and wine, and others claimed that he played upon the build-up of emotions such as anger, laughter or tears. Thus, the Devil had no real power over human reason and will but could only take advantage of an altered state or vulnerability caused by fever, drunkenness or sleep. Like other authors, Bohomolec defined a tripartite typology of miracles: *rzecz dziwna*, 'a strange thing', which cannot be explained; *niezwyczajna rzecz*, 'an unusual thing' which rarely happens, and *cud*, 'a miracle' such as healing the sick or exorcism. There were also references to traditional biblical accounts of supernatural events such as the flight of Habakkuk, that of Jesus and the familiar tale of Simon Magus.[37]

Bohomolec was one of the only Polish authors to employ concrete examples in his discourse, seeking to present proof to support his arguments, as opposed to Chmielowski, whose 'proofs' were somewhat fantastic. However, Bohomolec noted a correlation between poor, uneducated and superstitious people and belief in witchcraft. Reflecting the unclear nature of the provenance of supernatural powers, he attributed the ability to heal and perform exorcisms to witches, Jews and pagans. Several cases, such as that of Marthe Brossier, Elizabeth Blanchard (Garlick), the dévotes of Chambon and the events of Loudun, were cited to prove the fraudulent nature of accounts of witchcraft and possession and Bohomolec suggested that belief in Bald Mountain had been fostered through confusion between reality, dreams and the many tales heard in childhood. He illustrated this with an anecdote about two poor old and simple women accused of witchcraft. He describes them as under the delusion that they had flown to Bald Mountain and as suffering from a form of mental illness. There were many pages devoted to fantastic accounts of the sabbat and other beliefs associated with witchcraft and possession, presumably to paint a picture of the incredulity of the masses, as Bohomolec concluded with the words, 'whoever believes such tales knows neither the human heart nor himself'. Following much earlier sceptical voices such as Weyer and Scot, the Jesuit supported their views that some witches were victims of melancholy and suggested that the visit of an *incubus* could be explained by a thickening of blood in the lungs and head, which restrained breathing. One of Bohomolec's most ironic observations was that there were fewer accounts of witchcraft in Italy and France, where wine was drunk; but in the cold northern areas such as Scandinavia, Westphalia, Mecklenberg, Poland, Pomerania and Prussia, where beans, peas, fat and brown bread were eaten, there was an abundance of witches.[38] This view, expressed after the decline in European persecutions, supported opinions that Poland had indeed experienced a notable witchcraft persecution.

Bohomolec wrote at great length on the details of witchcraft belief, devoting much time to love magic. He described a common love-charm, which consisted of drying a hippomanes (the black fleshy substance said to occur on the forehead of a new-born foal) in a newly glazed pot in an oven which had been used to bake bread. He also claimed that certain phrases could evoke power, emphasizing the power of the written word in a predominantly illiterate society, and described how some people placed their faith in sewing certain words into a collar. Instructions were clear and had to be followed precisely. For example, Bohomolec described love magic which made use of bones bitten by flies from the right side of a frog (those from the left side would arouse hatred), smearing one's hands with ivy juice and touching the object of desire and carrying the head of the mushroom *lepiota procera* on the stomach. He also described a pomade made from the marrow of the left leg of a wolf and a grey amber and cypress powder, which should be given to the object of desire to smell.[39] In contrast to the popular tales of love magic usually ascribed to women, Bohomolec described at length the practices aimed at men worried about their wives' fidelity. One such example instructs a man to dry the heart of a pigeon and the head of a frog, and rub the subsequent powder onto his wife while she slept, and on waking she would reveal everything in her heart. Alternatively, the querent could put a frog in water, having removed its tongue, and then place it on the heart of the sleeping woman. The heart of a toad placed over her left breast, the heart of a blackbird or the heart and leg of an owl found in a hoopoe's nest, would, if placed on the head of the sleeper, have the same effect. A man wishing to discover whether his wife was faithful was instructed to put a diamond on the forehead of the sleeper: an honest woman would merely wake up, but an unfaithful woman would leap up out of the bed suddenly. Alternatively, the querent could collect a sunflower seed in August when the sun was in Leo, wrap it in a bay leaf with a wolf's tooth, put it in a church, and the woman who had been unfaithful would not be able to leave the church until the charm was removed. As with so many of the more elaborate practices ascribed to witches, or described as witchcraft, the printed sources again far outdo the trial records in their imaginative descriptions and Bohomolec's descriptions contrast with rare mentions of love magic in my sample.

In Poland, as elsewhere, accusations of deploying love magic were readily whispered against the powerful women of the court. Sigismund August's (1548–72) court was rife with gossip against his mistresses, his wife, Barbara Radziwiłłówna and his Italian mother Bona Sforza.[40] First, the king's mother was accused of employing a witch, whom Sigismund subsequently had arrested and taken to Brest to be burnt. However, after the king's astrologer, Proboszczewicz, warned him against fire in Brest, the witch was moved to Dubnik for execution. Sigismund's wife was also accused of using love magic to seduce the monarch, because of his deep love for her and because this match had been greatly opposed by most of the magnates except, of course, the Radziwiłłs. The accusations continued to dog the monarch when the influence wielded by his mistresses Susanna Orłowska and Barbara Giżanka was also blamed on witchcraft.[41]

Practices connected with love magic certainly survive in Polish customs to this day. Recommendations of popular rituals have always been exchanged, mainly among female members of a community in attempts to predict the identity of future husbands, to attract a partner, sour love for another or restore love lost. There is little doubt that such superstitions and rituals were employed predominantly by women and again this is an area fraught with ambiguity. One woman's efforts to make the object of her affections fall in love with her might impact negatively on another woman or on the object of her desire. We know from some trials in the fifteenth century that men claimed to have been the victims of love magic in order to cast off a lover or a wife and they also blamed their illnesses on a rejected lover seeking revenge and using witchcraft.[42]

The Context of the Sceptical Tradition

Although Polish authors, like most European critics of the persecution, focused on abuses of the judicial system, they advanced the specific argument on what some regarded as inappropriate jurisdiction, which limited debate somewhat and did not make for such a rich range of argument as that found elsewhere. However, the Polish emphasis on criticism of the judicial system echoes similar voices in the rest of Europe and particularly in Germany. The late sixteenth and seventeenth century saw a range of critical works including: Godelmann's *Tractatus de magis, veneficis et lamiis* (1591); Tanner's *Tractatus theologicus* (1617); Laymann's *Tractatus alter theologicus de sagis et veneficis* (1625); Spee's *Cautio Criminalis* (1631); and Meyfart's *Die Hochwichtige Hexen-Erinnerung* (1666), which not only succeeded in demolishing many of the previous arguments but also cited real cases as evidence. In contrast, Polish sources contained little discussion of the complex theology of witchcraft, demonic agency or linguistic interpretation.

From the middle of the seventeenth century in Europe, there was a slow trend towards demolishing the previous rationale underpinning belief in witchcraft and the focus on epistemology and rational, empirical truth precluded demonic existence, let alone demonic agency, undermining the ideological framework of witchcraft. However, characteristically for the witchcraft debate, there were complexities and differences in approaches and the old targets still remained popular – incompetent judges, abuse of the use of torture, lack of a defence lawyer and calling hostile witnesses. Although sceptical voices were an integral part of debate by the time the Polish witchcraft persecution began to gather momentum towards the end of the seventeenth century, there is little sign that they were greatly influential on the persecution, even though the ideas clearly permeated Polish sceptical debate. To recap, the first Polish voices against the persecution were published in Poznań in 1639, shortly after the works of Spee and Meyfart appeared.

The contexts within which the attacks were couched reveal much about the persecution and the clear limits within which sceptical discussion ranged in Poland. Surprisingly, one of the consequences of the main critics being members of the Roman Catholic clergy was that with the exception of Jan Bohomolec's work, the anti-witchcraft debate in

Poland did not explore the ontology of witches and witchcraft per se in the wake of sceptical European counterparts of the sixteenth century, Weyer and Scot. There was also no debate on the linguistic terminology used or on readings of Exodus, and instead the major framework for criticism was the judicial system's inherent abuses (in common with other European sources). I would suggest that in Polish writings, discussion of the appropriation of jurisdiction over witchcraft trials by the secular courts, to a large extent, suffocated any further development of an anti-witchcraft debate. Critics assumed that the solution lay in the reclamation of judicial jurisdiction by the clergy and avoided all but the shallowest of theological debate. Evidently, the paradox of anti-witchcraft rhetoric lay in the difficulty of criticizing the inherently non-empirical crime of witchcraft, when it was far safer to criticize the empirical abuse meted out by the judiciary. As the period progressed, a definite shift in the discourse of blame emerged as the binary paradigms of bad witch–good judge broke down and the idea of punishing the witch as the most heinous enemy of God and humankind gave way to a concern for the loss of innocent lives – Matt. 13 replaced Exod. 22.18 as the biblical citation of choice. It was evident to contemporaries that personal motives such as jealousy, revenge and perceived lapses in a range of female responsibilities played a part in naming suspects and could increase one's chances of being denounced.

The chronology of the publication of anti-witchcraft material also requires further investigation. There was evidently an enlightened circle of discussion around the publishing house of Wojciech Regulus, patronized by the Opaliński brothers in the mid-seventeenth century, and particularly between 1639 and 1650. Significantly, opposition to witchcraft was barely raised in public again until after the peak of the persecution in 1742 (although Gamalski's work was written prior to 1733). This coincides with one of the darkest periods in Poland's history and a point at which power was greatly decentralized, to the advantage of the nobility. The ire of the intellectuals and the Roman Catholic Church found many more pressing targets in an era that culminated in the partitions of Poland itself: it may well have been prudent to avoid speaking out about witchcraft if a majority supported the persecution. However, in comparison with some areas of Europe, Poland heard significant opposition to the persecution, possibly due to the relative autonomy of the nobility, especially enjoyed by the magnates. For example, enlightened nobles, such as the Opaliński brothers, enjoyed sufficient financial and political freedom. While decentralization and the power of the nobility enabled the persecution to occur, it also allowed opposition because the nobility was virtually omnipotent in its own possessions, as the Polish proverb *ja Pan, ja prawo*, 'I am Lord, I am Law', indicated. However, it is striking that both Czartoryski's and Gamalski's works (published during the peak of the persecution) were published posthumously and that *Czarownica* and *Wódka z elixirem* were published anonymously. We can only speculate as to whether this indicates caution on the part of both authors and publishers. Wiślicz suggests that because witchcraft trials were not mentioned in the usual town record books, that perhaps witchcraft trials were not discussed in 'writing or speech' and that the victims were not mentioned except during the intense time of the persecution:

> The subjective reality of witchcraft trials could not be a permanent context of human life, but it remained as a potential manner of describing the world. Its internal logic, different from ordinary [sic], allowed only for complete commitment – by accepting it one accepted all its possible consequences. Therefore in everyday life people tried to avoid any reference to the world of witchcraft trials, however, at the time of any crisis or even any disturbance of the community's emotional balance, it was easy to set an avalanche into motion.[43]

The evidence in this chapter supports the suggestion that Poznań was a centre of discussion, although its authors rarely identified specific trials, examples cited or locations. There are many factors that may have contributed to this: proximity to the German lands; relatively higher proportions of Protestant and German communities; supposed confessional tolerance; an enlightened nobility; and finally perhaps the constant refrain that Wielkopolska was positively overrun by witches.

8
Epilogue: Comparisons and Conclusions

This study set out to investigate the relationship between printed demonography and trials – a theme which has been interwoven throughout. However, it is worth explicitly comparing several of the key aspects of witchcraft beliefs in both their literary and trial contexts. As we have seen, the Wielkopolska trial records represent the juxtaposition of many elements, not necessarily binary opposites, but also co-authored narratives. The lack of Polish pamphlet material and the almost impossible task of discovering the reading habits of judges limit our ability to create a richer picture. The information in trial confessions should be regarded as having its origins in both the beliefs of the judges (suggested in the questions posed) and the information 'volunteered' (under torture) by the accused. By comparing these paradigms, my aim has not been to present a naïve contrast between the élite and the popular, nor between theory and reality, but to examine them in their contexts and identify who shaped the paradigms and what influenced them. This has allowed us to identify that there was in fact a composite body of attributes ascribed to a witch, but it was variously overlaid by different influences and was interpreted ambiguously. As we have seen, the same attributes could be viewed as positive or negative – desirable or demonic.

This study has analysed a wide range of printed sources and trial records in order to examine multiple ideas of the Devil, the witch and witchcraft in Wielkopolska specifically and in Poland more broadly. The paucity of scholarly research on the Polish persecution in English demanded a study that laid the foundations and provided a historical context for the reader. Of necessity, this restricted the analysis of witchcraft trials to one particular region, and sacrificed a more comparative approach. However, many different paradigms of the witch have come to light, which have challenged the assumed heterodoxy of the witch as a wholly negative concept. A pattern largely similar to that prevalent in the rest of Europe has emerged and the sources concur on the very basic essential characteristics of the witch, so we can conclude that there was indeed a composite, recognized body of attributes ascribed to a witch, although it was rather fluid and subject to elaboration. Witches were predominantly portrayed as female, with the ability bestowed by the Devil to control weather, inflict illness and death upon both animals and human beings and control fertility, which often required the agency of a material medium such as a powder or ointment, and which could be made from common, exotic or repulsive ingredients.

The similarities between trial narratives and élite demonography concur with the common basic characteristics of the witch and of the witchcraft from which they sprang. The differences occur in terms of elaborations on this theme and in the ambivalence therein. The trial accounts show a more cohesive and uniform ludic ideology of witchcraft, rather more rooted in the realities of everyday life; from familiarity with an individual devil to the locality of the sabbat. It is almost impossible to trace a transposition of ideology from demonography to the trial accounts, through a learned judge for example. However, we have been able to glean something about the interaction between the educated classes and the accused from the Opaliński case and Gamalski's writings.

On balance we can conclude that the Wielkopolska witchcraft persecution and Polish intellectual discourse were very similar to their counterparts in the rest of Europe, and not, as some historians would have it, 'backward'. The printed sources revealed a glaring contrast between the authors' use of extremely prurient motifs and the details that appeared in the trial records, which reflected popular lore more closely. Separate paradigms were understood by clerics drawing upon their predecessors (but not on pamphlet literature), by ordinary folk drawing on tradition and local beliefs and by satirists drawing on their observations that occasionally spanned the two. At the very heart of all these paradigms, we have the witch who can appropriate supernatural power, onto which a rich tapestry of variables were bolted. Whereas the fictional sources show a change in perceptions of the Devil, from a dangerous tempter and master of Hell in the sixteenth century to a figure of ridicule by the latter half of the eighteenth century, the witch also underwent many incarnations, as a stock character, a victim, a heroine, a servant of the Devil and a satirical emblem. So it is interesting to compare the depictions of some of the key aspects of the Devil and witchcraft in élite demonography and in the trials.

Naming the Devil

As in most cultures, the Devil took his name from a variety of sources or euphemisms if it was considered unlucky to mention his name directly. Common generic terms for the Devil, such as *szatan*, 'Satan', from the Hebrew *satan*, 'the obstructer' are widely used in both Polish texts and trials, along with the terms *diabeł*, *bies* and *czart*. Since neither Polish nor Latin has a definite article, it is often difficult to determine whether the authors were writing about *the* Devil or *a* devil.[1] The printed sources displayed a variety of names, predominantly biblical or Latin and Greek etymologies or calques echoing European trends. Biblical names included *Beelzebub*, 'Lord of Flies', *Satan*, and *Belial* alongside familiar Latin terminology such as *Lucifer*, *Dominus muscarum*, 'Lord of Flies', *Expertus*, *Accusator*, *Suggestor*, *Defluentes*, 'the fallen', *Tentator*, 'tempter' and *Malus*, 'evil'. Other euphemisms common to European sources included *Neptunus*, the Roman god of Hell[2] and *Bacchus*, the god of wine, confirming the link between the Devil and alcohol. Common Greek names such as *Diabolus*, διαβολος, 'devil' and *daemon* from δαιμων, 'a spirit', were also in use, along with *Astaroth*, the Phoenician god of the moon.[3] Polish equivalents of European names included, *Ojciec kłamstw*, 'Father of Lies', *Jędza*, 'hag', *Muchawiec*, 'fly man', *Latawiec*, 'incubus' and *Odmieniec*, 'changeling'. In contrast with many of the exotic borrowings, the polonized names tended to be functional epithets, as we have seen, such as *Szczebiot*, 'babbler' and *Bajor*, 'cheat'.[4] Devils were predominantly portrayed as male, but female devils appeared in *Postępek prawa czartowskiego*.[5] The emphasis on male devils complements theories and accusations of sexual activity between the female witch and the Devil.

The trials also reveal a varied terminology for the Devil or devils, but cannot compare to the richness of that found in the printed sources. One of the peculiarities of Polish trials is that a functional naming was more widely deployed by judges and officials, that is they used terms such as 'bridegroom' or 'cursed one', whereas the accused referred to their individual devils by rather mundane names such as Jaś or Jan, Marcin and Kuba.[6] There were also devils with surnames that traditionally indicated *szlachta* origins, typically ending in *-ski*, or *-czki*, such as Chrzanowski.[7] Many of those accused described consorting with a personal and individual devil, rather than *the* Devil, which introduced a degree of intimacy perhaps analogous to familiars. However, the Wielkopolska sample yielded only a few mentions of familiar-like creatures – for example, the Devil appeared as a cat to Ewa Rackowa according to a trial heard in Wronki in 1685.[8]

The Appearance of the Devil

Unsurprisingly, the characterization of the Devil allowed artistic licence to flourish, with authors drawing upon the early Church Fathers, Del Rio, Bodin and others to portray the Devil with a variety of features such as two horns (one on his neck, the other on his forehead), bristly hair, wide, round, inflamed eyes and the beard and body parts of a goat. He could be part human or have human hands with fingers of equal length, hawkish sharp nails, goose legs or the tail of a donkey, or even a human face under his tail. He might be two-faced like Janus or a spirit with no bodily form.[9] There was little consensus as to the Devil's appearance, instead, a fantastic array of combinations of male and animal forms and abnormalities were depicted.

In contrast, the emphasis in the trials appears to be on colourful clothing, rather than exaggerated features – the Devil did not differ so much from a normal man. For example, in only one of the cases in the sample is the Devil's transmogrification mentioned, when Jagnieszka claimed in 1710 that the Devil appeared to her as a monk in the forest. This is a detail more at home in Skarga's *Vitae*, perhaps underlining the connection between the witch and the saint.[10] The simple conceptualization of the Devil in the trials was reinforced by its repetition at public executions, through gossip and in denunciations, which may have explained the relative degree of uniformity in confessions. The Devil of the clergy was a truly frightening adversary of God, but the popular Devil could be colourfully dressed and was on first name terms with ordinary people.

Submission to the Devil

In Polish trial records the pact with the Devil was rarely described as explicit or written, with a few notable exceptions involving men, as we saw in Chapter 3. As far as I know, no Polish written pacts have survived. In fact, the most frequent accounts of submission to the Devil described it as a wedding with its subsequent consummation. The sexual element was further emphasized in descriptions in printed sources of women living with devils as husbands for long periods of time, echoed in trial records.[11] Demonographers held that the Devil answered the bidding of a woman and copulated with those who were willing, unwilling or asleep, with a preference for women with long hair. It was believed that the children (also known as *Wechselbaelge* or changelings) of these unions were tearful, sensitive and heavier (though slimmer) than normal children, and that even five wet nurses could not satisfy their voracious appetites.[12] The corollary, that is whether the Devil could impregnate women, was discussed on the basis of St Augustine's tale of the birth of Merlin, but disputed by the anonymous author of *Postępek prawa czartowskiego*. Bohomolec took the argument further, claiming that if the Devil could make women pregnant, it would make a mockery of marriage and inheritance laws. Social chaos was to be avoided and this theme, although popular in the printed sources, was completely absent from the trial records.

However, sex was not the only way of concluding a pact with the Devil and authors of printed sources revelled in descriptions of rituals, which included using sacred items for profane purposes, digging up the bodies of children from their graves, blaspheming, killing adults or children and making sacrifices. Many inversions of Roman Catholic ceremonies constituted conditions of the pact. For example, the Devil baptized the witch with a new name and made the sign of the Devil on her forehead with a chrism of goat fat and she, in turn, would give the Devil a piece of her dress to symbolize, paradoxically, submission of her worldly goods to him. A novice witch was to go to a church on a Sunday morning before the holy water had been brought in, where with her masters she would renounce Christ, the Christian faith, her baptism and the church.[13] Chmielowski described how a novice was forbidden to worship God or the Virgin Mary, or to venerate saints, their relics or images. Candidates were also forbidden to anoint themselves with holy water or holy salt, to go to confession or to genuflect. Another example tells of how a witch had to swear an oath and agree to have his or her name erased from the Book of Life, while standing in a circle drawn in the earth. The pact was secret and the witch was obliged to attend a *rada*, 'council', attract others into the service of the Devil and to always be at his beck and call to do his bidding.[14] The pact was an essential indicator of the witch's compliance since the Devil had no control over free will and had to tempt witches with promises of riches, revenge and success. These promises appear in earlier accounts such as the *Malleus Maleficarum*, but by the eighteenth century they seem to have disappeared, perhaps as people observed the witches' fate and poverty. Many of the authors may have concluded that these promises were never made or were broken. In the rare examples in the trial records in which the Devil made good on his promises, the rewards tended to disappear.[15]

If we return to the trials, a certain Regina claimed to have been introduced to the Devil and taught witchcraft by another woman,[16] and her devil, Jan, was described as a longstanding acquaintance. In a paradoxical morality, many women claimed to have stayed in faithful relationships with their devils for years – Oderyna claimed she had had sex with her devil Kuba for forty years. Ostling suggests that within the accusations of demonic infidelity, women tried to maintain some probity.[17] The initiatory weddings usually took place at Łysa Góra.

We danced, the devils took us home where we danced and had sex, just as with our husbands, three times and he was cold. Not every day, just on Thursdays and we had sex at home, my husband felt nothing and knew nothing although it was at home, because the Devil lay on the left side and my husband lay on the right.[18]

Zofia's confession revealed that even in the presence of a husband there were no obstacles to giving oneself to the Devil and that sexual penetration was an obvious symbol of submission. The repugnance of such apostasy was increased by the active sexual consummation, making a mockery of the sacrament of marriage through bigamy, adultery and even bestiality, as the Devil was not human. Agnieszka Odrobina of Opalenica begged the court not to tell her husband of her sexual exploits with her devil Jasiek, but since she was sentenced to the stake, her husband's wrath was the least of her worries.[19]

Apart from descriptions of sex, and despite claims that the Devil was supposed to urge witches to commit evil deeds, there was little description of any other interaction. Contrary to the prevailing assumption that all were in fear of the Devil, it appears that in some cases it was indeed the witches who exercised control, as in the *Sowiźrdzał* literature. In Grodzisk, for example, Kupidarzyna was able to cause rainfall by releasing her devil from behind the chimney, while in Gniezno, another devil was kept under a barrel in the cellar and yet another under a woman's skirts.[20] According to one of the earliest cases from Kalisz, in 1580 a devil was kept in a mirror and used to locate lost items.[21]

However, even as late as 1750, in the trial of Magdalena Klauzyna in Kalisz there was a rumour that the Devil was with her throughout the trial and it was commonly believed that the Devil prevented women from making their confession.[22] It is with no small measure of irony that the court recorded during the trial of a certain Franciszka, that a denizen of Hell excused himself because the prison was too hot.[23] However, sometimes the Devil revealed a softer side, as according to Agnieszka Kazacczyna, 'Organiscina's devil came to me and asked me from her not to denounce her twice in the evening'.[24]

A Lublin legend tells of a poor widow, who having unjustly lost a court case over her inheritance, complained that she would receive better justice from the Devil. Lo and behold, that night the Devil arrived with his cohorts and amended the court's decision in the records in favour of the widow.[25] The Devil certainly was seen as a good influence in this case.

Details of the Sabbat

Accounts of what actually took place at the sabbat vary greatly, but as we have come to expect, the printed sources offer the most lurid accounts, predominantly by inverting Christian rituals. According to Chmielowski, the Devil provided banquets for the witches with dishes of delicious stolen food, preceded by a benediction addressed to the Devil, but Bohomolec described revolting dishes of toads, the flesh of people who had been hanged, fresh corpses and unbaptized babies, eaten without salt and with bread made from black millet. Other accounts described tasty dishes that disappeared when placed before guests. At these ceremonies the witches indulged in a host of satanic practices where they worshipped the Devil as their master, danced either naked or clothed, sang songs and extinguished candles. At such orgies they prepared ointments from the corpses of those burned at the stake or hanged, to which they added the Host and Holy Oil and used it for witchcraft.[26] Chmielowski was no less graphic in his accounts of the sabbat, again inverting Christian rituals and claiming that witches offered their sons and daughters to the Devil and spread the Host over fields to cause crop failure.[27] Simple inversion was seen here at its apotheosis as a literary device and virtually every Roman Catholic office, personnel or sacrament had its lurid satanic counterpart, from diabolic psalms to a diabolic priest who dropped blood on the Host and ridiculed the Mass.[28] According to some descriptions they knelt with their backs to the Devil or in a circle in front of him, kissed him under the tail and presented children, babies and visitors to him. To show his content, he would make a hole in the ground, into which he urinated and then sprinkled everyone with the urine. If a witch did not bring a neighbour's children as promised, she had to present either her own or replacements or face punishment. The novice witch was welcomed with powder from the liver of an unbaptized baby or a chrism of blood from its left leg. She was ordered not to divulge her secret even under torture and to deny God and the saints. It was also at the sabbat that the so-called Devil's mark was given, usually under the eyelid, on the buttocks, in the mouth or on the right shoulder. The ears, the armpit and a woman's loins were also mentioned as likely spots and children were branded in the left eye, with the mark (made either with the Devil's horn or a hot steel brand) taking the shape of a hare, a black puppy, a cat or the legs of a toad. When the cock crowed, the gathering ended with the Devil turning his back on the revellers.[29] These descriptions illustrate a graphic disparity between trial records and the explicit printed discourse.

Lurid accounts of the sabbat were also to be found in some confessions, as for example in the case of Małgorzata Krystkowa, who described how her devil Jaś presented her to *starszemu*, 'the older one', to whom she gave her hand. When she renounced the Virgin Mary and God, the 'older one' announced 'now you are mine', she ate at the table with her Jaś, drank beer and danced with him. During the same trial, Anna Wraźka confessed that she had experienced a similar episode and had been asked if she would attend the sabbat often and whether she would do evil in the world.[30] Apart from the wedding and initiation ceremonies, the sabbat was an occasion for a variety of activities, including sex with the Devil, feasting and dancing, but it was also an occasion to pass on diabolic skills, for example Marusza Staszkowa was taught by Rogalka how to use horse ashes to ruin beer.[31]

Eleven year-old Dorota deposed as follows before the court in Gniezno:

> My mother led in the bridegroom, it was Thursday night, and the cocks were already crowing, when we got married. Mrs Siedlarka took a silk rope and gold wedding rings. Then she joined us together. There were six wax candles burning. Siedlarka said to me, do you take this man, and I said nothing and I didn't want to. But he said I take this woman, then immediately we danced back to back and I danced with my bridegroom. My stepmother danced with her partner, who was called Kazimierz. He played for us on the pipes... When he came to me, he hid me and did with me what he wanted, and he was cold. She gave birth to me, but I don't regard her as my mother, because she never taught me the Our Father, and I pity a dog more than her.[32]

We tend to find more lurid descriptions of the sabbat feast in trial records, because as we have seen, there were varied accounts of the feast, with Chmielowski describing dishes of tasty stolen food.[33] Anna Jasińska told of dining on horse droppings and horse urine,[34] and another of the accused tells of drinking horse urine wine from silver chalices made from horse manure.[35] In a case heard before the Kalisz court in

1613, the accused confessed that the devils provided foul-tasting beer, meat that tasted like dog meat, as well as horrible cabbage and turnip, whereas in Poniec, oats, cabbage and beer were on the menu, and yet other confessions reveal that the witches cooked and ate a stolen horse, stolen cows or meat.[36] Contrary to the élite conceptualization of the sabbat, which emphasized the almost monarchical role of the Devil, sitting in various guises on a throne, in the Wielkopolska trial records, as befitted a predominantly female gathering, there was most often a queen of the sabbat. In Gniezno, when the saddler's wife was queen, she was crowned with golden horns.[37] Also of note is the commonly reported role of men as musicians at the sabbat (also seen in German trials) who usually played a type of pipe and the presence of both peasants and lords.[38] The sabbat was an essential construct of the inverted diabolic system, on both a theoretical and pragmatic level, reminiscent of village festivals.

The Materials of Malefice

Descriptions of material agents such as powders, images, ointments and the personal possessions of those targeted in sympathetic magic (although the latter was rare in Polish trial confessions) provided motifs for literary sources, with two very practical purposes. First, it afforded yet another opportunity to describe repulsive matter used by witches such as corpses and excrement. Second, the powders and ointments found at the home of a suspected witch could be, and occasionally were, used as evidence. Both trial records and printed sources agree that ointment enabled flight, but the latter also claimed that ointment was also used to harness the elements and was scattered over the earth to cause a large black cloud leading to rainfall, storms, lightning, hail, floods, winds and tornadoes.[39] One witch apparently buried her ointment (said to contain thorn apple, corn cockle, herbs, poppy juice, pig lice and fox fat) at a crossroads at four o'clock in the morning, while uttering incantations to the Devil, and after three days she smeared it on her broomstick or herself in order to fly.[40]

According to demonological texts, witches also received powders from the Devil consisting of a variety of crushed matter but which included normal items such as oil, milk, herbs (especially those collected on St John's Eve, 23/24 June), metals, animal fur and feathers, but also goat's or donkey's brain, hyena womb and crocodile or frog bones. Magical properties were also ascribed to menstrual blood, semen, urine, bones and the tooth of a hangman, but it was powder that was most frequently mentioned in the witchcraft trials, provided by the witches' individual devils, in various colours.

It was not only the ingredients that were important, but also what the spells were intended to achieve, upon which demonologists loved to opine. In the *Malleus* a lizard buried under a corner of a house removed fertility from the occupiers and their animals for years, which was predictably restored when the remains were removed. In another description, the Host was buried together with a frog in a pot, and other favourite ingredients included snakes, mice and stones. These accounts concur with trial accounts, for example in a trial heard before the Kalisz court in 1613, three handfuls of bread, salt and water were buried in a pot. In other cases more abhorrent ingredients such as bones from a corpse, earth from a grave, cattle, horse manure and a rotting frog were typically mentioned.[41]

Distinctive Aspects of the Polish Persecution

Although the Polish persecution broadly follows the loose general European pattern, there are some aspects peculiar to Poland evident in the Wielkopolska trials. The lack of reference to identifiable trials and of any traceable circularity between trials, pamphlet materials and demonology is extremely regrettable, as it deprives the researcher of valuable contemporary or near-contemporary sources. We can perhaps speculate that those writing on witchcraft were less interested in the details of real trials because they tended to focus on criticism of the judicial procedures. Theological argument was obfuscated by the erroneous dispute over the loss of ecclesiastical jurisdiction, which concentrated the witchcraft debate around criticism of the judiciary. As in most parts of Europe, there were many critics of the persecution in Poland, who even prior to its peak, raged against typical abuses such as denunciation, swimming, failure to follow judicial procedures, failure to uphold witness and evidence criteria and the excessive use of torture. However, this study has revealed distinctive traits, such as the matted hair, a seigniorial pattern, the extremely high number of women, the 'giving' of the Devil, familiar-like devils and the apparent lack of witchfinders and searches for the Devil's mark.

Despite a host of methodological and ideological flaws, some tenets of Baranowski's work have at least been partially proved. His revised figures for a total of a few thousand executions bear a closer resemblance to my initial findings of around 800 trials and mentions of trials and to Pilaszek's 867 lay cases. Baranowski's claim of a peak between 1675 and

1725 has also been broadly confirmed, but must be considered in relation to Pilaszek's findings of a decrease from 25 to 19 per cent in trials between 1676 and 1700 compared with between 1701 and 1725, in comparison with Baranowski's increase from 23 per cent in the former to 32 per cent in the latter. According to the sample, the chronology of the persecution was similar to that elsewhere in Europe, beginning in the middle of the sixteenth century and increasing as the century progressed, coinciding with Groicki's Polish codifications of German law published in 1558–59 and the removal of jurisdiction over witchcraft cases from ecclesiastical to secular courts. By the middle of the seventeenth century, when the persecution had gained momentum, environmental factors clearly played a role. If the sample accurately indicates the peak of the persecution as between 1660 and 1740, the impetus to identify and persecute witches increased at a time when the Commonwealth was undergoing a crisis on both internal and external fronts. From 1750 the number of trials decreased, perhaps in part because of the Assessorial Edict of 1745 and the growth of the Polish Enlightenment.

Perhaps the most significant factor in the persecution was the degree to which power was concentrated in the hands of the local *szlachta*, which contributed immensely to abuses of the legal system. It is clear in the witchcraft trials published from Lublin and Cracow that witchcraft appeals made to the Court of Six Towns resulted in a greater degree of clemency, so future studies will contribute to a clearer overall picture and perhaps prove the apparent extreme harshness of the Wielkopolska judiciary to be somewhat of an anomaly. The Wielkopolska sample reveals little interest by the judges in acquiring evidential proof and it is clear that accusations were brought on the basis of varying motives, therefore, given the ease with which convictions were secured, the question remains of why so few trials occurred.[42]

Undoubtedly Wielkopolska's persecution correlated with the economic, political and social crises, which, together with increasing religious intolerance, dominated the century from 1650 onwards. These factors affected all aspects of life, but were exacerbated by the domination of the *szlachta*; whatever impacted on noble life was sure to trickle down to the peasantry. The deteriorating economic and social position of the petty and middling nobility may have sharpened tensions, rendering this estate more suspicious when misfortune struck. Such conditions also exacerbated the vulnerable subsistence eked out by the majority of the peasantry and landless *szlachta*, which made women's management of the household economy even more precarious. Symonowicz's idyll illustrates how women introspectively judged themselves as bad mothers or housewives and the trial records bring out some women's miserable propensity towards self-blame and guilt. In an era when most confessions judged women more harshly against ideas of the perfect Virgin Mary or female saints, or still maligned women along with Eve, it was all too easy for women to feel inadequate in a fiercely patriarchal society.

Nowhere was that patriarchal society more evident than in the Roman Catholic Church. The most extreme depictions by Roman Catholic writers served to heighten fear of the Devil and witchcraft, as well as to emphasize the church and its rituals as the only authentic remedies – frequent communion and confession and reverence of the sacramentals, rather than Protestant remedies of fasting and prayer. As this study has shown, the boundaries between sacred and profane were fluid and ambiguous and were often dependent on individuals and whim. The vocabulary of witchcraft was deployed literally to demonize other belief systems, both by Roman Catholics to vilify practices they deemed pagan and by Protestants to stigmatize Roman Catholic practices they deemed superstitious. At the heart of these issues we can detect anxieties about the control of power and its misuse, but also the application of the label of witch to those who lacked spiritual and/or behavioural probity – a motif common to both the printed sources and the trials. Most frequently it was deployed to accuse individuals (predominantly females) of appropriating special or magical power, something the Roman Catholic Church had striven to eradicate, replacing it with its own exclusive corporate male hierarchy. Both in early pagan times and during the reformations, the Roman Catholic Church had sought to assert its power over religious individualism to establish a religious sphere dominated by a celibate male hierarchy. Power, in the non-sanctioned hands of women, evoked Eve, strengthening the identification of evil with females.

Of course, this was not an exclusively Roman Catholic issue, but even in such a multi-confessional area such as Wielkopolska, those tried as witches were Roman Catholic, which provokes the question of whether Protestant communities were somehow free from fears of witchcraft (evidently not borne out by the rest of Europe), whether they had different ways of dealing with it, or whether they simply held different perceptions of the problem. Only one identifiable Protestant appeared in the sample even though many of the trials were heard before courts in predominantly Protestant towns.

The figure of the witch in literary sources was inherently complex, even encompassing the popular motif of women mocking men – a far cry from the power relations evident in most of the trials. In short, we can discern several tropes of the witch motif: the theoretical and mainly clerical diabolic and female witch; the diabolic witch of the judiciary; the male or female actually accused of witchcraft; and the witch of popular lower- and middle-class imagination. As we have seen in the *Sowiźdrzał* literature, a realistic attitude emerged based on common sense and even admiration for the 'real' witch's perceived powers, while Szymonowicz and Opaliński articulated a more realistic and contemporary image of the dynamics of the persecution and how women came to be accused of witchcraft.

However, definitions of witchcraft were dependent upon the period, regions, jurisdictions and personal beliefs of judges and individuals, which included victims, accusers and authors. In secular trials from the sixteenth century charges had generally been brought against individuals who could alternatively be identified as the so-called cunning folk.[43] From the sample of trial records a transitory period can be identified when traditional rituals, previously condoned, became criminalized, since many of the early secular cases are distinguished by the beneficent intent behind the rituals practised. As a stricter attitude emerged towards practices condemned by the church, punishment became more severe, increasing from a mere fine to the death penalty. In addition, the severity with which these cases were treated underlined the importance of milk and beer as commodities, reflecting the constant struggle to obtain basic resources and the fear engendered by a zero-sum ideology.[44]

Threads in a Rich Tapestry

As most historians of witchcraft swiftly discover, their work frequently raises more questions than it can satisfactorily answer and our conclusions are challenged by fresh research, new discoveries and developing theories. In the case of Poland, much remains to be done, but there is a growing cohort of researchers who are rising to this challenge. This study has established that in Wielkopolska the trials were broadly similar to those elsewhere in Europe. There also appeared to have been relatively small outbreaks in areas, rather than any mass trials involving many tens of victims, and it will be interesting to see whether future regional studies also bear out the Wielkopolska evidence for a later peak. Witches in Wielkopolska were often servants, according to the sample, and the crime of witchcraft evolved from cunning practices to alleged diabolism as the era progressed.

Although the interrogations were instigated and conducted by the judiciary, a vast amount of personal information emerges from confessions, revealing much of the past histories of the men, women and children on trial, as well as the grudges and complaints of witnesses and accusers. The confessions present a view of early modern society through a very specific prism, which unearths tensions, anger and quarrels, which often originated in complaints spanning many years, demonstrating how people held on to their grudges and suspicions accrued. It is largely these grudges, together with deprivation and misfortune, that were the drivers of witchcraft accusations.

I have also been able to identify cases that reference at least some of the explanations for witchcraft suggested by historians. Women clearly judged themselves as bad mothers, charity was often refused (encouraging grudges), and climatic change and subsistence fears may well have played a part in bringing accusations. Although witches were neighbours, they were also, in the Wielkopolska sample, servants or serfs, many had a bad reputation, some were cunning folk, and others had committed sexual indiscretions. The undoubtedly patriarchal society and perhaps even Groicki's aside to treat women accused of witchcraft more harshly than men may have contributed to the extremely high rate of women accused. The relatively few males who appeared before the courts on charges of witchcraft were named as sabbat attendees in the role of the musician, accused of *maleficia*, accused of writing a pact with the Devil or were related to witches, similarly to their counterparts in other areas of Europe.

In conclusion, Poland, like other European countries, experienced an intellectual, cosmopolitan debate on the nature of the witch, the Devil and witchcraft. Despite varying accounts and agendas, the paradigm of the witch emerged with a basic recognizable set of features, embellished with various additional motifs. The witch was a canvas on which not only to depict bad or unvirtuous behaviour, proscribed on religious, social or gendered grounds, but also on which to show positive, admirable qualities.

Despite differences in the legal, ecclesiastical and popular paradigms of the witch, there were still mechanisms in place for a persecution of significant proportions to occur. The statistics presented here are not conclusive, but merely indicate a pattern found in the sample for Wielkopolska. Significantly, a 'seigniorial pattern' has illustrated a particular dynamic identified within the Wielkopolska sample, in which the Lord of the Manor often brought charges of witchcraft against his servants. In this study I have provided a brief and preliminary overview of the intellectual, social, literary and legal aspects of witchcraft in Poland and Wielkopolska, based on archival research and the close reading of texts. It has added another dimension to the rich tapestry that is the history of witchcraft in Europe and, it is hoped, will provide the basis for future and more extensive work on the witchcraft persecution in Poland.

Notes

Prologue

1. APP AM Kalisz, I/158, pp. 347–60.
2. R. Briggs, '"*Many Reasons Why*": Witchcraft and the Problem of Multiple Explanation', in J. Barry, M. Hester and G. Roberts (eds), *Witchcraft in Early Modern Europe: Studies in Culture and Belief* (Cambridge, 1998), p. 53.
3. See M. Zakrzewska, *Procesy o czary w Lublinie w XVII i XVIII w.* (Łódź, 1947), p. 3; J. Wijaczka, 'Procesy o czary w regionie świętokrzyskim w XVII–XVIII wieku', in J. Wijaczka (ed.), *Z przeszłości regionu świętokrzyskiego od XVI do XX wieku. Materiały konferencji naukowej, Kielce, 8 kwietnia 2003* (Kielce, 2003); and idem, *Procesy o czary w Prusach Książęcych (Brandenburskich) w XVI–XVIII wieku* (Toruń, 2007).
4. F. Spee, *Cautio criminalis seu de processibus contra sagas* (Frankfurt, 1632), and *Czarownica powołana, abo krótka nauka y przestroga z strony czarownic...* (Poznań, 1639).
5. M. Bogucka, *Women in Early Modern Poland, against the European Background* (Aldershot, 2004), pp. 106–9; M. Pilaszek, *Procesy o czary w Polsce w wiekach XV–XVIII* (Cracow, 2008).
6. B. Baranowski, *Procesy czarownic w Polsce w XVII i XVIII w.* (Łódź, 1952).
7. S. Clark, *Thinking with Demons* (Oxford, 1999 [1997]); Briggs, *'Many Reasons Why'*; and A. Rowlands, 'Telling Witchcraft Stories: New Perspectives on Witchcraft and Witches in the Early Modern Period', *Gender and History* 10, no. 2 (1998), 294–302.

1 Witchcraft in Context: Histories and Historiographies

1. R. Briggs, *Witches and Neighbours* (London, 1996), p. 4.
2. For a better insight into Polish history between 1500–1800 see N. Davies, *God's Playground: A History of Poland* (2 vols, Oxford, [1981] 1991); R.I. Frost, *After the Deluge: Poland-Lithuania and the Second Northern War 1655–1660* (Cambridge, 1993); G. Lukowski and H. Zawadzki, *A Concise History of Poland* (Cambridge, 2001); A. Zamoyski, *The Polish Way: A Thousand Years' History of the Poles and Their Culture* (London, 1989); A. S. Kamiński, *Republic v Autocracy: Poland-Lithuania and Russia 1686–1697* (Cambridge, MA, 1993); M. Bogucka, *Historia Polski do 1864 roku* (Wrocław, 1999); J. Pieszczachowicz (ed.), *Wielka Historia Polski* (Cracow, 2000–01); J. Topolski (ed.), *Dzieje Polski* (Warsaw, 1975); and S. Kieniewicz, *History of Poland* (Warsaw, 1979).
3. For discussion on the Polish word *szlachta*, see Davies, *God's Playground*, I, p. 206; J. Topolski, 'The Structure of the Polish Nobility in the 16th and 17th Centuries: Some New Findings and Reflections', in idem, *The Manorial Economy in Early Modern East Central Europe* (Aldershot, 1994), pp. 60–70; W. Konopczyński, 'Wielkopolski w dobie Rzeczypospolitej szlacheckiej',

Roczniki Historyczne 1 (1925), 75–101; H. Litwin, 'The Polish Magnateria 1454–1648: The Shaping of an Estate', *APH* 53 (1986), 63–92; J.K. Fedorowicz, *A Republic of Nobles: Studies in Polish History to 1864* (Cambridge, 1982); R.I. Frost, 'The Nobility of Poland-Lithuania, 1569–1795', in H. Scott (ed.), *The European Nobilities in the 17th and 18th Centuries* (2 vols, London, 1995), II, pp. 183–222; R. Butterwick (ed.), *The Polish-Lithuanian Monarchy in European Context, c. 1500–1795* (Basingstoke, 2001); and I. Banać, *The Nobility in Russia and Eastern Europe* (New Haven, 1983). See W.N. Trepka, *Liber Generationis vel Plebeanorum*, ed. W. Dworzaczek (Wrocław, 1963).
4. Lukowski and Zawadzki, *History*, p. 48, and Frost, *Nobilities*, p. 192, where he suggests a figure of between 8 and 10 per cent according to contemporary traveller to Poland, Bernard Connor and between 6 and 7.5 per cent according to tax registers. Kaczmarczyk suggests 8 per cent or half a million by 1550, rising to one quarter in Mazowsze. See Z. Kaczmarczyk and B. Leśnodorski, *Historia Państwa i Prawa Polski od połowy XV do r. 1795*, vol. II. (Warsaw, 1957), p. 75.
5. Davies, *God's Playground*, I, pp. 218, 229.
6. Frost, *Nobilities*, p. 214, who refers to H. Olszewski, 'The Essence and Legal Foundation of the Magnate Oligarchy in Poland', *APH* 56 (1988), 29–49.
7. Frost, *Nobilities*, pp. 206–7, 212. See K. Przybos, 'Latyfundium Lubomirskich w połowie XVII wieku', *Studia Historyczne* 35 (1992), 19–33, where he notes that in 1642 Stanisław Lubomirski possessed 316 villages, 18 towns and 163 estates.
8. J. Kochanowicz, 'The Polish Economy and the Evolution of Dependency', in D. Chirot (ed.), *The Origins of Backwardness in Eastern European Economies and Politics from the Middle Ages until the Early Twentieth Century* (Berkeley and London, 1989), p. 98. Kochanowicz believes that in addition the system of German law strengthened seigniorial power at the expense of royal power.
9. Z. Sadowski, *Pieniądz a początki upadku rzeczypospolitej w XVII w.* (Warsaw, 1964), p. 355.
10. Kaczmarczyk and Leśnodorski, *Historia Państwa*, p. 175.
11. Kochanowicz, 'Economy', p. 113.
12. This was evident in the elections of Henri of Valois and Stefan Batory, which caused particular tensions among the Wielkopolska *szlachta*.
13. Davies, *God's Playground*, I, pp. 492, 502.
14. Frost, *Nobilities*, pp. 216–19.
15. J. Ptaśnik, *Miasta i mieszczaństwo w dawnej Polsce* (Warsaw, 1949), and M. Bogucka, 'Polish Towns between the 16th and 18th Centuries', in J. K. Fedorowicz (ed.), *A Republic of Nobles: Studies in Polish History to 1864* (Cambridge, 1982), pp. 138–52.
16. Kochanowicz, 'Economy', pp. 111–13.
17. Lukowski and Zawadzki, *History*, p. 55.
18. Davies, *God's Playground*, I, p. 288; Kochanowicz, 'Economy', pp. 94–5.
19. A. Mączak, 'The Structure of Power in the Commonwealth', in J. K. Fedorowicz (ed.), *A Republic of Nobles: Studies in Polish History to 1864* (Cambridge, 1982), pp. 131–3.
20. Kaczmarczyk and Leśnodorski, *Historia Państwa*, p. 178.
21. The dietines functioned on a local level, but wielded some power. For example, a dietine was held to elect representatives to the *Sejm*, to the

Crown Tribunal, and to consider reports from the *Sejm*. There was also a dietine to pass local resolutions or *lauda* and one that discussed the trade and finance of the province as well as taxes and military affairs. Lukowski and Zawadzki, *History*, p. 71.
22. K. Wilson, 'The Politics of Toleration: Dissenters in Great Poland (1587–1648)' (PhD thesis, SSEES, University College London, 2005), p. 133.
23. There are many differing opinions as to what exactly constituted Sarmatism and what its influence was. However, there is general acceptance that it was a belief which influenced noble attitudes and lifestyle based on the notion that the nobility was descended from the ancient tribe of the Sarmatians (some traced back to Noah) who originated from the region north of the Black Sea called Sarmatia. It was popular in the time of the Jagiellonian dynasty, but went into decline during the Saxon period, reaching its apotheosis in the course of the seventeenth century. Frost writes 'This identity-myth claimed that the *szlachta*, whether of Polish, Lithuanian, Ruthenian or German descent, formed one political nation, descended from the ancient Sarmatian tribe which had long resisted the Roman Empire. By the mid-seventeenth century the hallmarks of the "Sarmatian nation" were the use of the Polish language, adherence to the Catholic faith and the adoption of a distinctive style of dress, heavily influenced by Turkic and Tatar models, which symbolized the difference between the Polish constitution and the political systems of Western Europeans, whose effete, mincing fashions were taken to denote the domination of society by absolute royal power.' Frost, *Nobilities*, pp. 184–5. See also S. Cynarski, 'The Shape of Sarmatian Ideology in Poland', *APH* 19 (1968), 5–17; M. Bogucka, *The Lost World of the 'Sarmatians': Custom as the Regulator of Polish Social Life in Early Modern Times* (Warsaw, 1996); and J. Tazbir, 'Sarmatyzm a barok', *Kwartalnik Historyczny* 76 (1969), 815–30.
24. What Davies calls the 'Sandomierz Compromise' of 1569–70 was an attempted concord between the Protestant groups in Poland. Davies, *God's Playground*, vol. I, p. 185.
25. Pilaszek, *Procesy*, pp. 522–3.
26. Ibid., pp. 528–30.
27. J. Kłoczowski, *Dzieje chrześciaństwa polskiego* (Warsaw, 2000), pp. 188–91, 198. The intensification of attention and respect paid to the Eucharist and the significance of transubstantiation has great relevance to descriptions of its abuse in witchcraft.
28. J. Kłoczowski, *A History of Polish Christianity* (Cambridge, 2000), p. 155. He maintains that thousands of people died as a result of accusations of witchcraft at the end of the seventeenth century and that the witchcraft persecution came directly from Germany, as so many other Polish historians are keen to prove. He regards the decline in the number of cases as directly relative to an increase in accusations of blood libel against Jews.
29. Kaczmarczyk and Leśnodorski, *Historia Państwa*, p. 177.
30. J. Topolski, *Wielkopolska poprzez wieki* (Poznań, 1999), pp. 847, 510–11.
31. J. Topolski, 'Model gospodarczy Wielkopolski w XVIII wieku', *Studia i materiały do dziejów Wielkopolski i Pomorza* (20), 10, no. 2 (1971), 61; and idem (ed.), *Dzieje Wielkopolski* (2 vols, Poznań, 1969), I, pp. 515, 517, 522–3. Such conflict in the sixteenth century included withholding taxes, the

late arrival of forces on the eastern battlefield, and a strongly fuelled Executionist movement supported by the area's many Protestants.
32. Topolski (ed.), *Wielkopolski*, p. 490; E. Opaliński, *Elita władzy w województwach poznańskim i kaliskim za Zygmunta III* (Poznań, 1981); and Wilson, 'Toleration', p. 101.
33. U. Piotrkowska, 'Struktura i rozmieszczenie własności feudalnej w województwie Poznańskim w drugiej połowie XVI wieku', in *Społeczeństwo staropolskie*, IV (Warsaw, 1986), pp. 25, 28.
34. Wilson, 'Toleration', p. 272.
35. Topolski, 'Model', p. 66 and Kaczmarczyk and Leśnodorski, *Historia Państwa*, p. 11.
36. Davies, *God's Playground*, I, p. 305.
37. Wilson, 'Toleration', pp. 130–3.
38. Kłoczowski, *Polish Christianity*, p. 99.
39. J. Kłoczowski, *Kościół w Polsce w XV–XVII w.*, II (Cracow, 1969), p. 297.
40. Topolski (ed.), *Wielkopolska*, p. 731.
41. Pilaszek, *Procesy*, p. 527.
42. 'Przygody i sprawy trefne', in K. Badecki (ed.) *Polska fraszka mieszczańska* (Cracow, 1948 [n.d.]), pp. 104–5, shows just one example.
43. See M. Paradowska, *Bambrzy* (Poznań, 1998).
44. See W. Wyporska, 'Motive and Motif: Representations of the Witch in Early Modern Poland' (DPhil thesis, Hertford College, Oxford, 2007), ch. 2.
45. A. Dworkin, *Woman Hating* (New York, 1974), p. 130.
46. B. Ankarloo, S., Clark and W. Monter (eds), *The Athlone History of Witchcraft and Magic in Europe: The Period of the Witch Trials* (London, 2002), p. 13.
47. See in particular the introductions in J. Sharpe, *Instruments of Darkness* (London, 1996), pp. 1–33; L. Apps and A. Gow, *Male Witches in Early Modern Europe* (Manchester, 2003), pp. 1–24; Briggs, *Witches*; E.W. Monter, 'The Historiography of European Witchcraft: Progress and Prospects', *Journal of Interdisciplinary History* 2, no. 4 (1971–72), 435–51; A. Rowlands, *Witchcraft Narratives in Germany: Rothenburg, 1561–1652* (Manchester, 2003), pp. 1–15; J. Barry and O. Davies (eds), *Palgrave Advances in Witchcraft Historiography* (Basingstoke, 2007), T.A. Fudge, 'Traditions and Trajectories in the Historiography of European Witch-Hunting', *History Compass* 4, no. 3 (2006), 488–527; W. Behringer, 'Historiography', in R.M. Golden (ed.), *Encyclopedia of Witchcraft: The Western Tradition* (4 vols, Santa Barbara and Oxford, 2006), II, pp. 492–8.
48. L. Roper, *Oedipus and the Devil: Witchcraft, Sexuality and Religion in Early Modern Europe* (London, 1995 [1994]); S. Brauner, *Fearless Wives and Frightened Shrews: The Construction of the Witch in Early Modern Germany* (Amherst, 1995); D. Purkiss, *The Witch in History: Early Modern and Twentieth Century Representations* (London, 1996); D. Willis, *Malevolent Nurture: Witch-Hunting and Maternal Power in Early Modern England* (London, 1995); Rowlands, *Rothenburg*; M. Hester, *Lewd Women and Wicked Witches: A Study of the Dynamics of Male Domination* (London, 1992); and E. Whitney, 'The Witch "She"/The Historian "He": Gender and the Historiography of the European Witch-Hunts', *Journal of Women's History* 7, no. 3 (1995).
49. G. Henningsen, *The Witches' Advocate: Basque Witchcraft and the Spanish Inquisition (1609–1614)* (Reno, 1980), p. 12; N. Cohn, *Europe's Inner Demons*

(London, 1975), pp. 248–9; H.C.E. Midelfort, *Witch-Hunting in Southwestern Germany* (Stanford, 1972), pp. 178–82; and G. Quaife, *Godly Zeal and Furious Rage: The Witch in Early Modern Europe* (New York, 1967), p. 94.
50. See E.W. Monter, *Witchcraft in France and Switzerland: The Borderlands during the Reformation* (Ithaca and London, 1976), pp. 119–24; C. Larner, *Witchcraft and Religion* (Oxford, 1984), p. 65; and B. Levack (ed.), *The Witch-hunt in Early Modern Europe* (London, 1995 and 2006), pp. 138–9; L. Roper, *Witch Craze* (New Haven and London, 2004), pp. xi, 7; and L. Jackson, 'Wives, Witches and Mothers', *Women's History Review* 4 (1995), 63–83.
51. See Levack (ed.), *Witch-hunt*, pp. 89–90.
52. See Larner, *Witchcraft*; R. Kieckhefer, *European Witch Trials: Their Foundation in Popular and Learned Culture, 1300–1500* (London, 1976); and Baranowski, *Procesy*.
53. A. Macfarlane, *Witchcraft in Tudor and Stuart England* (London, 1970).
54. Roper, *Oedipus*, and Willis, *Malevolent Nurture*.
55. Baranowski, *Procesy*.
56. See J. Dydyński, *Wiadomości historyczne o mieście Kłecku* (Gniezno, 1848); S. Karwowski, *Gniezno* (Poznań, 1892); Ks. F. Siarczyński, *Wiadomości historyczne i statystyczne o miejście Jarosławiu* (Lwów, 1826); K. Kaczmarczyk, 'Proces o czarostwo w 1688 i 1699', *Lud* 7 (1908), 302–22; idem, 'Ze starych aktów. Proces o czary w Bochni 1679 r.', *Lud* 16 (1910), 45–53; M. Wawrzeniecki, 'Przyczynek do procesów o czary', *Lud* 24 (1925), 173; and idem, 'Dwa procesy o czary z 1684', *Lud* 24 (1925), 170–2.
57. See A. Karpiński, *Kobieta w mieście polskim w drugiej połowie XVI i w XVII wieku* (Warsaw, 1995); M. Pilaszek, 'Procesy czarownic w Polsce w XVI–XVIII w. Nowe aspekty. Uwagi na marginesie pracy B. Baranowskiego', *Odrodzenie i Reformacja w Polsce* 42 (1998), 81–103; S. Salmonowicz, 'O niegodziwości procesów o czary', *Czasopismo Prawno-Historyczne* 46 (1994), 115–20; W. Wyporska, 'Early Modern Exclusion – The Branding of the Witch in Demonological Literature 1511–1775', in E. Grossman (ed.), *Examining 'the Other', in Polish Culture: Studies in Language, Literature and Cultural Mythology* (Lampeter, 2002), pp. 153–165; idem, 'Jewish, Noble, German or Peasant? – The Devil in Early Modern Poland', in É. Pócs and G. Klaniczay (eds), *Demons, Spirits, Witches: Christian Demonology and Popular Mythology* (Budapest, 2006), pp. 135–47; idem, 'Witchcraft, Arson and Murder – The Turek Trial of 1652', *Central European Journal* 1 (2003), 41–54; and idem, 'Motive'.
58. Zakrzewska, *Czary w Lublinie*.
59. The title of a work on Polish religious tolerance in the seventeenth century by J. Tazbir, *Państwo bez stosów* (Warsaw, 1967).
60. A. Krzyżanowski, *Dawna Polska ze stanowiska jej udziału w dziejach postępującej ludzkości* (Warsaw, 1844). See also X.A.R., 'Relacja naocznego świadka o straceniu razem 14-tu mniemanych czarownic', *Przyjaciel Ludu* 16–18 (1835).
61. J. Łukaszewicz, *Krótki historyczno-statystyczny opis miast i wsi w dzisiejszym powiecie krotoszyńskim* (2 vols, Poznań, 1869–75), I, pp. 75–6.
62. Levack (ed.), *Witch-hunt*, pp. 215–18, and A. Llewellyn Barstow, *Witchcraze* (New York, 1994), pp. 58–9, 67.
63. Łukaszewicz, *Krotoszyńskim*, I, pp. 75–6.

64. F. Olszewski, 'Prześladowanie czarów w dawnej Polsce', in *Album uczące się mlodzieży poświęcone J. I. Kraszewskiemu* (Lwów, 1879), pp. 500, 504.
65. See J. Rosenblatt, *Czarownica powołana. Przyczynek do historii spraw przeciw czarownicom w Polsce* (Warsaw, 1883); J. Karłowicz, 'Czary i czarownice w Polsce', *Wisła* 1, no. 2 (1887), 14–20, 56–62, 93–9, 136–43, 172–3, 213–22; and Karwowski, *Gniezno*.
66. K. Koranyi, 'Studia nad wierzeniami w historii prawa karnego. Beczka czarownic', *Pamiętnik Historyczno-Prawny* 5, no. 2 (1927), 1–43; and idem, 'Czary i gusla przed sądami kościelnymi w Polsce w XV i pierwszej połowie XVI w.', *Lud* 26 (1927), 1–25.
67. Biblioteka Wojewódźka Publiczna w Bydgoszczu, rkp. III.534. T. Abdank Piotrowski, 'Sądy nad czarownicami w Fordonie' (1939), p. 2.
68. Koranyi, 'Beczka', p. 6, and J. Bystroń, *Kultura ludowa* (Warsaw, 1936), p. 236; Z. Gloger, *Encyklopedia staropolska illustrowana* (Warsaw, 1845–1910), p. 267; and J. Rafacz, 'Podejrzenie o czary w Krościenku', *Lud* 20 (1914/18), 303.
69. Rosenblatt, *Czarownica*, p. 7; J. Bystroń, *Dzieje obyczajów w dawnej Polsce wiek XVI–XVIII* (Warsaw, 1976 [1932]), p. 293; B. Baranowski, *Kultura ludowa XVII i XVIII wieku* (Łódź, 1971), pp. 203, 245; AGAD KB 252, fo. 252; and APP AM Pyzdry I/43, fos 59–62.
70. J. Putek, *Mroki średniowiecza*, 5th edn (Warsaw, 1985 [1935]), p. 159; and A. Fischer, F. Lorentz and T. Lehr Spławiński (eds), *Kaszubi: Kultura ludowa i język* (Toruń, 1934), p. 96.
71. Abdank Piotrowski, 'Sądy', p. 2; Gloger, *Encyklopedia*, p. 273; Karłowicz, 'Czary', p. 221; and Koranyi, 'Beczka', p. 5.
72. Gloger, *Encyklopedia*, p. 273; and Putek, *Mroki*, p. 148.
73. Karłowicz, 'Czary', p. 221; Olszewski, 'Prześladowanie', p. 500; Putek, *Mroki*, p. 145; and Rosenblatt, *Czarownica*, p. 23.
74. Gloger, *Encyklopedia*, p. 474; Łukaszewicz, *Krotoszyńskim*, I, p. 76; R. Berwiński, *Studia o gusłach, czarach, zabobonach i przesądach ludowych* (Warsaw, 1862), p. 187; and K. Kantak, 'Poznańska książka w obronie czarownic', *Kronika Miasta Poznania* 11 (1933), 268.
75. Gloger, *Encyklopedia*, pp. 266–7, 475; Olszewski, 'Prześladowanie', p. 495; and A. Fischer, 'Opowieści o czarownicach z doliny nowotarskiej', *Lud* 25 (1926), 78.
76. See R. Hassencamp, 'Ein Ostrowoer Hexenprozess aus dem Jahre 1719', *Zeitschrift der Historischen Gesellschaft für die Provinz Posen* 8 (1893), 223–8; H. Hockenbeck, 'Hexenbrände in Wongrowitz', *Zeitschrift der Historischen Gesellschaft für die Provinz Posen* 9 (1894), 175–8; J.A. Lilienthal, 'Die Hexenprozesse der beiden Städte Braunsberg, nach den Criminalacten des Braunsberger Archivs', Königsberg, 1861, *Neue Preussische Provinzial Blätter*, 2, 1858–60; J. Muhl, 'Zauberei und Hexenaberglauben im Danziger Land', *Mitteilungen des Westpreußischen Geschichtvereins* 32 (1933), H2; F. Reich, *Hexenprozesse in Danzig und in den westpreußischen Grenzgebieten* (Munich, 1940); and A. Warschauer, 'Die älteste Spur eines Hexenprozesses in Posen, *Zeitschrift der Historischen Gesellschaft für die Provinz Posen* 4 (1889).
77. Karłowicz, 'Czary', p. 142; and Gloger, *Encyklopedia*, p. 273.
78. Kantak, 'Poznańska książka', p. 269; and Koranyi, 'Beczka', p. 131.

79. J. Tuwim, *Czary i czarty polskie oraz wypisy czarnoksięskie* (Warsaw, 1960 [1924]), p. 54.
80. Gloger, *Encyklopedia*, p. 269.
81. Baranowski, *Procesy*, pp. 16–17, 179 and idem, *Kultura*, p. 245.
82. Pilaszek, 'Uwagi'.
83. Baranowski's signature is often found in the user records of the municipal court books. See B. Baranowski, *Najdawniejsze procesy o czary w Kaliszu* (Lublin-Łódź, 1951).
84. Baranowski, *Procesy*, p. 30.
85. Ankarloo et al. (eds), *Witch Trials*, p. 13.
86. K. Baschwitz, *Czarownice* (Warsaw, 1971 [1963]), p. 430.
87. G. Klaniczay, *The Uses of Supernatural Power: The Transformation of Popular Religion in Medieval and Early-Modern Europe* (Cambridge, 1990), p. 153.
88. Levack (ed.), *Witch-hunt*, pp. 214–8, and see pp. 279–81 of the 2006 edition.
89. G. Klaniczay, 'Witch-Trials in Hungary (1520–1777): The Accusations and the Popular Universe of Magic', in B. Ankarloo and G. Henningsen (eds), *Early Modern Witchcraft: Centres and Peripheries* (Oxford, 1998 [1990]), p. 230; Llewellyn Barstow, *Witchcraze*, p. 67; Levack (ed.), *Witch-hunt*, p. 216; J. Tazbir, 'Procesy o czary', *Odrodzenie i Reformacja w Polsce* 23 (1978), 152; G.K. Waite, *Heresy, Magic and Witchcraft in Early Modern Europe* (Basingstoke, 2003), p. 214; and R. Thurston, *The Witch Hunts: A History of the Witch Persecutions in Europe and North America* (Harlow, 2007), p. 150.
90. Ankarloo et al. (eds), *Witch Trials*, pp. 12–13, 49. Behringer dismisses Baranowski's 10,000 executions and concentrates on Lambrecht's statistics for Silesia; see W. Behringer, *Witches and Witch-Hunts* (Cambridge, 2004), pp. 153–4.
91. G. Adamczewska, 'Magiczna broń i jej rola w walce między wsią a dworem Sieradzkiem w XVII i XVIII wieku', *Łódzkie Studia Etnograficzne* 5 (1963), 5–16; Z. Kuchowicz, *Obyczaje staropolskie XVII–XVIII w.* (Łódź, 1975), pp. 134, 143; I. Orłowicz, 'Czarownice', *Acta Universitatis Nicolai Copernici* 51 (1998), 99–111; Salmonowicz, 'O niegodziwości', pp. 115–20; Tazbir, 'Procesy', pp. 151, 166; B. Janiszewska-Mincer, 'Bydgoskie procesy o czary w 1638 roku', *Prace Komisji Historii, Seria C* 4 (1966), 105; and B. Wojcieszak, *Opalenickie procesy czarownic z XVII wieku* (Opalenice, 1987).
92. K. Bukowska-Gorgoni, 'Procesy o czary i powołanie przez czarownice w orzecznictwie Sądu Wyższego prawa niemieckiego na Zamku Krakowskim', *Lud* 54 (1970), 156–67; Janiszewska-Mincer, 'Bydgoskie procesy', pp. 105–24; and Tazbir, 'Procesy', pp. 151–77.
93. Tazbir, 'Procesy', pp. 151–77.
94. J. Worończak, 'Procesy o czary przed Poznańskim sądem miejskim w XVI w.', *Literatura ludowa*, 3 (1972), 49–57; J. Derenda and B. Sygit, *Przez czarta opętane* (Bydgoszcz, 1990); J. Samp, *Droga na Sabat* (Gdańsk, 1981); A. Łuczak, *Czary i czarownice wczoraj i dziś* (Tarnów, 1993); and M. Kracik and J. Rożek, *Hultaje, złoczyńcy, wszetecznice w dawnym Krakowie. O marginesie społecznym w XVII I XVIII w.* (Cracow, 1986).
95. In addition to works mentioned above dealing with trials from Bochnia, Braniewo, Bydgoszcz, Cracow, Fordon, Gdańsk, Gniezno, Kalisz, Kłeck, Krotoszyń, Lublin, Lwów, Opalenica, Poznań, Sieradz, Turek and Wągrowiec, see: J. Stępień, *Kleczewskie procesy o czary* (Poznań, 1998), a rather sensationalist

account; J. Wijaczka, 'Men Standing Trial for Witchcraft at the Łobżenica Court in the Second Half of the 17th Century', *APH* 93 (2006), 69–85; W. Uruszczak and I. Dwornicka (eds), *Acta maleficorum Wisniciae. Księga złoczyńców sądu kryminalnego w Wiśniczu (1629–1665)* (Cracow, 2003); M. Adamczyk 'Procesy czarownic w Zbąszyniu', in J. Świerzowicz (ed.), *Wczoraj i dziś powiatu nowotomyślskiego. Jednodniówka* (Nowy Tomyśl, 1938); Z. Dydek, 'Czary w procesie inkwizycyjnym w Rzeszowie w XVIII wieku', *Rocznik Województwa Rzeszowskiego* 5 (1964–65); S. Klarner, 'Sprawy o czary w urzędach bełżyckich w wiekach XVI-XVIII. Z aktów urzędów radzieckiego i wójtowskiego miasta Bełżyc', *Wisła* 16 (1902); H. Połaczkówna (ed.) *Najdawniejsza księga sądowa wsi Trześniowa 1419–1609* (Lwów, 1923); Z. Malewski, 'Procesy o czarnoksięstwo i zabobony w Bydgoszczy. Przyczynek do dziejów czarownictwa w Polsce', *Przegląd Bygoski* 4 (1936); S. Szczotka (ed.), 'Sprawa Barbary Opielonki o czary 12 maja 1595', in *Materiały do dziejów zbójnictwa góralskiego z lat 1589–1782* (Łódź, 1952), pp. 24–5; W. Stachowski, 'Czarownice z Pępowa', *Kronika Gostyńska*, Series VI, 4 (1934); J. Adamczyk, 'Czary i magia w praktyce sądów kościelnych na ziemiach polskich w późnym średniowieczu (XV–połowa XVI w.)', in M. Koczerska (ed.), *Karolińscy pokutnicy i polskie średniowieczne czarownice. Konfrontacja doktryny chrześcijańskiej z życiem społeczeństwa średniowiecznego* (Warsaw, 2007); W. Uruszczak, 'Proces czarownicy w Nowym Sączu w 1670 roku. Z badań nad miejskim procesem karnym czasów nowożytnych', in E. Borkowska-Bagieńska and H. Olszewski (eds), *Historia prawa. Historia kutlura. Liber Memorialis Vitoldo Maisel dedicatus* (Poznań, 1994); J. Wijaczka, 'Procesy o czary w wsi Młotkowo w 1692 roku. Przyczynek do polowania na czarownice w Rzeczypospolitej XVII wieku.', *Odrodzenie i Reformacja* 48 (2004); Adamczewska, 'Magiczna'; B. Baranowski, 'Wielki proces o czary miłosne w Praszce w 1665 roku', *Łódzkie Studia Etnograficzne* 4 (1962), 5–14; Bukowska-Gorgoni, 'Procesy'; M. Wawrzeniecki, *Krwawe widma* (Warsaw, 1909); idem, 'Przyczynek', 173; idem, 'Dwa procesy', 170–2; idem, 'Namaszczanie się czarownic', *Lud* 26 (1927), 72–3; idem, 'Jak konstruowano u nas stos do palenia czarownic?', *Lud* 26 (1927), 71–2; idem, 'Szkoła magii w Krakowie', *Lud* 26 (1927), 69–70; idem, 'Proces o czary w Nieszawie w 1721', *Wisła* 11 (1898), 646–54; Kaczmarczyk, 'Proces o czarostwo'; idem, 'Przyczyńki do wiary w czary', *Lud* 13 (1907), 330–2; idem, 'Ze starych aktów'; idem, 'Straty archiwalne na terenie Poznania w latach 1939–1945', *Archeion* 28 (1957), 65–93; A. Komoniecki, *Dziejopis żywiecki* (Żywiec, 1987 [1704]); Rafacz, 'Podejrzenie'; M. Zakrzewska-Dubasowa, 'Proces o czary w Kraśniku z roku 1746', in *Z dziejów powiatu kraśnickiego* (Lublin, 1963); T. Tripplin, *Tajemnice społeczeństwa wykryte ze spraw kryminalnych krajowych* (3 vols, Wrocław, 1852); K. Koranyi, 'Czary w postępowaniu sądowym', *Lud* 25 (1926), 7–18; idem, 'Czary i gusla'; idem, 'Studia nad wierzeniami'; idem, 'Łysa Góra. Studium z dziejów wierzeń ludowych w Polsce w XVII I XVIII w.', *Lud* 27 (1928), 57–74; Z. Lasocki, 'Szlachta płońska w walce z czartem', *Miesięcznik Heraldyczny* 12 (1933), vol. 1, 1–8; vol. 2, 18–22; vol. 3, 37–42; M. Mikołajczyk, 'Jak obronić oskarżoną o czary. Mowy procesowe z 1655 roku w sprawie Gertrudy Zagrodzkiej', in M. Wąsowicz (ed.), *Dziejów kultury prawnej: Studia ofierowane Profesorowi Juliuszowi Bardzachowi w dziewięćdziesięciolecie urodzin* (Warsaw, 2004), pp. 389–410; Siarczyński,

Wiadomości; W. Smoleński, *Przewrót umysłowy w Polsce* (Warsaw, 1979 [1891]); Wojcieszak, *Opalenickie*.
96. See Wyporska, 'Turek', and www.witchcraftinpoland.com.
97. J. Wijaczka, 'Czary w regionie świętokrzyskim'; idem; 'Czary w Prusach Książęcych'; K.P. Szkurłatowski, 'Gdańskie procesy czarownic w XV–XVII w. na tle ówczesnych przemian religijnych', in J. Iluk and D. Mariańska (eds), *Protestantyzm i protestanci na Pomorzu* (Gdańsk-Koszalin, 1997); idem, 'Proces inkwizycyjny przeciwko czarownictwu w praktyce sądów sołtysich województwa malborskiego na przełomie VXII i XVIII w. na tle rozwoju europejskiego prawa karnego', *Rocznik Elbląski* 15 (1997); and T. Wiślicz, 'Czary przed sądami wiejskimi w Polsce w XVI–XVIII w.', *Czasopismo prawno-historyczne* 49 (1997), 47–63; and idem, 'Społeczeństwo Kleczewa i okolic w walce z czartem (1624–1700), *Kwartalnik Historyczny* 112 (2004), 37–60; Pilaszek, *Procesy*, and M. Ostling, *Between the Devil and the Host: Imagining Witchcraft in Early Modern Poland* (Oxford, 2011).
98. Wiślicz, 'Czary'; Karpiński, *Kobieta*, pp. 319–20; Pilaszek, 'Uwagi', pp. 81–103; Salmonowicz, 'O niegodziwości', pp. 115–20; and Bogucka, *Women*. A. Zdziechiewicz makes little significant contribution to the debate in *Staropolskie polowania na czarownice* (Katowice, 2004). See my website at www.witchcraftinpoland.com for reviews of Ostling's *Between the Devil* and Pilaszek's *Procesy*.
99. Stuart Clark, review of *Between the Devil and the Host: Imagining Witchcraft in Early Modern Poland*, by M. Ostling, *The Journal of Ecclesiastical History* 64, no. 1 (2013), 185–6.
100. M. Ostling, 'Konstytucja 1543 r. i początki procesów o czary w Polsce', *OiR* 49 (2005), 93–103; idem: 'Imagining Witchcraft in Early Modern Poland' (PhD thesis, University of Toronto, 2008); idem: *Between the Devil*, and Pilaszek, *Procesy*, p. 45.
101. Ostling, *Between the Devil*, pp. 244–53 and idem, pp. 7, 8, 32.
102. Ostling, 'Imagining', p. 35.
103. See Wyporska, 'Motive'; Pilaszek, *Procesy*, p. 45; Ostling, 'Imagining', pp. 33–4 and idem, *Between the Devil*, pp. 244–53. See cases from Wągrowiec, Akta Miasta Wągrowiec I/24 Księga rad i wojt 1686–88; Akta Miasta Wągrowiec I/25 Księga rad i wojt 1695–1737; Akta Miasta Wągrowiec I/42 Fragmenty księgi radzieckiej i wojtowskiej kryminalnej 1760–66; Akta Miasta Wągrowiec I/59 Ekstrakt z ksiąg wojtowskich m. Lękna – sprawy o czary Agnieszki Bednarki 1719–20; and Kryminalia–Fragmenty księgi radzieckiej i wojtowskiej kryminalnej 1760–66, 1774.
104. Ostling, *Between the Devil*, p. 201.
105. Ibid., appendix.
106. Ibid., p. 114.
107. Pilaszek, *Procesy*, p. 45.
108. Ibid., pp. 531–3.
109. Pilaszek, *Procesy*, pp. 337, 268, 525, 319, 528, 292, 299, 300, 281–3, 195, 203, 215, 533.
110. Ibid., pp. 522, 400.
111. Ibid., pp. 281–5, 529, 419, 283.
112. Ibid., pp. 184, 397, 281, 96.
113. Ibid., pp. 209–20.

114. Ibid., pp. 130-8.
115. Ibid., p. 527.
116. All local state archives were asked whether they were aware of material concerning witchcraft in their collections. The Black Books were examined from every archive and the Diocesan Archives were also asked for information. All but one (Gniezno) of the ecclesiastical archives claimed not to have any material concerning witchcraft. K. Dysa, 'Witchcraft Trials and Beyond: Right-bank Side Ukrainian Trials of the Seventeenth and Eighteenth Centuries' (PhD thesis, Central European University, 2004), p. 12; and M. Pilaszek, 'Witchhunts in Poland in the 16th–18th centuries', *APH* 86 (2002), 122. See APP AM Turek I/30, 1648-1667 entitled *Protocollon causarum criminalium seu potius maleficiorum*, which contains the trials of 39 women. The record APP AM Poniec I/50 *Proces o czary przed sądem wojtowskim m. Ponieca na sesji w Pawłowicach 1672* records one trial. PTPN rkps. 859, 1624-1738.
117. They cover 1652-53, 1656, 1660-61, 1663-70, 1671-1728, 1735, 1741, 1743-44, 1752-57, 1765-75 and 1775-88.
118. The rough copies run between 1553-58, 1581-85, 1590-1616, 1630-33, 1682, and 1721-23 and the testimony books cover 1718, 1722-69, 1772, 1774, and 1778.
119. Wiślicz, 'Czary'; J. Bardach, B. Leśnodorski and M. Pietrzak, *Historia państwa i prawa polskiego* (2 vols, Warsaw, 1966), p. 363; and R. Łaszewski, *Wiejskie prawo karne w Polsce XVII i XVIII w.* (Toruń, 1988), p. 137.
120. R. Golden (ed.), *Encyclopedia of Witchcraft: The Western Tradition* (Santa Barbara, 2006), *ad loc*. 'Nazi Interest in Witch Persecution'. Pilaszek does not mention it and to my knowledge no Polish historians use it for their research.
121. Baranowski, *Procesy*, p. 29, and A. Stebelski, *The Fate of Polish Archives during World War II* (Warsaw, 1964), p. 51.
122. Kaczmarczyk, 'Straty', pp. 92-3.
123. The material was gathered preliminarily from the archives in Poznań, Cracow, Warsaw, Przemyśl, Lublin, Bochnia, Bydgoszcz and Rzeszów and from references in secondary sources.
124. J. Tazbir (ed.), *Polska XVII wieku* (Warsaw, 1969), p. 89, quoted in J. Wormald, *Court, Kirk, and Community: Scotland 1470-1625* (London, 1997 [1981]), p. 166.
125. Pilaszek, *Procesy*, pp. 268, 297. Ostling, 'Imagining', p. 18.
126. During initial research, as an indicative control sample, all the municipal court records books for Rzeszów were examined with only three mentions of witchcraft.
127. PTPN rkps. 859, 1624-1738.
128. Primary sources examined also include printed sources such as episcopal letters, legal statutes and literature from the period. In order to determine which literary sources were likely to yield relevant material, dictionaries of sixteenth- and seventeenth-century Polish were consulted. See S. Urbańczyk et al. (eds), *Słownik Staropolski* (Warsaw, 1953–); S. Bąk et al. (eds), *Słownik polszczyżny XVI wieku* (Warsaw, 1966–); S.B. Linde, *Słownik języka polskiego* (Warsaw, 1807); S. Orgelbrand, *Wielka Encyklopedya Powszechna* (Warsaw, 1883); and Gloger, *Encyklopedia*.

129. Clark, *Thinking*, p. ix.
130. Others who have examined literature in tandem with witchcraft trials, such as Willis, *Malevolent Nurture*; Purkiss, *The Witch in History*; G. Roberts and L. Normand (eds), *Witchcraft in Early Modern Scotland: James VI's Demonology and the North Berwick Witches* (Exeter, 2000); and Brauner, *Fearless Wives*, have also produced illuminating studies.

2 The World of the Witches: Confessions and Conflicts

1. For an excellent discussion on reading archival sources, see N. Zemon Davis, *Fiction in the Archives: Pardon Tales and their Tellers in Sixteenth-Century France* (Cambridge, 1987).
2. Przybyszewski, *Czary*, p. 42. No trace of these records were found in APP Akta wojtowskie w Gostyniu 1768–73 and APP KM Gostyń I/33 Protocollon proconsulis gostinensis 1772–79.
3. M. Bogucka, 'Law and Crime in Poland in Early Modern Times', *Acta Polonica Historica* 71 (1995), pp. 187, 193.
4. Levack (ed.), *Witch-hunt*, p. 134.
5. Wiślicz, 'Kleczew', p. 73, and Pilaszek, *Procesy*, p. 45.
6. Pilaszek, *Procesy*, pp. 337, 268, 525, 319, 528, 292, 299, 300, 281–3, 195, 203, 215, 533.
7. W. Behringer, *Witches and Witch-Hunts* (Cambridge, 2004), p. 49.
8. M. Bogucka, 'Women and Economic Life in the Polish Cities During the 16th–17th Centuries', in S. Cavaciocchi (ed.), *La donna nell'economia secc. XIII–XVIII* (Florence, 1990), p. 108.
9. Wiślicz, 'Kleczew', p. 70.
10. Baranowski, *Kalisz*, pp. 17–23.
11. These rituals replicate a widespread Polish tradition described in Adam Mickiewicz's *Dziady*, for example.
12. Baranowski, *Kalisz*, pp. 24–6.
13. See Ostling, *Between the Devil*, pp. 107–39 for a lengthier discussion of spells.
14. Baranowski, *Kalisz*, pp. 31, 41, 57.
15. Ibid., pp. 200–9.
16. Ibid., pp. 56–66.
17. Ostling, *Between the Devil*, pp. 107–39.
18. APP AM Poznan I/638, fos 83v–6v and APP AM Turek I/30 – fos 2–7.
19. There are 13 clear cases in which one can clearly see separate accusations and sentences. However, there is another summary of a case without a sentence: AGAD KB 252: fo. 12v.
20. Ibid., fos 8v, 16v, 17.
21. Ibid., fo. 9v.
22. Ibid., fos 9, 27.
23. Ibid., fo. 16.
24. See Wyporska, 'The Devil' and idem, 'Branding', pp. 143–55.
25. Wiślicz, 'Kleczew', p. 92.
26. Kuchowicz, *Obyczaje*, pp. 132–6, and A. Czubryński, 'Z katalogu "imion diabłów"', *Euhemer* 6 (1958), 40–3.

27. AGAD KB 252, fo. 17; APP AM Dolsk I/7, pp. 104-8; APP AM Gniezno I/70, fos 178-9.
28. APP AM Pyzdry I/43, pp. 60, 52, 51.
29. AGAD KB 252, fos 15, 16v.
30. Ibid., fos 9v, 15 v, 18.
31. Ibid., fos 15, 25v.
32. Ibid., fos 28v, 41v.
33. AGAD KB 252, fos 9v, 15v, 18, 29, 41v; APP KM Gniezno, I/70, p. 385; Chmielowski, *Nowe Ateny*, pp. 92-4; J. Bohomolec, *Diabeł w swojej postaci* (Warsaw, 1772), pp. 151, 139; and S. Ząmbkowicz (trans.), *Młot na czarownice* (Cracow, 1614), p. 414. For a fuller discussion of portrayals of the Devil as black, see Ü. Valk, *The Black Gentleman* (Helsinki, 2001).
34. AGAD KB 252, fos 23v, 24.
35. Ibid., fos 54 and 25v.
36. Ibid., fos 23v, 54.
37. APP AM Dolsk I/7, p. 104.
38. H. Bonfigli, *De Plica Polonica Tractatus Mediophysicus* (Wrocław, 1712). In this work he comments on the condition, confirming that most Poles believed it to be the result of witchcraft. See also B. Connor, *The History of Poland in Several Letters* (2 vols, London, 1698), II, pp. 91-6.
39. Ząmbkowicz, *Młot*, pp. ii, 409.
40. Ks. B. Chmielowski, *Nowe Ateny albo Akademia wszelkiej scjencji pełna, część trzecia* (Cracow, 1966 [1754]), p. 122.
41. L. Przybyszewski, *Czary i czarownice* (Poznań, 1932), pp. 23-36.
42. AGAD KB 252, fo. 9.
43. Ibid., fo. 10v.
44. Ibid., fos 8, 17, 20v.
45. Ibid., fos 9v, 16v.
46. Ibid., fo. 89v.
47. Ibid., fos 9v, 18, 18v.
48. Ibid., fos8, 12v, 90.
49. Ibid., fo. 15.
50. Ibid., fos 18, 23, 29.
51. Ibid., fo. 54v, 90.
52. Ibid., fo. 16v.
53. Ibid., fos 10v, 15, 23.
54. Ibid., fo. 28v, 54v.
55. Ibid., fos 9v, 15, 18v, 19v.
56. Ostling, *Between the Devil*, pp. 140-82.
57. AGAD KB 252, fos 9-12v.
58. H. Węgrzynek, *'Czarna Legenda' Żydów: Procesy o rzekome mordy rytualne w dawnej Polsce* (Warsaw, 1995), pp. 47-9, and see idem, 'Dzieje poznańskiej legendy o profanacji hostii', *Kronika Miasta Poznania* 3-4 (1992), 45-56.
59. Węgrzynek, 'Dzieje', p. 52.
60. AGAD KB 252, fos 18, 20v, 23, 25v.
61. Ibid., fos 10, 10v, 29.
62. APP AM Poniec I/50, p. 6; AGAD KB 252, fos 41v, 29, 10, 10v; and APP AM Gniezno, I/70, pp. 370-95.
63. See Briggs, *Witches*, p. 13; Rowlands, *Rothenburg*, pp. 1-3.

64. Moszyński quoted in Pilaszek, *Procesy*, p. 394, and E. Bever, *The Realities of Witchcraft and Popular Magic in Early Modern Europe: Culture, Cognition, and Everyday Life* (Basingstoke and New York, 2008), p. 47.
65. W. Behringer, 'Weather, Hunger and Fear: Origins of the European Witch-Hunts in Climate, Society and Mentality', *German History* 13, no. 1 (1995), p. 23.
66. Rowlands, *Rothenburg*, p. 68; Roper, *Oedipus*, p. 182; APP AM Poznań, I/638, fos 89, 148v; and APP AM Kalisz I/158, pp. 347–8.
67. Roper, *Oedipus*, pp. 180, 216; Roper, *Witch Craze*, p. 10; APP AM Turek I/30, fo. 11.
68. Roper, *Witch Craze*, p. 123, and APP AM Gniezno, I/70, pp. 395–405.
69. Rowlands, *Rothenburg*, p. 122, and APP AM Gniezno, I/70, pp. 370–95.
70. Behringer, *Witches*, p. 87.
71. For an excellent comparison between peasant communities and their relationship with the Junkers in East-Elbian Germany and their counterparts in Poland during the period see W.W. Hagen, 'Village Life in East-Elbian Germany and Poland, 1400–1800: Subjection, Self-Defence, Survival', in T. Scott (ed.), *The Peasantries of Europe* (London, 1998), pp. 145–89.
72. Rowlands, *Rothenburg*, p. 59.
73. S. Hoszowski, *Klęski elementarne w Polsce w latach 1587–1648* (Warsaw, 1960), p. 464.
74. B. Fagan, *The Little Ice Age: How Climate Made History 1300–1850* (2000), pp. 105, 113.
75. H. Flohn and R. Fantechi, *The Climate of Europe: Past, Present and Future* (1984), p. 48, and B. Baranowski and Z. Kamieńska (eds), *Historia kultury materialnej Polski w zarysie* (Wrocław, 1978), IV, p. 13.
76. C.P. Pfister, 'Monthly Temperature and Precipitation in Central Europe 1525–1979', in R.S. Bradley and P.D. Jones (eds), *Climate since A.D. 1500* (1995 [1992]), pp. 127, 137.
77. See A. Karpiński, *W walce z niewidzalnym wrogiem* (Warsaw, 2000), pp. 26–7.
78. Ibid., pp. 303–5. Karpiński, *Kobieta*, p. 399; Hoszowski, *Klęski*, p. 462; and J. Kwak, *Klęski elementarne w miastach górnośląskich (w XVIII i w pierwszej połowie XIX w)* (Opole, 1987), p. 17.
79. AGAD KMB 252, fos 12v–13, 15–20v, 23–6v, and P. Anders, *Grodzisk Wielkopolska* (Poznań, 1995), p. 20.
80. Hoszowski, *Klęski*, pp. 460, 464, and H. Lamb, *Climate, History and the Modern World* (1995), p. 232.
81. Łukaszewicz, *Krotoszyński*, II, pp. 300, 318.
82. P. Anders, *Pyzdry miasto nad Wartą* (Poznań, 1993), pp. 14–15; W. Łęcki, *Gostyń* (Poznań, 1997), p. 11; G. Patro, *Wągrowiec zarys dziejów* (Warsaw, 1982), pp. 26–9, 36; and K. Dąbrowski and A. Gieysztor (eds), *Osiemnaście wieków Kalisza*, II (3 vols, Kalisz, 1960–62), p. 470.
83. Topolski, *Wielkopolska*, pp. 118, 120–4, 133.
84. I. Gieysztorowa, *Wstęp do demografii staropolskiej* (Warsaw, 1976), p. 189.
85. Ibid., pp. 195–6, 199.
86. Hagen, 'Village Life', p. 172.
87. Rowlands, *Rothenburg*, p. 198.
88. AGAD KB 252, fos 20v–21.

89. *Postępek prawa czartowskiego przeciw narodowi ludzkiemu* (Cracow, 1872 [1570]), p. 114, and Ząmbkowicz, *Młot*, pp. 434.
90. Ząmbkowicz, *Młot*, pp. 21, 152; *Postępek*, p. 114; Chmielowski, *Nowe Ateny*, p. 134; and J. Bohomolec, *Diabeł w swojej postaci, Część druga* (Warsaw, 1777), p. 275.
91. APP AM Kalisz I/158, fo. 88v.
92. Rowlands, *Rothenburg*, p. 68, and APP AM Poznań I/638. fos 88v–90, 148v–54.
93. Ostling, *Between the Devil*, and idem, 'Imagining'.
94. Pilaszek, *Procesy*, pp. 280–85.
95. W. Kriegseisen, 'Between Intolerance and Persecution. Polish and Lithuanian Protestants in the 18th Century', *APH* 73 (1996), 13–27.
96. T. Wiślicz, '"Miraculous Sites" in the Early Modern Polish-Lithuanian Commonwealth', in T. Wünsch (ed.), *Religion und Magie in Ostmitteleuropa: Spielräume theologischer Normierungsprozesse in Spätmittelalter und Früher Neuzeit* (Berlin, 2006), pp. 287–99. See p. 294.
97. Bogucka, *Women*, pp. 63–4, 68–9.
98. Kłoczowski, *Polish Christianity*, pp. 78–83, 108, 111, 113, 116, 146, 109, 133.
99. Behringer, 'Weather', pp. 21–2.
100. APP KM Turek I/30 fos 2–9.
101. Despite Poland's frequent comparison with Hungary, it is clear that only the later peak was common to both persecutions. Hungary's persecution continued to rage long after trials in Wielkopolska had become an anomaly. In the 1750s there were 143 trials in Hungary, 47 in the 1760s, and eight in the 1770s – the last execution was in 1777. Behringer, *Witches*, p. 190.
102. Topolski, *Wielkopolska*, p. 131.

3 Witchcraft and Gender: Intimate Servants and Excluded Masculinities

1. APP AM Gniezno I/70, pp. 395–405; Bogucka, 'Women'; Karpiński, *Kobieta*, p. 135; A. Karpiński, 'Female Servants in Polish Towns in the Late 16th and 17th Centuries', *APH* 74 (1996), 21–44.
2. APP AM Poznań I/639, fos 216v–8v.
3. APP AM Kalisz I/158, pp. 129–31.
4. APP AM Gniezno I/135, pp. 23–39.
5. Their trials would have been noted in the *Sąd grodzki* records.
6. M. Bogucka, 'Great Disputes over Woman in Early Modern Times', *APH* 78 (1998), 27–52, and A. Wyrobisz, 'Woman, Man and Historical Change: Case Studies in the Impact of Gender History', *APH* 71 (1995), 69–82; APP AM Gostyń I/41, pp. 9–13; M. Bogucka, 'The Foundations of the Old Polish World: Patriarchalism and the Family. Introduction into the Problem', *APH* 69 (1994), 10.
7. AGAD KM Sieradz 41, fos 9–11v.
8. M. Bogucka, 'Gender in the Economy of a Traditional Agrarian Society: The Case of Poland in the 16th–17th Centuries', *APH* 74 (1996), 6–15, and idem, 'Patriarchalism', pp. 37–53.

9. A. Karpiński, 'The Woman on [sic] the Market Place. The Scale of Feminization of Retail Trade in Polish Towns in the Second Half of the 16th and in the 17th Century', in S. Cavaciocchi (ed.), *La donna nell'economia secc. XIII–XVIII* (Florence, 1990), pp. 283–92.
10. S. Waszak, 'Dzietność rodziny mieszczańskiej w XVI i XVII w. i ruch naturalny ludności miasta Poznania w końcu XVI i w XVII wieku', *Roczniki Dziejów Społecznych i Gospodarczych* 16 (1954), 316–84, and Karpiński, *Kobieta*, p. 186; APP AM Gniezno I/70, pp. 370–95; M. Bogucka, 'Rodzina w polskim mieście XVI–XVII wieku: wprowadzienie w problematykę', *Przegląd Historyczny* 74, no. 3 (1983), 495–507.
11. See Jackson, 'Wives', p. 71.
12. Ibid., pp. 63–84.
13. APP KM Poznań I/638, fo. 89v, 1544.
14. U. Rublack (ed.), *Gender in Early Modern Germany* (Cambridge, 2002), pp. 1–18. See also L. Roper, *The Holy Household: Women and Morals in Reformation Augsburg* (Oxford, 1989), for a more in-depth discussion.
15. APP AM Kalisz I/158, pp. 17–29, 200–209, 377–84.
16. Brauner, *Fearless Wives*, pp. 114 –15.
17. APP AM Gniezno I/135, pp. 12, 86.
18. L. Roper, 'Witchcraft and Fantasy in Early Modern Germany', in J. Barry, M. Hester and G. Roberts (eds), *Witchcraft in Early Modern Europe: Studies in Culture and Belief* (Cambridge, 1998), pp. x, xi, 7, 8, 10, 207–36.
19. APP AM Turek I/30. Thirty-eight women were tried in 12 trials in this book between 1648–67.
20. Ibid., fos 2–7.
21. Ibid., fos 25–7v, 30v, 45–45v.
22. Rowlands, *Rothenburg*, pp. 141–79, 157. Here she discusses gender in a chapter entitled 'Seduction, Poison and Magical Theft: Gender and Contemporary Fantasies of Witchcraft'. APP AM Gniezno I/135, pp. 12, 1.
23. C. Holmes, 'Women: Witnesses and Witches', *Past and Present* 140 (1993), 45–6, 56, 78. See also the discussion in R. Briggs, 'Women as Victims? Witches, Judges and the Community', *French History* 5, no. 4 (1991), and idem, *Witches*, pp. 285–6. Feminist historians have also argued that under a patriarchal society women will conduct themselves in such a way as to seek masculine approval, which results in criticizing or ousting other women who jeopardize this by their unconventional behaviour.
24. J. Sharpe, 'Witchcraft and Women in Seventeenth Century England: Some Northern Evidence', *Continuity and Change* 6, no. 2 (1991), 183, 193; W. Monter, 'The Pedestal and the Stake: Courtly Love and Witchcraft', in C. Koontz and R. Bridentahl (eds), *Becoming Visible: Women in European History* (Boston, 1987), p. 134, and S. Clark, 'The "Gendering" of Witchcraft in French Demonology: Misogyny or Polarity?', *French History* 5 (1991), 429–31. Whitney criticized this view for reducing gender to a mere cipher.
25. C. Larner, *Enemies of God: The Witch-Hunt in Scotland* (Baltimore, 1981), pp. 1–2, 92, 100, and Rowlands, *Rothenburg*, pp. 160, 169–70.
26. In 1745 in Poznań a German Protestant accused his wife of witchcraft. APP AM Poznan I/671, pp. 1–4.
27. Rowlands, *Rothenburg*, p. 160.
28. APP AM Kalisz I/158, pp. 289–90.

29. APP AM Pyzdry I/43, pp. 54–5, and AGAD KB 252, fos 20v, 21.
30. See Midelfort, *Witch Hunting*, where he argues that where there was a critical mass of cases. Inevitably men would also feature among the accused.
31. See key in AGAD KB 252, fo. 23v.
32. Both of these cases are recorded in APP AM Wągrowiec 1/25, which is unnumbered.
33. This is an interesting contrast to demonological accounts, which maintained that the witch was still visible in bed when attending the sabbat.
34. APP AM Wągrowiec 1/25, unnumbered.
35. AGAD KB 252, fos 89–92v.
36. APP AM Wągrowiec 1/25, unnumbered. For a discussion of accusations of sodomy in tandem with witchcraft in Fribourg, Lausane and Ajore, see Monter, *Witchcraft*, pp. 135–6.
37. This term could be translated as either material or cloth.
38. APP AM Kalisz I/158, pp. 404–14.
39. APP AM Wągrowiec 1/25, unnumbered.
40. Ibid.
41. APP AM Poznań I/647, fo. 293.
42. Ibid., fos 292–3v, 295–6v.
43. APP AM Poznań I/644, fos 24–5.
44. This theme will be explored in Chapter 5.

4 Framing the Witch: Legal Theories and Realities

1. Pilaszek, *Procesy*, pp. 45, 204, Ostling, *Between the Devil*, p. 73. APP AM Pyzdry I/43, pp. 7, 52 (*Speculum Saxonum*); AGAD KB 252, fo. 8v (Carpzov); AGAD KB 252, fo. 27 (Damhouder); and ibid., fos 42, 92 (Mollerius). See APP AM Poznań I/641, fo. 1055.
2. Koranyi, 'Czary i gusla', pp. 1–3, 16.
3. AGAD KB 252, fo. 25.
4. R. Bugaj, *Nauki tajemne w Polsce w dobie odrodzenia* (Wrocław, 1976), p. 151.
5. Koranyi, 'Czary i gusla', p. 1. Discussion of ecclesiastical cases and visitations is beyond the scope of this work, but would make an excellent research topic.
6. H. Karbownik, 'Management of Witchcraft Trials in the Light of Synod Resolutions and Bishops' Regulations in Pre-partition Poland', *The Review of Comparative Law* 2 (1988), 66.
7. For the case of Katarzyna Ceynowa in 1836, see A. Majkowski, 'Pławienie i śmierć rzekomej czarownicy w Chałupkach', *Gryf* 2 (1910), 168–75, 201–8.
8. Koranyi, 'Czary i gusla', p. 8.
9. *Volumina Legum*, I, 578. Bardach et al. (eds), *Historia państwa* (1976), p. 288.
10. Pilaszek, *Procesy*, pp. 45, 194, 209–20 for her criticism of Ostling.
11. Ibid., pp. 166–77.
12. Karbownik, 'Management', pp. 67, 71–5.
13. J. Czechowicz, *Praktyka kryminalna* (Chełmno, 1769), p. 195; J. Wijaczka, 'Procesy o czary w Polsce w dobie Oświecenia. Zarys problematyki', *Klio* 7 (2005), 21, 42; and Pilaszek, *Procesy*, p. 168.

14. For a full discussion of these regulations see Karbownik, 'Management', pp. 65–78.
15. Bardach et al. (eds), *Historia państwa* (1976), p. 195.
    For a discussion on judges see: Bogucka, 'Law and Crime'; M. Pilaszek, 'W poszukiwaniu prawdy o działalności sądów kryminalnych w Koronie XVI–XVIII w.', *Przegląd Historyczny* 89, no. 3 (1998), 361–81; and M. Kamler, 'Rola tortur w polskim sądownictwie miejskim drugiej połowy XVI i pierwszy połowy XVII w.', *Kwartalnik Historyczny* 95, no. 3 (1988), 107–25.
16. See Wiślicz, 'Czary', and Pilaszek, *Czary*, pp. 199–202.
17. Koranyi, 'Czary i gusla', p. 16.
18. J. Kitowicz, *Opis obyczajów za panowania Augusta III* (Warsaw, 1985 [1840]), pp. 136–7.
19. W. Maisel, *Poznańskie prawo karne do końca XVI wieku* (Poznań, 1963), pp. 17–20.
20. S. Sarnicki, *Statuta y metrika przywileiów koronnych* (Cracow, 1594), p. 214.
21. S. Kutrzeba, *Polskie ustawy i artykuły wojskowe od XV do XVII wieku* (Cracow, 1937), p. 210.
22. B. Groicki, *Porządek sądów i spraw miejskich prawa maydeburskiego w Koronie polskiej* (Cracow, 1567), pp. vi–vii.
23. Reprinted in 1562, 1565, 1568, 1582 and 1587 according to K. Estreicher, *Bibliografia Polski. Część III. Obejmująca druku stóleci XV–XVIII w układzie abecadłowym* (11 vols, Cracow, 1910).
24. Bardach et al. (eds), *Historia państwa* (1976), p. 193.
25. Bartłomiej Groicki was thought to have been born in the second decade of the sixteenth century. In 1559 he became a scribe in the High Court of German Law in Cracow and then moved to a similar position in Royal Customs and Excise in 1567. He returned to his former job in 1573 and died around 1605. Therefore, as Bardach et al. point out, his experience was practical rather than theoretical. He based his work on the Bible and Damhouder's *Practica rerum criminalium*, among others. See the introduction to B. Groicki, *Artykuły prawa majdeburskiego: Postępek sądów około karania na gardło. Ustawa płacej u sądów* (Warsaw, 1954 [1558, 1559, 1568]), pp. v–vi.
26. Reprinted in 1559, 1560, 1565, 1568, 1582 and 1587, see Estreicher, *Bibliografia*.
27. Ibid., reprinted in 1562, 1566, 1567, 1582 and 1587.
28. Koranyi, 'Czary i gusla', p. 16 and Bardach et al. (eds), *Historia państwa* (1976), p. 194.
29. See Pilaszek, *Procesy*, pp. 185–91.
30. B. Groicki, *Artykuły prawa maydeburskiego, które zową Speculum Saxonum...* (Warsaw, 1954 [1558]), p. 3.
31. B. Groicki, *Porządek sądów i spraw miejskich prawa maydeburskiego w Koronie polskiej* (Warsaw, 1953 [1559]), pp. 229–33.
32. Groicki, *Porządek* (1567), fo. B.
33. Groicki, *Artykuły... które*, p. 102.
34. See also: Maisel, *Poznańskie prawo*; J. Rafacz, *Dawne polskie prawo karne* (Warsaw, 1932); W. Maisel, 'Sąd miejski prawa polskiego w Kaliszu w XVI wieku', *Czasopismo prawno-historyczne* 23, no. 2 (1971), 129–39; Ptaśnik, *Miasto*; J. Bardach, B. Leśnodorski and M. Pietrzak (eds), *Historia ustroju i prawa polskiego* (Warsaw, 1994); K. Kamińska, *Sądownictwo miasta Torunia*

do połowy XVII wieku na tle ustroju sądów niektórych miast Niemiec i Polski (Warsaw, 1980); D. Makiłła and Z. Naworski, *Prawa na ziemiach polskich – Polska predrozbiorowa zarys wykłady* (2 vols, Toruń, 2000), I; Pilaszek, 'W poszukiwaniu', pp. 361–81; M. Kamler, 'Penalties for Common Crimes in Polish Towns 1550–1650', *APH* 71 (1995), 161–74; idem, 'Struktura i liczebność środowisk przestępczych Poznania i Krakowa w drugiej połowie XVI w.', *Przeszłość demograficzna Polski: materiały i studia* 15 (1984), 71–93; Bogucka, 'Law and Crime', pp. 175–95; idem, *Staropolskie obyczaje w XVI i XVII w.* (Warsaw, 1994); and H. Łaszkiewicz, 'Kary wymierzone przez sąd miejski w Lublinie w drugiej połowie XVII wieku', *Czasopismo prawno-historyczne* 41, no. 2 (1989), 139–51.
35. Bardach et al. (eds), *Historia ustroju*, pp. 250, 272–3.
36. W. Maisel, 'Prawo karne w statutach polskich', *Czasopismo prawno-historyczne* 26 (1974), 102–3.
37. Adamczyk, 'Czary', pp. 245–6 and Maisel, *Poznańskie prawo*, p. 212.
38. In times of the interregnum and rebellion special courts such as the *sądy kapturowe* and *sądy konfederackie* respectively were convened to hear criminal cases. For example the Trybunał Zamoyski was an appeal court for the villages and towns of the Zamoyski estates, which consisted of one delegate from each of the five private towns, the alderman and the Professor of Law at the *Akademia Zamoyska*, and this court was led by the burgrave, with its own guards, chancellery and archive. There were also the *sądy podkomorskie*, 'Chamberlain's Courts'.
39. Bardach et al. (eds), *Historia ustroju*, pp. 283, 239–44, 262. For more information on witchcraft cases heard by village courts, see Wiślicz, 'Czary', and Łaszewski, *Wiejskie prawo*.
40. Bardach et al. (eds), *Historia ustroju*, p. 243.
41. Kamińska, *Sądownictwo*, p. 45, and Ptaśnik, *Miasta*, p. 39.
42. M. Bogucka and H. Samsonowicz, *Dzieje miast i mieszczaństwa w Polsce przedrozbiorowej* (Wrocław, 1986), p. 456.
43. Makiłła and Naworski, *Prawa*, I, p. 177. They maintain that witchcraft trials were recorded in the village and municipal courts, but were most often to be judged on the basis of the municipal laws.
44. J. Bardach, B. Leśnodorski and M. Pietrzak (eds), *Historia państwa i prawa polskiego od połowy XV do r. 1795* (2 vols, Warsaw, 1966), II, p. 158, and Kamińska, *Sądownictwo*, pp. 45–6.
45. Bardach et al. (eds), *Historia państwa* (1966), p. 414.
46. B. Baranowski, *Życie codziennie małego miasteczka w XVII i XVIII wieku* (Warsaw, 1975), p. 224.
47. Bardach et al. (eds), *Historia państwa* (1966), pp. 424, 153–4.
48. Groicki, *Artykuły... które*, p. 103.
49. Groicki, *Porządek* (1953), p. 26.
50. Groicki, *Artykuły... które*, p. 134.
51. Groicki, *Porządek* (1953), p. 27–8. In a case from Gostyń a female seigneur sent a team of three men to hear the case. See AM Gostyń, I/141, pp. 9–13. Opinions on this subject vary, despite many contemporary accounts of the abuses carried out by judges. For further comment see Pilaszek, 'W poszukiwaniu' and Kamler, 'Rola tortur'.
52. M. Pilaszek, 'Witchhunts', pp. 111, 115.

53. Pilaszek, 'W poszukiwaniu'.
54. Kamler, 'Rola tortur', p. 108, and Pilaszek, 'W poszukiwaniu', p. 363.
55. Bogucka, 'Law and Crime', pp. 176–7.
56. Bystroń, *Dzieje*, II, p. 337.
57. J. Sokołowska and K. Żukowska (eds) *Poeci polskiego baroku* (Warsaw, 1965), I, pp. 337, 631.
58. Baranowski, *Życie*, pp. 38, 41.
59. Bogucka, 'Law and Crime', pp. 178–9, 187, 189, 192.
60. Ibid., pp. 106–7, and PTPN, rkp 859, fos 74, 125v.
61. Groicki, *Porządek* (1953), pp. 123, 131–5, and Groicki, *Artykuły...które*, pp. 29, 30, 130.
62. Baranowski, *Kultura*, p. 259; APP AM Wronki I/22, fos 17v, 74–7; Bardach et al. (eds), *Historia państwa* (1976), p. 284; and Groicki, *Artykuły...które*, p. 126. This was also the case in areas such as Rothenburg for example, see Rowlands, *Rothenburg*, pp. 9, 30, 32.
63. Groicki, *Porządek* (1953), pp. 191–2, 198.
64. Groicki, *Postępek* (1953), pp. 105, 108, 128–9.
65. APP AM Poznań I/639 fos 43v-44 and APP AM Poznań I/644, pp. 355–70.
66. Groicki, *Porządek* (1953), pp. 195–6, 199.
67. Maisel, *Poznańskie prawo*, p. 128.
68. Groicki, *Artykuły...które*, pp. 71, 138–9.
69. Bukowska-Gorgoni, 'Procesy o czary', pp. 156–67, and Groicki, *Porządek* (1953), pp. 155–7, 162.
70. Pilaszek, *Procesy*, pp. 227–8.
71. Bardach et al. (eds), *Historia państwa* (1976), pp. 127, 245. The six cities were Cracow, Olkusz, Bochnia, Sandacz, Wieliczka and Kazimierz. Of the nine appeals mentioning witchcraft heard by this court, Pilaszek says that in six cases the sentences were relaxed. Pilaszek, *Procesy*, pp. 228–39. See also Bukowska-Gorgoni, 'Procesy o czary'.
72. Koranyi, 'Beczka', p. 24, and AGAD KB 252, fo. 27.
73. See note 1. According to Pilaszek, *Procesy*, p. 194, Berlich, Carpzov and Binsfeld were cited in trials in Grodzisk, Nowe nad Wisłą and Fordon.
74. Bardach et al. (eds), *Historia ustroju*, pp. 273–9; Łukaszewicz, *Krotoszyński*, II, pp. 39–41; APP AM Pyzdry I/51, pp. 40–5; and Kamler, 'Struktura', p. 74.
75. Kochanowicz, 'Economy', p. 107.
76. Mikołajczyk, 'Jak obronić', pp. 389–410.
77. Łukaszewicz, *Krotoszyński*, II, pp. 39–41.
78. APP AM Gniezno I/70, p. 395.
79. APP AM Gniezno I/135, p. 11.
80. Pilaszek, 'W poszukiwaniu', p. 370 and APP AM Poznań I/644, p. 302.
81. APP AM Poznań I/644, fo. 165, p. 302 and APP AM Kalisz I/159, p. 564.
82. APP AM Poznan I/645 fo. 127v.
83. Ptaśnik, *Miasta*, p. 45.
84. Maisel, 'Kalisz', p. 133. This happened in over half of trials in the sample for which information is available.
85. APP AM Gniezno I/135, p. 73.
86. Ibid., p. 14.
87. AGAD, KM Szczercowa 2, fos 130–1, 134–6.
88. APP AM Kalisz I/159, pp. 554–573, 598–602.

89. APP AM Gniezno I/135, p. 70, p. 11.
 90. Bogucka, *Obyczaje*, p. 176.
 91. APP AM Gniezno I/135, p. 71.
 92. APP AM Kalisz I/159, p. 602.
 93. AGAD KMB 252, fo. 15v.
 94. APP AM Gniezno I/135, pp. 71–2 and APP AM Poznań, I/168, fos 88v–90, 148v.
 95. For example, see APP AM Poznań 1/639, fos 216v–21v (beheading), APP AM Gniezno I/70, pp. 395–405, 414–31, 355, 357–8 (flogging), PTPN, rkp 859, k. 97–9v, and AM Wagrowiec 1695–1737, unnumbered.
 96. Pilaszek, *Procesy*, pp. 245–50.
 97. Ibid., p. 264.
 98. Ibid., p. 259.
 99. Wiślicz, 'Kleczew', p. 76.
100. Ibid., pp. 75–6.
101. Ibid., p. 83.
102. Ibid., p. 82 and PTPN, fos 154–5.
103. S. Gamalski, *Przestrogi duchowne sędziom inwestygatorom i instygatorom czarownic* (Poznań, 1742), fo. C3. Hagen talks about neglect of manorial obligations, such as the *załoga* or *Hofwehr* and of repairs to housing. See Hagen, 'Village Life', p. 173.
104. KM Nieszawa, 19, k.189.
105. Łukaszewicz, *Krotoszyński*, II, pp. 39–41.
106. APP AM Kalisz I/158, pp. 17–29.
107. Hagen, 'Village Life', p. 154.
108. APP AM Kalisz I/159, pp. 554–73, 598–602.
109. Dydyński, *Wiadomości*, pp. 101–3.
110. APP AM Pyzdry I/51, pp. 40–5.
111. Baranowski, *Procesy*, pp. 66–8.
112. In the second half of the eighteenth century the number of trials had declined according to my Wielkopolska sample, and other historians agree on this point. See Pilaszek, *Procesy*, pp. 219–26.
113. Levack (ed.), *Witch-hunt*, pp. 247–9.
114. AGAD KM Dobra 9, fos 158–9v.

5 *Nullus Deus, Sine Diabolo*: The Ecclesiastical Witch

1. J.A. Simpson and E.S.C. Weiner (eds), *Oxford English Dictionary*, 2nd edn (Oxford, 1991), 'demonology'.
2. W. Stephens, *Demon Lovers: Witchcraft, Sex, and the Crisis of Belief* (Chicago and London, 2002), p. 9.
3. Klaniczay, 'Witch-Trials', p. 234. There were apparently only three Hungarian demonological works.
4. Stephens, *Demon Lovers*, pp. 7, 8, 29.
5. Ibid., pp. 35–55.
6. See Clark, *Thinking*, pp. 43–79.
7. L. Pełka, *Polska demonologia ludowa* (Warsaw, 1987), pp. 13–14, and S. Urbańczyk, *Religia pogańskich Słowian* (Cracow, 1947), p. 8.

8. L. Słupecki, *Slavonic Pagan Sanctuaries* (Warsaw, 1994), p. 8.
9. Pełka, *Demonologia*, p.12.
10. Urbańczyk, *Religia*, pp. 9, 18.
11. See Adam Mickiewicz's popular work *Dziady*, whose various parts were based on the return of ancestral spirits.
12. Pełka, *Demonologia*, p. 8, and P. Urbańczyk, 'The Meaning of Christianization for Medieval Pagan Societies', in idem (ed.), *Early Christianity in Central and East Europe* (Cracow, 1947), pp. 31–7.
13. Pełka, *Demonologia*, p. 5.
14. See the anonymous work, *Postępek*. See 'Devil Books', in Golden, *Encyclopedia*, and K. Roos, *The Devil in Sixteenth Century German Literature: The Teufelbücher* (Frankfurt, 1972).
15. Urbańczyk, 'Christianization', pp. 31–7.
16. Pełka, *Demonologia*, p. 5.
17. Słupecki, *Sanctuaries*, p. 229.
18. A. Brückner, 'Wierzenia religijne i stosunki rodzinne', in A. Brückner, L. Niederle and K. Kadlec (eds), *Początki kultury Słowiańskiej* (Cracow, 1912), pp. 155, 158, 160.
19. Explanations of the history and intricacies of the Devil in the Bible are beyond the scope of this study, but are addressed by, among others, E. Pagels, *The Origin of Satan* (London, 1996); P. Stanford, *The Devil: A Biography* (London, 1996); G. Massadié, *A History of the Devil* (New York, 1997); and R. Muchembled, *A History of the Devil: From the Middle Ages to the Present* (Cambridge, 2003).
20. Again provenance is of the utmost importance here. The so-called witch of Endor called up the spirit of Samuel for the good of King Saul, so this provenance was regarded as divine rather than diabolic. See the *Canon Episcopi* (c. 906) and *Summis Desiderantes* (1484).
21. APP AM Kalisz I/158, pp. 17–29, 80–2, 129–31.
22. A. Vlasto, *The Entry of the Slavs into Christendom* (Cambridge, 1970), pp. 154–6; Lukowski and Zawadzki, *History*, p. 6; Brückner, 'Wierzenia', p. 158; APP AM Turek, I/30, fo. 9; and Pełka, *Demonologia*, p. 14.
23. Vlasto, *Slavs*, p. 136.
24. Ankarloo et al. (eds), *Witch Trials*, pp. 11, 124. Midelfort suggests that many Calvinists' providential view of witchcraft coincided with the so-called Little Ice Age. See H.C. Erik Midelfort, 'Witchcraft and Religion in Sixteenth-Century Germany: The Formation and Consequences of an Orthodoxy', in B. Levack (ed.), *Articles on Witchcraft, Magic and Demonology: The Literature of Witchcraft* (12 vols, London, 1992), IV, p. 301. This article was originally published in 1971.
25. Ankarloo et al. (eds), *Witch Trials*, p. 129.
26. Erasmus had many correspondents in Poland, and Grodzisk noble Stanisław Ostroróg exchanged letters with Melanchthon.
27. For discussions on demonology, see among others: Ankarloo et al. (eds), *Witch Trials*; S. Anglo, *The Damned Art: Essays in the Literature of Witchcraft* (London, 1977); Clark, *Thinking*; B. Levack (ed.), *New Perspectives on Witchcraft, Magic and Demonology: Demonology, Religion, and Witchcraft* (London, 2001); and J. Caro Baroja, 'Witchcraft and Catholic Theology', in B. Ankarloo and G. Henningson (eds), *Early Modern Witchcraft: Centres and Peripheries* (Oxford, 1993), pp. 19–43.

28. Clark, *Thinking*, p. 543. Here he raises the point that although little research has been carried out on 'radical' groups' attitudes to demonology, they appeared to be the least 'demonological' of religious groups.
29. R. Scribner, 'Ritual and Popular Religion in Catholic Germany at the Time of the Reformation', *Journal of Ecclesiastical History* 35 (1984), 47–77.
30. M. Czechowic, *Rozmowy Chrystyjańskie* (Cracow, 1575), fo. 194v. He was exiled from Poznań in 1566; M. Krowicki, *Obrona nauki prawdziwej* (Pinczów, 1560), fos 119, 72v, 73, 82, 95v; and J. Seklucjan, *Katechizm prosty dla ludu* (Olsztyń, 1948 [1545–46]), fo. F2v.
31. Krowicki, *Obrona*, pp. 68, 92v, 121v.
32. S. Budny, *O przedniejszych wiary* (Łosk, 1576), p. 5.
33. P. Gilowski, *Wykład katechizmu Koscioła chrzesciańskiego z Pism Świętych* (Cracow, 1579), pp. 187–9, 64, 161, and fo. 191v.
34. In Poland there is a long tradition of Roman Catholics preparing nine dishes on Christmas Eve.
35. APP AM Kalisz I/158, p. 25.
36. A. Gdacjusz, 'Ardens irae divinae ignis', in K. Kolbuszewski (ed.), *Postyllografia polska XVI i XVII wieku* (Cracow, 1921 [1644]), pp. 245–7.
37. S. Clark, 'Protestant Demonology: Sin, Superstition, and Society (c. 1520–c. 1630)', in Levack (ed.), *New Perspectives on Witchcraft*, p. 190. He also writes that the tone of Protestant demonology was affected by the fact that 'Protestant witchcraft writings were thus dominated by the pastorate and its concerns – not by jurists or philosophers – and their tone is not so much intellectual as evangelical and homiletic.'
38. James I and VI, *Daemonologie* (Edinburgh, 1597); W. Perkins, *A Discourse of the Damned Art of Witchcraft* (Cambridge, 1610); H. Holland, *A Treatise against Witchcraft* (Cambridge, 1590); and J. Stearne, *A Confirmation and Discovery of Witch-Craft* (London, 1648).
39. For discussion of this topic see Clark, *Thinking*, pp. 526–45.
40. M. Białobrzeski, *Katechizm albo wizerunek wiary chrześciańskiej* (Cracow, 1567), pp. 245, 220.
41. J. Bossy, 'Moral Arithmetic: Seven Sins into Ten Commandments', in E. Leites (ed.) *Conscience and Casuistry in Early Modern Europe* (Cambridge, 1988), pp. 214–34.
42. W. Konopczyński (ed.), *Polski Słownik Biograficzny* (Cracow, 1935–), s.v. Laterna.
43. M. Laterna, *Harfa duchowna* (Cracow, 1585), pp. 113–14, 115–17, 622–4.
44. A. Tylkowski, *Tribunal Sacrum* (Warsaw, 1690), fos F2, H3, A5, B5.
45. Ibid., fos V3, LV.
46. Ibid., fos K5, L.
47. Ibid., fos K4, K5. This work will be examined later in the chapter. For cases where the accused died before a sentence could be passed, see: APP AM Wronki I/22, fos 74–77 and PTPN rkp. 859, fos 28, 63–4.
48. M. Nowakowski, *Kolęda duchowna* (Cracow, 1749), fo. B25 and pp. 116, 121, 391, 62, 65.
49. Nowakowski, *Kolęda*, pp. 126–47, 128, 135, 137.
50. Skarga's work will be explored later in this chapter.
51. Nowakowski, *Kolęda*, pp. 146–7.
52. Chmielowski, *Ateny*, pp. 5–8.

53. *Volumina legum*, VIII, pp. 546–7.
54. Chmielowski, *Ateny*, pp. 17–9, 29, 30, 80.
55. Ibid., pp. 106, 108, 110, 120–2.
56. APP AM Wronki I/22, fo. 51.
57. Chmielowski, *Ateny*, pp. 127–8.
58. Stephens calls these inversions counter-sacraments. See Stephens, *Demon Lovers*, pp. 181–6, 200.
59. There is also mention of a trinity of devils in the case of Grzegorz heard at Wągrowiec. See the unnumbered book APP AM Wągrowiec I/25. Chmielowski, *Ateny*, pp. 130–3.
60. Chmielowski, *Ateny*, p. 135.
61. Ibid., pp. 122, 132–3.
62. There are similar details in German trials. See Rowlands, *Rothenburg*, p. 112.
63. Chmielowski, *Ateny*, pp. 111, 135; APP AM Gniezno I/70, p. 374; AGAD KM Warta 46, fo. 529v.
64. Chmielowski, *Ateny*, pp. 84, 97, 86, 97.
65. Ibid., pp. 89–90. AGAD KB 252, fos 9–12 and AGAD KM Radziejewska 15, fos 256, 258.
66. Chmielowski, *Ateny*, pp. 147–51.
67. 'Through him, with him, in him', the words with which the Host is consecrated and raised above the altar during Mass.
68. Chmielowski, *Ateny*, pp. 151–4.
69. M. Rożek, *Diabeł w kulturze polskiej: dzieje postaci i motywu* (Warsaw, 1993), p. 136. Skarga also published collections of his sermons to the *Sejm*, which were extremely critical of many aspects of Polish life, the nobility and confessional issues. The edition used is based on the last to have been prepared by Skarga, published posthumously in 1615. P. Skarga, *Żywoty Świętych*, ed. M. Kozielski (2 vols, Cracow, 1995 [1615]).
70. Skarga, *Żywoty* (1995), I, pp. 44–9.
71. M. Warner, *Alone of All Her Sex – The Myth and Cult of the Virgin Mary* (London, 2000), pp. 234–5.
72. Skarga, *Żywoty* (1995), II, pp. 179–81, 303–14 and I, p. 101.
73. Ibid., II, pp. 179–81.
74. Klaniczay, *Transformation*, pp. 4, 2.
75. APP AM Poznań I/638, fo. 88v; APP AM Kalisz I/158, pp. 202, 347; and APP AM Turek I/30, fo. 14v.
76. J.-M. Sallmann, *Naples et ses saints à l'âge baroque 1540–1750* (Paris, 1994), pp. 98, 208, 117, 128, 177, 183, 186, 189.
77. Warner, *Alone*, pp. 117, 128.
78. Although the debate here discusses almost exclusively female examples, it must be remembered that men were also subject to these dichotomies, although less frequently. The case of Urbain Grandier and the Ursulines of Loudun is a good example. See Klaniczay, *Transformation*, for an excellent discussion of female saints.
79. Wiślicz, 'Miraculous Sites', pp. 287–8, 295, 297, 299.
80. M. Kałowski, *Informacya o początkach y dalszym progressie cudnowego mieysca Łagiewnickiego* (Kalisz, 1723), pp. 1, 13, 19, 148–51, 120–25, 142–3.
81. F. Kolert, *Krynice cudownych łask Maryi z Jurowickich Gór wynikaiące* (Nieśwież, 1755), fos C, D2.

82. Baranowski, *Procesy*, p. 49.
83. H.P. Broedel, *The Malleus Maleficarum and the Construction of Witchcraft: Theology and Popular Belief* (Manchester, 2003), p. 34. He effectively demolishes this argument.
84. Ząmbkowicz, *Młot*, p. 5.
85. Ibid., pp. 1–3. Copies of the Polish version are still to be found in libraries in Wrocław, Cracow, Kórnik, Poznań and Bydgoszcz, most of which originate from collections in convents and monasteries.
86. Clark writing in Ankarloo et al. (eds), *Witch Trials*, p. 136.
87. These subjects form the basis of the following two chapters.
88. Stephens, *Demon Lovers*, p. 260; Klaniczay, *Transformations*, p. 46; and M. Douglas, *Purity and Danger: An Analysis of the Concepts of Pollution and Taboo* (London, 1985 [1966]), p. 174.

6 Beyond Demonology: Blame the Witches

1. For works that examine the witchcraft persecution in tandem with demonology or literature see: Purkiss, *The Witch*; Brauner, *Fearless Wives*; Willis, *Malevolent Nurture*; M. Gibson, *Early Modern Witches: Witchcraft Cases in Contemporary Writing* (London, 2000); J.M. Schmidt, *Glaube und Skepsis. Die Kurpfalz und die abendländische Hexenverfolgung, 1446–1685* (Bielefeld, 2000); and Roberts and Normand (eds), *Witchcraft*.
2. Clark, *Thinking*, p. viii. In fact Clark even goes so far as to proclaim the death of the term demonologist.
3. Koranyi, 'Czary i gusla', p. 2, and M. Siennik, *Lekarstwa doświadczone* (Cracow, 1564), pp. 118, 199. This work was not reprinted.
4. S. Syreniusz, *Zielnik, z herbarzem z ięzyka łacinskiego zowią to iest opisane własne imion, kształtu* (Cracow, 1673 [1613]), pp. 124–6. Syreniusz was doctor to the Jesuits in Cracow for over twenty years. APP AM Kalisz I/158, pp. 17–29, 202.
5. J. Haur, *Skład albo skarbiec znakomitych sekretów ekonomiej ziemiańskiej* (Cracow, 1693 [1689]), p. 418. *Oekonomia ziemiańska* was reprinted in 1679 and the compilation work was reprinted in 1744 (there were two editions published that year by the Jesuits in Warsaw and Cracow), 1756, 1757, 1788, 1790 and 1793. The compilation editions were published by the Barefoot Carmelite order at Berdychów and by Jesuits in Warsaw and Cracow. The Jesuit editions (1730, 1744, 1756 and 1757) contained additions by Dr Bystrzycki.
6. AGAD KM Dobra 9, pp. 158–9 and APP AM Dolsk I/7, p. 105.
7. Bonfigli, *De Plica Polonica*. In this work he comments on the condition, confirming that most Poles believed it to be the result of witchcraft. See also Connor, *History*, II, pp. 91–6.
8. Haur, *Skład*, pp. 418, 427.
9. The notion of the East as a hotbed of witchcraft is a recurring motif in Polish sources.
10. Haur, *Skład*, pp. 450, 452–6; APP AM Dolsk I/7, p. 104; and AGAD KB 252, fo.10.
11. Haur, *Skład*, p. 455.
12. APP AM Kalisz I/158, fo. 202.

13. Haur, *Skład*, pp. 157–8, 141–7. The witches' sabbat was supposed to take place at Bald Mountain.
14. Some of the few exceptions are to be found in APP AM Turek I/30 fos 14v–21v; AGAD KB 252, fos 20v–1; and PTPN rkp. 859, fos 23v–6. In German trials weather magic was mentioned much more frequently and there were also Roman Catholic rituals designed to ward off bad weather. See Scribner, 'Ritual'.
15. S. Duńczewski, 'Kalendarz Duńczewskiego 1759 r.', in B. Baczko and H. Hinz (eds), *Kalendarz Półstuletni 1750–1800* (Warsaw, 1975), pp. 55–8.
16. APP AM Kalisz I/158, pp. 80, 202.
17. J. Januszowski, *Wróżki Iana Podworzeckiego* (Cracow, 1589), pp. 5, 6, 9, 20, 24–30.
18. Behringer, *Witchcraft*, p. 112; H. Kamen, *The Iron Century: Social Change in Europe, 1550–1669* (London, 1971); and F. Giedroyc, *Mór w Polsce w wiekach ubiegłych: zarys historyczny* (Warsaw, 1899), pp. 52–3, bears out this claim. The winter of 1588 was reported as extremely severe in Poland.
19. S. Poklatecki, *Pogrom, czarnoksięskie błędy, latawców zdrady i alchimickie fałsze jako rozplasza* (Cracow, 1595), fos A, Aii, Bii, Fiii, Gv.
20. Willis, *Malevolent Nurture*, pp. 160–1.
21. Willis constructs her explanation around fear of female power during Elizabeth I's reign, and subsequently James I and VI's complicated relations with both Elizabeth and his mother.
22. Rumour abounded of aristocratic witches at Sigismund August's court, which included mistresses of the king and his mother Bona Sforza.
23. Purkiss, *The Witch*, pp. 182, 263.
24. J. Sokolski, *Zaświaty Staropolskie* (Wrocław, 1994), p. 218; S. Feyrabend, *Theatrum diabolorum das ist: Warhaffte eigentliche und kurtze Beschreibung allerley grewlicher, schrecklicher und abschewlicher Laster* (Frankfurt am Main, 1575); *Theatrum de veneficis, das ist: Von Teuffelsgespenst, Zauberern und Giffthereitern, Schwartzküstlern, Hexen und Unholden, vieler fürnemmen Historien und Exempel* (Frankfurt am Main, 1586); and *Postępek*, pp. 97,106, 114, 118–19. Estreicher notes a Russian translation of *Postępek* in 1687.
25. This concept was also elaborated in the play *Komedia Justyny i Konstanciej* by Marcin Bielski, published in 1557, but is much more developed in the German early modern genre of *Teufelbücher*.
26. *Postępek*, pp. 50, 97–8, 102–4.
27. See J. Rytel, 'Barok' in J. Jakubowski (ed.) *Literatura Polska od średniowiecza do pozytywizmu* (Warsaw, 1974), pp. 140–44; P. Oppenheimer, *A Pleasant Vintage of Till Eulenspiegel* (Middletown, 1972), pp. xvii, xviii; L.-L. Sosset, *Le Personnage de Tiel Eulenspiegel à travers l'Histoire, la Légend et le Folklore* (Rodez and Andrimont, 1938); K. Badecki (ed.), *Pisma Jana Dzwonowskiego* (Cracow, 1910 [1608–25]); idem (ed.), *Polska satyra mieszczańska* (Cracow, 1950); J. Miśkowiak, *Ze Studiów nad 'Sowizdrzałem' w Polsce* (Poznań, 1938); J. Ziomek, *Renesans* (Warsaw, 1998), pp. 144–9; B. Verheyen, *Till Eulenspiegel. Revolutionär, Aufklärer, Assensater: zur Eulenspiegel-Rezeption in der DDR* (Frankfurt am Main and Oxford, 2004); R. Tenberg, *Die deutsche Till Eulenspiegel* (Würzburg, 1996); W. Virmond, *Eulenspiegel und seine Interpreten* (Berlin, 1981); G. Bollenbeck, *Till Eulenspiegel* (Stuttgart, 1985); and C. Wolf and G. Wolf, *Till Eulenspiegel* (Frankfurt am Main, 1976).

216 *Notes*

There is also a museum dedicated to the character; see www.eulenspiegelmuseum.de.
28. Ziomek, *Renesans*, pp. 144–9.
29. Rytel, 'Barok', p. 142.
30. Miśkowiak, *Ze Studiów*, pp. 60, 101.
31. S. Grzeszczuk, *Antologia literatury sowizdrzalskiej XVI i XVII wieku* (Wrocław, 1985), pp. v, vi, lxx–iv.
32. There is a Polish tradition of pouring wax through a key onto water in order to predict future husbands on the evening of 29/30 November, and it was mentioned in trial records. See APP AM Poznań I/638, fos 83v. APP AM Opalenica I/5, pp. 46–7. This also reflects German customs of the fifteenth century. Scribner writes about consecrated water on Saint Blasius's Day being sprinkled on poultry and geese to protect them. See Scribner, 'Ritual', pp. 62–3 for further discussion of these practices in Germany.
33. 'Komedia rybałtowska nowa', in K. Badecki (ed.), *Polska komedia rybałtowska pierwsze zbiorowe i krytyczne wydanie* (Lwów, 1931 [1615]), line 268.
34. 'Statut Jana Dzwonowskiego', in K. Badecki (ed.), *Pisma Jana Dzwonowskiego* (Cracow, 1910 [1608–25]), pp. 67–71.
35. Several Wielkopolska trials described noblewomen using the services of cunning women subsequently accused of witchcraft.
36. Ostling, *Between the Devil*, pp. 221–32.
37. This reflects Olszewski's theory explained in Chapter 1.
38. 'Peregrynacja dziadowska' (1612), in Badecki (ed.), *Polska komedia rybałtowska*, pp. 205–10. Estreicher gives 1614 as the publication date.
39. 'Synod klechów Podgorskich' (1607), in Badecki (ed.), *Polska komedia rybałtowska*, ll. 226–9, 803–11.
40. 'Z nowinami torba kursorska Iozefa Pięknorzyckiego z Mątwiłaiec, naleziona v Nalewayków', in K. Badecki (ed.) *Polska satyra mieszczańska* (Cracow 1950 [1645]), p. 304.
41. APP AM Gniezno I/70, fo. 374 and AGAD KB 252, fos 9v, 16v.
42. 'Z nowinami', p. 313.
43. 'Przygody i sprawy trefne', pp. 104–5.
44. 'Statut Jana Dzwonowskiego', p. 60.
45. S. Szymonowicz, *Sielanki* (Cracow, 1921 [1614]), ll. 88–92, which takes Theocritus' Idyll II as its model.
46. K. Opaliński, *Satyry* (Cracow, 1652 [1650]), p. 11.
47. D. Wisner, *Tractatus brevis de extramagi, lamii, veneticis* (Poznań, 1639).
48. APP AM Opalenica I/5, pp. 16–19; A. Sajkowski, *Krzysztof Opaliński Wojewoda Poznański* (Poznań, 1960), pp. 69, 71, 82, 219; and R. Pollak (ed.) *Listy Krzysztofa Opalińskiego do brata Łukasza 1641–53* (Wrocław, 1957).
49. APP Castr. Poznań. Rel. nr 166, Protestatio Rogowczyków contra Łukomska et cives Pobiedziscenses, fos 951–6.
50. *Wódka z elixierem* (Poznań, 1729), fos A3, I2, D3, D, C2, A3, B3, C, G3, H, H2. See also K. Thomas, *Religion and the Decline of Magic* (London, 1997 [1971]), and Macfarlane, *Witchcraft*.
51. *Wódka*, fos G3, H2, H3.
52. APP AM Poznań I/643 fo. 39v.
53. *Wódka*, fo. I and APP AM Turek I/30, fos 14v–21v.
54. F. Bohomolec, 'Czary' in J. Kott (ed.) *Komedie na teatrum* (Warsaw, 1960 [1775]), pp. 353–5.

7 Sceptical Voices: Ending the Era

1. Olszewski, 'Prześladowanie', p. 489, and Baranowski, *Procesy*, p. 57.
2. Three of the five Bohomolec brothers were Jesuits.
3. APP AM Gniezno I/70, pp. 458–60.
4. In typical synthetic style, the author cited authors such as Del Rio, Farinacci, St Augustine, St Thomas Aquinas, Suarez and Layman, as well as biblical authority. *Czarownica*, pp. 2, 3, 20, 22, 26, 32. Baranowski, *Kultura*, p. 238.
5. See Pilaszek, *Procesy*, pp. 45, 209, 212–13.
6. *Czarownica*, 'dla poratowania y ochrony sumnienia ich', pp. 2, 5, 6, 9, 10, 13–14, 19, 46, 47, 49, 58–61, 89–90, 92; Ptaśnik, *Miasta*, p. 34; and W. Maisel, *Tortury w praktyce sądu kryminalnego miasta Poznania w XVI–XVIII w.* (Poznań, 1978), p. 116.
7. *Czarownica*, pp. 62–3, 90.
8. AGAD KB 252, fo. 15v.
9. Ibid., pp. 79, 82 and APP AM Turek I/30, fos 14v–21v.
10. *Czarownica*, p. 74, and *Carolina*, article 31.
11. *Czarownica*, pp. 74–5, 77–8.
12. Majkowski, 'Pławienie'.
13. APP AM Wronki, I/22, fo. 17v.
14. *Czarownica*, pp. 64–8, 85, 87–8, and Rowlands, *Rothenburg*, pp. 9, 30, 32.
15. *Czarownica*, pp. 89–92, 95; AGAD KB 252, fos 63–4; and PTPN, rkp. 859, fo. 28.
16. *Czarownica*, pp. 4, 4b.
17. Ibid., pp. 21–2, 24.
18. In the town of Biecz in 1600, a so-called witch was employed by the town council to trace missing goods. APK, KŁ Biecza 1549–1693, pp. 127–49. In other trials locating stolen goods was regarded as witchcraft; see APP AM Poznań I/638, fos 83v–6v.
19. *Czarownica*, pp. 25–6, 28–30, 34, 40; APP AM Kalisz, I/158, p. 350; APP AM Poznań I/644, fos 24–5.
20. *Czarownica*, pp. 8, 35–7, 39.
21. Ibid., pp. 41–5, 96–8.
22. See the introduction to Wisner, *Tractatus* and pp. 1–3.
23. Ibid., pp. 5–9, 16, 22.
24. Ibid., pp. 9, 11–12, 14, 17–19, 20–21, 23–5.
25. K.F. Czartoryski, *Instructio circa judicia sagarum judicibus eorumque consiliariis accomodata Romae primum 1657...* (Gdańsk, 1682), fos A1, A2. Although it is beyond the scope of this work to examine possession in Poland, this is clearly a concern.
26. Ibid., fo. A2.
27. Ibid., fo. B.
28. Ibid., fo. B2.
29. Ibid., fos B2, B3.
30. S. Gamalski, *Przestrogi duchowne sądziom inwestygatorom i instygatorom czarownic* (Poznań, 1742), fos A, A2, B. For a discussion of Gamalski's work, see Kantak, 'Poznańska'.
31. Ibid., fos B, B2.
32. Ibid., fos B3, C.
33. Ibid., fo. C3.

34. This also occurred in witchcraft trials. See Chapter 7 and APP AM Kalisz I/158, pp. 404–14.
35. Gamalski, *Przestrogi*, fos C3, D, D2, D3.
36. J. Załuski, *Objaśnienie błędami zabobonów zarażonych oraz opisanie niegodziwości, która pochodzi sądzenia przez probę plawienia w wodzie niniemanych czarownic jako takowa proba jest omylna różnymi dowodami stwierzone* (Berdyczów, 1766), pp. 4–5, 13, 9–12, 27, 34, 40–1, 45–6, 58–60, 65–6, 71–2.
37. Bohomolec, *Diabeł* (1772), pp. 11, 4, 53, 56, 77–8, 83, 87, 115, 120, 140–3, 147–9, 157, 374. See also Bohomolec, *Diabeł* (1777), p. 178.
38. Ibid., pp. 53, 56–7, 62, 70, 72, 78, 115, 120, 129, 131, 139, 359.
39. Bohomolec, *Diabeł* (1772), pp. 364–5, 367.
40. A. Brzezińska, 'Accusations of Love Magic in the Renaissance Courtly Culture of the Polish-Lithuanian Commonwealth', *East Central Europe* 20–3 (1993–96), 117–40.
41. Ibid. pp. 117–40. There was also great interest in magic at the court of Stefan Batory (1576–86), who invited John Dee among others to court. See Bugaj, *Nauki*.
42. Koranyi, 'Czary i gusla', pp. 1–25, and Olszewski, 'Prześladowanie', p. 498.
43. Wiślicz, 'Kleczew', p. 88.

8 Epilogue: Comparisons and Conclusions

1. For a full discussion of Polish terminology, see Wyporska, 'Motive', ch. 2.
2. Chmielowski, *Nowe Ateny*, pp. 85–6, 94; Bohomolec, *Diabeł* (1772), p. 116; and Ząmbkowicz, *Młot*, p. 336.
3. *Postępek*, pp. 15, 19, 20, 31, 65, 70, 98, and Czubryński, 'Z katalogu', p. 37.
4. Many more names appear in Polish demonological fiction.
5. *Postępek*, p. 97.
6. For example, of 19 names given for devils in the Grodzisk collection of trials, Jasiek, Kuba and Jan appear three times each, Woyciech twice, and the following once each; Jarek, Maciek, Stach, Rokitka, Andrzej, Marcin and Malachoski.
7. APP AM Gniezno I/70, fo. 386.
8. APP AM Wronki I/22, fos 49–52.
9. Ł. Górnicki, *Demon Socratis albo rozmowa złodzieja a czartem* (2 vols, Warsaw, 1961 [1624]), p. 534, and Ząmbkowicz, *Młot*, p. 410.
10. APP AM Pyzdry I/43, p. 54.
11. APP AM Dolsk 1/7, p. 104 and AGAD KB 252, fo. 16v.
12. Ząmbkowicz, *Młot*, pp. 56, 67, 198, 204, 372, and Bohomolec, *Diabeł* (1772), p. 158.
13. Bohomolec, *Diabeł* (1772), p. 157; Chmielowski, *Nowe Ateny*, p. 130; and Ząmbkowicz, *Młot*, p. 43.
14. Chmielowski, *Nowe Ateny*, p. 111.
15. Levack (ed.), *Witch-hunt*, pp. 149–50, and APP AM Poznań I/644, fos 24–5.
16. Rowlands, *Rothenburg*, pp. 55, 62, 168.
17. APP AM Pyzdry I/43, p. 52; PTPN, rkp. 859, fo. 65v, AGAD KB 252, fo. 16v, and Ostling, *Between the Devil*, pp. 217–18.

18. APP AM Gniezno I/70, fo. 385.
19. AGAD KB 252, fos 54, 25v and APP AM Opalenica I/5, pp. 17, 48.
20. Ibid., fos 27–30, and Przybyszewski, *Czary*, pp. 23–36.
21. APP AM Kalisz I/158, p. 27.
22. APP AM Kalisz I/159, p. 567 and APP AM Poniec I/50, p. 10.
23. APP AM Pyzdry I/43, p. 69.
24. APP AM Dolsk I/7, p. 51.
25. A. Gauda and Z. Nasalski, *Czarcia łapa* (Lublin, 1991), p. 9.
26. Chmielowski, *Nowe Ateny*, pp. 131–2, and Bohomolec, *Diabeł* (1772), pp. 137–8.
27. AGAD KB 252, fos 20v–1.
28. Chmielowski, *Nowe Ateny*, pp. 130–3, and Ząmbkowicz, *Młot*, pp. 21–2.
29. Bohomolec, *Diabeł* (1772), pp. 135–9, and Chmielowski, *Nowe Ateny*, p. 135.
30. APP AM Poniec I/50, pp. 8, 23–36.
31. AGAD KB 252, fos 8, 12v, 90 and APP AM Opalenica I/5, p. 18.
32. APP AM Gniezno I/70, fo. 374.
33. Chmielowski, *Nowe Ateny*, pp. 122, 132–3.
34. AGAD KB 252, fo. 15.
35. APP AM Pyzdry I/43, p. 129.
36. APP AM Kalisz I/158, p. 357; APP AM Poniec I/50, p. 3; AGAD KB 252, fos 54v, 90; and APP AM Pyzdry I/43, p. 130.
37. Przybyszewski, *Czary*, p. 34.
38. AGAD KB 252, fos 8, 17, 20v, 41v.
39. Bohomolec, *Diabeł* (1772), p. 170; *Postępek*, p. 113; and Chmielowski, *Nowe Ateny*, p. 127.
40. *Postępek*, p. 99, and Bohomolec, *Diabeł* (1772), p. 360.
41. Bohomolec, *Diabeł* (1772), pp. 80, 311, 375; APP AM Kalisz I/158, p. 347; APP AM Opalenica I/5, pp. 17, 44; and APP AM Pyzdry I/43, pp. 52, 54.
42. Briggs, *Witches*, pp. 13, 399–402, and Rowlands, *Rothenburg*, pp. 1–3.
43. APP AM Kalisz I/158, pp. 28, 80, 202, 348.
44. Przybyszewski, *Czary*, p. 26, and APP AM Opalenica I/5, p. 17.

Bibliography

Manuscript and Archival Sources

Archiwum Główne Akt Dawnych (AGAD), Warsaw
Księga Czarna Krzemieniecka 1764(sic)–77
Księgi Baworowskich 252
Księgi Miejskie Dobra 9, 12
Księgi Miejskie Nieszawa 19
Księgi Miejskie Ostrzeszów 458 rel. i obl. 15
Księgi Miejskie Praszka 2
Księgi Miejskie Radziejów 15
Księgi Miejskie Szczerców 2, 3
Księgi Miejskie Sieradz 41, 44
Księgi Miejskie Uniejów 3
Księgi Miejskie Warta 46, 48

Archiwum Państwowe w Bochnii
Akta Staropolskie Bocheńskie 69
Księgi Ławnicze Uścia Solnego
MB-H/3326/b
MB-H/3491/31
MB-H/3491/31, 37, 22
MB-H/3630/3, 3708, 3712

Archiwum Państwowe w Bydgoszczu (APB)
Akta Miasta Łobżenice 6
Akta Miasta Nowego nad Wisłą pow. Swiezie t.I. 1416–1918, syg. 131
Akta Miasta Fordonu 5
Księgi Ławnicze Bydgoskie DI/6

Archiwum Państwowe w Kielcach
Akta Miasta Sandomierza 11

Archiwum Państwowe w Krakowie (APK)
Acta damnatorum seu maleficorum alias smola 1554–1625 – 864
Advocatalia et Scabinalia Wisnicensia 1701–1712
Akta Castr. Crac. 1101, 1102, 1102a
Akta nigra maleficorum Wisniciae ab 1665
Akta Miasta Kazimierz 266, 267, 269
Akta Miasta Kraków Criminalia 872, 873, 876, 881, 883, 897, 898
Księgi Ławnicze Biecza 1549–1693
Księgi Miejskie Kraków 900a

Bibliography

Archiwum Państwowe w Lublinie
Akta Miasta Lublina Advocatalia 38, 48, 50
Akta Miasta Lublina Maleficorum 140, 141, 142, 143, 144
Księga Miejska Kraśnika 1745-49

Archiwum Państwowe w Poznaniu (APP)
Akta Criminalia Poznań 474
Akta Miasta Borek I/2
Akta Miasta Dolsk I/7
Akta Miasta Gostyń I/41
Akta Miasta Gniezno I/70, I/135
Akta Miasta Kalisz I/158, I/159
Akta Miasta Kopanica I/21
Akta Miasta Kryzwiń I/76
Akta Miasta Opalenica I/5
Akta Miasta Ostrzeszów I/14
Akta Miasta Poniec I/50
Akta Miasta Poznań I/400, I/638, I/639, I/640, I/641, I/643, I/644, I/645, I/647, I/662, I/664, I/848
Akta Miasta Pyzdry I/43, I/51
Akta Miasta Turek I/25, I/30
Akta Miasta Wągrowiec 1/24, 1/25, 1/59
Akta Miasta Wronki I/22
Akta Miasta Zagórów I/5
Castr. Poznań. Rel. nr 166, Protestatio Rogowczyków contra Łukomska et cives Pobiedziscenses, fos. 951-6

Archiwum Państwowe, Przemyśl (APP)
Criminalia Scabinalia 81, 84, 85

Archiwum Państwowe w Rzeszowie (APR)
Akta Miejskie Rzeszowa 19

Biblioteka PAN-u, Kórnik
Rkp. 1037

Biblioteka Uniwersytecka w Warsawie (BUW)
Sprawa Pani Forsterowej rektorowej w Lesznie przeciw organiscie Dresslerowi o obrazę czci 1773 r. syg. 715
Miscellanea historico-politica saecula XV-XVII w. syg. 48

Poznańskie Towarzystwo Przyjaciół Nauk, Poznań (PTPN)
Rkp. 859

Biblioteka Wojewódźka Publiczna, Bydgoszcz
Rkp. III.534 - Abdank Piotrowski, T., 'Sądy nad czarownicami w Fordonie' (1939)
Actio Criminalis contra Catherine Mrówczyna III/158

Websites

www.eulenspiegel-museum.de
www.witchcraftinpoland.com

Printed Primary Sources

'Acta capitulorum nec non iudiciorum ecclesiasticum selecta', in B. Ulanowski (ed.), *Monumenta medii aevi res gestas Poloniae illustrantia* (3 vols, Cracow, 1894–1908).
Badecki, K. (ed.), *Pisma Jana Dzwonowskiego* (Cracow, 1910 [1608–25]).
—— *Polska satyra miesczańska* (Cracow, 1950).
Białobrzeski, M., *Katechizm albo wizerunek wiary chrześciańskiej* (Cracow, 1567).
—— *Postilla Orthodoxa* (Cracow, 1581).
Biblija sacra podług edycji Gdańskiey (Magdeburg, 1726).
Biblija święta (Brześć Litewski, 1563).
Biblija święta (Nieśwież, 1572).
Biblija święta (Cracow, 1577).
Biblija święta (Gdańsk, 1632).
Biblija święta podług Gdańskiego exemplarza (Amsterdam, 1660).
Bielski, M., *Komedia Justyny i Konstanciej* (Cracow, 1557).
—— *Kronika to jest historia świata* (Warsaw, 1976 [1551]).
Bohomolec, F., 'Czary, komedya we trzech aktach', in J. Kott (ed.), *Komedie na teatrum* (Warsaw, 1960 [1775]).Bohomolec, J., *Diabeł w swojej postaci* (Warsaw, 1772).
—— *Diabeł w swojej postaci, część druga* (Warsaw, 1777).
Bonfigli, O., *De plica tractatus* (Cracow, 1711).
—— *De Plica Polonica Tractatus Mediophysicus* (Wrocław, 1712).
Budny, S., *O przedniejszych wiary* (Łosk, 1576).
Calagius, A., *Synonyma latina* (Wrocław, 1579).
Calepinus, A., *Dictionarum undecem linguarum* (Lyons, 1588 [1574]).
Canon Episcopi (c. 906).
Carpzov, B., *Practicae novae rerum criminalium imperialis saxonica in tres partes divisa* (Viteberg, 1684).
Chmielowski, Ks. B., *Nowe Ateny albo Akademia wszelkiej scjencji pełna, część trzecia* (Cracow, 1966 [1754]).
Connor, B., *The History of Poland in Several Letters* (London, 1698).
Czarownica powołana, abo krótka nauka y przestroga z strony czarownic... (Poznań, 1639).
Czartoryski, K.F., *Instructio circa judicia sagarum judicibus eorumque consiliariis accomodata Romae primum 1657...* (Gdańsk, 1682).
—— *Mandatum pastorale ad universum clerum et populum Dioecesis suae de cantelis in processu contra sagas adhibendis die XI Aprilis* (n.p., 1669).
Czechowicz, J., *Praktyka kryminalna* (Chelmno, 1769).
Czechowicz, M., *Rozmowy Chrystyjańskie* (Cracow, 1575).
Damhouder, J., *Praxis rerum criminalium* (Rotterdam, 1650).
Długosz, J., *Historia Polonica Libri XII* (2 vols, Cracow, 1711–12).
Duńczewski, S., 'Kalendarz Duńczewskiego 1759 r.', in B. Baczko and H. Hinz (eds), *Kalendarz Półstuletni 1750–1800* (Warsaw, 1975 [1759]).

Erazm z Rotterdamu, *Księgi, które zową język, z łacinskiego na polski wyłożony* (Cracow, 1542).
Falimierz, H., *O ziołach i o moczy gich* (Cracow, 1534).
Feyrabend, S., *Theatrum diabolorum das ist: Warhaffte eigentliche und kurtze Beschreibung allerley grewlicher, schrecklicher und abschewlicher Laster* (Frankfurt am Main, 1575).
Gamalski, S., *Przestrogi duchowne sędziom inwestygatorom i instygatorom czarownic* (Poznań, 1742).
Gdacjusz, A., 'Ardens irae divinae ignis', in K. Kolbuszewski (ed.), *Postyllografia polska XVI i XVII wieku* (Cracow, 1921 [1644]).
Gifford, G., *A Discourse of the Subtle Practice of Devils by Witches* (London, 1587).
—— *A Dialogue concerning Witches and Witchcraftes* (London, 1593).
Gilowski, P., *Wykład katechizmu Kościoła chrzesciańskiego z Pism świętych* (Cracow, 1579).
Górnicki, Ł., *Demon Socratis albo rozmowa złodzieja a czartem* (2 vols, Warsaw, 1961 [1624]).
Grillandus, P. *Tractatus de hereticis et sortilegis* (Lyons, 1536).
Groicki, B., *Ten postępek wybrań jest z praw cesarskich* (Cracow, 1559).
—— *Porządek sądów i spraw miejskich prawa maydeburskiego w Koronie polskiej* (Cracow, 1567).
—— *Porządek sądów i spraw miejskich prawa maydeburskiego w Koronie polskiej* (Warsaw, 1953 [1559]).
—— *Artykuły prawa maydeburskiego, które zową Speculum Saxonum*...(Warsaw, 1954 [1558]).
——*Artykuły prawa majdeburskiego: Postępek sądów około karania na gardło. Ustawa płacej u sądów* (Warsaw, 1954 [1558, 1559, 1568]).
—— *Obrona sierot i wdów* (Warsaw, 1958 [1605]).
Haur, J.K., *Skład albo skarbiec znakomitych sekretów ekonomiej ziemiańskiej* (Cracow, 1693 [1689]).
Holland, H., *A Treatise against Witchcraft* (Cambridge, 1590).
James I and VI, *Daemonologie* (Edinburgh, 1597).
Januszowski, J., *Wróżki Iana Podworzeckiego* (Cracow, 1589). Kałowski, M., *Informacja o początkach i dalszym progresie cudownego miejsca łagiewnickiego* (Kalisz, 1723).
Kitowicz, J., *Opis obyczajów za panowania Augusta III* (Warsaw, 1985 [1840]).
Klonowic, S., *Flis* (Wrocław, 1951 [1598]).
Knapski, G., *Thesaurus Polono–Latino–Graecus seu promtuarium linguae Latinae et Graecae, Polonorum usui accomodatum* (3 vols, Cracow, 1621).
Kolert, F., *Krynice cudownych łask Maryi z Jurowickich Gór wynikające* (Nieśwież, 1755).
'Komedia rybałtowska nowa', in K. Badecki (ed.), *Polska komedia rybałtowska pierwsze zbiorowe i krytyczne wydanie* (Lwów, 1931 [1615]).
Komoniecki, A., *Dziejopis żywiecki* (Żywiec, 1987 [1704]).
Krowicki, M., *Obrona nauki prawdziwej* (Pinczów, 1560).
Laterna, M., *Harfa duchowna* (Cracow, 1585).
Leopolita, J., *Biblija* (Cracow, 1561).
Majkowski, A., 'Pławienie i śmierć rzekomej czarownicy w Chałupkach', *Gryf* 2 (1910), 168–75, 201–8.
Mączyński, J., *Lexicon latinopolonicum* (Regiomonti, 1564).
Miczyński, Ks. S., *Zwierciadło Korony Polskiej* (Cracow, 1618).

Mymerus, F., *Dictionarium trium linguarum* (Cracow, 1528).
Nowakowski, M., *Kolęda duchowna* (Cracow, 1749). Opaliński, K., *Satyry* (Cracow, 1652 [1650]).
'Peregrynacja dziadowska', in K. Badecki (ed.), *Polska komedia rybałtowska pierwsze zbiorowe i krytyczne wydanie* (Lwów, 1931 [1612]).
Perkins, W., *A Discourse of the Damned Art of Witchcraft* (Cambridge, 1610).
Poklatecki, S., *Pogrom, czarnoksięskie błędy, latawców zdrady i alchimickie fałsze jako rozplasza* (Cracow, 1595).
Pollak, R. (ed.), *Listy Krzysztofa Opalińskiego do brata Łukasza 1641–53* (Wrocław, 1957).
Postępek prawa czartowskiego przeciw narodowi ludzkiemu, ed. A. Benis (Cracow, 1872 [1570]).
'Przygody i sprawy trefne', in K. Badecki (ed.), *Polska fraszka mieszczańska* (Cracow, 1948 [n.d.]).
Rej, M., *Apokalipsis* (Cracow, 1565).
Remy, N., *Demonolatreiae* (Lyons, 1595).
Sarnicki, S., *Statuta y metrika przywileiów koronnych: językiem polskim spisane* (Cracow, 1594).
Scot, R., *The Discoverie of Witchcraft* (London, 1584).
Sejm piekielny – satyra obyczajowa (Cracow, 1903 [1622]).
Seklucjan, J., *Katechizm prosty dla ludu* (Olsztyń, 1948 [1545–6]).
Siennik, M., *Lekarstwa doświadczone* (Cracow, 1564).
—— *Herbarz, to jest ziół tutecznych, postronnych i zamorskich opisanie* (Cracow, 1568).
Skarga, P., *Żywoty Świętych* (Warsaw, 1579).
—— *Żywoty Świętych*, ed. M. Kozielski (2 vols, Cracow, 1995 [1615]).
Sokołowska, J. and Żukowska, K. (eds), *Poeci polskiego baroku* (Warsaw, 1965).
Spee, F., *Cautio criminalis seu de processibus contra sagas* (Frankfurt, 1632).
'Statut Jana Dzwonowskiego', in K. Badecki (ed.), *Pisma Jana Dzwonowskiego* (Cracow, 1910 [1608–25]).
Stearne, J., *A Confirmation and Discovery of Witch-Craft* (London, 1648).
Stryjkowski, M., *Kronika Polska* (Warsaw, 1782 [1582]).
Summis Desiderantes (1484).
'Synod klechów Podgorskich', in K. Badecki (ed.), *Polska komedia rybałtowska pierwsze zbiorowe i krytyczne wydanie* (Lwów, 1931 [1607]).
Syreniusz, S., *Zielnik, z herbarzem z ięzyka łacinskiego zowią to iest opisane własne imion, kszaltu* (Cracow, 1673 [1613]).
Szczurowski, T., *Missya Bialska. Prawo kanoniczne o wszystkich ustawach i dekretach synodalnych we wszelkich materiach i wydarzeniach* (Supraśl, 1792).
Szymonowicz, S., *Sielanki* (Cracow, 1921 [1614]).
Theatrum de veneficis, das ist: Von Teuffelsgespenst, Zauberern und Giffthereitern, Schwartzküstlern, Hexen und Unholden, vieler fürnemmen Historien und Exempel (Frankfurt am Main, 1586).
Trepka, W.N., *Liber Generationis vel Plebeanorum*, ed. W. Dworzaczek (Wrocław, 1963).Tylkowski, A., *Tribunal sacrum seu de arte faciendae et audiendae sacramentalis confessionis. Opus Regno Poloniae specialiter accomodatum* (Warsaw, 1690).
Volumina legum, przedruk zbioru praw staraniem XX. Pijarów w Warszawie od roku 1732 do 1793 (vols 1–10, Warsaw, 1980).
Weyer, J., *De Praestigiis Daemonum* (Basel, 1583).

—— De Lamiis (Basel, 1577).
Wisner, D., *Tractatus brevis de extramagi, lamii, veneticis* (Poznań, 1639).
Wódka z elixierem (Poznań, 1729).
Wuyek, J., *Biblia* (Cracow, 1599).
'Z nowinami torba kursorska Iozefa Pięknorzyckiego z Mątwiłaiec, naleziona w Nalewayków', in K. Badecki (ed.), *Polska komedia Polska satyra mieszczańska* (Cracow, 1950 [1645]).
Załuski, J.A., *Objaśnienie błędami zabobonów zarażonych oraz opisanie niegodziwości, która pochodzi sądzenia przez probę plawienia w wodzie niniemanych czarownic jako takowa proba jest omylna różnymi dowodami stwierzone* (Berdyczów, 1766).
Ząmbkowicz, S. (trans.), *Młot na czarownice* (Cracow, 1614).

Printed Secondary Works

Adamczewska, G., 'Magiczna broń i jej rola w walce między wsią a dworem w Sieradzkiem w XVII i XVIII wieku', *Łódzkie Studia Etnograficzne* 5 (1963), 5–16.
Adamczyk, J., Maisel i magia w praktyce sądów kościelnych na ziemiach polskich w późnym średniowieczu (XV–połowa XVI w.)', in M. Koczerska (ed.), *Karolińscy pokutnicy i polskie średniowieczne czarownice. Konfrontacja doktryny chrześcijańskiej z życiem społeczeństwa średniowiecznego* (Warsaw, 2007).
Adamczyk, M., 'Procesy czarownic w Zbąszyniu', in J. Świerzowicz (ed.), *Wczoraj i dziś powiatu nowotomyślskiego. Jednodniówka* (Nowy Tomyśl, 1938).
Amussen, S., 'Gender, Family and the Social Order, 1560–1725', in A. Fletcher and J. Stevenson (eds), *Order and Disorder in Early Modern England* (Cambridge, 1985).
Anders, P., *Pyzdry miasto nad Wartą* (Poznań, 1993).
—— *Grodzisk Wielkopolska* (Poznań, 1995).
Anglo, S., *The Damned Art: Essays in the Literature of Witchcraft* (London, 1977).
Ankarloo, B. and Henningsen, G. (eds), *Early Modern Witchcraft: Centres and Peripheries* (Oxford, 1998 [1990]).
Ankarloo, B., Clark, S. and Monter W. (eds), *The Athlone History of Witchcraft and Magic in Europe: The Period of the Witch Trials* (London, 2002).
Apps, L. and Gow, A., *Male Witches in Early Modern Europe* (Manchester, 2003).
Backvis, C., *Szkice o kulturze staropolskiej* (Warsaw, 1975).
Banać, I., *The Nobility in Russia and Eastern Europe* (New Haven, 1983).
Baranowski, B., *Polskie procesy czarownic jako zjawisko społeczno-kulturalne* (Łódź, 1949).
—— *Najdawniejsze procesy o czary w Kaliszu* (Lublin-Łódź, 1951).
—— *Procesy czarownic w Polsce w XVII i XVIII wieku* (Łódź, 1952).
—— *Sprawy obyczajowe w sądownictwie wiejskim w Polsce w XVII i XVIII wieku* (Wrocław, 1955).
—— 'Wielki proces o czary miłosne w Praszce w 1665 roku', *Łódzkie Studia Etnograficzne* 4 (1962), 5–14.
—— *Pożegnanie z diabłem i czarownicą* (Łódź, 1965).
—— *Kultura ludowa XVII i XVIII wieku* (Łódź, 1971).
—— *Życie codziennie małego miasteczka w XVII i XVIII wieku* (Warsaw, 1975).
—— *Nietolerancja i zabobony w Polsce w XVII i XVIII wieku* (Łódź, 1987 [1950]).
—— *O hultajach, wiedźmach i wszetecznicach* (Łódź, 1988).

Baranowski, B. and Kamieńska, Z. (eds), *Historia kultury materialnej Polski w zarysie* (Wrocław, 1978).
Bardach, J., Leśnodorski, B. and Pietrzak, M. (eds), *Historia państwa i prawa polski od połowy XV do r. 1795* (2 vols, Warsaw, 1966).
—— *Historia państwa i prawa polskiego* (2 vols, Warsaw, 1976).
—— *Historia ustroju i prawa polskiego* (Warsaw, 1994).
Barry, J. and Davies, O. (eds), *Palgrave Advances in Witchcraft Historiography* (Basingstoke, 2007).
Barry, J., Hester, M. and Roberts, G. (eds), *Witchcraft in Early Modern Europe: Studies in Culture and Belief* (Cambridge, 1998).
Baschwitz, K., *Czarownice* (Warsaw, 1971 [1963]).
Bąk, S. et al. (eds), *Słownik polszczyzny XVI wieku* (Warsaw, 1966–).
Behringer, W., 'Weather, Hunger and Fear: Origins of the European Witch-hunts in Climate, Society and Mentality', *German History* 13, no. 1 (1995), 1–27.
—— *Witchcraft Persecutions in Bavaria* (Cambridge, 1997).
—— *Witches and Witch-Hunts* (Cambridge, 2004).
—— 'Historiography', in Golden, R.M. (ed.), *Encyclopedia of Witchcraft: The Western Tradition* (4 vols, Santa Barbara and Oxford, 2006), vol. II.
Berwiński, R., *Studia o gusłach, czarach, zabobonach i przesądach ludowych* (Warsaw, 1862).
Bever, E., *The Realities of Witchcraft and Popular Magic in Early Modern Europe: Culture, Cognition, and Everyday Life* (Basingstoke and New York, 2008).
Bieroński, W., *Czary i zabobony* (Kołomyja, 1885).
de Blécourt, W., 'The Making of the Female Witch: Reflections on Witchcraft and Gender in the Early Modern Period', *Gender and History* 12, no. 2 (2000), 287–309.
Bogucka, M., *Dzieje kultury polskiej do 1795 roku* (Warsaw, 1964).
—— 'Polish Towns Between the 16th and 18th Centuries', in J.K. Fedorowicz (ed.), *A Republic of Nobles: Studies in Polish History to 1864* (Cambridge, 1982).
—— 'Rodzina w polskim mieście XVI–XVII wieku: wprowadzenie w problematykę', *Przegląd Historyczny* 74, no. 3 (1983), 495–507.
—— 'Women and Economic Life in the Polish Cities During the 16th–17th Centuries', in S. Cavaciocchi (ed.), *La donna nell'economia secc. XIII–XVIII* (Florence, 1990).
—— 'The Foundations of the Old Polish World: Patriarchalism and the Family. Introduction into the Problem', *Acta Polonicae Historica* 69 (1994), 37–53.
—— *Staropolskie obyczaje w XVI i XVII w.* (Warsaw, 1994).
—— 'Law and Crime in Poland in Early Modern Times', *Acta Polonica Historica* 71 (1995), 175–95.
—— 'Gender in the Economy of a Traditional Agrarian Society: The Case of Poland in the 16th–17th Centuries', *Acta Poloniae Historica* 74 (1996), 6–15.
—— *The Lost World of the 'Sarmatians': Custom as the Regulator of Polish Social Life in Early Modern Times* (Warsaw, 1996).
—— 'Great Disputes over Woman in Early Modern Times', *Acta Poloniae Historica* 78 (1998), 27–52.
—— *Historia Polski do 1864 roku* (Wrocław, 1999).
—— *Women in Early Modern Poland, against the European Background* (Aldershot, 2004).

Bogucka, M. and Samsonowicz, H., *Dzieje miast i mieszczaństwa w Polsce przedrozbiorowej* (Wrocław, 1986).
Bollenbeck, G., *Till Eulenspiegel* (Stuttgart, 1985).
Bossowski, J., *Sądy Boże na Pomorzu* (Poznań, 1937).
Bossy, J., 'Moral Arithmetic: Seven Sins into Ten Commandments', in E. Leites (ed.), *Conscience and Casuistry in Early Modern Europe* (Cambridge, 1988).
Brauner, S., *Fearless Wives and Frightened Shrews: The Construction of the Witch in Early Modern Germany* (Amherst, 1995).
Briggs, R., 'Women as Victims? Witches, Judges and the Community' *French History* 5 (1991), 438–50.
—— *Witches and Neighbours* (London, 1996).
—— '"Many Reasons Why"': Witchcraft and the Problem of Multiple Explanation', in J. Barry, M. Hester and G. Roberts (eds), *Witchcraft in Early Modern Europe* (Cambridge, 1998).
Broedel, H.P., *The Malleus Maleficarum and the Construction of Witchcraft: Theology and Popular Belief* (Manchester, 2003).
Bruchnalski, W., 'Dyabeł z Okszy 1649', *Lud* 7 (1901), 146–50.
Brückner, A., 'Wierzenia religijne i stosunki rodzinne', in A. Brückner, L. Niederle and W. Kadlec (eds), *Początki kultury Słowiańskiej* (Cracow, 1912).
—— *Encyklopedia staropolska* (Warsaw, 1939).
—— *Dzieje kultury polskiej* (Warsaw, 1957).
—— *Kultura, piśmiennictwo, folklor* (Warsaw, 1974).
Brzezińska, A., 'Accusations of Love Magic in the Renaissance Courtly Culture of the Polish Lithuanian Commonwealth', *East Central Europe* 20-3 (1993–96), 117–40.
Buchowski, M., 'Spór o racjonalność magii', *Lud* 67 (1983), 73–90.
Budzyk, K. et al., *Literatura mieszczańska w Polsce od końca XVI do końca XVII wieku* (Warsaw, 1954). Bugaj, R., *Nauki tajemne w Polsce w dobie odrodzenia* (Wrocław, 1976).
Bukowska-Gorgoni, K., 'Procesy o czary i powołanie przez czarownice w orzecznictwie Sądu Wyższego prawa niemieckiego na Zamku Krakowskim', *Lud* 54 (1970), 156–67.
Burke, P., *Popular Culture in Early Modern Europe* (London, 1978).
Burszta, J. et al. (eds), *Kultura ludowa Wielkopolski* (3 vols, Poznań, 1967).
Butterwick, R. (ed.), *The Polish-Lithuanian Monarchy in European Context, c. 1500–1795* (Basingstoke, 2001).
Bystroń, J.S., *Megalomanja narodowa* (Warsaw, 1935).
—— *Kultura ludowa* (Warsaw, 1936).
—— *Dzieje obyczajów w dawnej Polsce wiek XVI-XVIII* (Warsaw, 1976 [1932]).
Caro Baroja, J., 'Witchcraft and Catholic Theology', in B. Ankarloo and G. Henningson (eds), *Early Modern Witchcraft: Centres and Peripheries* (Oxford, 1993).
Charewiczowa, Ł., *Kobieta w dawnej Polsce okresu do rozbiorów* (Lwów, 1938).
Cheyne, T.K. and Blade, J.S. (eds), *Encyclopedia Biblica* (4 vols, London, 1902).
Clark, S., 'The "Gendering" of Witchcraft in French Demonology: Misogyny or Polarity?', *French History* 5 (1991), 429–31.
—— 'Protestant Demonology: Sin, Superstition, and Society (c. 1520–c. 1630)', in B. Ankarloo and G. Henningson (eds), *Early Modern Witchcraft: Centres and Peripheries* (Oxford, 1993).

—— *Thinking with Demons: The Idea of Witchcraft in Early Modern Europe* (Oxford, 1999 [1997]).

—— Review of *Between the Devil and the Host: Imagining Witchcraft in Early Modern Poland*, by M. Ostling, *The Journal of Ecclesiastical History* 64, no. 1 (2013), 185–6.

Cohn, N., *Europe's Inner Demons* (London, 1975).

Cynarski, S., 'The Shape of Sarmatian Ideology in Poland', *Acta Polonicae Historica* 19 (1968), 5–17.

Czacki, T., *O litewskich i polskich prawach* (2 vols, Cracow, 1987 [1861]).

Czubryński, A., 'Z katalogu "imion diabłów"', *Euhemer* 6 (1958), 36–43.

Daly, M., *Gyn/Ecology: The Metaethics of Radical Feminism* (Boston, 1979).

Davies, N., *God's Playground: A History of Poland* (2 vols, Oxford, 1991 [1981]).

Dąbrowski, K. and Gieysztor, A. (eds), *Osiemnaście wieków Kalisza* (3 vols, Kalisz, 1960–62).

Derdziuk, A., *Grzech w XVIII w.* (Lublin, 1996).

Derenda, J. and Sygit, B., *Przez czarta opętane* (Bydgoszcz, 1990).Doroszewski, W., *Słownik języka polskiego* (11 vols, Warsaw, 1958–69).

Douglas, M., *Purity and Danger: An Analysis of the Concepts of Pollution and Taboo* (London, 1985 [1966]).

Dworkin, A., *Women Hating* (New York, 1974).

Dydek, Z., 'Czary w procesie inkwizycyjnym w Rzeszowie w XVIII wieku', *Rocznik Województwa Rzeszowskiego* 5 (1964–65), 383–401.

Dydyński, J., *Wiadomości historyczne o mieście Kłecku* (Gniezno, 1848).

Dysa, K., 'Witchcraft Trials and Beyond: Right-bank Side Ukrainian Trials of the Seventeenth and Eighteenth Centuries' (PhD thesis, Central European University, Budapest, 2004).

Ehrenreich, B. and English, D., *Witches, Midwives, and Nurses: A History of Women Healers* (Old Westbury, NY, 1973).

Estreicher, K., *Bibliografia Polski. Część III. Obejmująca druku stóleci XV–XVIII w układzie abecadłowym* (11 vols, Cracow, 1910–).

Fagan, B., *The Little Ice Age: How Climate Made History 1300–1850* (2000).

Fedorowicz, J.K., *A Republic of Nobles: Studies in Polish History to 1864* (Cambridge, 1982).

Fischer, A., 'Opowieści o czarownicach z doliny nowotarskiej', *Lud* 25 (1926), 78–94.

Fischer, A., Lorentz, F. and Lehr Spławiński, T. (eds), *Kaszubi: Kultura ludowa i język* (Toruń, 1934).

Flohn, H. and Fantechi, R., *The Climate of Europe: Past, Present and Future* (1984).

Frost, R.I., *After the Deluge: Poland-Lithuania and the Second Northern War 1655–1660* (Cambridge, 1993).

—— 'The Nobility of Poland-Lithuania, 1569–1795', in H. Scott (ed.), *The European Nobilities in the 17th and 18th Centuries* (2 vols, London, 1995), vol. II.

Fudge, T.A., 'Traditions and Trajectories in the Historiography of European Witch-hunting', *History Compass* 4, no. 3 (2006), 488–527.

Gacki, Ks. J., 'Klasztor Święto-Krzyzki Księży Benedyktynów na Łysej Górze', *Pamiętnik Religijno-Moralny* 7, no. 1 (1861), 10–38.

Gansiniec, R., 'Eucharystia w wierzeniach i praktykach ludu', *Lud* 44 (1957), 75–117.

Gaskill, M., 'The Devil in the Shape of a Man: Witchcraft, Conflict and Belief in Jacobean England', *Historical Research* 71 (1998), 42–171.
Gauda, A. and Nasalski, Z., *Czarcia łapa* (Lublin, 1991).
Gawełek, F., 'Przyczynek do czarów', *Lud* 15 (1909), 356–7.
Gibson, M., *Early Modern Witches: Witchcraft Cases in Contemporary Writing* (London, 2000).
Giedroyc, F., *Mór w Polsce w wiekach ubiegłych: zarys historyczny* (Warsaw, 1899).
Gieysztorowa, I., *Wstęp do demografii staropolskiej* (Warsaw, 1976).
—— 'Rodzina staropolska w świetle badań demograficznych: zarys problematyki', in *Społeczeństwo staropolskie* (Warsaw, 1979), vol. II.
Ginzburg, C., *The Night Battles: Witchcraft and Agrarian Cults in the Sixteenth and Seventeenth Centuries* (Baltimore, 1983 [1966]).Gloger, Z., *Encyklopedia staropolska illustrowana* (Warsaw, 1845–1910).
Golden, R.M. (ed.), *Encyclopedia of Witchcraft: The Western Tradition* (4 vols, Santa Barbara, 2006).
Gołębiowski, Ł., *Lud polski, jego zwyczaje, zabobony* (Warsaw, 1983 [1830]).
Górski, R. and Krzyżanowski, J., *Z zagadnień twórczości ludowej. Studia folkorystyczne* (Warsaw, 1970).
Grzeszczuk, S., *Antologia literatury sowizdrzalskiej XVI i XVII wieku* (Wrocław, 1985).
Guldon, Z., *Procesy mordy rytualne w Polsce w XVI–XVIII wieku* (Kielce, 1995).
Hagen, W.W., 'Village Life in East-Elbian Germany and Poland, 1400–1800: Subjection, Self-Defence, Survival', in T. Scott (ed.), *The Peasantries of Europe* (London, 1998).
Harley, D., 'Historians as Demonologists: The Myth of the Midwife-witch', *Social History of Medicine* 3 (1990), 1–26.
Hassencamp, R., 'Ein Ostrowoer Hexenprozess aus dem Jahre 1719', *Zeitschrift der Historischen Gesellschaft für die Provinz Posen* 8 (1893), 223–8.
Hastrup, K., 'Iceland: Sorcerers and Paganism', in B. Ankarloo and G. Henningsen (eds), *Early Modern Witchcraft: Centre and Peripheries* (Oxford, 1990).
Heikkinen, A. and Kervinen, T., 'Finland: The Male Domination', in B. Ankarloo and G. Henningsen (eds), *Early Modern Witchcraft: Centre and Peripheries* (Oxford, 1990).
Henningsen, G., *The Witches' Advocate: Basque Witchcraft and the Spanish Inquisition (1609–1614)* (Reno, 1980).
Hester, M., *Lewd Women and Wicked Witches: A Study of the Dynamics of Male Domination* (London, 1992).
Hockenbeck, H., 'Hexenbrände in Wongrowitz', *Zeitschrift der Historischen Gesellschaft für die Provinz Posen* 9 (1894), 175–8.
Holmes, C., 'Women: Witnesses and Witches', *Past and Present* 140 (1993), 45–78.
Hoszowski, S., *Klęski elementarne w Polsce w latach 1587–1648* (Warsaw, 1960).
Jackson, L., 'Wives, Witches and Mothers', *Women's History Review* 4 (1995), 63–83.
Janiszewska-Mincer, B., 'Bydgoskie procesy o czary z 1638 roku', *Prace Komisji Historii, Seria C* 4 (1966), 105–24.
Janów, J., 'Exemplum o czarcie włódącym do zbrodni przez opiłstwo', *Lud* 11 (1932), 12–24.
Jodkowski, J., 'O czarowniku Znaku na inkwizycji w Grodnie w 1691 r. i o ziołach czarodziejskich', *Lud* 30 (1931), 202–11.

Kaczmarczyk, K., 'Przyczyńki do wiary w czary', *Lud* 13 (1907), 330–2.
—— 'Proces o czarostwo w 1688 i 1699', *Lud* 7 (1908), 302–22.
—— 'Ze starych aktów. Proces o czary w Bochni 1679 r.', *Lud* 16 (1910), 45–53.
—— 'Straty archiwalne na terenie Poznania w latach 1939–1945', *Archeion* 28 (1957), 65–93.
Kaczmarczyk Z. and Leśnodorski, B., *Historia Państwa i prawa Polski od połowy XV do r. 1795* (2 vols, Warsaw, 1957).
Kamen, H., *The Iron Century: Social Change in Europe, 1550–1660* (London, 1971).
Kamińska, K., *Sądownictwo miasta Torunia do połowy XVII wieku na tle ustroju sądów niektórych miast Niemiec i Polski* (Warsaw, 1980).
Kamiński, A.S., *Republic v Autocracy: Poland-Lithuania and Russia 1686–1697* (Cambridge, MA, 1993).
Kamler, M., 'Struktura i liczebność środowisk przestępczych Poznania i Krakowa w drugiej połowie XVI w.', *Przeszłość demograficzna Polski: materiały i studia* 15 (1984), 71–93.
—— 'Rola tortur w polskim sądownictwie miejskim drugiej połowy XVI i pierwszy połowy XVII w.', *Kwartalnik Historyczny* 95, no. 3 (1988), 107–15.
—— 'Penalties for Common Crimes in Polish Towns 1550–1650', *Acta Poloniae Historica*, 71 (1995), 161–74.
Kantak, K., 'Poznańska książka w obronie czarownic', *Kronika Miasta Poznania* 11 (1933), 268–77.
Karbownik, H., 'Management of Witchcraft Trials in the Light of Synod Resolutions and Bishops' Regulations in Pre-partition Poland', *The Review of Comparative Law* 2 (1988), 65–78.
Karłowicz, J., 'Czary i czarownice w Polsce', *Wisla* 1 and 2 (1887), 14–20, 56–62, 93–9, 136–43, 172–8, 213–22.
Karpiński, A., 'The Woman on [sic] the Market Place. The Scale of Feminization of Retail Trade in Polish Towns in the Second Half of the 16th and in the 17th Century', in S. Cavaciocchi (ed.), *La donna nell'economia secc. XIII–XVIII* (Florence, 1990).
—— 'Prostytutki, złodziejki i czarownice. Z badań nad kobiecą przestępczością w Poznaniu w drugiej połowie XVI i w XVII w.', *Kronika Miasta Poznania* 1–2 (1993), 110–32.
—— *Kobieta w mieście polskim* (Warsaw, 1995).
—— 'Female Servants in Polish Towns in the Late 16th and 17th Centuries', *Acta Poloniae Historica* 74 (1996), 21–44.
—— *W walce z niewidzalnym wrogiem* (Warsaw, 2000).
Karwot, E., *Katalog magii Rudolfa* (Wrocław, 1955).
Karwowski, S., *Gniezno* (Poznań, 1892).
Kieckhefer, R., *European Witch Trials: Their Foundation in Popular and Learned Culture, 1300–1500* (London, 1976).
Kieniewicz, S., *History of Poland* (Warsaw, 1979).
Klaits, J., *Servants of Satan: The Age of the Witch Hunts* (Bloomington, 1985).
Klaniczay, G., *The Uses of Supernatural Power: The Transformation of Popular Religion in Medieval and Early-Modern Europe* (Cambridge, 1990).
—— 'Witch-Trials in Hungary (1520–1777): The Accusations and the Popular Universe of Magic', in B. Ankarloo and G. Henningsen (eds), *Early Modern Witchcraft: Centres and Peripheries* (Oxford, 1998 [1990]).

Klarner, S., 'Sprawy o czary w urzędach bełżyckich w wiekach XVI–XVIII. Z aktów urzędów radzieckiego i wójtowskiego miasta Bełżyc', *Wisła* 16, 1902.
Kłoczowski, J., *Kościół w Polsce w XV–XVII w.*, II (Cracow, 1969).
—— *Dzieje chrześcijaństwa polskiego* (Warsaw, 2000).
—— *A History of Polish Christianity* (Cambridge, 2000).
Kochanowicz, J., 'The Polish Economy and the Evolution of Dependency', in D. Chirot (ed.), *The Origins of Backwardness in Eastern European Economies and Politics from the Middle Ages until the Early Twentieth Century* (Berkeley and London, 1989).
Konopczyński, W., 'Wielkopolski w dobie Rzeczypospolitej szlacheckiej', *Roczniki Historyczne* 1 (1925), 75–101.
Konopczyński, W. (ed.), *Polski Słownik Biograficzny* (Cracow, 1935–).
Kopaliński, W., *Słownik mitów i tradycji kultury* (Warsaw, 1985).
Koranyi, K., 'Czary w postępowaniu sądowym', *Lud* 25 (1926), 7–18.
—— 'Czary i gusła przed sądami kościelnymi w Polsce w XV i pierwszej połowie XVI w.', *Lud* 26 (1927), 1–25.
—— 'Studia nad wierzeniami w historii prawa karnego. Beczka czarownic', *Pamiętnik Historyczno-Prawny* 5, no. 2 (1927), 1–43.
—— 'Łysa Góra. Studium z dziejów wierzeń ludowych w Polsce w XVII i XVIII w.', *Lud* 27 (1928), 57–74.
Korcz, W., *Współniczki diabła czyli o procesach czarownic na Śląsku w XVII w.* (Katowice, 1985).
Kosciełniak, W. and Walczak, K., *Kronika miasta Kalisza* (Kalisz, 1989).Kracik, M. and Rożek, J., *Hultaje, złoczyńcy, wszetecznice w dawnym Krakowie. O marginesie społecznym w XVII–XVIII w.* (Cracow, 1986).
Kraushar, A., *Czary na dworze Batorego* (Cracow, 1888).
Krejči, K., *Wybrane studia slawistyczne. Kultura, literatura, folklor* (Warsaw, 1971).
Kriegseisen, W., 'Between Intolerance and Persecution. Polish and Lithuanian Protestants in the 18th Century', *Acta Poloniae Historica* 73 (1996), 13–27.
Krzyżanowski, A., *Dawna Polska z stanowiska jej udziału w dziejach postępującej ludzkości* (Warsaw, 1844).
Krzyżanowski, J., *Paralele. Studia porównawcze z pogranicza literatury i folkloru* (Warsaw, 1961).
—— *Słownik folkloru polskiego* (Warsaw, 1965).
Krzyżewski, W. (ed.), *Encyklopedia powszechna* (4 vols, Warsaw, 1985).
Kuchowicz, Z., *Lęki i gusła dawnej wsi* (Warsaw, 1957).
—— *Z dziejów obyczajów polskich w wieku XVII i pierwszej połowej XVIII* (Warsaw, 1957).
—— *Wizerunki niepospolitych niewiast staropolskich XVI–XVIII wieku* (Łódź, 1972).
—— *Obyczaje staropolskie XVII–XVIII w.* (Łódź, 1975).
—— *Żywoty niepospolitych kobiet polskiego baroku* (Łódź, 1989).
Kuchta, J.,'Nauki tajemne w Polsce w XV i XVI w.', *Lud* 27 (1928), 75–107.
Kutrzeba, S., *Polskie ustawy i artykuły wojskowe od XV do XVII wieku* (Cracow, 1937).
Kwak, J., *Obyczajowość mieszkańców miast górnośląskich w XVI–XVIII w.* (Opole, 1986).
—— *Klęski elementarne w miastach górnośląskich (w XVIII i w pierwszej połowie XIX w)* (Opole, 1987).

Labouvie, E., 'Men in Witchcraft Trials: Towards a Social Anthropology of "Male" Understandings of Magic and Witchcraft', in U. Rublack (ed.), *Gender in Early Modern Germany* (Cambridge, 2002).
Lamb, L., *Climate, History and the Modern World* (1995 [1982]).
Larner, C., *Enemies of God: The Witch-Hunt in Scotland* (Baltimore, 1981).
—— *Witchcraft and Religion* (Oxford, 1984).
Lasocki, Z., 'Szlachta płońska w walce z czartem', *Miesięcznik Heraldyczny* 12 (1933), vol. 1, 1–8; vol. 2, 18–22; vol. 3, 37–42.
Lea, H.C., *Materials toward a History of Witchcraft* (Philadelphia, 1939).
Lehr-Spławiński, T., *Rozprawy i szkice z dziejów kultury Słowian* (Warsaw, 1954).
Levack, B. (ed.), *Witch-hunting in Continental Europe: Local and Regional Studies* (London, 1992).
—— *The Witch-hunt in Early Modern Europe* (London, 1995 and 2006).
—— *New Perspectives on Witchcraft, Magic and Demonology* (12 vols, New York and London, 2001).
Lilienthal, J.A., 'Die Hexenprozesse der beiden Städte Braunsberg, nach den Criminalacten des Braunsberger Archivs', Königsberg 1861, *Neue Preussische Provinzial Blätter* 2, 1858–60.
Linde, S.B., *Słownik języka polskiego* (6 vols, Warsaw, 1807–14).
Litwin, H., 'The Polish Magnatéria 1454–1648: The Shaping of an Estate', *Acta Polonicae Historica* 53 (1986), 63–92.
Llewellyn Barstow, A., *Witchcraze* (New York, 1994).
Lukowski, J. and Zawadzki, H., *A Concise History of Poland* (Cambridge, 2001).
Łaszewski, R., *Wiejskie prawo karne w Polsce XVII i XVIII w.* (Toruń, 1988).
Łaszkiewicz, H., 'Kary wymierzone przez sąd miejski w Lublinie w drugiej połowie XVII wieku', *Czasopismo prawno-historyczne* 41, no. 2 (1989), 139–51.
Łęcki, W., *Gostyń* (Poznań, 1997).
Łuczak, A., *Czary i czarownice wczoraj i dziś* (Tarnów, 1993).
Łukaszewicz, J., *Krótki historyczno-statystyczny opis miast i wsi w dzisiejszym powiecie krotoszyńskim* (2 vols, Poznań, 1869–75).
Macfarlane, A., *Witchcraft in Tudor and Stuart England* (London, 1970).
Maciejewski, T., *Narzędzia tortur, sądów bożych i prób czarownic* (Koszalin, 1997).
Madar, M., 'Estonia I: Werewolves and Poisoners', in B. Ankarloo and G. Henningsen (eds), *Early Modern Witchcraft: Centre and Peripheries* (Oxford, 1990).
Maisel, W. *Ortyle sądów wyższych miast wielkopolskich z XV i XVI w.* (Wrocław, 1959).
—— *Poznańskie prawo karne do końca XVI wieku* (Poznań, 1963).
—— 'Sąd miejski prawa polskiego w Kaliszu w XVI wieku', *Czasopismo prawno-historyczne* 23, no. 2 (1971), 129–39.
—— 'Prawo karne w statutach polskich', *Czasopismo prawno-historyczne* 26, no. 2 (1974), 99–117.
—— *Tortury w praktyce sądu kryminalnego miasta Poznania w XVI–XVIII w.* (Poznań, 1978).
Makiłła. D. and Naworski, Z., *Prawa na ziemiach polskich – Polska predrozbiorowa zarys wykłady* (2 vols, Toruń, 2000).
Malewski, Z., 'Procesy o czarnoksięstwo i zabobony w Bydgoszczy. Przyczynek do dziejów czarownictwa w Polsce', *Przegląd Bygoski* 4 (1936), 71–81.
Massadié, G., *A History of the Devil* (New York, 1997).
Matusiak, S., 'Tria idola na Łysej Górze', *Lud* 14 (1908), 313–25.

Matuszewski, I., *Dyabeł w poezji* (Warsaw, 1894).
Mączak, A., 'The Structure of Power in the Commonwealth', in J.K. Fedorowicz (ed.), *A Republic of Nobles: Studies in Polish History to 1864* (Cambridge, 1982).
—— *Money, Prices and Power in Poland, 16th–17th centuries* (Aldershot, 1995).
Midelfort, H.C., 'Witchcraft and Religion in Sixteenth-Century Germany: The Formation and Consequences of an Orthodoxy', in B. Levack (ed.), *Articles on Witchcraft, Magic and Demonology: The Literature of Witchcraft*, IV (12 vols, London, 1992 [1971]).
—— *Witch Hunting in Southwestern Germany 1562–1684: The Social and Intellectual Foundations* (Stanford, 1972).
Mikołajczyk, M., 'Przestępstwa przeciw religii i Kosciołowi w prawie miast polskich XVI–XVIII wieku', *Czasopismo Prawno-Historyczne* 52, 1–2 (2000), 225–38.
—— 'Jak obronić oskarżoną o czary. Mowy procesowe z 1655 roku w sprawie Gertrudy Zagrodzkiej', in M. Wąsowicz (ed.), *Dziejów kultury prawnej: Studia ofierowane Profesorowi Juliuszowi Bardzachowi w dziewięćdziesięciolecie urodzin* (Warsaw, 2004).
Miśkowiak, J., *Ze Studiów nad 'Sowizdrzałem' w Polsce* (Poznań, 1938).
Monter, E.W., 'The Historiography of European Witchcraft: Progress and Prospects', *Journal of Interdisciplinary History* 2, no. 4 (1971–72), 435–51.
—— *Witchcraft in France and Switzerland: The Borderlands during the Reformation* (Ithaca and London, 1976).
—— 'The Pedestal and the Stake: Courtly Love and Witchcraft', in C. Koontz and R. Bridentahl (eds), *Becoming Visible: Women in European History* (Boston, 1987).
—— 'Toads and Eucharists: The Male Witches of Normandy, 1564–1660', *French Historical Studies* 20 (1997), 563–95.
Moszyński, K., *Kultura ludowa Słowian* (Cracow, 1934).
Muchembled, R., *A History of the Devil: From the Middle Ages to the Present* (Cambridge, 2003).
Muhl, J., 'Zauberei und Hexenaberglauben im Danziger Land', *Mitteilungen des Westpreußischen Geschichtvereins* 32 (1933), H2.
Murray, M., *The Witch-Cult in Western Europe* (Oxford, 1921).
Nowicki, A., 'O renesansowej magii', *Euhemer* 2 (1960), 15–22.
Nowodworski, M., 'Jaka jest nauka kościoła o diable!', *Pamiętnik Religijno-Moralny* 7, no. 2 (1861), 151–61.
Ogonowski, Z., *Z zagadnień tolerancji w Polsce XVI w.* (Warsaw, 1958).
Olszewski, F., 'Prześladowanie czarów w dawnej Polsce', in *Album uczące się mlodzieży poświęcone J.I. Kraszewskiemu* (Lwów, 1879).
Olszewski, H., 'The Essence and Legal Foundation of the Magnate Oligarchy in Poland', *Acta Poloniae Historica* 56 (1988), 29–49.
Opaliński, E., *Elita władzy w województwach poznańskim i kaliskim za Zygmunta III* (Poznań, 1981).
Oppenheimer, P., *A Pleasant Vintage of Till Eulenspiegel* (Middletown, 1972).
Orgelbrand, S., *Wielka Encyklopedya Powszechna* (12 vols, Warsaw, 1883–84).
Orłowicz, I., 'Czarownice', *Acta Universitatis Nicolai Copernici* 51 (1998), 99–111.
Ostling, M., 'Konstytucja 1543 r. i początki procesów o czary w Polsce', *OiR* 49 (2005), 93–103.
—— 'Imagining Witchcraft in Early Modern Poland' (PhD thesis, University of Toronto, 2008).

234 Bibliography

—— *Between the Devil and the Host: Imagining Witchcraft in Early Modern Poland* (Oxford, 2011).

Pagels, E., *The Origin of Satan* (London, 1996).

Paprzyca, H., 'Poglądy religijne przodków naszych', *Wisła* 16 (1902), 219–35, 507–33.

Paradowska, M., *Bambrzy* (Poznań, 1998).

Patro, G., *Wągrowiec zarys dziejów* (Warsaw, 1982).

Pelc, J., 'Wiek XVII, kontrreformacja, barok; prace z historii kultury' *Studia Staropolskie*, 29 (Wrocław, 1970).Pełka, L., *Polska demonologia ludowa* (Warsaw, 1987).

Pellowski, L., *Świat aniołów i demonów* (Wąbrzezno, 1930).

Pfister, C.P., 'Monthly Temperature and Precipitation in Central Europe 1525–1979', in R.S. Bradley and P.D. Jones (eds), *Climate since A.D. 1500* (1995 [1992]).

Pieszczachowicz, J. (ed.), *Wielka Historia Polski* (Cracow, 2000–01).

Pilaszek, M., 'Procesy czarownic w Polsce w XVI–XVIII w. Nowe aspekty. Uwagi na marginesie pracy B. Baranowskiego', *Odrodzenie i Reformacja w Polsce* 42 (1998), 81–103.

—— 'W poszukiwaniu prawdy o działalności sądów kryminalnych w Koronie XVI–XVIII w.', *Przegląd Historyczny* 89, no. 3 (1998), 361–81.

—— 'Witchhunts in Poland, 16th–18th Centuries', *Acta Polonicae Historica* 86 (2002), 103–32.

—— *Procesy o czary w Polsce w wiekach XV–XVIII* (Cracow, 2008).

Piotrkowska, U., 'Struktura i rozmieszczenie własności feudalnej w województwie Poznańskim w drugiej połowie XVI wieku', in *Społeczeństwo staropolskie*, IV (Warsaw, 1986).

Plezia, M., *Słownik łaciny średniowiecznej w Polsce* (Warsaw, 1953–).

Podgórscy B. and A., *Wielka księga demonów polskich* (Katowice, 2005).

Polaszewski, L., 'Szlachta wielkopolski na podstawie rejestrów pogłównego z lat 1673–1676', in *Społeczeństwo staropolskie*, III (Warsaw, 1983).

Polska Akademia Nauk, *Słownik Łaciny Średniowiecznej w Polsce* (Warsaw, 1953–).

Połaczkówna, H. (ed.), *Najdawniejsza księga sądowa wsi Trześniowa 1419–1609* (Lwów, 1923).

Przybos, K., 'Latyfundium Lubomirskich w połowie XVII wieku', *Studia Historyczne* 35 (1992), 19–33.

Przybyszewski, L., *Czary i czarownice* (Poznań, 1932).

Przybyszewski, S., *Synagoga szatana* (Warsaw, 1902).

Ptaśnik, J., *Miasta i mieszczaństwo w dawnej Polsce* (Warsaw, 1949).

Purkiss, D., *The Witch in History: Early Modern and Twentieth Century Representations* (London, 1996).

Putek, J., *Mroki średniowiecza*, 5th edn (Warsaw, 1985 [1935]).

Quaife, G., *Godly Zeal and Furious Rage: The Witch in Early Modern Europe* (New York, 1967).

Rafacz, J., 'Podejrzenie o czary w Krościenku', *Lud* 20 (1914/1918), 302–3.

—— *Dawny proces Polski* (Warsaw, 1925).

—— *Dawne polskie prawo karne* (Warsaw, 1932).

Reich, F., *Hexenprozesse in Danzig und in den westpreußischen Grenzgebieten* (Munich, 1940).

Roberts, G. and Normand, L. (eds), *Witchcraft in Early Modern Scotland: James VI's Demonology and the North Berwick Witches* (Exeter, 2000).

Rokitniak, T., 'Z notatnika wakacyjnego', *Wieś* 32–3 (1948), 1.
Roos, K., *The Devil in Sixteenth Century German Literature: The Teufelbücher* (Frankfurt, 1972).
Roper, L., *The Holy Household: Women and Morals in Reformation Augsburg* (Oxford, 1989).
—— *Oedipus and the Devil: Witchcraft, Sexuality and Religion in Early Modern Europe* (London, 1995 [1994]).
—— 'Witchcraft and Fantasy in Early Modern Germany', in J. Barry, M. Hester and G. Roberts (eds), *Witchcraft in Early Modern Europe: Studies in Culture and Belief* (Cambridge, 1998).
—— *Witch Craze* (New Haven and London, 2004).
Rosenblatt, J., *Czarownica powołana. Przyczynek do historii spraw przeciw czarownicom w Polsce* (Warsaw, 1883).
Rowlands, A., 'Telling Witchcraft Stories: New Perspectives on Witchcraft and Witches in the Early Modern Period', *Gender and History* 10, no. 2 (1998), 294–302.
—— *Witchcraft Narratives in Germany: Rothenburg, 1561–1652* (Manchester, 2003).
Rowlands, A. (ed.), *Witchcraft and Masculinities in Early Modern Europe* (Basingstoke, 2009).
Rożek, M., *Diabeł w kulturze polskiej: dzieje postaci i motywu* (Warsaw, 1993).
Rublack, U. (ed.), *Gender in Early Modern Germany* (Cambridge, 2002).
Russell, J.B., *Witchcraft in the Middle Ages* (Ithaca, 1972).
—— *A History of Witchcraft* (London, 1997 [1981]).
Ryan, W., *The Bathhouse at Midnight: An Historical Survey of Magic and Divination in Russia* (Stroud, 1999).
Rytel, J., 'Barok', in J. Jakubowski (ed.), *Literatura Polska od średniowiecza do pozytywizmu* (Warsaw, 1974).
Sadowski, Z., *Pieniądz a początki upadku rzeczypospolitej w XVII w.* (Warsaw, 1964).
Sajkowski, A., *Krzysztof Opaliński Wojewoda Poznański* (Poznań, 1960).
Sallmann, J.-M., *Naples et ses saints à l'âge baroque 1540–1750* (Paris, 1994).
Salmonowicz, S., 'O niegodziwości procesów o czary', *Czasopismo Prawno-Historyczne* 46 (1994), 115–20.
Samp, J., *Droga na Sabat* (Gdańsk, 1981).
Schindler, N., *Rebellion, Community and Custom in Early Modern Germany*, trans. Pamela E. Selwyn (Cambridge, 2002).
Schmidt, J.M., *Glaube und Skepsis. Die Kurpfalz und die abendländische Hexenverfolgung, 1446–1685* (Bielefeld, 2000).
Schulte, Rolf, *Man as Witch: Male Witches in Central Europe*, trans. Linda Froome-Doring (Basingstoke, 2009).
Scribner, R., 'Ritual and Popular Religion in Catholic Germany at the Time of the Reformation', *Journal of Ecclesiastical History* 35 (1984), 47–77.
Sharpe, J., 'Witchcraft and Women in Seventeenth Century England: Some Northern Evidence', *Continuity and Change* 6, no. 2 (1991), 179–99.
—— *Instruments of Darkness* (London, 1996).
Siarczyński, Ks. F., *Wiadomości historyczne i statystyczne o miejście Jarosławiu* (Lwów, 1826).
Simpson, J.A. and Weiner, E.S.C. (eds), *Oxford English Dictionary*, 2nd edn (Oxford, 1991).

Słupecki, L., *Slavonic Pagan Sanctuaries* (Warsaw, 1994).
Smoleński, W., *Przewrót umysłowy w Polsce* (Warsaw, 1979 [1891]).
Sochaniewicz, K., 'O potrzebie systematycznego wydawnictwa materiałów do historii procesów o czary w Polsce', *Lud* 24 (1925), 165-9.
Sokolski J., *Zaświaty Staropolskie* (Wrocław, 1994).
Soldan, W., *Geschichte der Hezenprozesse* (2 vols, Monachium-Lipsk, 1880).
Sosset, L.-L., *Le Personnage de Tiel Eulenspiegel à travers l'Histoire, la Légend et le Folklore* (Rodez and Andrimont, 1938).
Stachowski, W., 'Czarownice z Pępowa', *Kronika Gostyńska, Series VI* 4 (1934).
Stanford, P., *The Devil: A Biography* (London, 1996).
Stanisławski, J., *Wielki Słownik Polsko-Angielski* (Warsaw, 1983).
Stebelski, A., *The Fate of Polish Archives during World War II* (Warsaw, 1964).
Stephens, W., *Demon Lovers: Witchcraft, Sex, and the Crisis of Belief* (Chicago and London, 2002).
Stępień, J., *Kleczewskie procesy o czary* (Poznań, 1998).
Sulisz, J., 'Przyczynek do historii prawa niemieckiego w Polsce', *Lud* 13 (1907), 282-90.
Szczotka, S. (ed.), 'Sprawa Barbary Opielonki o czary 12 maja 1595', in *Materiały do dziejów zbójnictwa góralskiego z lat 1589-1782* (Łódź, 1952).
Szkurłatowski, K.P., 'Gdańskie procesy czarownic w XV-XVII w. na tle ówczesnych przemian religijnych', in J. Iluk and D. Mariańska (eds), *Protestantyzm i protestanci na Pomorzu* (Gdańsk-Koszalin, 1997).
—— 'Proces inkwizycyjny przeciwko czarownictwu w praktyce sądów sołtysich województwa malborskiego na przełomie VXII i XVIII w. na tle rozwoju europejskiego prawa karnego', *Rocznik Elbląski* 15 (1997), 44-55.
Tazbir, J., *Święci, grzesznicy i kacerze* (Warsaw, 1959).
—— *Państwo bez stosów* (Warsaw, 1967).
—— 'Sarmatyzm a barok', *Kwartalnik Historyczny* 76 (1969), 815-30.
—— *Dzieje polskiej tolerancji* (Warsaw, 1973).
—— *Polska XVII w: państwo, społeczeństwo, kultura* (Warsaw, 1974).
—— 'Procesy o czary', *Odrodzenie i Reformacja w Polsce* 23 (1978), 151-77.
—— 'Krakowski stos. Katarzyna Weiglowa (ok 1450-1539)', *Człowiek i Światopogląd* 10 (1985), 38-47.
—— *Mity i stereotypy w dziejach Polski* (Warsaw, 1991).
—— *Okrucieństwo w nowożytnej Europie* (Warsaw, 1993).
Tazbir, J. (ed.), *Polska XVII wieku* (Warsaw, 1969).
Tenberg, R., *Die deutsche Till Eulenspiegel – rezeption bis zum Ende des 16 Jahrhunderts* (Würzburg, 1996).
Thomas, K., *Religion and the Decline of Magic* (London, 1997 [1971]).
Thurston, R., *The Witch Hunts: A History of the Witch Persecutions in Europe and North America* (Harlow, 2007).
Topolski, J., 'Model Gospodarczy Wielkopolski w XVIII wieku', *Studia i materiały do dziejów Wielkopolski i Pomorza I* (20), 10, no. 2 (1971), 57-71.
—— 'The Structure of the Polish Nobility in the 16th and 17th Centuries: Some New Findings and Reflections', in idem, *The Manorial Economy in Early Modern East Central Europe* (Aldershot, 1994).
—— *Wielkopolska poprzez wieki* (Poznań, 1999).
Topolski, J. (ed.), *Dzieje Gniezna* (Warsaw, 1965).
—— (ed.), *Dzieje Wielkopolski* (2 vols, Poznań, 1969).

—— (ed.), *Dzieje Polski* (Warsaw, 1975).
Trevor-Roper, H., *The European Witch-Craze of the Sixteenth and the Seventeenth Centuries* (London, 1990 [1969]).
Tripplin, T., *Tajemnice społeczeństwa wykryte ze spraw kriminalnych krajowych* (3 vols, Wrocław, 1852).
Tuwim, J., *Czary i czarty polskie oraz wypisy czarnoksięskie* (Warsaw, 1960 [1924]).
Urbańczyk, P., 'The Meaning of Christianization for Medieval Pagan Societies', in idem (ed.), *Early Christianity in Central and Eastern Europe* (Cracow, 1947).
Urbańczyk, S., *Religia pogańskich Słowian* (Cracow, 1947).
Urbańczyk, S. et al. (eds), *Słownik Staropolski* (Warsaw, 1953–).
Uruszczak, W., 'Proces czarownicy w Nowym Sączu w 1670 roku. Z badań nad miejskim procesem karnym czasów nowożytnych', in E. Borkowska-Bagieńska and H. Olszewski (eds), *Historia prawa. Historia kultura. Liber Memorialis Vitoldo Maisel dedicatus* (Poznań, 1994).
Uruszczak, W. and Dwornicka, I. (eds), *Acta maleficorum Wisniciae. Księga złoczyńców sądu kryminalnego w Wiśniczu (1629–1665)* (Cracow, 2003).
Valk, Ü., *The Black Gentleman* (Helsinki, 2001).
Verheyen, B., *Till Eulenspiegel. Revolutionär, Aufklärer, Assensater: zur Eulenspiegel-Rezeption in der DDR* (Frankfurt am Main and Oxford, 2004).
Virmond, W., *Eulenspiegel und seine Interpreten* (Berlin, 1981).
Vlasto, A., *The Entry of the Slavs into Christendom* (Cambridge, 1970).
Waite, G.K., *Heresy, Magic and Witchcraft in Early Modern Europe* (Basingstoke, 2003).
Walawender, A., *Kronika klęsk elementarnych w Polsce i w krajach sąsiednich w latach 1450–1586* (Lwów 1935).
Warner, M., *Alone of All Her Sex – The Myth and Cult of the Virgin Mary* (London, 2000).
Warschauer, A., 'Die älteste Spur eines Hexenprozesses in Posen', *Zeitschrift der Historischen Gesellschaft für die Provinz Posen* 4 (1889), 213–15.
Waszak, S., 'Dzietność rodziny mieszczańskiej w XVI i XVII w. i ruch naturalny ludności miasta Poznania w końcu XVI i w XVII wieku', *Roczniki Dziejów Społecznych i Gospodarczych* 16 (1954), 316–84.
Wawrzeniecki, M., 'Proces o czary w Nieszawie w 1721', *Wisła* 11 (1898), 646–54.
—— *Krwawe widma* (Warsaw, 1909).
—— 'Dwa procesy o czary z 1684', *Lud* 24 (1925), 170–2.
—— 'Przyczynek do procesów o czary', *Lud* 24 (1925), 173.
—— 'Jak konstruowano u nas stos do palenia czarownic?', *Lud* 26 (1927), 71–2.
—— 'Namaszczanie się czarownic', *Lud* 26 (1927), 72–3.
—— 'Szkoła magii w Krakowie', *Lud* 26 (1927), 69–70.
Węgrzynek, H., 'Dzieje poznańskiej legendy o profanacji hostii', *Kronika Miasta Poznania* 3–4 (1992), 45–56.
—— *'Czarna Legenda' Żydów: Procesy o rzekome mordy rytualne w dawnej Polsce* (Warsaw, 1995).
Whitney, E., 'The Witch "She"/The Historian "He": Gender and the Historiography of the European Witch-Hunts', *Journal of Women's History* 7, no. 3 (1995), 77–101.
Wijaczka, J., 'Procesy o czary w regionie świętokrzyskim w XVII–XVIII wieku', in idem (ed.), *Z przeszłości regionu świętokrzyskiego od XVI do XX wieku. Materiały konferencji naukowej, Kielce, 8 kwietnia 2003* (Kielce, 2003).

—— 'Procesy o czary w wsi Młotkowo w 1692 roku. Przyczynek do polowania na czarownice w Rzeczypospolitej XVII wieku.', *Odrodzenie i Reformacja* 48 (2004), 161–70.

—— 'Procesy o czary w Polsce w dobie Oświecenia. Zarys problematyki', *Klio* 7 (2005), 17–62.

—— 'Men Standing Trial for Witchcraft at the Łobżenica Court in the Second Half of the 17th Century', *Acta Polonicae Historica* 93 (2006), 69–85.

—— *Procesy o czary w Prusach Książęcych (Brandenburskich) w XVI–XVIII wieku* (Toruń, 2007).

Willis, D., *Malevolent Nurture: Witch-Hunting and Maternal Power in Early Modern England* (London, 1995).

Wilson, K., 'The Politics of Toleration: Dissenters in Great Poland (1587–1648)' (PhD thesis, SSEES, University College London, 2005).

Winiarz, A., 'Sądy Boże w Polsce', *Kwartalnik Historyczny* 5 (1891), 1–24.

Wiślicz, T., 'Czary przed sądami wiejskimi w Polsce w XVI–XVIII w.', *Czasopismo prawno-historyczne* 49 (1997), 47–63.

—— 'Społeczeństwo Kleczewa i okolic w walce z czartem (1624–1700), *Kwartalnik Historyczny* 112 (2004), 37–60.

—— ' "Miraculous Sites", in the Early Modern Polish-Lithuanian Commonwealth', in T. Wünsch (ed.), *Religion und Magie in Ostmitteleuropa: Spielräume theologischer Normierungsprozesse in Spätmittelalter und Früher Neuzeit* (Berlin, 2006).

Wojcieszak, B., *Opalenickie procesy czarownic w XVII wieku* (Opalenice, 1987).

Wolf, C. and Wolf, G., *Till Eulenspiegel* (Frankfurt am Main, 1976).

Wormald, J., *Court, Kirk, and Community: Scotland 1470–1625* (London, 1997 [1981]).

Worończak, J., 'Procesy o czary przed Poznańskim sądem miejskim w XVI w.', *Literatura ludowa* 3 (1972), 49–57.

Wyporska, W., 'Early Modern Exlcusion – The Branding of the Witch in Demonological Literature 1511–1775', in E. Grossman (ed.), *Examining 'the Other', in Polish Culture: Studies in Language, Literature and Cultural Mythology* (Lampeter, 2002).

—— 'Witchcraft, Arson and Murder – The Turek Trial of 1652', *Central European Journal* 1 (2003), 41–54.

—— 'Jewish, Noble, German or Peasant? – The Devil in Early Modern Poland', in É. Pócs and G. Klaniczay (eds), *Demons, Spirits, Witches: Christian Demonology and Popular Mythology* (Budapest, 2006).

—— 'Motive and Motif: Representations of the Witch in Early Modern Poland' (DPhil thesis, Hertford College, Oxford, 2007).

Wyrobisz, A., 'Economic Landscapes: Poland from the Fourteenth to the Seventeenth Century', in A. Maczak, H. Samsonowicz and P. Burke (eds), *East-Central Europe in Transition from the Fourteenth to the Seventeenth Century* (Cambridge, 1985).

—— 'Woman, Man and Historical Change: Case Studies in the Impact of Gender History', *Acta Polonicae Historica* 71 (1995), 69–82.

X.A.R., 'Relacja naocznego świadka o straceniu razem 14-tu mniemanych czarownic', *Przyjaciel Ludu* (1835), 16–18.

Zakrzewska, M., *Procesy o czary w Lublinie w XVII i XVIII w.* (Łódź, 1947).

Ziomek, J., *Renesans* (Warsaw, 1998).

Zakrzewska-Dubasowa, M., 'Proces o czary w Kraśniku z roku 1746', in *Z dziejów powiatu kraśnickiego* (Lublin, 1963).
Zamoyski, A., *The Polish Way: A Thousand Years' History of the Poles and Their Culture* (London, 1989).
Zdziechiewicz, A., *Staropolskie polowania na czarownice* (Katowice, 2004).
Zemon Davis, N., *Fiction in the Archives: Pardon Tales and Their Tellers in Sixteenth-Century France* (Cambridge, 1987).

Index

abortion, 108, 119
abuse, domestic/sexual 29, 56, 61
  of legal system, 70, 73, 83, 84, 102,
    108, 153, 154, 155, 156, 160, 170,
    173, 174, 185, 186
  adultery, 59, 108, 116, 133, 181
  alcohol, 34, 129, 130, 134, 144–7, 156,
    170, 178
  abuse of, 144
ambiguity, 3, 12, 22, 32, 35, 40, 102,
  118, 120, 121, 129, 138, 151, 158,
  172, 176, 187
anonymous works
  Czarownica powołana, xv, 4, 45, 125,
    151–9
  Komedia rybałtowska nowa, 137
  Peregrynacja dziadowska, 138–40
  Sejm piekielny, 137
  Statut Jana Dzwonowskiego, 137–8
  Wódka z elixierem, 144–7
  Z nowinami torba kursorska Iozefa
    Pięknorzyckiego z Mątwiłaiec,
    naleziona w Nalewayków, 140
Antitrinitarians, 49, 102
apostasy, 12, 35, 49, 66, 71, 107, 109,
  163, 164, 181
appeals (judicial), 7, 28, 45, 73, 78, 82,
  87, 109, 164, 168, 186, 208 n.38
archives, 22, 23, 25–8, 200 n.116
Augsburg, 44, 50, 58

Bamberg, 15, 44
banishment, 49, 64, 87
baptism, 100, 110, 111, 113, 180
Baranowski, Bogdan (Bohdan), 4, 16,
  17, 18, 19–23, 30, 79, 185, 186
barrel, 61, 67, 147, 166, 181
beer, 1, 34, 39, 42, 44, 55, 56, 57, 64,
  67, 69, 79, 88, 89, 183, 184, 188
Behringer, Wolfgang, 32, 45, 46, 50
bestiality, 65, 68, 113, 181
Białobrzeski, Marcin, 107, 114

Bible, 82, 100, 124, 132, 207 n. 25;
  see also individual books
blasphemy, 36, 66, 158, 160
Bogucka, Maria, 4, 21, 23, 24, 30, 32,
  49, 54, 55, 80, 85
Bohomolec, Franciszek, 147–8, 150
Bohomolec, Jan, 152, 169–73, 180,
  182
Borek, 84, 90
Boruta, 37, 99
Brandenburg, 10, 13, 14
bribery, 79, 167
Briggs, Robin, 3, 4, 5, 6, 15, 42, 53, 60
Budny, Szymon, 102–3
Calvinism, 7, 11, 14, 49, 103, 105, 110,
  146
Carolina, 43, 45, 74, 75, 76, 82
Carpzov, Benedikt, 23, 24, 82
cattle, 1, 2, 32, 42, 43, 46, 47, 48, 55,
  61, 62, 63, 67, 71, 87, 88, 89, 90,
  103, 121, 128, 130, 158, 185
childbirth, 58, 138
Chmielowski, Benedykt, 38, 111–15,
  125, 170, 180, 182, 183
Christ Child, abuse of, 40
Christianity, 18, 22, 40, 50, 66, 96,
  98, 99, 100, 117, 159
Clark, Stuart, 5, 22, 28, 97, 102, 105,
  125, 127
clemency, 63, 81, 87, 163, 186; *see also*
  death sentence, remission of
clergy, Roman Catholic, 4, 9, 12, 13,
  24, 55, 65, 70, 73, 74, 76, 91, 95,
  99, 105, 106, 108, 109, 110, 119,
  120, 121, 126, 136, 144, 145, 154,
  168, 173, 174, 179
climate, 4, 14, 30, 45–8, 129
Constitution (1543), 24, 72, 154, 160
Commonwealth of Poland-Lithuania,
  6–7, 9–11, 13, 14, 45, 49, 51, 83,
  90, 91, 93–4, 124, 186

counter-magic, 34, 112, 114, 128, 132, 159
Counter-Reformation, 4, 11, 14, 21, 40, 49–52, 101, 118, 119, 121
court record books, 16, 18, 25–8
courts, 7, 19, 31–2
  structure of, 76–77
  ecclesiastical, 72–3
  secular, 73–6
Cracow, 8, 9, 21, 72, 82, 123, 129, 186
crop destruction, 32, 42, 43, 46, 48, 51, 62, 103, 124, 128, 182
cunning folk, 3, 18, 33, 35, 55, 89, 137, 188–9
Czartoryski, Kazimierz Florian, 73, 92, 150, 151, 154, 162–5, 167, 175
Czartoryski, Teodor, 73
Czechowic, Marcin, 73, 102

Damhouder, Joos de, 24, 76, 82
death sentence, 18, 19, 26, 73, 74, 76, 82, 92, 144, 157, 165; *see also* execution, remission of, 33; *see also* clemency
Decalogue, 107, 108, 156; *see also* sins
Del Rio, Martin, 106, 114, 179
Deluge; *seePotop*
demons, 95, 98, 99, 103, 108, 128, 139
denunciation
depression, 66, 157; *see also* melancholy
devils, 3, 18, 28, 36–8, 44, 62, 64, 72–4, 88, 99, 103, 115–16, 134, 137, 148
  female, 99
Devil's mark, 37, 45, 106, 109, 182, 185
Długosz, Jan, 41, 98, 128
Doruchów, 16, 19, 20, 30
Duńczewski, Stanisław, 108, 130–2, 150
Dziewanna, 99, 135

Easter, 50, 64, 65, 84, 103, 110
Endor (witch of), 134, 211 n. 20
Enlightenment, 52, 93, 109, 112, 170, 186
epidemics, 4, 10, 12, 14, 30, 45–8, 51
Eucharist, 40, 47, 50, 62, 64–5, 92, 102, 109, 112–13, 131, 139; *see also* Host, theft of

Eulenspiegel, 44, 135–40
execution, 15, 20, 21, 23, 27, 32, 36, 68, 93, 127, 146, 154, 166, 169, 172, 179, 185; *see also* death sentence
executioner, 18, 26, 33–4, 78, 83, 85, 121, 142, 143, 157, 167
Exodus, Book of, 50, 75, 100, 125, 127, 174
exorcism, 102, 103, 114, 117, 119, 121, 131, 159, 169, 170

familiars, 112, 139, 178, 185
feminist theories, 15, 17, 50, 205 n. 23
fertility, 15, 50, 56, 58–9, 61, 68, 91, 108, 109, 131, 177, 185
functionalism, 15, 17, 19

Gamalski, Serafin, 125, 151, 165–8, 174, 175, 177
Gdacjusz, Adam, 79, 104, 105
Germany/Germans, 10, 11, 13–15, 17–18, 26, 27, 30, 39, 41, 43, 51, 93, 98–9, 102, 109, 124, 130, 134, 153, 173, 175, 184
  devils, 36–7, 67–8, 137
  law, 21, 25, 74, 77–8, 82, 186
  Poland as extension of, 20, 95
Gilowski, Paweł, 103, 104, 107
Gloger, Zygmunt, 18
Gniezno, 23, 32, 44, 45, 46, 54, 64, 72, 84, 85, 86, 88, 91, 92, 93, 153, 156, 181, 183, 184
gods, Slavonic, 97–100
Good Friday, 65, 110
Gostyń, 14, 30, 47
Grodzisk, 13, 14, 32, 35, 36, 39, 41, 42, 46, 62, 63, 66, 84, 143, 154, 156, 181
Groicki, Bartłomiej, 24, 43, 69, 74–6, 78–9, 80–2, 86, 137, 138, 145, 155, 186, 189

Haur, Jakub, 129–30, 150
herbs, 2, 12, 33, 34, 42, 48, 55, 71, 74, 89, 99, 102, 108, 110, 130, 131, 137, 138, 139, 148, 159, 184
heresy, 11, 24, 25, 40, 82, 102, 104, 107, 113, 119, 128, 155, 162, 166
Himmler, Heinrich, 26

Host, theft of, 21, 39–42, 44, 50, 85, 88, 182, 185
Hungary, 20, 21, 31, 50, 95, 130

idolatry, 66, 103, 107, 110, 120, 158
impotence, 71, 112, 129
incantations, 22, 33, 48, 81, 92, 108, 132, 137, 158, 163, 184
incubi, 133, 139, 171, 178
infanticide, 24, 56, 119
interrogation, 35, 36, 62, 79, 81, 84–5, 86, 156, 157, 161, 162, 163, 164, 167, 176
Inquisition, Holy Office of, 72, 162

Januszowski, Janusz, 132, 149

Kałowski, Marcin, 121
Karpiński, Andrzej, 21, 55
Klaniczay, Gabor, 20, 118
Kolert, Franciszek, 122
Krowicki, Marcin, 102–3

de Lancre, xiv, 106
Larner, Christina, 60
latawiec, 178
Laterna, Marcin, 107–8, 110, 114
legal system, Wielkopolska, 77–8
judiciary, 78–80
Levack, Brian, 20, 91, 93
Leviticus, Book of, 124, 132
Little Ice Age, 46, 47
lord, 1, 2, 33, 55, 87–91, 142, 175, 184, 190; *see also* seigneur
Lublin, 4, 21, 22, 77, 182, 186
Lutheranism, 11, 14, 110, 146
Lwów, 21, 67
Łagiewniki, 105, 121, 125, 145
Łysa Góra, 38–9, 41, 62–5, 88, 113, 121, 148, 181; *see also* sabbat

magic, 3, 21, 33, 40, 84, 99, 102, 108, 112, 118, 120, 128, 129, 133, 139, 160, 184, 187
high, 68, 100
image, 138
ligature, 141
love, 35, 58, 61, 89, 129, 137, 148, 171–3

sympathetic, 62, 184
weather, 45, 47, 48, 61, 112, 131, 146
magical theft, 90, 138
maleficia, 56, 60, 68, 71, 107, 112, 131, 164, 189
Malleus Maleficarum, 4, 18, 20, 21, 38, 76, 96, 104, 105, 106, 122–4, 160, 180, 185; *see also Młot na czarownice*
Marianism, 8, 12, 49, 50, 118, 120
Marzana, 99, 135
Matthew, Book of, 155
medicine, 73, 128–33, 138
melancholy, 66, 106, 166, 171; *see also* depression
metamorphosis, 102, 170
midwives, 15, 58, 61, 85, 91
milk theft, 1, 2, 22, 32, 33, 39, 48, 61, 93
miracles, 41, 96, 100, 115, 119, 120, 121, 122, 132, 170
miscarriage, 58, 61, 160
Młot na czarownice, 18, 122–4; *see also Malleus Maleficarum*
Molitor, Ulrich, 105, 123
mothers, 1, 15, 24, 32, 40, 44, 57, 58–9, 63, 91, 104, 113, 129, 139, 172, 183, 187, 189
musicians, 39, 64, 184, 189

neighbours, 13, 19, 35, 53, 62, 73, 90, 107, 119, 140, 143, 145, 146, 147, 148, 182, 189
Nider, Johannes, 105, 123
nobility, 6–12, 22–5, 70, 73, 75, 80, 87–91, 142, 157, 174–5
noble women, 18, 54–5, 135, 138
Nowakowski, Marcin, 110–11, 115, 125, 126

Opalenica, 143, 181
Opaliński, Krzysztof, 13, 14, 79, 89, 142–4, 145, 149, 150, 151, 152, 160, 174, 177, 188
Opaliński, Łukasz, 143–4, 152, 160, 174
Ostling, Michael, 21–3, 27, 34, 40, 48, 139, 181

pact with the Devil, 20, 38, 62–3, 66–8, 97, 105, 106, 108–9, 124, 137, 166, 170, 179–80, 189
paganism, 21, 38, 80, 97–101, 104, 107, 114, 120, 128, 129, 135, 149, 170, 187
pamphlet literature (lack of), 106, 115, 125, 149, 150, 176, 177, 185
peasantry, 7, 10, 11, 17, 18, 19, 21, 45, 46, 47, 61, 89, 90, 101, 142, 184; *see also* serfs
Pilaszek, Małgorzata, 4, 5, 11, 12, 21, 22, 23–5, 27, 31, 72, 75, 79, 82, 87, 96, 160, 185, 186
plague, 43, 46–7, 51, 103, 110, 135
Pobiedziska, 91, 93, 143
poison, 34, 35, 42, 48, 56, 76, 82, 90, 92, 129, 140, 143, 170
Poklatecki, Stanisław, 132–3, 149
Poland; *see also* Commonwealth of Poland-Lithuania
history of, 6–12
Pomerania, 13, 14, 27, 171
Poniec, 14, 184
possession, 122, 130, 131, 163, 171
Potop (Deluge), 8, 10, 14, 24, 47, 73
poverty, 2, 3, 15, 47, 80, 92, 140, 145, 180
powder, 2, 39, 42, 48, 62, 86, 88–9, 91–2, 112, 131, 171, 172, 177, 182, 184
Poznań, 4, 13–15, 18, 19, 20, 21, 26, 27, 30, 32, 40, 41, 44, 47, 48, 53, 55, 56, 57, 65, 66, 67, 71, 72, 76, 77, 78, 84, 142, 144, 146, 160, 165, 173, 175
Circle, 151–9
prayer, 22, 101, 114, 116, 133, 159, 167, 169, 181
pregnancy, 33, 81, 82, 157, 159, 180
prison (jail), 59, 65, 84, 121, 143, 153, 160, 162, 163, 165, 166, 168, 169, 181
procuring, 53, 57, 59, 83
profit, 10, 35, 39, 80, 138, 158, 167
in prayers, 32, 33, 90
prostitution, 53, 57, 80, 117
Protestantism, 11, 14, 41, 49, 51, 57, 60, 79, 96, 97, 99, 100, 101–5, 106, 107, 113, 114, 115, 124, 125, 132, 146, 158, 175, 187
Psalms, Book of, 166
publications, chronology of, 4, 115, 125, 149–50, 151, 153, 174
Pyzdry, 32, 46, 47, 61, 67, 91, 92

Reformation, 11, 101–5
Regulus, Wojciech, 142, 151–2, 174
religious toleration, 11, 13, 105
revenge, 2, 18, 51, 138, 139, 140, 141, 147, 149, 153, 156, 158, 164, 166, 173, 174, 180
rituals, 1, 3, 32, 33, 34, 44, 47, 52, 97, 98, 99, 102–5, 109, 111–13, 119, 120, 125, 126, 129, 132, 145, 148, 172, 180, 182, 187, 188
Rokita, 36, 37, 99
Roma (gypsy), 10, 18, 42
Roman Catholicism, 11–15, 18, 19, 24, 29, 40, 41, 44, 49, 50, 57, 72, 86–7, 92, 96, 100–16, 119, 123, 124, 125, 131, 133, 152, 159, 165, 169, 174, 180, 182, 187; *see also* Counter-Reformation
Rothenburg, 44, 48, 61, 83, 157
Rowlands, Alison, 5, 45, 47, 59, 60, 61
Ruthenia, 10, 23, 130, 146

sabbat, 1–3, 38–9, 44, 61–4, 71, 86, 88, 92, 106, 108, 13, 119, 131, 140, 156, 164, 167, 171, 182–4; *see also Łysa Góra*
sacramentals, 24, 49, 102, 109, 112, 113, 120, 125, 131, 132, 187
sacraments, 40, 102, 109, 110, 111, 112, 113, 125, 159, 181, 182
saints (female), 49, 115–19, 135, 187
Sarmatism, 11, 94, 136, 193, n. 23
Scot, Reginald, 102, 171, 174
serfs, 47, 53, 55, 90, 189; *see also* peasantry
sex, diabolic, 37, 39, 91, 109, 119, 183
shaving, 18, 74, 169
Siennik, Marcin, 128–9
Silesia, 10, 13, 14, 27, 99, 130
sins, 36, 44, 50, 82, 100, 103, 107, 110, 134, 137; *see also* Decalogue
Skarga, Piotr, 111, 115–9, 179

scepticism, 93, 110, 123, 142, 151–75, 179
slander, 23, 88, 93, 176
Slavonic spirits, 97, 103, 139
  domovoi, 37
  południca, 98
  przypołudnica, 139, 144
  topielec, 98
  uboże, 98
sodomy, 65, 68, 97, 109, 113
Sowiźdrzał, 135–40, 143, 149, 181, 188; see also Eulenspiegel
Spee, Friedrich, 4, 45, 142, 151–9, 173
Speculo Saxonum, 43, 82, 92
statistics, witchcraft trials, 4, 189
  Poland, 19–20, 21–7
  Wielkopolska, 29–32
succubi, 133
Sułkowski, A., 92
supernatural, 3, 12, 15, 35, 42, 111, 118, 122, 126, 144, 147, 149, 151, 167, 170, 177
superstition, 14, 18, 47, 52, 101, 103, 104, 107, 108, 110, 111, 120, 124, 127, 134, 143, 145, 147, 148, 150, 153, 154, 157–9, 160, 163, 167, 168, 170, 172, 187
Swedes, 8, 9, 13, 14, 80, 121
swimming, of witches, 32, 46, 58, 71, 72, 85, 92, 99, 110, 131, 144, 146
Syreniusz, Szymon 129
szlachta; see also nobility and noble women
Szymonowicz, Szymon, 141, 145, 149, 150, 188

taxes, 7, 11, 47, 56, 78, 87, 142
teachers, 59, 62, 136, 139, 142
Teufelbücher, 99, 137
Thursday, 1, 33, 39, 41, 42, 63, 67, 113, 134, 140, 181, 183
torture, 81–2, 85
  abuse of, 45, 157, 160, 162, 164, 173, 185
  death during, 73, 165, 169
  exemptions from, 156–7
  restrictions upon, 76

Toruń, 49, 66, 67
transubstantiation, 22, 40
Turek, 22, 32, 58, 101
Tylkowski, Woyciech, 108–9, 112, 113, 115, 130, 131, 150

Vatican, 73, 150, 162–4
vodka, 79, 144–7

Wągrowiec, 32, 46, 47, 62, 64
Waliszew, 19
war, 4, 6, 8–10, 12, 14, 16, 17, 19, 20, 23, 26, 27, 30, 43, 46–7, 51, 55, 80, 94
Warner, Marina, 116, 119
Warta, 23, 32, 46, 78
Wartegau, 26
Weyer, Johan, 100, 102, 106, 171, 174
widows, 15, 39, 53, 55, 56, 61, 157, 182
Wielkopolska, 1–4
  history of, 12–6
  archives, 25–8
  persecution, 30–2
Wijaczka, Jacek, 21
Wiślicz, Tomasz, 21, 22, 31, 32, 36, 49, 87, 120, 175
Wisner, Daniel, 142, 151, 152, 160–1, 167
witch
  demographics of, 53–69
  finder, 45, 158, 185
  gender of, 54–69
  representations of, 3–4, 28, 53, 100, 112, 127–8, 143, 149
  male, 61–9
  occupations of, 53–4
witchcraft, decline in trials, 91–4
witnesses, 59, 68, 80–6, 91, 146, 156, 161, 167, 170, 173, 189
Wronki, 32, 46, 178

Załuski, Andrzej, 151, 168–9
Ząmbkowicz, Stanisław, 123–6
zero-sum, 22, 90, 119, 138, 188
Ziarnko, Jan, xiv, 106

www.ingramcontent.com/pod-product-compliance
Lightning Source LLC
Chambersburg PA
CBHW050555100325
23228CB00005B/234